Compass Points
Navigating the 20th Century

Edited by Robert Chodos

Between the Lines, Toronto   **Compass Foundation, Toronto**

Compass Points: Navigating the 20th Century
© Between the Lines and the Compass Foundation, 1999

Between the Lines gratefully acknowledges financial assistance for our publishing activities from the Ontario Arts Council, The Canada Council for the Arts, and the Government of Canada through the Book Publishing Industry Development Program.

Special publishing support for this book was provided by the Canadian Studies Program of the Department of Canadian Heritage and by the Upper Canada Province of the Society of Jesus.

Every reasonable effort has been made to find copyright holders. The publisher would be pleased to have any errors or omissions brought to its attention.

Canadian Cataloguing in Publication Data
Main entry under title:
Compass points : navigating the 20th century
Many articles originally published in Compass : A Jesuit Journal.
ISBN 1-896357-32-6
1. Canada - Civilization - 20th century.
2. Civilization, Modern - 20th century.
I. Chodos, Robert, 1947- .

FC600.C66 1999   971.06   C99-932055-6
F1021.2.C66 1999

THE CANADA COUNCIL | LE CONSEIL DES ARTS
FOR THE ARTS | DU CANADA
SINCE 1957 | DEPUIS 1957

Editor: Robert Chodos
Book design: Philip Street
Cover collage: David Laurence

Layout and typesetting: Gail van Varseveld
Cover design: Gordon Robertson
Printed in Canada by Transcontinental

This book was composed in Corel Ventura™
using Bembo and Univers Condensed.

1 2 3 4 5 6 7 8 9 10   06 05 04 03 02 01 00 99

Between the Lines
720 Bathurst Street, # 404
Toronto, Ontario, M5S 2R4
Canada
(416) 535-9914
btlbooks@web.net
www.btlbooks.com

Compass Foundation
P.O. Box 6605, Station A
Toronto, Ontario M5W 1X4
Canada

compass@gvanv.com
www.gvanv.com/compfndn/

*In memory of Stephanie Vincec CSJ,
colleague and friend (1936–1998)*

More than most books, this is a collective enterprise. Among the people who have brought it to fruition are:

- talented and perceptive writers whose articles appear in these pages;

- my colleagues on the *Compass* editorial board who participated in the conception and editing of the *Compass* decades issues and this book: Louisa Blair, Jack Costello SJ, Michael Czerny SJ, Mary Rose Donnelly, David Eley SJ, Curtis Fahey, Edward Hyland, Peter Larisey SJ, Judy MacDonald, Douglas McCarthy SJ, Brian Massie SJ, Jacques Monet SJ, Jerald Owczar, Martin Royackers SJ, Wanda Romer Taylor and the late Stephanie Vincec CSJ;

- other members of the *Compass* team: Philip Street, whose work as *Compass*'s art director began with the 1900–1910 issue of the magazine and has continued through this book; office manager Barbara Barrett, who capably anchored the farflung and often haphazard editorial operation that was *Compass*; the late Peter McGehee, desktop publisher for the 1900–1910 issue; and his successor Gail van Varseveld, whose contributions have gone well beyond desktop publishing to include every aspect of the magazine and this book;

- Jamie Swift, who saw a potential book in this material, and his colleagues at Between the Lines, who accepted his invitation.

Sister Stephanie Vincec, an enthusiast for this project from the beginning, battled cancer during most of the period in which the decades series appeared. In the spring of 1998 she was looking forward to attending the upcoming *Compass* editorial board meeting that would determine the shape of this book, but her condition worsened and she died a few days before the meeting. Our satisfaction in seeing *Compass Points* in print is tempered by our sorrow that Sister Stephanie is not here to see it.

—**Robert Chodos**

Contents

Frans Masereel (1898–1972)

 1	Leisurely Review of a Fascinating Century	by Robert Chodos

6 THE FIRST DECADE

7	Opening a Window on Our Century	by Michael Czerny
9	The Janus Decade	by George Woodcock
17	Saskatoon: The Instant City	by Don Kerr
23	New, Fast and Big	by Rosemary Donegan and Jamie Swift
28	Kipling and Yeats: The Apologist and the Visionary	by Stephanie Vincec
30	Rethinking the Universe	by John Honner
37	The Crisis of Modernism	by Roger Haight
44	Bloody Dress Rehearsal for 1917	by Stanley B. Ryerson

46 THE SECOND DECADE

47	A Decade of Suffering and Violence	by Jacques Monet
49	In 1910 Human Character Changed	by Modris Eksteins
56	Alarm Bells for Civilization	by Gwynne Dyer

KEY: Introduction   Arts and Culture   Notable Individuals   Politics

♖	61	The Social Gospel: Christianity for the Here and Now	by Ramsay Cook
♟	67	Filling the Gap on the Homefront	by Kori Street
🏛 ♟	70	A Strike with an Elusive Meaning	by Doug Smith
🏛	73	Ontario's Bitter Language Fight	by Robert Choquette
♟	76	Influenza: Disease of the Wind	by Eileen Pettigrew
👣	78	T.E. Lawrence: Military Hero, Anguished Searcher	by Dennis Duffy
🏛	81	Russia: Power Was in the Streets	by Mary McAuley
🏛	84	Ireland: Destructive Adventure	by John Francis Larkin

86   THE TWENTIES

🧭	87	The Exuberance and Despair of the 1920s	by Stephanie Vincec
🎺 ♟	89	Prologue to Our Own Era	by Jean Clair
🎺	96	Literary Fistfight in Paris	by Louis Dudek
♖	100	Rocky Road to Church Union	by John Webster Grant
🏛	104	No Heroes, No Defeats: A New Era in Canadian Politics	by H. Blair Neatby
🏛	109	Agnes Macphail in Parliament	by Terry Crowley
🏛	112	Fascism's Mystique of Power	by Alkis Kontos
🏛 ♟	116	Marcus Garvey: Black Moses	by Robert Hill
🏛	119	Ascendancy of the Chiangs	by Mary Rose Donnelly
⚛	122	Breath Came and They Lived: The Discovery of Insulin	by Michael Bliss
⚛ ♟	125	The Public Health Offensive	by Jutta Mason
👣	128	St. Miguel Pro and the Secret Kingdom	by John Matheson

130   THE THIRTIES

🧭	131	Why Do the 1930s Seem So Familiar?	by Martin Royackers
🏛	133	From Stock Market Crash to Phony War	by Lukin Robinson
🏛	141	Desperate Canadians Turned to Political Messiahs	by Allan Levine
♟	146	On the Prairies, You Had to Learn to Peel a Nickel	by Gail Burns
🏛	150	Latin America's Response to the Depression	by Liisa North
♖ ♟	153	Education and Economic Democracy: The Antigonish Movement	by Greg MacLeod

and Economy   ♖ Religion and Spirituality   ⚛ Science and Technology   ♟ Society

	158	Emmanuel Mounier: Catalyst for a Generation	by John Hellman
	160	Norman Bethune: Driven to Be an Actor on the World Stage	by Andrée Lévesque
	163	Grey Owl's Masquerade for Conservation	by Donald B. Smith
	165	The Soviet Union's Literary Underground	by Ioan Davies
	168	Guernica: Icon of the Century	by Peter Larisey

170   THE FORTIES

	171	The Second World War's Long Shadow	by Robert Chodos
	173	Are We Losing Sight of the Trees?	by Gil Drolet
	176	The Lasting Trauma of the Holocaust	by Michael Lerner
	180	The Atomic Bomb: Face to Face with Infinite Destruction	by Robert Jay Lifton
	184	Connections to the War Still Vibrate	by Brian McKenna
	189	Country Girl at Intelligence HQ	by Imogen Ryan
	192	In the Movies, Even Lassie Went to War	by Marc Gervais
	196	In Canada, a Legacy of Welfare and Political Division	by Eric Kierans
	200	An Ambiguous International Role for Canada	by Denis Smith
	204	Postwar Social Life Stressed Conformity	by Mary Louise Adams
	208	Alfred Pellan and the Quebec Painters' Quiet Revolution	by Malcolm Reid

212   THE FIFTIES

	213	A Sense of Time Standing Still	by Curtis Fahey
	215	The Cold War Masked a Geopolitical Agenda	by Anatol Rapoport
	220	Power, Confusion and Corporate Interests: McCarthy and Hoover	by Peter Dale Scott
	225	The Fifties Look: Selling a Self-Image	by Philip Street
	228	My Adventures in Darkest Suburbia	by Miriam Blair
	231	Maire-Alain Couturier: The Priest Who Championed Modern Art	by Peter Larisey
	235	A Peasant Pope Breathed New Life into the Church	by Romeo Maione

KEY: Introduction   Arts and Culture   Notable Individuals   Politics

🗞️ 🏛️	238	The Federal Institution that United Quebecers	by Louis Balthazar
🗞️ 🏛️	241	TV Hard-Wired Canada into Two Solitudes	by Mark Starowicz
🗞️	244	We Created an Elvis to Meet Our Need	by Malcolm Reid
🗞️	248	Beckett's Poetic Rendering of Faith and Doubt	by Craig Stewart Walker
👣	251	Tony Walsh: A Gentle Man Who Challenged Others	by Stephen Hagarty

254   THE SIXTIES

🧭	255	The Multi-Ring Sixties Brought Lasting Change	by Peter Larisey
🏛️ 🪑	257	A Generation that Said No to Plastics	by Robert Chodos
⛪	262	Vatican II: Outpouring of the Spirit and Human Shift	by Janet Somerville
🏛️	268	Showing the Maple Leaf in Vietnam	by Victor Levant
🏛️	272	From Hope to a Hole in the Park: The Columbia Revolt	by Peter Larisey
🪑	277	Expo 67: Theme Park for a Happy Future	by David Eley
🪑	279	Fit, Young and Casual Were the Trinity	by Margaret Visser
🪑	281	Hockey Had Not Yet Lost Its Soul	by Curtis Fahey
	284	Three Sixties Stories	
🏛️ 🪑		The Jungle Collided with Rochdale College	by Ray Bennett
🗞️ 🪑		My Discovery of Bob Dylan	by Robert Morgan
🗞️ 🪑		Changing The World with My Guitar	by Bob Bossin
🏛️ 🪑	288	Taking the Longer View	by Judy MacDonald
👣	290	Georges and Pauline Vanier: The Vice-Regal Couple Who Inspired Canadians	by Jacques Monet

292   THE SEVENTIES

🧭	293	Watching the 1970s Weave and Unravel	by Mary Rose Donnelly
🏛️	295	From Boom to Economic Crisis	by Mel Watkins
⛪ 🪑	300	Christians Made Justice a Vital Concern	by Michael Czerny
🏛️	306	New Horizons for Canada	by Doug Smith
🏛️ 🪑	310	Canadians Listened to "Ni-wha Judge"	by Louisa Blair
🗞️	314	Nobel Moved Away from the Mainstream	by Malcolm Reid

and Economy   ⛪ **Religion and Spirituality**   ⚛️ **Science and Technology**   🪑 **Society**

317 Watergate: We Still Don't Know Why — by Rae Murphy

320 Woody's World: Beyond Sex and Death — by Marc Gervais

322 Finding Feminism, Rediscovering Faith — by Denise Nadeau

326 I Came Too Late for Sixties Magic — by Charlie Angus

328 Oscar Romero: El Salvador's Archbishop to the Poor — by Frances Arbour

330 THE EIGHTIES

331 The Decade in Our Blind Spot — by Louisa Blair

333 The Rise of Neoconservatism — by Rae Murphy

339 The Church in Canada: A Golden Autumn and a Dark Night — by Doug McCarthy

343 Quebecers Were Asked a Question, and Gave their Answer — by Daniel Latouche

348 Revolution on the Desktop — by Gail van Varseveld

354 The Eighties' Environmental Legacy: Death (of Nature) by Natural Causes? — by Moira Farr

359 Jean Vanier: Community Builder — by Carolyn Whitney-Brown

362 THE NINETIES

363 The Age of America — by Judy MacDonald

365 After the (Cold) War Is Over... — by Rick Salutin

372 A Gambler's Society: The End of Job Security — by Jamie Swift

377 Hannibal's Mirrors: Cyberintelligence and the Zapatista Revolution — by Louisa Blair

382 Canada in the Information Age — by Ronald Deibert

385 Spirituality in the Nineties: Rediscovering Sacred Spaces — by Peter McIsaac

391 Is Aboriginal Self-Government a Mirage? — by Miles Morrisseau

397 Rwanda: Alone with Its Deep Wounds — by Augustin Karekezi

402 South Africa's Election: Inspiring yet Sobering — by Josephine C. Naidoo

407 Mother Teresa: Champion of the Poor — by Lucinda Vardey

KEY: Introduction   Arts and Culture   Notable Individuals   Politics and Economy   Religion and Spirituality   Science and Technology   Society

Leisurely Review of a Fascinating Century

Compass Points is the view not of one person but of many; not all-of-a-piece but composite; the twentieth century seen through a hundred and five different lenses. Woody Allen is here but not Walt Disney; T.E. Lawrence but not D.H. Lawrence; Mother Teresa but not Dorothy Day; Jean Béliveau but not Maurice Richard. Analytically minded readers will no doubt discern patterns in what is included and what is left out. All I can say is that the determinants of these decisions included personal taste, whim, and which writers completed their assignments and which did not.

The collection casts a wide net: political, social, economic, cultural, scientific, religious. It reflects the circumstance that it was conceived, edited and published in Canada, but is not a book of Canada's century alone; and while it bespeaks its origins in a Catholic magazine, it is not solely a book of the century in the Catholic Church.

The material is organized by decade, and there are elements of arbitrariness to this as well. The development of the desktop computer began in the mid-1970s and has taken some startling turns in the 1990s; nevertheless, it was arguably in the 1980s that computers really took hold, and so our look at the computer is slotted into this decade. Nor do we mean to suggest that fascism came out of nowhere in the 1920s or that feminism was confined to the 1970s—only that these decades were especially important times for these phenomena.

Featured here are historians, archivists, journalists, artists, priests, poets, novelists and people who just have interesting stories to tell. What they have produced is insightful, analytical, personal, sprawling, rough around the edges, contradictory and incomplete. Welcome to the twentieth century.

It was Michael Czerny's idea to start with. Many things were Michael's idea to start with, including my being editor of *Compass: A Jesuit Journal*. Indeed, without Michael I might never have heard of the publication. It was Michael, then the director of the Jesuit Centre for Social Faith and Justice in Toronto, who called me in the spring of 1986 to let me know that the Jesuits published a magazine and to ask me if I wanted to be its editor. Once we had established that having a Jewish editor of a Jesuit magazine was not a problem for either of us, it quickly developed that the kind of magazine the Jesuits were interested in publishing and the kind I was interested in editing were not so far apart.

By 1989 I had settled into the job and developed a close collegial relationship with the editorial board, which included Michael and a few other Jesuits as well as several highly articulate lay Catholics. The hallmark of *Compass* was that every issue had a theme. In those three years we had explored themes as diverse as fundamentalism, free trade, sexuality, the environment and the role of the laity in the church. But Michael's idea was the most ambitious one yet.

The 1990s were about to begin—the last decade of the twentieth century. Why not use the nineties to do a "leisurely retrospective" on the century, one decade at a time? We would begin in 1990 with a theme issue devoted to the years 1900–1910 and then continue with one "decade issue" per year until we reached the nineties in 1999. When the series was finished we would have an album of the century that could be compiled into a book.

The editorial board was generally favourable to the idea, although someone commented that it reflected perhaps unwarranted confidence that *Compass* would still be around in 1999—something that could not be taken for granted with a small, reader-supported magazine. Despite such doubts, we decided to launch the series, and in the fall of 1989 we began planning the 1900–1910 issue of *Compass*, scheduled for publication in March/April 1990.

From the beginning, a number of principles governed our work. Our scope would be international, but we would have a special focus on Canada. We would cover the ongoing life of the Roman Catholic Church, but not to the exclusion of other religious bodies or the secular world. Each decade would be approached from as many angles as possible. We wanted to maintain a balance between getting inside the mentality of the decade we were examining and relating its events and developments to our own day (thus Stephanie Vincec's juxtaposition in the 1900–1910 issue of Kipling, the writer who loomed large in his own time, and Yeats, whose poetry has had much greater resonance for subsequent generations).

We also agreed that we would publish articles about events, developments and personalities that were interesting and characteristic of their times, but we would make no attempt to be comprehensive. Hence the somewhat arbitrary nature of what is included in this book. The Bretton Woods monetary conference of 1944 was undoubtedly a landmark event, but there is only a passing reference to it in our 1940s issue, and in these pages. Other subjects that were covered in the magazine—the Balfour Declaration of 1917, the writing of Franz Kafka, the Hungarian Revolution of 1956—had to be dropped as the material was pared down for the book. I hope that the range, variety and quality of what *is* here will lead readers to forgive us for the gaps.

For the first issue we elected Michael, as the originator of the series, to write the leader—the short article at the front of the magazine that would introduce the theme and orient readers to the material. We wanted someone eminent and venerable to write the main overview article; after Northrop Frye turned us down, we were very fortunate to get George Woodcock. Roger Haight SJ, then teaching at Regis College in Toronto, across the street from the *Compass* office, was able to write authoritatively about the modernist crisis, the defining event of the decade in the life of the Catholic Church. In Saskatoon we found Don Kerr, who told the improbable story of his city's early years. The first decade of the twentieth century also saw the advent of the theory of relativity and other momentous changes in humanity's understanding of the universe; an Australian Jesuit, John Honner, turned out to be the best person to explain these changes in terms accessible to the nonspecialist.

The issue came together. And as it did, a terrible event in war-torn El Salvador wrenched the Jesuit world, including the *Compass* editorial board. On November 16, 1989, six Jesuits, their cook and her teenage daughter were murdered by government soldiers in San Salvador. A call went out to Jesuits in other countries to come to El Salvador to continue their work. One of those who responded to the call was Michael Czerny. The March/April 1990 issue of *Compass*, the one that inaugurated the twentieth century series, also contained a letter from Michael explaining his decision to go teach at the University of Central America. He spent two years in San Salvador, and then went on to Rome as secretary for social justice of the worldwide Jesuit order. While Michael would continue to be a strong supporter of *Compass* and write for it on occasion—including an article on Christian social justice movements in the 1970s issue—the work of planning and shaping the decades series continued without him.

I do not mean to slight Michael in any way, or to discount the tremendous debt that this project owes him, but it seems to me that the series really hit its stride after he left, in our issue on the years 1910–1920. Perhaps this was because the decade of the First World War was a watershed period in the life of the century itself. Perhaps this was because the two writers we commissioned to put the war in perspective, Modris Eksteins and Gwynne Dyer, between them succeeded in capturing the impact of the slaughter in

Europe on its own time and on us. In any case, the 1910–1920 issue remains one of my two favourites in the series—the other being the 1950s issue, which won a silver National Magazine Award in the Editorial Package category.

The 1950s issue was memorable in a very different way from our treatment of 1910–1920. For most decades, the subjects for at least the main articles suggested themselves without much difficulty: for the 1920s, that decade's peculiar combination of carefree exuberance and postwar despair; for the 1930s, the Depression and the rise of Hitler; for the 1940s, the Second World War, the Holocaust, the atomic bomb and postwar reconstruction. But what was there to say about the 1950s? Even our leader writer, historian and editor Curtis Fahey, characterized the decade as leaving us with "a curious sense of time standing still."

Once we started planning the issue, however, it turned out there was lots to say about the fifties: suburbia, the Cold War, McCarthyism, Pope John XXIII, Elvis Presley, Samuel Beckett. In fact, there was so much material that we had to expand the issue to fifty-six pages from the usual forty-eight. And it was good material too, if the opinion of the National Magazine Award judges counts for anything.

Soon afterward, ongoing Jesuit financial problems forced us to cut back on the size of *Compass*. The 1960s and 1970s theme sections, despite the wealth of material to be covered, had to be squeezed into fewer pages. The financial problems continued, and in 1997 the Jesuits precipitated the demise of the magazine by ending their funding of *Compass*, along with numerous other projects they had supported. Our confidence at the outset of the series that *Compass* would survive through the 1990s proved unwarranted. We were left with a truncated decades series that covered only the first eighty years of the century.

However, Between the Lines of Toronto, which had expressed interest in publishing a book using the material from the series, still wanted to proceed with the project, and so we were left with the problem of what to do about the 1980s and 1990s. We decided to commission new material specifically for the book, and were pleased that some very talented and perceptive writers responded positively to our invitation to contribute to these sections. There were also articles in other issues of *Compass* that had appeared during those years—on the Quebec referendum of 1980, the changing nature of work, South Africa's first post-apartheid election, the genocide in Rwanda—that seemed suitable for inclusion in this book.

What follows is a compilation of articles from all these sources. We hope you recognize the times that are depicted in these pages as the times you have lived through, while learning something new about those times as well.

And what did we learn about the twentieth century in the course of preparing the decades series and this book? Perhaps the only grand conclusion to be drawn is that there are no grand conclusions—especially after Rick Salutin's salutary warning about the perils of such conclusions in his essay on the post–Cold War period of the 1990s.

We are not at the end of history. We may well be at the end of a phase of history that we think of as the modern era, although future generations will no doubt come up with a better name for it. The unravelling of modernity has been accompanied by horror and bloodshed on an unprecedented scale, facilitated by the advanced technology that has been another characteristic of this century. The century ends on a much more sombre note than it began. Moira Farr concludes her account of developments on the environmental front in the 1980s with the observation that if there is any room for hope it lies in our having learned some hard truths. Her observation applies to more than the environment.

For those of us who do retain some hope, the emergence of the environmental movement is one of the developments of the latter part of the century that could be labelled prophetic in the sense that it points to what the next phase of history will need to look like if the horrors of the twentieth century are not to be dwarfed by those of the twenty-first. There are other such developments, notably the rise of feminism, the growth of a new global consciousness and the persistence and even revival of spirituality (at least, as Peter McIsaac SJ suggests, on the margins). While these developments may be prophetic, the historical record from biblical times onward attests to the fact that people don't always listen to prophets.

But enough for now of my late-twentieth-century pessimism. Come back with us to the more hopeful world of 1900, and then follow the twentieth century through its meandering, rarely smooth but undeniably fascinating course.

Robert Chodos
October 1999

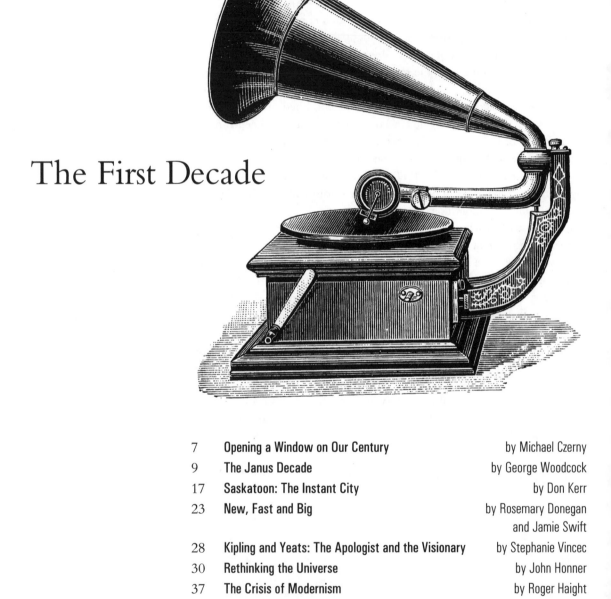

The First Decade

7	**Opening a Window on Our Century**	by Michael Czerny
9	**The Janus Decade**	by George Woodcock
17	**Saskatoon: The Instant City**	by Don Kerr
23	**New, Fast and Big**	by Rosemary Donegan and Jamie Swift
28	**Kipling and Yeats: The Apologist and the Visionary**	by Stephanie Vincec
30	**Rethinking the Universe**	by John Honner
37	**The Crisis of Modernism**	by Roger Haight
44	**Bloody Dress Rehearsal for 1917**	by Stanley B. Ryerson

Opening a Window on Our Century

by Michael Czerny

On a visit to Czechoslovakia, I listened as friends told me about a terrible fight at Bila Hora (White Mountain): so vivid, so dramatic, so sad. A battle during the Warsaw Pact invasion of 1968? A turning point in the Second World War? No, it happened on November 8, 1620. Yet to hear tell of it, Bila Hora wasn't history at all. What makes it not old and dead but living? It's the fact, I suppose, that Czechs have kept on letting it determine their identity, century after century.

Few Canadians carry around much history like that. Maybe that's both a cost and a benefit of being the New World. Still, it's safe to say that the whole twentieth century keeps on shaping us.

To begin this leisurely review of our century, we'll look back at 1900–1910, a very curious decade indeed. Nana, Grampa, you were there: how was it? Can we get behind the certainties ("common sense") and the dogmas (ideology) of today? Can we pick out the big changes that keep on shaping us?

Our forebears came bursting out of the Industrial Revolution with a formula they were sure would last forever. Our century began with a limitless confidence, a deep-seated complacency, and an outrageous conformism that take our breath away.

But very important dogmas were on their way out. Who is to say even now whether the biggest revolution was inner (Freud) or atomic (Planck), chemical (Curie) or automotive (Ford) or political (Russia), cultural (Picasso) or literary (Pound) or religious (the modernist crisis in Catholicism)? The keynote may be the relativity (Einstein) that began in theoretical physics and ended up in everything.

"On or about December, 1910," according to Virginia Woolf, "human character changed," and some of us were not amused. Who knows but that having spent the century tampering with it we may end up with an immutable human nature once again?

It was the end of a glorious era, or the glorious end of an era. The Victorian and Hapsburg empires may have been in decay, but what a wonderful backdrop for culture, business, science and (for those who didn't have to work too hard) daily life! And in the colonies, Sir Wilfrid Laurier declared that "the twentieth century belongs to Canada," a claim we had neither the faith to believe nor the courage to reject.

Knowing as we do how utterly it would be punished and transformed in the First World War, that world may seem unreal to us. Now it's devilishly difficult to get back past the Great War, which acts as a sinkhole, drawing the years before and after into itself. Thus 1900–1910 are the dark ages of the twentieth century.

But the people of 1900–1910 were largely unconscious of living in a prewar decade. Can we gain access? How did *they* think? What was different about living then? We want to catch that decade's awareness of itself, and how it differs from our dim images of it.

Are we about to change our minds? Are we about to revise the intertwined myths of individualism (*I*), rationalism (*know*), secularism (*everything*) and progress (*better*) that until recently have been the story of our century?

Welcome to 1900–1910. May this review prove no less mirror than window.

Michael Czerny SJ was a member of *Compass*'s publishing policy committee until 1990, and has been secretary for social justice at the Jesuit Curia in Rome since 1992.

The Janus Decade

by George Woodcock

History is both an abstract and a symbolic art. Faced with the chaos of actuality and the intimidating abundance of information that the social "sciences" offer, the historian depends on the abstracting intuition that arranges this material, extracting like a painter a form that encloses the leading concept and a series of images that symbolically concentrate the facts and give them meaning beyond themselves. The great practitioners, from Herodotus and Thucydides on, understood this, and so the ancients gave history a muse like the other creative arts and made her a daughter of Zeus.

This ancient abstracting and symbolizing process has to be called up especially when one deals with what at first sight seems an entirely arbitrary concept, the history of a decade, clipped neatly from the calendar between January 1, 1900, and December 31, 1910. There are indeed periods of history that cohere naturally in convenient time capsules. But the decade of which I write can be seen just as easily either as the culmination of the nineteenth century, the last liberating fling of the Victorian era, or as a prelude to the unprecedented catastrophe of the Great War, for indeed it was both. It was not merely a January decade—opening a century as if it were a greater year—but a Janus decade, facing both forward and back. To many who lived in it, it was a tranquil ending to a long age of peace and progress. To those who survived it, it was the prelude to an age of war and of revolutions both political and cultural, as the world would struggle towards a unity few people in 1910 except a handful of utopian idealists thought possible or even desirable.

In literature, from which we gain our first impressions, it was a hesitant, ambiguous decade. The modernists were already at work, like moles under the lawn—Joyce and Lawrence, Eliot and Pound and Lewis—in one sense opening out new concepts of literature and its purpose, in other ways sustaining the genuine insights of the decadent-estheticist movement that had gone underground after the trial of Oscar Wilde in 1896. Yet though books like Joyce's *Dubliners* were already completed by 1910, none of these writers, except for Pound, actually made contact by publication with their potential readerships until the next decade. For those who did not have the privilege of hearing at first hand the views of the young modernists, the cutting edge of literature was still provided by didactic voices that had first been heard in the 1880s and 1890s, like those of Bernard Shaw and H.G. Wells, or by masters of psychological realism, as they were then seen, like Arnold Bennett, Henry James, and the French late-nineteenth-century masters.

The situation in philosophy—and in psychology which was only beginning to detach itself from philosophy—was similar. William James, who drew both disciplines together in such seminal books as *The Variety of Religious Experience* and *Pragmatism*, and John Dewey who also began to publish during this decade (*Studies in Logical Theory*) were at this point transitional figures. Like Henri Bergson in France (whose memorable *L'évolution créatrice* appeared in 1907), they were engaged in creating a post-Nietzschean philosophy that would apply the discoveries of nineteenth-century scientists in new ways. And while Freud published his most important work, *Die Traumleitung* (so misleadingly translated as *The Interpretation of Dreams*), in the first year of our decade, it would not be until the 1920s that his view of the human mind, with its corollary for human culture, would become evident and exert its transformative influence.

There were other fields in which humanity's view of itself and of the universe would be changed by discoveries that began first in the sciences and later spread into philosophy and literature before being apprehended by the general public. The publication in 1900 of the mid-Victorian Gregor Mendel's observations on hybridization seemed at first a mere pendant to the pioneering work on evolutionary biology in the nineteenth century, but eventually it would turn out to be the foundation stone of a new science, genetics. At the same time, a whole new vision of the universe was arising behind the conservative notions of orthodox religion, to which most people in the western world still adhered. Max Planck in 1900 first adumbrated his quantum theory and Albert Einstein in 1905 shook the Newtonian order with his special theory of relativity. However, other discoveries—X-rays, by W.C. Roentgen, and radium, by Marie Curie—were more rapidly applied and immediately recognized through the new Nobel prizes (of which the first were awarded in 1901). As a result, these discoveries were much more influential in arousing awareness of the future that science, which had so rapidly changed the world in the nineteenth century, might still have to offer humanity.

In the visual arts too, that other great area of changing perception, the decade was one of potentiality rather than great achievement. The Postimpressionist masters were already either dead, like Van Gogh, or would die by the middle or end of the decade, like Gauguin and Cézanne. Outside relatively narrow artistic circles in France, their reputation was not yet appreciable. By this time what we call modernist art had appeared in Paris in two movements that carried to a logical conclusion the rebellion against traditional representationalism the Postimpressionists had launched. One was that of the Fauves (the "wild men" as their critics called them), who shocked the critics and the public with their distorted figures, flat planes and gaudy colours and whose rebellion was essentially anarchic; the leading painter of this group was Henri Matisse. The other movement, as intentionally formal as the Fauves appeared to be antiformal, was Cubism, which broke down the shapes of nature but reconstituted them at the shamanic command of the imagination. Pablo Picasso and Georges Braque initiated Cubism between 1905 and 1909, and the key work, painted in 1907, was Picasso's *Les Demoiselles d'Avignon*.

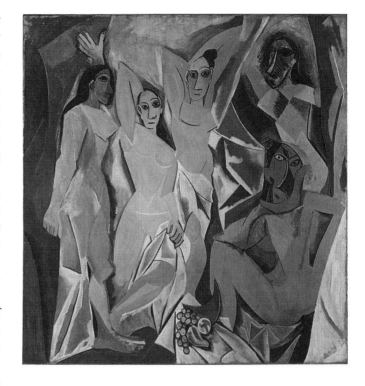

Pablo Picasso (1881–1973), *Les Demoiselles d'Avignon*, 1907. Oil on canvas, 243.9 x 233.7 cm. New York, The Museum of Modern Art, the Lillie P. Bliss Bequest. © Succession Pablo Picasso/SODRAC (Montreal) 1999

One of the important developments of those earlier years of the twentieth century was the concept of an artistic and literary avant-garde. The process probably began in the 1890s in France, when many experimental writers and painters were associated with the militant anarchists, the political avant-garde of the time. Wedded to the antibourgeois conceptions of romanticism, this concept presented the artist by the early years of the twentieth century as the forerunner, leading humanity through new perceptions towards a less imperfect world of relationships. It paralleled the concept of progress that held sway in the nonartistic world. By the early 1900s the hostile reactions to machinery that had inspired not only the Luddites but also social prophets like John Ruskin and William Morris had died away, and this was largely because the undeniable and rapid technological progress of the times was, in western Europe and North America at least, enhancing the lifestyles and standards of all except the poorest of people.

The Rulers: Edward VII, Kaiser Wilhelm, Franz Josef, Czar Nicholas

The steamboat and the railway, the telegraph and telephone and typewriter, had already changed communication and transport dramatically before the new century began. Now, with the launching of the first Zeppelin in 1900, with Marconi's successful transatlantic radio communication in 1901, with Henry Ford's creation of a practicable "car for the people" (the Model T) in 1908, the advances of the nineteenth century were dramatically magnified. Even in areas like the development of synthetic materials and plastics, which we generally think of as associated with much more recent times, the first practical advances were made in the early years of the twentieth century; rayon was first patented and put on the market in 1902, and bakelite, the earliest plastic, was developed in 1909.

Perhaps it was the spread of electricity, which demonstrated that industry could be efficient, productive and clean, that had the broadest effect. Urban transport was changed and suburban spread was encouraged by the development of electric tramways and railways; the number of horses used to drag trams in Britain declined from 36,000 in 1900 to 900 in 1914. In the home, the widespread introduction of electric light, and shortly afterwards of electrically operated appliances, helped to create a domestic self-sufficiency that strengthened the urge of the English middle classes to own their homes.

Greying photographs of Edwardian garden parties and balls, and on a humbler level picnics and bicycle jaunts, give an impression of a kind of sunny late afternoon of contentment before the storm of the Great War. The impression is not entirely false. More people, at least in the industrialized world, were indeed living a better life than during the greater part of the nineteenth century, for apart from the general rise in the standard of living, this was a time when social security was much on the minds of governments and voters. In the late nineteenth century, countries as varied as Bismarck's Germany and tiny New Zealand had introduced health insurance and pensions for the old. These examples were slowly influencing other countries.

Yet times when things are improving are usually also times of growing discontent over prospects incompletely realized. The decade beginning in 1900 was marked by failed revolutions in Spain and Russia as well as by the organization of dissent on peaceful lines in the more educated countries. In Britain, the Labour Party, founded in the early years of the twentieth century, won twenty-nine seats in the elections of 1906.

It was on the high level of international politics that progress showed its most powerful and destructive face and magnified the discontent of populations into situations that would change the face of the world by the end of the succeeding decade. Two movements were on foot that, although few people yet imagined it, would lead to the Great War and its consequences. One was Imperialism, which had reached its apogee during the late Victorian era in the division of what King Leopold II of Belgium, one of the least reputable beneficiaries, called "ce magnifique gâteau africain." By 1900 every European power of any consequence had its slice or slices of the African cake, and the turn of the century was celebrated by the hard-won war in which the British broke the opposition of the Boers and established their rule in South Africa.

Imperialism was not merely a fashion among rulers. The peoples of Europe took its pretensions seriously, and the English especially gloried in the extent to which the map of the world was coloured by the peculiar pink that indicated British rule. The war against the Boers commanded almost total support at home. The relief of Mafeking was greeted with vast popular celebrations during which the homes and premises of critics of the war ("Pro-Boers" as they were called) were vandalized and looted. In the rival imperial countries popular resentment against the British ran high during the Boer War, not because they were imperialists but because they were imperialists of the wrong race.

The crisis of Monarchism was closely linked to the crisis produced by an Imperialism at saturation point. Apart from France—and even there royalism had a noted revival during the decade—the great powers of Europe were still monarchies. Three were old and established ones: Franz Josef's Dual Monarchy of Austria-Hungary with its dependent Slavic territories; Nicholas II's Russia, stretching over Europe and Asia from the Baltic to the Pacific; Edward VII's United Kingdom, which gained imperial status because of the Indian Raj. One monarchy was a new one, the German Reich of William II, which had come into existence as recently as 1871 (four years after the confederation of Canada) through the union of many small kingdoms and principalities and city-states. The difficulties of reconciling the established interests of the old monarchies (and the aging republic of France) with those of this ambitious and industrially efficient new power created hidden tensions in Europe before 1905 and overt ones thereafter.

Germany came late to the imperial feast, picking up mostly unprofitable territories. Even more, Kaiser William II and his advisors were irked by the worldwide naval ascendancy Britain had achieved and sustained from the Napoleonic wars onward. The only way Germany could challenge the Pax Britannica was by creating a navy superior to Britain's and this was the policy that Admiral Tirpitz persuaded William II to accept in 1898. Progress now showed its darker face as new types of deadly and specialized craft were created: destroyers, cruisers and battleships, all heavily armoured with steelplate, propelled by powerful steam turbines, and equipped with increasingly accurate and destructive weapons. Britain was soon led to compete by developing similar craft; the first of them, the celebrated *Dreadnought*, was launched in 1906.

Already, by this time, the political alignments that would fatally divide Europe in the next decade were taking shape, as Britain, which had remained isolated from European affairs since 1815, embarked on a series of alliances and arrangements designed to protect itself as well as other countries from German threats. In 1904 the Entente Cordiale with France was concluded; it led to mutual defence talks in 1906, and to a British entente with Russia, which had recently formed a defensive alliance with France. Germany and Austria-Hungary had already formed a Triple Alliance, with Italy as an unreliable junior partner; it would be used to protect the European adventures of the Hapsburg empire, such as the 1908 annexation of Bosnia and Herzegovina, which provided the eventual provocation for war in 1914.

Peoples as well as governments were taken up in the mounting fever of hostility, and Germany was widely seen by the British people from 1905 onwards as an economic as well as a military threat, largely because new customs regulations required that the country of origin should be shown on imported goods. In this way the amount of foreign goods entering under existing free trade policies was revealed, and the British believed their jobs were being threatened by the introduction of what they persistently referred to—though they continued to buy it—as "shoddy foreign junk."

In the attempts to cool the mounting antagonisms, King Edward VII appeared as the last British monarch to play an active diplomatic role. The longevity of his mother, the Queen-Empress Victoria, who died on January 22, 1901, meant that Edward did not come to the throne until he had grown old in expectancy, and it was the last season of his life he lived out in his reign. But his royal cousins, William in Berlin and Nicholas in St. Petersburg, and his imperial colleague Franz Josef in Vienna became even

more truly winter kings than Edward, for by the end of the next decade all their thrones would be fallen and they themselves would be dead or exiled. Edward visited these kings in the hope of averting the conflict he clearly foresaw, but the other three monarchs, still ruling with almost absolute power of war and peace, were obdurate. A conscientious and unusually popular monarch, Edward died on May 6, 1910, his reign not quite spanning the decade.

The Writers: D.H. Lawrence, T.S. Eliot, James Joyce, Ezra Pound, Wyndham Lewis

Though Europe remained the main political storm centre during this period, and would do so until the middle of the century, Asia was beginning to stir out of its nineteenth-century passivity. In China, the antiforeign Boxer Rebellion of 1900 invited the intervention of European expeditionary forces and weakened the Chinese Empire. In 1905 Sun Yat-sen began organizing a revolutionary alliance in exile and preparing the way for the revolution in February 1911 that would end the ancient empire and begin China's long march into the twentieth century. Japan, rapidly adapting western concepts and techniques, had already entered the modern age. In 1902 it formed an alliance with Britain; in 1905 its imperial aims in Korea and Manchuria led it into conflict with Russia, which in 1903 had completed the Trans-Siberian railway with the aim of extending its power in the Far East.

In the resulting war of 1904–5 the world was astonished to see a great European power defeated for the first time by an Asian one. The event had lasting consequences in Asia, where the Japanese surge towards domination would not be halted until 1945, and also in Europe, where Russia's defeat was one of the causes of its first revolution, in 1905. The Russian people would temporarily lose the constitutional gains they made in that early uprising, but the 1917 Revolution became a virtual inevitability on that cold day in January 1905 when troops fired into the midst of a crowd of a quarter of a million St. Petersburg workers who had come to the Winter Palace to lay their grievances before their "little father," Nicholas II. The soldiers' guns not only killed many people but also destroyed the faith of the survivors in the autocracy.

1900–1910 was a Janus decade indeed: its achievements seemed to crown the nineteenth century; it bred the seeds of the twentieth century's sorrows as well as its joys. Good and bad lay in its promises, and one of its most significant events took place in its very last weeks.

On November 9, 1910, thousands of Russian intellectuals and peasants, defying the disapproval of the Tsarist state, sang "Eternal Memory" as they carried one of the great figures of the time, Leo Tolstoy, to his grave in the woods of Yasnaya Polyana. The young Boris Pasternak was among them, and so a continuity of great Russian writing was sustained. But Tolstoy's most important contact in his last months had been a young Indian lawyer who began to write to him from the Transvaal late in 1909. The lawyer was Mohandas Karamchand Gandhi, later known as the Mahatma, who was just beginning—largely under Tolstoy's influence—the great nonviolent struggle that would eventually liberate India from alien rule without violent revolution and spell the end of the British empire. It was another sign both of the growing role of even a defeated Russia in world affairs and of the increasing importance Asia was assuming in the twentieth-century world as its first decade drew to a close.

George Woodcock, historian, literary critic and author of numerous books on a wide variety of subjects, was a leading figure in Canada's intellectual life. He died in 1995.

Saskatoon: The Instant City

by Don Kerr

In Canada's prairie west, the first decade of the twentieth century brought railways that tied distances together, settlers to fill the great spaces, and towns and cities appearing almost overnight. But most prairie cities already had some existence in the 1880s or 1890s. Only one was entirely a creature of the first, and amazing, decade of this century: Saskatoon.

When the new century began, Saskatoon was a barely visible collection of shacks on the great western plains, a few on one side of the South Saskatchewan River, a few on the other. There was a train bridge, "over which a most miserable mixed passenger and freight train came and went upon no schedule," a tiny depot, a roundhouse that doubled as a Sunday school, two hotels, four stores, a church, a scattering of houses and a ferry that was less reliable than the train. There were "no streets, no sidewalks; neither sewers nor waterworks; no light, no newspaper, no telephones—in fact nothing that bore the slightest resemblance of simplest comfort." There were not even the fifteen houses necessary for Saskatoon to become a village.

Seven years later 4,000 people lived in a newly incorporated city. Three great bridges were under construction, including two railway bridges and a traffic bridge to replace the wretched ferry, for Saskatoon had won the railway sweepstakes for central Saskatchewan and become, in its words, a new Winnipeg. Sewer, water and electricity services were also installed in 1907, and once those support systems were in place permanent brick and stone buildings could start to grow, including one that was three storeys high and plastered with architectural ornamentation. Saskatoon —the instant city.

By 1910 the great western boom had begun and over the next two years the city doubled and doubled again, dwarfing the Saskatoon of 1907 and obliterating the Saskatoon of 1900. Everything went straight up: a building grew eight storeys tall; land rose from $2 an acre in the 1890s to as high as $1,900 a front foot; the total value of building permits rose from a few hundred dollars to $7 million in 1912, a figure that wouldn't be reached again until 1952. Dirt roads gave way to pavement; wooden side-walks to cement ones; coal oil to electricity; pioneer baseball, played without gloves, to a professional team playing in a stadium that seated 3,000; Christmas concerts to travelling theatre companies from the United States and Britain; trade in buffalo bones—the main 1890s export—to trade in everything the new farmers and new towns in Saskatoon's trading area needed.

But the greatest growth was in people, from 113 in the 1901 census to 11,000 people in the 1911 census, when Saskatoon declared itself the "fastest growing city in the world," and then, by its own count, to 28,000 people in the *annus mirabilis*, 1912, the most optimistic of all years throughout the prairie west and in much of the western hemisphere.

The prairies were finally settled. The west was won because Europe needed Canada's wheat to fuel its industrial expansion, key items like iron and steel and ocean freight rates were relatively cheap, and the price of grain was rising. Once freight rates were equalized between points, a city proved a profitable venture every three or four hundred miles. Saskatoon grew as a farmers' city, a warehouse and trading centre. It called itself the Hub City and the City of Bridges. It also provided services like hospitals and entertainment and schools—most notably a university, already under construction and offering classes before the decade was over.

There were newspaper headlines like "Last Year a Hamlet—Next Year a City" and "Truth Stranger than Fiction." There were population predictions of 50,000 to 100,000 people in five to ten years, the "City Rising Steadily as the Temperature." The dominant theme of the period was growth and the ideology of growth. It's easy to see why. Throughout every summer of the decade, the hammer and saw were at work from dawn to dusk constructing the city, and people who invested in real estate on the ground floor, as they put it, were wealthy in five years. So the dollar was almighty and the unearned increment a blessing. Three or four Saskatoons were sold for the one that was built, and avarice was the deadly sin Saskatonians most delighted in and practised.

Almost no one said a word against capital accumulation or growth. They were the unexamined good of the period. Though Christianity was strong in overwhelmingly Protestant Saskatoon as elsewhere in the early west, the pulpit was quiet on such issues. The sabbath was kept holy and liquor reviled. Each new liquor licence was met with new recruits to the temperance forces, and when a local brewery called its beer Liquid Bread a local minister called it liquid poison. Middle-class women organized themselves into the Women's Christian Temperance Union, the Young Women's Christian Association and the Imperial Order of the Daughters of the

Empire to inculcate Christian values, and so gained a hegemony over morality parallel to the one their husbands held over economics and politics. But almost no one spoke against the accumulation of wealth or the claims of progress as the true gods of the new century. This may have been because prominent realtors and businessmen were also prominent members of their congregations and fundraisers for the new churches being built as part of the great boom. More deeply, however, I think it was because of what all Saskatonians could see in front of their eyes, and what they could imagine.

Much can be said about how people lived in that decade, and much detailed information can be gleaned, mainly from newspapers, about working and living conditions. But if we compare the small pioneer community of the 1880s and 1890s with the city that suddenly replaced it, Saskatoon's instant growth can also offer a unique opportunity to view sharply differing value systems side by side.

Pioneer life placed a high value on neighbourliness. It had to because there were few settlers, and they were separated by long distances and faced many hazards, like prairie fires and blizzards. People didn't lock their houses, and travellers were expected to enter even if no one was home. Community gatherings were for everyone. Women who had grown up in the early Saskatoon remarked on the informal friendliness of that life, and there is a marvellous image of those women as girls riding horseback to visit one another. In the city social life was formalized—Mrs. so-and-so will be at home Tuesday afternoon at 3:00 p.m.—and distinctions of class, wealth and race sharpened.

One race prominent in the early life of Saskatoon, the Indians, disappeared almost entirely from sight. The Dakota Sioux were important to the settlers. Chief Whitecap advised on the best site for the city and there was much trade and interaction between the Dakota and the early settlers. Mrs. Trounce, a somewhat formal woman from Devon, called the Indians "such dirty horrible looking creatures" when she first met them, but as her husband had a store and they were often present, she was much more comfortable with them two years later—"you would laugh to see our table with 7 or 8 Indians round it"—and she had made a good friend in Maggie Whitecap. During the 1885 rebellion, when the settlers were afraid of the Indian and Métis, an armed contingent was talked into skirting Saskatoon. Chief Whitecap had tea on the other side of the village, and when the mounted men rode on into the Kusch homestead and the children were frightened and hiding in the snow, an Indian they knew rode them back home where Whitecap warmed the hands of one of the little girls before riding on to battle. In a world where the two groups were equal, there was much human commerce between them.

But the settlers of the new century swamped the nomadic peoples, who had already been put on reserves so that the west might be settled and were kept there with a pass system. For the first sixty years or so of the twentieth century, Indians appeared in Saskatoon only in a camp at Exhibition time and in the Travellers' Day parade. Saskatoon was built where the buffalo roamed, where the Cree camped and made arrows from the saskatoon bushes, where the trail to Batoche went down the main street. For at least half a century, all that world became invisible.

Finally there's the matter of how people lived with the land. The people in the village and on the surrounding homesteads lived easily with nature as had the nomadic peoples before them. They broke perhaps ten acres in a good year, with a hand plough and horses or oxen, and they lived off the land: "We had only to make up our mind to have fish or prairie chicken for supper and go out and get it." They rode horseback or walked, planted gardens, picked berries, and lived lightly on the land—which they would however have developed as rapidly as those that followed had they been able to. There was simply no market and they practised subsistence agriculture.

The wave of settlers that washed into the west after 1900 believed in developing as far as humanly possible what they called "unimproved" land, assuming in that word that the earth was there solely to serve humanity, which we might see today as her most recent and most predatory species. Development, progress, industrialization were unexamined values. Everyone's prosperity, wellbeing and self-image depended on the ploughdown of prairie grassland. Saskatoon came into existence because of that ploughdown and there were thirteen machinery warehouses in the city by 1912. Today you can visit the Western Development Museum and see the prehistoric threshers of those early days, giant machines it's hard not to love though they are an early symbol of that combination of technology and belief that has made southern Saskatchewan one of the most highly cultivated places on the face of the earth. The rich grasslands of a century ago have been as obliterated by monoculture wheat as the Saskatoon of 1900 was by the Saskatoon of 1910.

Yet everyone in early Saskatoon (myself included had I been there) would have welcomed with delight the creation out of "nothing" of a splendid artifact, a city. As we hired an architect to put classical columns on our portico; joined the first drama club and performed *Nellie, the Fireman's Ward*; bought lots in Fairhaven to support the city's growth; voted for the Liberals who had opened the country to immigration; attacked liquor because of all the transient men who drank too much and expectorated on the new sidewalk; recognized the importance of the Grain Growers' Association, whose battles for farmers were everybody's battles; supported the YWCA in its attempts to protect young women; attacked a federal census that said Regina had three times as many people as Saskatoon; welcomed every settler, every building, every new machine like the telephone and the motor car; and believed the world was getting better all the time—as we did all these things and were in our time progressive, we could feel thoroughly satisfied. Who need worry about the environment? There had always been new frontiers (though this was one of the last). We believed in culture more than creatures. How could it have been otherwise for such an amazing event as the settling of the west and the creation of new cities in the first decade of the twentieth century?

But in the first decade of the twenty-first century, we may need a value system in direct opposition to the one that created my city, one that will place the supreme value on nature as our only home and look on the optimistic, joyful ploughdown of the grasslands and the building of prairie cities as an age of innocence. Now not just the west but the whole world is a frontier and things other than cities have to be built, while those things the cities engulfed, cohesive communities and tribal societies living easily with the land, must now challenge the preeminence of the city in our imagination.

Don Kerr is a Saskatoon playwright and poet and the coauthor with Stan Hanson of *Saskatoon: The First Half Century* (1982).

New, Fast and Big

by Rosemary Donegan and Jamie Swift

In *fin de siècle* Paris, the artistic and cultural capital of the West, the salon was giving way to the public café. The theatre was thriving, and the avant-garde, much discussed by the *boulevardiers* of the Latin Quarter, was being born. Montmartre boasted three permanent circuses and a hippodrome. During the International Exposition of 1900, Parisians erected a Venetian façade along the Seine. Across the river was the tallest structure in the world. The Eiffel Tower, originally built to last only through the 1889 Exposition, was retained as "a monument to modernism."

"Upper-class leisure—the result not of shorter working hours but of no working hours at all—produced a life of pompous display, frivolity, hypocrisy, cultivated taste, and relaxed morals," wrote Roger Shattuck in his study of the avant-garde. His book *The Banquet Years* was named for sumptuous bourgeois feasts so elaborate that an intermission was needed between courses. Sherbet doused with champagne cleansed the collective palate. Clearly, affluent patrons of the arts had ample time to indulge their passions.

This was *la belle époque*. As traditional social and moral values were being turned upside down, a new esthetic was arising, and experiments abounded. One such experiment was Cubism, developed by Pablo Picasso along with Georges Braque. With his painting *Les Desmoiselles d'Avignon* (1906–7), Picasso was to reshape the way people see and think about art.

The Cubists rejected the animated and colourful realism of the Impressionists. Inspired by African motifs and influenced by Paul Cézanne's notion of "perceptual realism," they attempted to portray the solid reality of objects in space. Violins, guitars, cigarette packages and the human figure were analysed and dissected, the fragments reassembled on the painting's surface. The Cubists abandoned the attempt to create the illusion of three-dimensional perspective or visual depth, which had preoccupied artists since the Renaissance.

Not to be outdone by the Paris scene, the Italians put their own stamp on the artistic experimentation of the time. The Italian Futurists have often been compared to the Cubists, from whom they drew lessons of technique and representation. But they rejected the static nature of Cubist images, and were fascinated by movement, emotion and action.

The first Futurist Manifesto appeared on the front page of the Paris newspaper *Le Figaro* on February 20, 1909. Written by the Italian poet Filippo Tommaso Marinetti, this fractious polemic demanded a harsh break with the past and an abrupt move into the new century. With characteristic bombast, Marinetti proclaimed the ascendancy of youth, which he and his fellow Futurists represented:

> The oldest among us are thirty; we have thus at least ten years in which to accomplish our task. When we are forty, let others—younger and more daring men—throw us into the wastebasket like useless manuscripts! We desire it!...Our decaying minds already [will be] promised to the catacombs of libraries.

The Futurists were dazzled by the speed and grace of the machine. The new cars and airplanes promised a radiant future. The speed limit on English roads had already been increased to twenty miles an hour. The Wright Brothers had taken off at Kitty Hawk, North Carolina. "We declare that the splendour of the world has been enriched with a new form of beauty, the beauty of speed," proclaimed the Futurist Manifesto. "A race-automobile adorned with great pipes like serpents with explosive breath...a race-automobile which seems to rush over exploding powder is more beautiful than the *Victory of Samothrace*."

Frustrated with Italy's preference for studying its past over attending to its present, the Futurists railed against "historical art." They saw themselves as iconoclasts, destroying museums and libraries while fighting against "moralism, feminism and all utilitarian cowardice." Their glorification of war and patriotism led many of the early Futurists to become involved politically with the young Benito Mussolini.

Yet what appears at first glance to be bombastic rhetoric is in fact something more. When Marinetti wrote of "broad-chested locomotives pawing at the rails like huge steel horses bridled with steel tubes," he was presaging some of the dominant themes of the century to come: a preoccupation with size and speed and technical innovation; a fascination with "the latest" or "the youngest"; the replacement of autonomy with automation.

Even as they wrote, the Futurists' vision was being played out in North America. At Daytona Beach, Florida, in 1910, Barney Oldfield pushed a "race-automobile" to the astonishing speed of 133 miles an hour. The age of the automobile had indeed begun. The car would do more than anything else to change the face of life in industrial society. Henry Ford, the Michigan farm boy who hated farming but loved machines, echoed Marinetti's Futurist bravado in his oft-quoted assessment of history: "History is more or less bunk. We don't want tradition. We want to live in the present and the only thing that is worth a tinker's damn is the history we make today."

Although he later recanted and built a huge historical theme park based on "rural Americana," at the turn of the century Ford had eyes only for the future of the automobile. When he set up his company with twelve investors and $28,000

Henry and Edsel Ford in the Model F, 1905

in capital in 1903, his workers were able to crank out 1,700 Model A's (not to be confused with the 1927 Ford Model A) in just over a year. With the perfecting of the assembly line, Ford's workers became individual parts in a great labour machine. Within seventy-five years Ford was making 4.5 million cars in each "model year."

This was big business, and big business was the order of the day in North America. Whole industrial sectors were moulded into huge single enterprises, or trusts. And while many American populist politicians made reputations as trustbusters, few were able to halt the wave of consolidation.

Among the biggest of the big was J.P. Morgan, founder of a bank bearing his name and the U.S. Steel Corporation. At one point he controlled 741 directorships in 112 companies. Morgan's interest in monopolizing steel led him to seize control of the nickel industry with the formation of the International Nickel Company (Inco), incorporated in New Jersey but with assets at Sudbury, Ontario. Morgan had a solid foothold in the growing arms business and it made sense for his steel trust to reach into the Laurentian Shield. Nickel was essential for hardening the steel skins of the huge battleships, or dreadnoughts, that the great powers were launching.

In addition to his far-flung business interests, Morgan was a patron of the arts. A man fond of grand gesture, he liked to spend several months in Europe every year acquiring objets d'art, rare manuscripts, statues and

J.P. Morgan

paintings to bring back to the U.S., where he adorned his private mansions and the museums and libraries he endowed.

We have no factual record of what J.P. Morgan thought of Henry Ford, although it's likely he suspected that the new industry based on motorized metal boxes hurtling about the countryside would not be bad for business—especially the steel business. We do, however, have E.L. Doctorow's fictional vision of Morgan's meeting with the motor magnate, in the novel *Ragtime*:

> Pierpoint Morgan was that classic American hero, a man born to extreme wealth who by dint of hard work and ruthlessness multiplies the family fortune till it is out of sight....He had sensed in Ford's achievement a lust for order as imperial as his own....He had no illusions that Ford was a gentleman. He recognized him for a shrewd provincial, as uneducated as a piece of wood. But he thought he saw in Ford's use of men a reincarnation of Pharaoism.

The development of art, however, need not depend on wealth, power or the avant-garde. The early years of the century also gave birth to a totally new art form, jazz, developed by a people who were themselves scarcely a generation out of slavery comparable to that employed by the Pharoahs of ancient Egypt. It had little connection with the latest Paris sensation or the world of sharp-eyed enterprisers amassing immense fortunes.

If the 1920s were "the Jazz Age," as F. Scott Fitzgerald maintained, that was true only in the sense that white audiences were first exposed to jazz music on a mass level in that period. While it is difficult to trace the precise genesis of jazz, the music did emerge around the turn of the century; the great pianist Jelly Roll Morton once claimed that jazz music began in 1902.

What we now know as jazz was then called ragtime, or simply "playing hot." But what emerged from the streets, honky-tonks and brothels of New Orleans was something different from the more formal ragtime of Scott Joplin, who had been trained in the tradition of European music. It was a "cultural clambake" with roots in Africa: a combination of the rhythms of black American folk music, often called the blues; the rags played by trained musicians like Joplin; and the music of the marching bands that played in the streets of New Orleans.

People in the early years of the century liked to gather in huge numbers to make their own entertainment, for there were no image merchants plugging the latest pop star. Great spectacles—picnics, parades and public concerts—were the order of the day. In New Orleans the crowds gathered on the shore of Lake Pontchartrain, eating chicken gumbo, red beans and rice, drinking beer and claret wines. Forty bands would gather as people danced, swam and strolled about.

"One of my pleasantest memories as a kid growing up in New Orleans was how a bunch of us kids, playing, would suddenly hear sounds," said jazz guitarist Danny Barker:

> But we wouldn't be sure where they were coming from. So we'd start trotting, start running—"It's this way! It's that way!" And sometimes, after running for a while you'd find you'd be nowhere near that music. But that music could come on you any time like that. The city was full of the sounds of music.

Despite its complex origins, jazz was rooted in the daily experience of black culture and was first played by poor black working people. The washtub bass and cigar-box guitar were the first instruments available to the black blues artists. Joplin himself first laid his hands on a piano in a house where his mother worked as a domestic servant. As New Orleans was one of the American ports closest to Cuba and after the Spanish-American War many units were demobilized there, the town was suddenly flooded with used band instruments: cornets, trombones, clarinets, drums.

The early music was syncopated, with cross-rhythms played between the beats, reflecting European-influenced ragtime; it had plenty of off-pitch blue notes that came from black folk music directly descended from Africa; and it was played *fast*, away from the ground beat with a lot of vibrato. Jazz players call this "fooling around with the beat." "If you gotta ask," said Louis Armstrong in response to someone who asked him what this music was, "you'll never know."

As the pace of American industrialization accelerated after 1900, southern blacks were drawn north to factories like those of Henry Ford. The New Orleans jazz musicians also began to migrate north to Chicago, Detroit, New York, Philadelphia and even Montreal. The closing down of Storyville, New Orleans's fabled red light district, at the request of the U.S. Navy during the First World War, helped speed the diaspora. The music that travelled in this way flourished throughout North America.

Jazz was to influence much of the music of the twentieth century. Rock, soul, popular show tunes, modern concert music: all owe a debt to jazz. By the 1920s, the music had captured the capitals of the world, including Paris. The French, ever conscious of image and symbol, would come to realize that *la musique hot*, played with extraordinary intensity at top speed, somehow said something about the way the era combined the "latest" with primal sources.

"Jelly Roll" Morton

At the time of writing, **Rosemary Donegan** was an art historian and freelance curator living in Toronto and a member of the editorial collective of *BorderLines* magazine. **Jamie Swift** is a writer living in Kingston, Ontario. His books include *Wheel of Fortune: Work and Life in the Age of Falling Expectations* (1995) and *Civil Society in Question* (1999).

Kipling and Yeats: The Apologist and the Visionary

Rudyard Kipling

by Stephanie Vincec

In the first decade of the century, most people regarded Rudyard Kipling as a greater writer than his exact contemporary William Butler Yeats. Kipling was awarded the Nobel Prize for literature in 1907, when he was forty-two; Yeats's Nobel had to wait until 1923, when he was fifty-eight. But Kipling, the energetic apologist for his age, has declined in reputation as the times changed; Yeats, the avant-garde observer of society and human nature, endures as a great poet of this century.

In 1909 Kipling was so popular that his recovery from a critical illness made world headlines. Born in India, he had moved from journalism to short stories, "barrack-room ballads," declamations and novels. He sincerely believed that the white race, especially if English, was born to set standards and bring the benefits of civilization to others. He assumed the divine rights of empire in his hymn "Recessional" (1897) which, *lest we forget*, ascribes military power to the *lord of the farflung battle line*. Even his animal fables in the *Jungle Books* (1904–5) promote the status quo. A human child adopted by wolves learns the rule of Law (of the Jungle, of course) through the pack's Council sessions, and eventually slays a threatening outsider, the tiger.

Sayings of Kipling's have entered our language, but are now often quoted only to be questioned. "*East is east*—or is it?" asked a recent headline, and the phrase *white man's burden*, with its racist assumptions, comes from Kipling's poem appealing to the United States to colonize the Philippines.

The British writer and critic Marghanita Laski puts Kipling's short stories with the "best in the world," especially when read aloud. However, even she has to admit that, out of thirty-six volumes of collected works, much is "dross" and only a few of Kipling's poems are "worth serious consideration."

By contrast, Yeats's smaller output (about ten volumes comprising poetry, plays, speeches, literary essays and the rather far-fetched *Vision*) contains much gold, notably in the single 500-page volume of his collected poems. In mid-career Yeats left behind the incantations and dreamy hypnotic rhythms that had characterized his poetry before 1900. He relearned his craft through writing for the Abbey Theatre and, in 1909, from Ezra Pound, who expounded Imagism and convinced Yeats to seek a greater economy of words.

Already in revolt against Victorianism, the "irrelevant descriptions of nature, the scientific and moral discursiveness of [Tennyson]...the political eloquence of Swinburne, the psychological curiosity of Browning, and the poetical diction of everybody," Yeats used the new theories and his historical studies to discipline his art. The result of his transformation emerged after 1910. Yeats's later poetry is accessible on many levels, from the immediate to the esoteric.

William Butler Yeats

Yeats's aristocratic values of pride, courage, independence and beauty do not blind him to bitter realities. If in armed conflict *a terrible beauty is born* ("Easter 1916"), he has no illusion about glorious motives. In "An Irish Airman Foresees his Death" (1919), his persona admits: *Those that I fight I do not hate,/Those that I guard I do not love.* Yeats's general observation of society in "The Second Coming" (1922) applies just as well today: *The best lack all conviction, while the worst/Are full of passionate intensity.*

Passion itself is the stuff of Yeats's verse. The mystery of life comes through in the sexual imagery of "Leda and the Swan" and the speculations of *a sixty-year-old smiling public man*, who "Among School Children" (1928) thinks of a *youthful mother* whom *honey of generation had betrayed.* His famous line *How can we know the dancer from the dance?* comes from the latter poem. In his sixties, he faced the reality of physical decline: *An aged man is but a paltry thing,/A tattered coat upon a stick* ("Sailing to Byzantium," 1928). A person *can embody truth* but *never know it*, wrote Yeats in 1939, epitomizing his life's goal and the limitations of human achievement.

In their differences, Kipling and Yeats hint at the wide range of English writing between 1900 and 1910. Kipling's considerable talent now seems dated; Yeats forged an utterance that often transcended its occasion.

Stephanie Vincec CSJ was a member of the editorial board of *Compass* magazine and its successor, the board of directors of the Compass Foundation, from 1987 until her death in 1998. She was also a teacher, a literary scholar, and communications director of the Sisters of St. Joseph of Hamilton.

Rethinking the Universe

by John Honner

M odern physics rests on two principal foundations, both of which have their origins in the first decade of the twentieth century. The theory of relativity, a unification of space, time and matter, offers a framework for describing the vastness of the universe. Quantum mechanics, on the other hand, enables us to describe what is happening inside the very small world of the atom. Like rival deities in primeval mythologies, these fundamental theories are in many respects irreconcilable with each other. And yet, again like primitive gods, the origins and fortunes of the two theories are bound up with each other and provide the basis for our understanding of our milieu. Modern physics contains the seeds of a return to a totemic outlook on reality.

The theories of relativity and quantum mechanics have changed humanity irretrievably not merely by spawning nuclear weapons and microchip technology. More fundamentally, they have subverted the naïve experimental positivism of classical physics: the universe can no longer be imagined as a billiard table of rebounding balls or the motion of a perfectly wound-up clock. Physicists today deal much more with fields of force, the paradox of wave-particle duality, and the necessity of revising our inflated respect for the fundamental reality of material objects.

Since the rise of Newtonian mechanics and the fall of Aristotelian cosmology only a few centuries ago, an ideological wall has separated physics and metaphysics; today that wall is crumbling. The story of physics in the first decade of this century is thus also the story of the beginnings of a great shift in the way we understand the universe and, more significantly, in the way we understand human participation in the description of nature.

Physics used to pride itself on its absolute detachment and objectivity. Modern physics implies that such a view of reality is as limited as flat-earth theory: our separations between subject and object are more arbitrary and pragmatic than we realize. In other words, our connections with one another and our world go deeper than we can physically dissect, and there may well be an underlying Being that makes sense of all we observe and experience.

Our common-sense view of the world will continue to work (just as flat-earth theory works quite well on the small scale of building tennis courts or rolling pastry), but physicists are forcing us to realize that—as some philosophers have always suggested—the universe is not quite what our common sense tells us it is. Physics had become a partner with metaphysics again.

Planck's "Purely Formal Assumption"

One cannot mark precisely when it all began, but the turn of the century is as likely a candidate as any. Perhaps the change in centuries brought the courage to think differently. Physicists were puzzled by anomalies in the observed levels of energy radiated from the surface of a heated object. This so-called "black-body radiation" was at odds with the predictions of existing classical theory. Max Planck had wrestled unsuccessfully with this puzzle for years. In early February 1900, he at last found a way to derive an equation that would satisfactorily explain the problem.

Stretching the limits of classical theory, Planck introduced the stratagem of treating the oscillating sources of radiation as if they entailed discrete bundles of energy and not a continuous stream. This ploy he called "a purely formal assumption." The energy of each of these bundles was denoted as E. Next he conceived a constant, h, that linked E with v, the energy of radiation measured as its frequency. Hence he proposed the epoch-making equation:

$$E = hv$$

In later papers the elements of energy were referred to as quanta and h became known as Planck's constant or the quantum of action.

Planck did not entirely resolve the dilemma posed by black-body radiation. Nor had he sensed that, with the introduction of a kind of segmentation into the radiation process, the future of classical physics would be placed in jeopardy. As he wrote later, his work brought about "a break with classical physics far more radical than I had initially dreamt of."

"You Are a Smart Boy, Einstein"

Enter Albert Einstein. In 1900 he graduated in mathematics and physics from the Polytechnic Academy in Zurich. He was the only member of his graduating class not to get a position as an assistant at the academy. His professor, H.F. Weber, was supposed to have told him, "You are a smart boy, Einstein, a very smart boy. But you have one great fault: you do not let yourself be told anything."

Max Planck

In 1901 Einstein submitted a doctoral thesis on the kinetic theory of gases to the University of Zurich, but it was not accepted. At the beginning of 1905 he was twenty-five years old and a consultant in the Swiss Patent Office in Bern. In this remarkable year he wrote, virtually in isolation, five papers in physics: two of these furthered the beginnings of quantum theory; the others established the theory (and consequences) of special relativity. In a list of the most important writings ever produced in physics, three of Einstein's 1905 papers would surely be found in the first ten places (and his 1915 study of general relativity would probably be given first place). Perhaps it was just as well that he did not let himself be told anything!

Einstein's first paper in 1905, on the generation of light, continued Planck's work. What Planck has called "a purely formal assumption," however, Einstein described as "a heuristic viewpoint." Einstein shifted attention from the oscillating particle that was the source of radiation (Planck's hypothesis) to the nature of the radiation itself. Where Planck focused on black-body radiation, Einstein included in his attention another anomaly, the so-called photoelectric effect observed by Heinrich Hertz late in the nineteenth century. It seemed possible to dislodge electrons by beaming radiation onto the surface of metals. The curiosity, once again, was that the dislodgement appeared discrete rather than continuous.

The photoelectric effect seemed to imply that light radiation was not a continuous stream, as James Clerk Maxwell's classical theory presupposed, but particle-like. This was the basis for Einstein's cunning "heuristic viewpoint." As Planck had done for the oscillating particle, Einstein stipulated that the energy of the radiated light itself is composed of "light quanta." That is, light can be considered as consisting of particles of energy, E, where, as with Planck's equation, the energy was related to the frequency of vibration of radiation by the quantum of action, h. In this single equation a wave property (frequency) was related to an assumed particle property, a nonsense that was equivalent to advertising chalk as cheese and permanently confounded Einstein.

A year later, in his paper on the theory of light emission and absorption, Einstein admitted that his new radiation theory was at odds with Maxwell's theory. A set of stairs is, after all, completely different from an inclined ramp: one can stand anywhere, and hence at any height, on a ramp; but on stairs one can stand only on predetermined levels. The consequences of Einstein's quantum theory would rebound on him later, after Niels Bohr's discovery of the quantum mechanics of atomic structure. Meanwhile, however, Einstein had another interest: relativity.

It is a popular myth that Einstein sublimated the theory of relativity out of his own imagination. The recently published first volume of Einstein's papers show that as early as 1899 Einstein was corresponding with his first wife, Mileva Maric, about the "electrodynamics of moving bodies," the title of his paper on relativity in 1905. Einstein himself later stated that the theory of relativity was ripe for anybody to discover in 1905.

Certainly there were great advances in theory being made and, at the same time, curiously inexplicable experimental results being reported. Results of the Michelson-Morley experiment of 1879–81 suggested that the speed of light is unaffected by the velocity of its source and hence that time cannot be absolutely defined. At stake, ultimately, were the Newtonian notions of absolute space and time. One persisting heritage of classical physics is the idea that the universe follows its fixed mechanical agenda in some vast, invisible, calibrated bucket of absolute space, by reference to which all that is in the universe can be given a definite location and timetable.

Albert Einstein

In his 1905 paper on relativity Einstein offered a theoretical framework in which all motion was taken to be relative. That is, the common-sense idea of a body possessing invariantly fixed dimensions and existing in a fixed, absolute time-frame was rejected. Instead, lengths and times were real only within the observer's own space-time frame of reference. Events that are simultaneous in one system are thus not necessarily simultaneous in systems moving relative to each other. What appears to be one length in one reference frame will be another length in another reference frame. Einstein also postulated that the speed of light (the speed of electromagnetic radiation) is always constant, whatever the velocity of its source.

If Einstein was right, then Newtonian views of space and time had to be revised. In ordinary life, of course, no differences would be felt. In high-speed particle physics, however, the effects of time dilation would become very obvious. The mass of a body at rest would increase dramatically as a particle approached the velocity of light. (Such effects are indeed observed in particle accelerators today.) There was thus uncovered a connection between mass and energy.

In another 1905 paper on the inertia and energy-content of a body, Einstein explored the famous equation $E=mc^2$, which connected mass (m), energy (E), and the velocity of light (c) in a manner ultimately to have dramatic and drastic consequences not only for Nagasaki and Hiroshima but for the entire future of the planet Earth. Indeed, Einstein's 1905 paper concluded with the thought that bodies "whose energy content is variable to a high degree, for example radium salts," could be used to test the mass-energy equation. Little did he realize then how close he was to suggesting the future uranium-fission experiments and the atomic bomb.

Einstein's paper on relativity received no sudden amazed response. Eventually it was Planck himself, the leading physicist of the time, who published the first paper picking up on Einstein's work. Quite prophetically Planck wrote, "Like the quantum of action in the quantum theory, so the velocity of light is the absolute central point of the theory of relativity." These two fundamental constants of nature, h and c, were to dominate future physics.

To some it might seem that Einstein was relativizing the universe. Einstein, however, saw himself doggedly pursuing the scent of "the Old One," his affectionate name for his impersonal God. The very comprehensibility of the universe was for him a miracle of the highest order. Despite the revolution he introduced into physics, he was, in the end, a classical thinker, after the fashion of his hero, Isaac Newton. What would shatter Einstein's dream would be a theory that denied the possibility of human beings giving an ordered mechanical account of all motion in the universe. Such a theory, as is inevitable in human affairs, was soon to appear.

Bohr and the "Jesuit Maxim"

In 1909 Einstein declared his confidence that the light-quanta and light-wave ideas could be reconciled. In that same year, however, a Danish student called Niels Bohr, then twenty-five, began his doctoral thesis on the electron theory of metals formulated by Hendrik Antoon Lorentz. One of his main results was that the theory failed to account for observed phenomena. In 1910, Ernest Rutherford began the scattering experiments that were to indicate that the so-called "uncuttable" atom in fact consisted of a heavy, positively charged nucleus surrounded by distant electrons.

Just as a shaken bookcase emits distinctive sounds of falling books, so also "excited" atoms had been known to produce distinctive radiation energies: Johann Balmer had provided a neat mathematical formula for the spectrum of hydrogen in 1884. Just why his formula worked remained unexplained. Even more difficult to explain, however, was the stability of the Rutherford atom. Because rotating electrons (unlike planets around the sun) are moving charges, according to Maxwell's classical electromagnetic theory they should spiral into the positive nucleus and give off a huge flash of energy. This rather sweetly named "Rayleigh-Jeans catastrophe" was never observed. What, then, was happening in the atom?

The basic strategy for approaching this question was provided by Niels Bohr in 1913. All that was required (and it was quite a requirement!) was a limitation to the applicability of classical physics. Bohr proposed that just as a closely examined photograph shows up grainy rather than even in colour, so also, on the scale of the very small, there are gaps or discontinuities in nature: the electrons are confined to certain orbits (or energy levels) and hence are unable to spiral into the nucleus. Rather than "sliding" from one orbit to the next through the intervening space, the electron went from one level to the next without trespassing on the space between (at least not in a way physics could detect).

Niels Bohr

Counterintuitive as it was, Bohr's theory was immediately successful: it explained the stability of the Rutherford atom, it explained the patterns of the hydrogen spectrum, and it explained the values of the constants used in Balmer's formula. But it left an uneasy taste in physicists' mouths: to arrive at his conclusions Bohr had to use aspects of the very classical physics he was elsewhere rejecting. Bohr would joke that this was a sign of deep truth, where both what one had to say and its opposite were equally true!

In proposing this correspondence principle, Bohr was having his cake and eating it at the same time. Einstein was horrified, and wrote to Max Born in 1919, "The quantum theory gives me a feeling very much like yours. One really ought to be ashamed of its success, because it has been obtained with the Jesuit maxim: 'Let not thy left hand know what thy right hand doeth.'" Where continuity in the physical world was lost, mechanical connectedness and strict causality were also at risk. And if causal connections were no longer plausible, the objective mathematical explanation of nature could also be seriously questioned. How then could a physicist describe the universe? In 1924 Einstein was so horrified at Bohr's interpretation of quantum mechanics that he wrote, "I would rather be a cobbler, or even an employee in a gaming house, than a physicist."

Much later on in their debate Einstein conceded to Bohr that there was a consistency in quantum mechanics, but it was a consistency with which Einstein was most unhappy. Einstein was optimistic that more comprehensive theories could be developed that would reconcile the two views and save the ordered mechanics of the universe implicit in classical physical theory; indeed, most of his later life was spent searching for a unified field theory that would reconcile all physics. Given his view of God as one who provided order rather than randomness, Einstein had no other choice. More recently again, however, experimental evidence seems to support Bohr's more radical views: we do not, in theory, live in a world of isolated objects.

The Totemic Universe

Totemism is a term that attempts to describe primitive patterns of living in a particular ecology. Key to these patterns are associations between tribal clans and particular features of the landscape: the survival of the clan is tied to the survival of a particular species of flora or fauna, and vice versa. This most elementary form of religion implies that individual, clan, tribe and environment are connected. A spirit that is literally Aboriginal hovers over the present and makes it one with the past.

In totemic societies the sense of sequential time is not strong. Neither is skill in counting significant, for counting entails individuation or distinguishing one object from another. Nor is any strong distinction made between matter and spirit: the material environment is replete with spirits, and it is but a short step of human imagination from totemism to animism.

Newtonian physics influenced the rise of empiricist philosophies and critical methods. Its norms permeated our culture. We have got used to the idea of ourselves as being isolated objects living in the absolute space and time of ideal histories. We have developed one outlook towards the material universe, and another towards the spiritual. We have, for too long, lived dualistically, in quite separated realms of the temporal and the transcendental. If modern physics continues along its present course, in many ways it will teach us once again to live totemically: connected with one another, connected with our pasts and futures, and with a healthy skepticism about material objects as ultimate models for what is real.

For Christians, this represents a welcome change of mind. Our diverse and almost incomprehensible orthodox theologies of incarnation (hypostasis), eucharist (transubstantiation) and resurrection (body and soul) hold little meaning today and are ripe for reformulation. So also, once the Newtonian walls are broken down, our imagination of ways in which God can be present in the world is enlivened.

There are dangers, of course, in letting one's imagination get too far ahead of physical theory. Our world will not change in its appearance. How we think about it and how we see ourselves living in it, however, are ready for radical revolution. Niels Bohr said that the theory of relativity represents the greatest change in human knowledge since the words "here" and "now" were first invented. He is probably right, and it all began at the start of our century.

John Honner has degrees in science, philosophy, and theology. From 1988 to 1998 he was editor of *Pacifica: Australian Theological Studies*, and for many years he was a member of Jesuit Theological College and lectured in philosophy and theology at the United Faculty of Theology in Melbourne. His publications include *The Description of Nature: Niels Bohr and the Philosophy of Quantum Physics* (1988).

The Crisis of Modernism

by Roger Haight

Until the Second Vatican Council, one would have been hard put to define what modernism was. There are a few basic facts on which people might have agreed: modernism was a theological movement within the Roman Catholic Church during the first decade of this century (although some even hesitate at the notion of a movement lest it imply a unified consensus); what came to be called modernist writings began to appear in the 1890s in France, and then in England, Italy, and to some extent the United States; modernism reached its apogee in 1907 when it was identified and condemned by the Vatican; in the following years the so-called modernists were simply suppressed by church authority; and by the beginning of the Great War in 1914 modernism was dead.

But beyond those facts, what kind of Catholics were the modernists? What was really going on in their writings? In their own minds, these thinkers were loyal defenders of the faith, building bridges across the growing gap between the church and the intellectual culture of Europe at the end of the nineteenth century. In the judgement of the condemning papal authority, these writers were heretics; they were a fifth column, a conspiracy corroding the faith of the church from within.

To appreciate how much the foundations of the church needed rethinking, one has to imagine the cleavage between the Catholic Church and the intellectual world of the time. Beneath the shifting social and political movements of the nineteenth century, science and historical research gradually opened up new vistas for human understanding. Since Kant, philosophy had taken on an anthropocentric character; it appealed to human experience. Achievements in all realms were often accompanied by a heady confidence in human reason and a disdain for authority. Against this modernity the Catholic Church simply reasserted its own authority, principally in the person of the pope. In 1864 the Vatican condemned the proposition that the church should in any way accommodate itself to modern civilization. A few years later, it declared the pope infallible. Its entire system of theology at the end of the century was based on an appropriated divine authority, paradoxically buttressed by a rationalistic apologetics, and imposed on the clergy and faithful by didactic methods of teaching. Catholics who were fearful that new ways of thinking would undermine faith itself looked beyond the Alps for a papal pillar of security. The reaction to modernism was called integralism: a neat system based on authority in which nothing could be sacrificed.

The fear of the modernists lay in the other direction. To them it appeared that the church was literally cutting itself off from a growing body of knowledge and closing its doors to intellectual inquiry. They believed that faith did not entail suppression of thought. Their strategy was to enter into the patterns of thinking of the time and draw out of them a renewed apologetics, faith and church. This approach, however, raised a serious question. Was this a compromise or even a sellout of faith to the contemporary antireligious culture? Or was it what would later be called an inculturation, bringing faith to bear on culture through expression in the forms of culture? That question can be answered by a brief survey of the people involved.

Maurice Blondel (1861–1949), of Dijon, France, defended and published his doctoral thesis, *L'Action*, in Paris in 1893, a convenient date for marking the beginning of the modernist movement. A loyal and pious Catholic layman, Blondel accepted the seemingly antireligious philosophical presuppositions of the day as the point of departure for his thesis. Then, by a meticulous analysis of human action, he led the reader to the religious question and the brink of faith. Philosophy, he said, cannot evade the religious question. The presuppositions and method underlying this work, completely misunderstood by the scholastics of the period, would provide a model for the gradual revival of Catholic theology from the 1930s onward.

Alfred Loisy (1857–1940) was a priest who began his academic career as a Scripture scholar at the Institut Catholique in Paris. He was dismissed from his post the same year Blondel defended his thesis because of his progressive views on Scripture. Then in 1902, he published his famous *L'Évangile et l'église*, which touched off the real crisis. In this book, Loisy proposed a radically historical view of the Catholic Church, defending the church as a historical organism that grew out of the Gospel of Jesus and adapted to different circumstances in history. The problem was that the contemporary Catholic Church did not conceive itself as a product of historical development. Although it received some critical acclaim, *L'Évangile et l'église* was placed on the Index of forbidden books. Loisy was even attacked by Blondel in 1904; there was no conspiracy between these two. Not until 1943, in the encyclical letter *Divino Afflante Spiritu*, did the church recognize the legitimacy of historical critical method in the study of Scripture, which would be so influential in the reforms of Vatican II.

Lucien Laberthonnière (1860–1932) was an Oratorian priest-teacher whose interest in philosophy and theology drew him into the modernist controversy. Early on, his reading of *L'Action* caused him to write Blondel a letter, which led to friendship and collaboration. Laberthonnière defended Blondel's "method of immanence," and in 1905 Blondel bought and Laberthonnière edited the influential *Annales de philosophie chrétienne*, in which many of the modernist issues were discussed.

Also in 1905 Édouard Le Roy (1870–1954) appeared on the modernist scene in Paris with the publication of a short article entitled "Qu'est-ce qu'un dogme?" Although he was professionally a mathematician and philosopher of science, he had internalized the philosophy of Henri Bergson, and he aligned himself with the thought of Blondel and Laberthonnière, in the end without their approval. Through the category of "thought-action," he developed a theory of dogma that interpreted the propositions of belief in terms of a faith lived in action, and thus put the question of dogma at the heart of the controversy. Put forward in a very simple way, his theory only added fuel to the polemics, which in turn elicited several attempts at clarification. Throughout the modernist crisis, Le Roy defended Loisy on principles he thought consistent with those of Blondel and Laberthonnière—who in turn distanced themselves from Le Roy and Loisy.

The English Jesuit George Tyrrell (1861–1909) is considered, along with Loisy, an archetypal modernist. Tyrrell began his career as a teacher, then became a writer on the staff of *The Month*, was noted as a director of spiritual retreats, and wrote a good deal in the area of popular spirituality. He sensed the strain placed on educated Catholics by the prevailing theology. His explicitly theological writings deal with issues touching on the foundations of faith such as revelation, the method of theology, and the development of doctrine. He was an eclectic rather than a systematic thinker. The recurring theme in his work is experience, and how both historical and inward experience must be integrated into theology. The decade was not kind to Tyrrell: he was expelled from the Jesuits and excommunicated, and he died rather suddenly at the age of forty-eight.

Perhaps the most fascinating of the modernists, Baron Friedrich von Hugel (1852–1925) was also based in England although he was given to travel and had connections all over Europe, including the Vatican. A man of diverse interests, von Hugel is best known for his writings on religious mysticism. He was the glue that held these disparate thinkers together in some solidarity. He knew all the protagonists, encouraged them, mediated

Alfred Loisy

between them, tried to protect them in Rome, and himself entered into the academic list on the basis of his technical knowledge of Scripture and his views on religious experience.

There were of course other modernists as well. In the end any given modernist may have held an extreme position on one topic or another. But it is difficult to find anything in the thought of the leading modernists that is seriously objectionable or that is not held, perhaps in modified form, today.

The first decade of the century, then, was a period of intellectual excitement and confusion within the Catholic Church. The lack of clarity was due in part to the profusion of social and political movements occurring at the same time. Especially in France, the relation between the church and the state was changing rapidly. Catholic-inspired social movements, loosely connected with modernism, commanded attention. The relation of national churches to the Roman centre of authority was also an underlying issue. But strictly theological confusion reigned as well. The modernists frequently and justly claimed that they were misunderstood.

It is clear that the first intention of the movement was not inward- but outward-looking. All of these writers stood firmly within the Catholic Church and their primary motivation was to address intellectual currents outside the church. But in so doing it was necessary to adjust the language of the church to new forms of speech. Blondel's first audience consisted of the rationalist philosophers of his day. As for Loisy, his thought rested on a desire to take history seriously and use it to interpret the meaning of revelation, faith and the Church. But whatever the original intention, modernist ideas were almost immediately redirected into an inner-church controversy. The tone was highly polemical, even emotional and strident. The modernist debate became a highly charged crisis.

Two characteristics of the period help explain the crisis religiously. First, the church's theology at the time was completely devoid of historical consciousness. It had no sense of being in time, of the historical dimensions of the church's origins and development. Despite the advances made by John Henry Newman in this area, the ideological structure of the church's self-understanding simply did not take historical change and movement into account.

At the same time, this lack of historical consciousness generated fear. Only religious fear can explain the exaggerated reaction against modernist ideas. When the whole world seems to be changing, the pressure on an institution that will not budge can only rise. Certainly the church feared the modern world, but the outside world was manageable as long as it remained outside. However, the logic of modernist thinking was drawing the hostile elements of the modern world inside the church. What was feared, then, were internal forces that would change the very structure of the church.

The focal point of this fear was the nature of religious authority, which was also an absolute institutional authority. The forces from outside the church that were impelling change could only be read as a challenge to this authority. What happens when historical study demonstrates the historicity and thus relativity of ideas and institutions? How can an absolute institutionalized religious authority tolerate an appeal to human experience as the medium for truth and the validity of dogma?

The logic of fear explains the way the modernist controversy was solved. In July 1907 the Vatican issued a decree (*Lamentabili Sane Exitu*) that condemned a series of propositions taken out of context from modernist writings. On September 8 of the same year, the papal encyclical *Pascendi Dominici Gregis* defined and condemned what it called "modernism," a term not previously in common use. Looking back at *Pascendi*, one has to recognize a document that was politically brilliant, deadly effective, intellectually dishonest, and totally comprehensible in the historical situation. It presented modernism as an abstract system of thought with first premises, an integral logic and a series of conclusions. This whole system was then labelled accurately as an insidious combination of all heresies. The argument was dishonest because the system did not accurately describe the thought of any modernist, nor did any modernist subscribe to it. Quite literally the Vatican created the modernism it condemned. But it cleverly used modernist writers to construct the heretical theological system, drawing together their themes, ideas, even phrases.

These decrees were only one element of a two-pronged attack on modernist thinking. The other consisted of institutional repression. Committees of vigilance were to be set up in every diocese to monitor what was being taught in seminary classrooms. Writings were to be censored and those suspected of modernist ideas were to be reported. In the end all those who held office in the church, from bishops to seminary professors to candidates for ordination, were to profess an extensive oath against modernism as it was defined by the encyclical. By 1914, when Europe became caught up in a wider cataclysm, modernism as a movement ceased to exist. And yet the fabricated heresy lived on in the fear of it and the reaction against it. Candidates for ordination were still taking the oath against modernism in the late 1960s. In these later years this practice caused no little anxiety among those who were aware of what they were doing. They were obliged to take an oath, often in the chapel before the Blessed Sacrament, to something that they knew was not true.

If we look at the significance of the decade of modernism for the Roman Catholic world, two areas of reflection fairly leap off the pages of this history. The first concerns the discipline of theology, the second the exercise of religious authority.

Modernist theology may be considered analogous to the Protestant liberal theology that developed during the course of the nineteenth century. By 1920 Protestant liberal theology had in some respects run its course and a neo-orthodox theological reaction set in. While returning to biblical themes and the classical ideas of the Reformers, this neo-orthodoxy internalized much of the ground gained by liberal theology. Most important, it responded to liberal theology *theologically*.

In the Roman Catholic Church this natural theological development never occurred. The budding equivalent of liberal theology never got off the ground, so that no Roman Catholic equivalent of neo-orthodox theology ever developed. The Catholic Church has never really had a theology that learned from and internalized the problems of modernity and at the same time responded to the modernist program with careful theological reasoning. The response to modernism was an exercise in pure authoritarian power. And the gradual theological reawakening before the Second Vatican Council was really a cautious resumption of the modernist agenda unfolding within the context of fear of authority.

Tyrrell was correct in his complaint against the confusion of Roman theology with revelation. But the church was unable to grasp this distinction; it identified the prevailing scholastic theology with revelation and imposed it on the basis of authority. The legacy of this identification has been more than a mistrust of theology: it has been a deep rift between theology and authority. It consists in a chasm between a creative discipline of theology and a "theology" supported primarily not by argument but by sheer authority.

The second problem, the problem of authority, is closely related. Two distinct kinds of authority—religious authority, the authority of the leaders of a religious community to mediate God's authority to religious sensibility, and disciplinary authority, the authority of office-holders in a large institutional church who try to maintain discipline—run together in the magisterium. In the modernist period, this distinction was not operative and probably was never perceived by the church's leadership. Religious authority was reduced to disciplinary authority and became confused with a need for order and institutional uniformity. In exercising authority in this way, the Vatican laid aside all concern for truth and practically dismissed the value of inquiry. It took fifty years before humility in the face of mystery, courage in the face of change, and fearless confidence in the Spirit of God came together in Pope John XXIII's decision to call the Second Vatican Council.

The fear of modernism and the modern world seemed to die all at once at Vatican II. The oath against modernism is no longer taken. Insofar as it was a historical movement and its particular language was tied to the first decade of this century, modernism is a phenomenon of the past. Most of its significant ideas have been incorporated into Catholic theology today. But the deeper structural elements of the crisis are perennial and are destined to live on, at least in the near future.

Roger Haight SJ taught systematic theology at Regis College in Toronto at the time of writing, and later at Weston Theological College in Cambridge, Mass.

Bloody Dress Rehearsal for 1917

by Stanley B. Ryerson

Czar Nicholas II

In 1905, hundreds of working men and women—socialists, radicals, democrats—gathered in Winnipeg and Vancouver in support of the Russian revolution of that year. They helped form a current of world awareness that is crucial for social consciousness and action, in Canada as elsewhere, and they deserve to be remembered.

What was that revolution? And why should it concern Canadians? Moments of contact with our remote "northern neighbours" have been fleeting and far apart. In 1854, an Upper Canada College "old boy," Major Dunn, won the Victoria Cross for valor in the Crimean War. In 1956 this writer, also a onetime UCC pupil, accompanied Canadian Communist Party leader Tim Buck to the Twentieth Congress of the Communist Party of the Soviet Union in Moscow. Midway between those dates was the defeated revolution of 1905—the "dress rehearsal" for October 1917.

The turn of the century was marked by wars of empire—South African, Spanish-American, and shortly thereafter Russo-Japanese—which with the warped vision of hindsight we now see as prelude-tremors to 1914 and 1939. War (the encounter of competing empires' greed) and revolution (the challenge to despotic power structures of exploitation) intersected, as Russian and Japanese expansionisms collided in Manchuria, Siberia and the Pacific rim. Having blockaded Russia's fleet at Port Arthur (1904), Japan defeated its main army at Mukden and destroyed its great fleet, brought all the way from the Baltic, at Tsushima (March and May 1905). These defeats of the tsarist autocracy triggered workers' revolts and a peasants' war. On St. Petersburg's Bloody Sunday in January 1905, troops fired on a huge, peaceful, icon-bearing crowd headed by a priest. There followed strikes in heavy industry, on the railroads and in the Baku oil-fields; peasant risings over a vast area; and in December an insurrection in Moscow that was bloodily suppressed.

Peace having been made with Japan in August, in October the tsar conceded a limited parliamentary regime (the Duma) and a semblance of agrarian reform. But the ensuing Stolypin administration restored "order": opposition deputies to the Duma were arrested, some were sent to Siberia, and others sought refuge abroad—one or more would address workers' meetings in Canada. Pogroms occurred in the Ukraine, Bessarabia, White Russia and Poland: the tsar, it was said, was trying to cure social unrest with racial bleeding.

Among exiles who found a home here in Canada, more than a few "nineteen-o-fivers" became staunch activists in labour and socialist movements. Their experience of this first Russian revolution included the spontaneous emergence of a new kind of political institution, the "soviet" (a council of soldiers, workers and peasants), with its promise of a rank-and-file democracy from below; the fact of the revolution's defeat; and a historic question mark about its potential for the future.

Stanley B. Ryerson was for many years Canada's leading Marxist historian. His books include a two-volume history of Canada, *The Founding of Canada* (1960) and *Unequal Union* (1968). He died in 1998.

The Second Decade

47	A Decade of Suffering and Violence	by Jacques Monet
49	In 1910 Human Character Changed	by Modris Eksteins
56	Alarm Bells for Civilization	by Gwynne Dyer
61	The Social Gospel: Christianity for the Here and Now	by Ramsay Cook
67	Filling the Gap on the Homefront	by Kori Street
70	A Strike with an Elusive Meaning	by Doug Smith
73	Ontario's Bitter Language Fight	by Robert Choquette
76	Influenza: Disease of the Wind	by Eileen Pettigrew
78	T.E. Lawrence: Military Hero, Anguished Searcher	by Dennis Duffy
81	Russia: Power Was in the Streets	by Mary McAuley
84	Ireland: Destructive Adventure	by John Francis Larkin

A Decade of Suffering and Violence

by Jacques Monet

The second decade of the century, 1910–1920, brought the violent end of a world, and also a new and radical beginning. It was not made up of four years of war and six of peace. Rather, it was ten years of the worst suffering and violence in history. It opened with the Italian bombing of Tripoli in 1911 and closed with reports in late 1920 that the influenza virus, spread on the battlefields of Europe in 1918, had by then killed almost five times as many people as had perished in the Great War itself.

The war was a mad, distorted dream that mobilized some sixty-five million people and killed more than eight million. In the beginning, it was a crusade to defend the integrity of small communities and protect the safety of orphaned children. In the end, in the words of Winston Churchill, "it had brought out all the horrors of all the ages." But also the epic valor of ordinary people.

For Canadians, the Great War brought out the worst as well as the best. Overseas, tranquil courage, great deeds and noble sacrifice. At home, in-ability to cope. A government born out of the opportunistic and unnatural union of Tories and Quebec *nationalistes* succeeded only in dividing our founding peoples from each other and our newest citizens from their com-patriots. Sir Wilfrid Laurier, whose reconciling vision had shone like a bea-con over our century's first decade, became the leader of a broken minor-ity, his achievement in pieces before the bigotry of Ontario's language laws and the Dominion's legal harassment of the Germanic and Slavic Canadians he had invited to our land. *"C'est fini,"* he whispered, and they were his last words, February 17, 1919.

The decade was indeed an end. The century-long British Peace was broken—first in Ireland at Easter 1916. But the British Empire survived for several more decades, while four other great empires fell: the Chinese first, later the Austro-Hungarian and Russian, and finally the Ottoman, which was the oldest. On December 9, 1917, General Allenby secured Jerusalem, the first "crusader" to succeed since the Holy Places had fallen to Sultan

Saladin in 1187. Did he have in mind that a month earlier a national home in the Holy Land had been promised to the Jewish people?

The second decade also bore a new consciousness. Albert Schweitzer's reading of the Parables brought him to Gabon in 1913, and Benedict XV's reflections led him in 1919 to decisive direction for native leadership in the Roman Catholic Church. It bore a new social passion: a new language and politics for unions, new votes and a daring new place for women, new organizations and a new voice for the churches.

For the Bolsheviks, who seemed to be making true Chancellor Beth-mann-Hollweg's 1914 prediction that "the future belongs to Russia," and for the nationalists, it was a decade of triumph. In the womb of these triumphs the pulse of the dictator's spirit was beginning, faintly but surely, to beat. Benito Mussolini founded the Fasci del Combattimento in March 1919, Josef Stalin won laurels as the Bolsheviks defended their revolution in a civil war, and Adolf Hitler took charge of the Nazi party's propaganda at Munich's Hofbrauhaus in August 1920.

Still, the principal date of the decade must be November 11, 1918, and the place Compiègne. Soldiers of tired and shattered armies trekked out of the wood in silence, heroes unable even to raise a cheer. What was their prayer? Surely that some time peace would have its heroes then, not war.

Jacques Monet SJ is a historian and has been president of both Regis College in Toronto and the University of Sudbury. He was a member of the *Compass* editorial board from 1990 to 1992.

In 1910 Human Character Changed

by Modris Eksteins

On or about December, 1910, human character changed....All human relations have shifted.

—Virginia Woolf

Without being as chronologically specific, many others have agreed with Virginia Woolf that some fundamental changes occurred in the early years of the second decade of this century. Ben Tillett, the British dockers' leader who led a nationwide strike in 1911, reflected on the mood of the age: "A strange, hectic period of our economic history! It was a great upsurge of elemental forces." In Germany in 1912, after stunning electoral gains by a liberal-socialist alliance, Friedrich Naumann, a liberal leader, commented: "Something new has begun in Germany in these past days; an era is approaching its end; a new age has dawned." And observing a new energy in many aspects of life but especially in the arts, Ford Madox Ford had the impression that the years 1910 to 1914 as a whole were "like an opening world."

If years in a life seem to accelerate, so do decades in a century. By 1911 our century had acquired a distinct momentum. The automobile, the airplane and the moving picture, all so recently developed, were inescapable and enthralling symbols of this movement and change. So were the new dances: the turkey trot and the tango. Urban industrial civilization, with its ethic of enterprise and progress but also its reality of commotion and cacaphony, had clearly conquered the West. The tram and the motor car had taken over the city. Urban sprawl was well underway. By 1910 greater London and New York had populations of more than five million, Paris nearly three, and Berlin two. Further growth seemed certain.

Many were excited by the change; others were less sanguine. Filippo T. Marinetti and his fellow Futurists worshiped the machine; to them it was a source of liberation. E.M. Forster, however, was greatly troubled: "Science, instead of freeing man...is enslaving him to machines....God

Giacomo Balla (1871–1958), *Automobile in Corsa* (*Car in a Race*), 1914. Tempura and ink on paper mounted on canvas, 53.8 x 73.4 cm. Toronto, Art Gallery of Ontario. © Giacomo Balla/SODRAC (Montreal) 1999

what a prospect!"

Emancipation, so central a theme in this century, had already emerged as a major concern by the early years of the second decade. Women, youth, homosexuals, labour and native populations were all beginning to mobilize for action. The metropolitan centre was under attack from the periphery.

The women's suffrage movement turned to radical measures. In Britain the Pankhursts, mother and daughters, led a campaign of militancy that saw not only smashed windows in smart Oxford and Regent Street department stores but also the tragic death of Emily Davison, trampled by the king's horse at the Epsom Derby on June 4, 1913. To Olive Schreiner in 1911, the "new woman" was "no Helen of Troy passed passively from male hand to male hand; but that Brynhild whom Segurd found, clad in helm and byrne, the warrior maid."

Youth saw itself as an agent of renewal. The scouting movement grew; youth groups sprang up in political parties and churches; and in 1913 thousands of German youths gathered on the Hohe Meissner mountain to gorge themselves on myth and ritual and to condemn bourgeois mediocrity and materialism. André Gide made public his homosexual orientation; Sergei Diaghilev, Marcel Proust and Jean Cocteau all seemed intent on avenging Oscar Wilde.

Labour agitation grew. The years 1911 to 1914 saw much strike activity. On the continent, socialism attracted many new members and even more voters. In the national elections in Germany in 1912 one out of three Germans voted socialist and the German Social Democratic Party was confirmed as by far the largest and most successful socialist party in the world. In his novel *Jean Barois*, written between 1910 and 1913, Roger Martin du Gard raised the possibility of a victorious push for power by labour. The working class represented a new frontier from which would spring new life.

A more literal frontier that enchanted many was the colonial world. There too a motif of revolt was to be observed. In Europe's colonies native unrest was growing, as were tendencies towards self-government among white settler populations. The German expressionist painter Emil Nolde sailed for the South Pacific in 1913 in search of inspiration. The general fascination with the frontier and the exotic made orientalism, chinoiserie, rugs from Bokhara, silk trousers and the Russian ballet all the rage in Europe.

In the intellectual and scientific community the activity was astonishing. Niels Bohr announced his theory of atomic structure in 1913. Among scientists a new physical worldview was emerging in which uncertainty and discontinuity were important notions. But the questioning and experimentation had spread, and former fixities began to disintegrate in all realms of understanding. If immutable laws did not exist in nature, then they could hardly exist in history or society or art.

Art continued to move from representation to abstraction. Only in abstraction is affirmation possible, said Paul Klee, a leading member of the Blaue Reiter group formed in Munich in 1911. In music, in a similar manner, Igor Stravinsky and Arnold Schönberg continued to break new ground, moving away from traditional rhythms and harmonic patterns. And in the new architecture of poured concrete and straight lines—in the work of Auguste Perret, Walter Gropius and Hans Poelzig—the lack of ornament, of historical clutter, was positively defiant.

Liberation was a central urge in all of this activity. There was much optimism and much excitement. Energy, provocation and action would revitalize the world. Among the most popular words of the day, wrote the critic Van Wyck Brooks, were "renascence" and "creative."

The commotion was such that Rupert Brooke began to doubt the notion of progress. What was "certain," he said, was "change." In Germany in 1912 the expressionist painter Franz Marc was convinced that "a turning point in history" had been reached, "a period in which all that is great and ancient has passed away and the new and the unforseeable have taken its place." And the French poet Charles Péguy could assert in 1913 that the world had changed less since Jesus Christ than it had in the last thirty years. Striking an ominous note, Péguy said the speed of change had become such that some kind of débâcle was inevitable within a few years.

But why a débâcle? Because newness had become a value rather than an attribute, and because there was much resistance to all this turmoil and change. The European bourgeoisie had a powerful sense of achievement, stability and permanence. It had built huge empires, magnificent bridges, awesome battleships. Its accomplishment was based on hard work and a social code central to which were notions of duty, respectability and service. Of the atmosphere in his stolid middle-class home as he was growing up, Hermann Hesse said that beauty and art were "*only* beauty and *only* art." Morality, character and will were far more important and encompassing concepts. The solidity of Victorian furniture symbolized the bourgeois perception of self.

Schönberg's music caused muddle-class outrage in Vienna; Stravinsky and Nijinsky's efforts caused a riot in Paris. "The terroristic arrogance of the new artists" was a phrase heard often in theatre vestibules and middle-class salons.

The European war that broke out in August 1914 was an outcome of this struggle between a vision of change and an urge for stability and gradualism. In the international community, Germany, more than any other country, represented the new. Despite many stuffy and conservative aspects to German life, Germany led the revolt against the longstanding Anglo-French domination of the world. Britain, on the other hand, experienced the modern movement the least and showed the least interest in it. When Freud's *Interpretation of Dreams* was published in translation in England in 1913, the publisher stated that the sale of the book would be limited "to members of the medical, scholastic, legal and clerical professions."

German activism and dynamism, at the very heart of Europe, were profoundly unsettling. Germany's naval and colonial ambitions, its extraordinary industrial growth to world leadership in a little over a generation, and a cultural effervescence that questioned many of the assumptions of an Anglo-French hegemony—all this had thrown Europe into a diplomatic, military and cultural quandary. The German government and high command had no precise territorial ambitions when the Schlieffen Plan was unleashed against Belgium and France in August 1914, but notions of regen-

eration, renewal and spiritual revitalization dominated German thinking. "Everything will have to be new after this profound, mighty visitation," wrote Thomas Mann in December; Germany would resurrect Europe from decay and degeneration. For Germans, the war was *eine innere Notwendigkeit*, a spiritual necessity.

In all belligerent states, a key feature of the mood of August 1914 was the expectation that the war would be over quickly—before the leaves fell, said the Kaiser, or at least by Christmas, according to more pessimistic forecasts. No one, except for the odd eccentric like the wealthy Warsaw banker Ivan Bloch, predicted a long war of trenches and attrition. But when the German attack stalled at the Marne in September, the two sides began to dig in—initially of course to recuperate and regroup. As the entrenchments became increasingly sophisticated, the much-sought-after breakthrough became correspondingly less likely. By 1916 a gruesome war of attrition had become the reality. Strategy was reduced to one primitive interest: to force the other side to take more casualties than one's own.

The cost in human life was horrific, and the emotional toll was equally appalling. That men continued to "go over the top," wave after wave, year after year, despite the likelihood of mutilation or death, says much about the powerful social code that drove the war effort. Service, duty, commitment, hard work, patriotism and sacrifice—these solid Victorian notions carried men forward into the hell that was no man's land. Nineteenth-century values fuelled this war, and those values won. Yet in the process of victory they were cruelly wounded.

If nineteenth-century values drove the war, twentieth-century technology fought it: machine guns, monstrous artillery, tanks, submarines, airplanes, zeppelins, gas, flamethrowers. The individual was obliterated. The hero of this war was the unknown soldier. The German role in developing the new technology and especially in pushing back the frontiers of the permissible in warfare was considerable. The Germans were the first to attack civilian targets from the sea and the sky and to resort to gas and to unrestricted submarine warfare.

Technology butchered values. As the war progressed, it seemed to take on an energy of its own, beyond the control of civilian and military strategists alike. Military strategists knew neither how to win the war nor how to stop it. In the process the war decimated not only men and matériel but also the moral authority of the old world. The great stirring phrases—"for king and country," "do your duty," "a war to end war"—exploded like so many shells. "All the great words," wrote D.H. Lawrence, "were cancelled out."

Confronted by material force and personal helplessness, soldiers withdrew into themselves. Sandor Ferenczi, who treated psychologically disturbed soldiers in Budapest, noted, "Libido withdraws from the object into the ego, enhancing self-love and reducing object love to the point of indifference." This seemed to be true of western culture as a whole in the wake of the Great War. The destruction, both literal and figurative, was such that the objective world appeared to have lost its meaning. On seeing Verdun during the great battle there, César Méléra said, "Every sign of humanity has been swept away." The upshot was a turning inward and a preoccupation with self.

The armistice on November 11, 1918, was celebrated by some civilians; among soldiers it elicited little rejoicing. Guy Chapman was with his unit in Bethencourt:

> At eleven o'clock we slung on our packs and tramped on along the muddy pavé. The band played but there was little singing....We took over our billets and listlessly devoured a meal. In an effort to cure our apathy, the little American doctor from Vermont who had joined us a fortnight earlier broke his invincible teetotalism, drank half a bottle of whisky, and danced a cachucha. We looked at his antics with dull eyes and at last put him to bed.

Yes, the Entente arrayed against Germany had won, but at what cost? While they lost the physical war, the Germans may have won the spiritual war. All the rational connections of the prewar world—the nexus of cause and effect—seemed riddled with shell shot. The postwar world would be consumed by a passion for newness and a neurotic self-centredness. A preoccupation with technique and self would produce a culture of antics, spectacle and escape. Rainer Maria Rilke was attending a lecture in Munich on November 11, 1918, when a note was handed to the lecturer who told the audience the news of the armistice. There was a commotion. Rilke then turned to his companion and said, "Now the future can begin."

Before the war intellectual barriers had crumbled. Now all sorts of barriers crumbled, for everyone. Empires collapsed. Dynasties disappeared. Civil war rocked much of Europe. Bolshevism struggled to assert itself in Russia after its initial coup in November 1917. Women received the vote. Socialists joined governments. Those people who had lived "downstairs" before 1914 moved not "upstairs" but out of the house altogether. The eight-hour day was introduced in several countries. At the same time, a sense of social order wilted. Historical continuity was gone. The Austrian Hans Weigel said of 1919, "We woke up one day, and our grandparents were foreigners."

In the arts violent experimentation took hold. In Zürich, Paris, Berlin, Munich and Cologne, Dada played its war games of the mind. Tristan Tzara gave instructions on how to write a poem: cut words out of a newspaper, put them into a paper bag, shake the bag, remove the words one by one, and you have your poem. Marcel Duchamp took the Mona Lisa and gave her both a moustache and an obscene title. The architect Bruno Taut called for "Death to everything stuffy! Down with everything serious!" Art had become anti-art, the only sense nonsense.

A treaty was imposed on the Germans in June 1919. The sentiments it represented augured ill for the future. "What is the use of this treaty?" Gabriel Hanotaux asked. "The same use as a lie in relieving embarrassment." Versailles tried to reconstitute an old world, and as a result was probably doomed to failure. The British economist John Maynard Keynes, who along with his Bloomsbury friends represented the gentler wing of the modern movement, predicted as much. He resigned from the Treasury in June 1919 in disgust at the peace settlement. In December he published *The Economic Consequences of the Peace*, a stinging critique of the Versailles Treaty that sold 100,000 copies in eight months.

The decade that had begun with such energy and confidence ended in desperate sadness. On November 11, 1920, the Unknown Warrior was borne from France in a coffin and buried at Westminster Abbey. Britain and the dominions had not suffered as directly or as extensively as Germany, France or Russia, but there were more than a million British and Empire dead. One observer tried several years later to conjure up those dead marching past the Cenotaph in Whitehall:

> Imagine them moving in one continuous column, four abreast. As the head of that column reaches the Cenotaph, the last four men would be at Durham. In Canada, that column would stretch across the land from Quebec to Ottawa; in Australia, from Melbourne to Canberra; in South Africa, from Bloemfontein to Pretoria; in New Zealand; from Christchurch to Wellington; in Newfoundland, from coast to coast of the island; and in India, from Lahore to Delhi. It would take these men eighty-four hours, or three and a half days, to march past the Cenotaph in London.

In Paris Emmanuel Berl said, *"Il fait beau. Allons au cimetière."* It's nice out. Let's go to the cemetery.

Modris Eksteins's books include *Rites of Spring: The Great War and the Birth of the Modern Age* (1989) and *Walking since Daybreak: A Story of Eastern Europe, World War II and the Heart of Our Century* (1999).

Alarm Bells for Civilization

by Gwynne Dyer

It would have taken quite a hardy soul to see a bright side to the First World War at the time, but it may have served a useful purpose nevertheless. Like the alarm bells of a stricken ship, it still rings insistently across the decades: do something decisive right now, or this ship is going down with all hands. The ship is civilization.

It would be another two and a half decades before the first nuclear weapon was dropped on a city, another four decades before Dame Barbara Ward began talking about "spaceship earth," another six before Carl Sagan and his colleagues stumbled onto the ironically unifying concept of a "nuclear winter." But the First World War gave people their first glimpse of the abyss.

People began responding to the message right away. The war literature of the twenties and thirties was quite revolutionary in its style and its sensibility: ordinary men writing extraordinary things. Humble men like British infantryman Frank Richards would never before have had the temerity to write about their experiences; *Her Privates We*, Richards called his book about infantrymen in war. Or consider the League of Nations, that first, foredoomed attempt to bridge the abyss that the First World War revealed. Even governments realized that everything had changed.

The problem, as people in 1914 did not understand but people in 1918 were beginning to, was basically one of scale. Governments and states were still behaving in ways that had hardly changed since the eighteenth century, and (apart from the exacerbating effects of popular nationalism) the political causes and the initial strategic moves of the First World War differed little from those of the War of the Spanish Succession two centuries before. But if you quintuple the population, increase the per capita GNP tenfold, and replace single-shot muzzle-loading muskets with machine guns that fire six hundred bullets a minute, then you have changed the very nature of the game.

Conscript armies millions strong, supported by huge industrialized economies, fight very different wars from those that were waged by small armies of professional soldiers. It is not just that the butcher's bill is a lot higher; the political consequences of going to war are also different.

To be precise, the European empires went to war in 1914 believing that the conflict would serve the traditional purpose of adjusting the pecking order among the great powers. Instead, it ended up by destroying the losers utterly. Whole empires vanished, more than a dozen new countries appeared, and radical political movements like fascism and communism rose to power in great states—which was not what the initiators of the war had intended at all.

We have drunk quite deep of the horrors of the First World War over the years, so there is little point in going over them again here. Besides, the horrors suffered by the soldiers in the trenches were largely the same as those experienced by soldiers in any major nineteenth-century war (give or take a couple of novel weapons like poison gas and flamethrowers), except that they went on for much longer and affected many more people. It is the question of scale, in the war's physical and political aspects alike, that should hold our attention, as indeed it drew the attention of those who actually fought the war.

The shocking discovery that old institutions produce different and highly unwelcome results when you multiply the inputs tenfold or a hundredfold was what drove the many determined postwar attempts to change or replace those old institutions, from the creation of the League of Nations to Lenin's victory in the Soviet Union. The shock of the First World War also killed the smug confidence of the late nineteenth century that "history" knew what it was doing when it gave the Europeans such enormous power: one of the characteristics of twentieth-century European consciousness is a sense that history is in deep trouble and needs help.

But one can expand the argument quite a long way beyond that. There is nothing unique in the twentieth century's view of itself as the vital turning point of human history, of course—half the ages of humanity have believed that they lived in the final days. But the peculiar twentieth-century version of this apocalyptic vision relies on some quite tangible evidence, and the fact that people have cried wolf many times before does not disprove the existence of wolves.

I believe that our times, broadly defined—say, the nineteenth through the twenty-first centuries—really are a critical era that will make or break the experiment of human civilization. We have lived with one model of civilization for around five thousand years, but our powers over each other, over weapons, over the balance of the environment have grown so great that the transition to a different model has become a question of survival.

C.J. Patterson, *Your Chums Are Fighting—Why Aren't You?* Colour offset lithograph, 96.5 x 63.0 cm. National Archives of Canada, First World War Collection C-029484

The model that has predominated in almost all civilized societies since early in the third millennium BCE is one in which war was actually the centrepiece. So-called "patriarchal" civilizations, typified in the ancient Middle Eastern tradition by god-kings, elaborate hierarchies, rigid class systems, slavery, armies, and the systematic depoliticization and suppression of women, were so efficient at warfare that they eliminated virtually all rival models.

There were once a variety of such rival models, and the earliest civilized societies were mostly a good deal less warlike, less autocratic, less brutal in almost every respect. Some, like those of Egypt and Crete, retained that character as late as 1500 BCE, but in the parts of the Middle East that were less isolated by geography, the patriarchal model had triumphed everywhere by the early part of the third millennium BCE. Moreover, there is strong reason to suspect that this transformation, however regrettable, may have been inevitable.

It is significant in this regard that the civilizations that grew more or less independently in east Asia and the New World appear to have undergone a similar collapse into "patriarchal" value systems and social structures at approximately similar points in their development. The fact that the same lurch into the patriarchal model occurred in so many societies, and that we have no examples of significant movement in the opposite direction until quite recently, suggests strongly that this may have been a highly functional adaptation—and I suspect that this may have been related, once again, to the question of scale.

Imagine an early urban society struggling to maintain social cohesion and political purpose through the traditional means of kinship ties and personal friendship. As it grows from a few thousand to tens and then hundreds of thousands of individuals, the old rough democracy is less and less able to cope. Just once let a militarized hierarchy gain sway over this society, and it will never lose control again, for it is simply more efficient at running things, both internally and in relations with other states.

It is more efficient, among other things, at conquering neighbours, so that soon there are no nonmilitarized states left in the region. Thenceforward, militarized kingdoms and empires predominate everywhere, and warfare is chronic. Gresham's Law applied to whole societies: bad social models drive out good.

The resulting international system flourished for five thousand years (despite a steady toll of casualties among the member states, not to mention their inhabitants) because it was functional. It answered a variety of needs, it rewarded those who collaborated and punished those who defied it, and the warfare that was its constant accompaniment did not do enough damage to threaten the survival of civilization itself.

Neither, to be frank, did the First World War. Eight million military dead (or thirteen million total fatalities, or whichever figure you favour) is an awesome toll, but it is not the end of civilization. However, it felt like the end of everything to the participants, and the perception is as important as the fact: it set the alarm bells off.

The political leaders no less than the soldiers who survived the First World War were frightened by the implications of industrialized warfare, and quite rightly so. People could not have identified the specific threat of nuclear weapons in 1919, but they were only twenty-five years away from the first nuclear test, and in a broader sense they already knew, or at least suspected, what was coming next. Thus the revolutionary conclusion that was born as a propaganda slogan in the war and has been a constant theme of public discourse ever since: that it is now necessary to end not just some particular war, but the whole institution of war.

I am not suggesting that this was an entirely original thought that occurred to people only after the assassination of Archduke Franz Ferdinand and the events that followed. The traditional moral and philosophical arguments about just and unjust wars had already developed, in the late nineteenth and early twentieth centuries, into a critique of the institution itself: Marxists flogged their simplistic nostrums, the Tsar of Russia called conferences on the subject, and early peace activists (with the suffragists prominent among them) struggled to gain the public's attention.

Moreover, one can argue with the benefit of hindsight that this was part of a considerably broader erosion of the patriarchal model. The democratic revolutions in America and France had swept away the divine right of (god-)kings even before the end of the eighteenth century, and the nineteenth century saw the abolition of slavery, the spread of democracy and even the first stirrings of the women's emancipation movement. Other aspects of the patriarchal model were coming into question, so it was only natural that the central institution of warfare would also come under attack sooner or later.

Why, after five thousand years without any serious challenge, should the patriarchal institutions have come into question in this period? If we admit the hypothesis that the rise of patriarchy, including the institution of warfare, filled a need for strong hierarchy and central direction in newly formed mass societies that had no other means of articulating themselves, then the advent of alternative, more democratic means for deciding a society's values and goals was bound to challenge patriarchy.

From the invention of printing to today's CNN, the modern mass media have begun to supply those means and thus have restored the possibility of democracy in mass societies. As a result, all the patriarchal institutions are under threat—and hardly before time, for the change in scale has made them potentially lethal.

The people who fretted about patriarchal institutions (though they didn't use that term) in the late nineteenth century did not know one tenth of it, of course. They had no idea of how destructive warfare could become, of how calamitous the environmental consequences of massive industrialization might be, even of the implications of unlimited childbearing. Yet without knowing any of the specific projections that have obsessed people in the late twentieth century, some of them knew enough to be worried anyway, and worried aloud for the benefit of everybody else.

It had virtually no effect: we are a species that responds better to crises than to predictions. Before all these well-founded fears could coalesce into an analysis of the problem and a prescription for dealing with it, there had to be some apocalyptic event to focus people's attention. The First World War was that event.

Although that war frightened millions of people into thinking seriously about the prospects for civilization itself for the first time, it solved nothing. Seventy-three years later, we are still in the midst of a struggle to alter the characteristic behaviours of civilized societies in ways that will give human civilization a better chance of survival.

It is a struggle that will probably continue long past our own lifetimes, and it is clearly not a foregone conclusion that we will win it. We have both the United Nations and nuclear weapons, the environmental movement and global warming, the rapid spread of democracy and the widening North-South economic gulf. We must continue to regard civilization as an experiment in progress.

But it is just as well that we had the First World War when we did. At a relatively modest cost, it gave us early warning of what kinds of perils we were about to encounter and caused us to start thinking about how to survive them a few decades earlier than we might otherwise have done. For all we know, that could be the margin between success and failure.

That is one of the speculations that can never be proved. But if you doubt that the margin is narrow, consider a twentieth century in which the old empires and the old complacency continued into the 1940s or 1950s, and acquired all the technology that accrued in the meantime, before they stumbled into their first fully industrialized war. We would probably be in a lot deeper trouble than we are—if, indeed, we were here at all.

Gwynne Dyer is a syndicated columnist, military historian and filmmaker. His books include *War* (1985).

The Social Gospel: Christianity for the Here and Now

by Ramsay Cook

In July 1918, just a few months before the Armistice that ended four years of brutal warfare, a new church was founded in Winnipeg. The Winnipeg Labour Church, led by a dissident Methodist named William Ivens, asked its members to subscribe to a seemingly simple creed. "I am willing to support an independent and creedless church," the statement ran, "based on the Fatherhood of God and the Brotherhood of Man. Its aim shall be the establishment of justice and righteousness among men of all nations."

Less than a year later, many of the Protestant clergy and laypeople who were attracted to these generous sentiments—James Shaver Woodsworth, Salem Bland, William Ivens and A.E. Smith, most notably—threw their support behind Winnipeg workers who successfully paralysed the city with a brief but dramatic general strike. At least at the beginning, the strike seemed to confirm Woodsworth's conviction that during the Great War "the workers have received a revelation of a new heaven and a new earth for the first heaven and the first earth have passed away." Things looked different by July 1919 when the strike had been crushed by a ruthless combination of federal, provincial and municipal authorities. "Bloody Saturday" would live on in the minds of workers, but as the decade ended the nostrums proclaiming the new earthly heaven seemed as far from fulfillment as ever.

The Winnipeg General Strike remains a symbol of much that was simultaneously noble and naïve in the movement known as the social gospel. For the strike was the culmination of a decade that severely tested some of the most widely accepted shibboleths of the Edwardian age. These included an optimistic evaluation of humanity's capacity for moral improvement, even perfection, and a conviction that, once purified of "social" sin, people and nations would readily replace competition with cooperation and turn swords into ploughshares. Traditional Protestant doctrines of sin,

Nellie McClung

punishment, judgement and salvation were watered down or replaced with a melioristic creed that stressed the idea of humanity as made in the image of a benign Father.

Almost everything that took place on the battlefields of Europe between 1914 and 1918 and even at the Paris Peace Conference ran counter to this sentimental liberal perfectionism. Yet paradoxically, optimism about making the world safe for democracy and building the Kingdom of Heaven on earth persisted. Perhaps the horrors of war combined with government-sponsored war propaganda made that optimism inevitable. In his contribution to a book revealingly entitled *The New Era in Canada* (1917), the normally hard-nosed —even cynical—Sir Clifford Sifton wrote:

> While our sons have been fighting in Europe the moral leaven has been working at home. Conventions of earnest-minded citizens have been held to consider schemes of social improvement….Many of them have given their sons to die a violent death in battle for a noble ideal, and they will not readily permit themselves to be influenced by anything except the highest motive.

Others—suffragist Nellie McClung, socialist Jimmy Simpson, agrarian radical Henry Wise Wood—might have been skeptical about the sincerity of a member of the self-made Canadian ruling class like Sifton, but they shared the assumptions underlying his rhetoric. A new and improved phoenix was widely expected to arise from the ashes of war.

The strange mix of patriotism, social idealism and political unrest owed much to the liberal Protestantism that pervaded English Canadian culture. And that liberal Protestantism, or modernism, with its humanistic emphasis, nurtured the movement known as the social gospel. The roots of this movement were deep in the intellectual and material transformation of North American society during the last decades of the nineteenth century. Those changes represented several direct challenges to traditional Christian teaching, both Catholic and Protestant. Protestants responded earliest and embraced new, secularizing doctrines more fully than Catholics, though Pope Leo XIII's 1891 social encyclical *Rerum Novarum* was part of the Catholic response.

The rise of industrial capitalism urgently demanded reevaluation of Christian social ethics. In its earliest years, the new economic order produced outrageous contrasts between rich and poor, luxury and slums, leisure and endless work. As capitalist expansion created a new working class that laboured long hours for low wages in unhealthy and dangerous conditions, the cities spawned slum housing, poverty and disease. Often the new urban populations were composed of recent immigrants who brought foreign languages, customs and even religions to Canada. For Christians the new social order represented a bewildering challenge. How could the traditional injunction to love one's neighbour be made real and practical in a society where the apparent imperatives of capitalism awarded the race to the swift and the battle to the strong? Increasingly Protestant leaders wondered out loud about the prospect for churches that failed to attract the new working classes. And if they were lost to Christian churches might they not end up in the sway of secular doctrines like socialism, doctrines that threatened both the established social order and Christian belief itself?

While many Christians recognized the social ills of emerging industrial capitalism, only a minority came to the conclusion that a radical revision of Christianity was called for if the challenge was to be met. Salem Bland summed up this tendency in his *New Christianity* (1920) when he wrote, "Labour and Christianity are bound together. Together they stand or fall. They come into the Kingdom together or not at all." This social gospel meant that Christians must turn their attention to curing the ills of this world by developing a sociology based in Christian teachings focused on the here and now. The movement demanded a "practical Christianity" with a relevant message to replace "Churchianity" with its emphasis on individual salvation and justice in the hereafter.

But the social gospel was more than just a response to material conditions and social injustice. Traditional Christianity faced other challenges as well. For Protestants who founded their faith on the rock of biblical teachings two new sciences, evolutionary biology and historical criticism, raised profoundly unsettling questions. The Darwinian hypothesis that the origin of the species could best be explained by the process of natural selection struck at the heart of Christian belief about creation and utterly devastated the accepted chronology of humanity's history on earth. And Protestants were also unsettled by the increasingly troubling findings and claims of the historical school of biblical criticism that originated in Germany. Historical, archeological and linguistic studies raised large questions about the authenticity of events and teachings that had been central to Christian belief for centuries. For many, the Bible became little more than an important but deeply flawed human record rather than a divinely inspired revelation of God's word. Even the divinity of Jesus was brought into question.

While the controversies sparked by Darwinism and historical criticism were at first confined to the halls of theological learning, by the end of the nineteenth century many clergy and even their parishioners were troubled by these subversive doctrines. In Canada there were well publicized debates between Christians and Free Thinkers, heresy trials of "modernist" ministers, and the usual range of bad jokes about our tree-climbing ancestors.

What emerged from this intellectual turmoil was a modernist theology that coincidentally was well suited to the growing demand for a socially relevant Christianity. Evolution, usually stripped of its natural selection component, was viewed as bolstering rather than destroying humanity's potential for growth in the direction of Christian perfectionism. And whatever else historical criticism had done, it had stripped away often confusing sections of the Bible without destroying the uplifting story of the carpenter's son who came to teach humanity the principles of the ethical life. William Irvine, a Methodist-turned-Unitarian-turned-agrarian-radical, summed up the new belief in somewhat extreme form when he recalled his ministry in southwestern Ontario in 1914. "I was preaching sheer humanism," he proudly admitted. "The supernatural had vanished. There were no miracles, no virgin birth, no atonement and no resurrection….I was not preaching to get people into heaven but...I was much more interested in getting heaven into people."

It was perhaps convenient that the social crisis of industrial capitalism offered Protestant thinkers and believers an opportunity to turn their eyes from the large, intractable intellectual questions posed by the new science and the new biblical criticism. Constructing a Christian sociology seemed more fruitful than reconstructing Christian theology. In the firm conviction that the sacred and the secular were one, Protestants could turn to slum clearance, prohibition, votes for women, industrial safety legislation, milk pasteurization, public ownership of public utilities, "Christianizing and Canadianizing" immigrants, and public and cooperative ownership.

Since the social gospel was neither a precise political philosophy nor a party platform, its advocates ranged over a wide spectrum. All agreed that changing people's environment would open the way to social regeneration. Sin was a social defect alienating people from society rather than a sign of alienation from God. For moderate adherents of the new liberal theology of social reform, Sunday closing, prohibition, city mission work and improved housing and sanitation constituted a large enough program. Others took up the cause of trade unionism, devising schemes for arbitration and conciliation to prevent strikes and avoid class conflict. But for the more radical, Christian socialism, labour churches and the identification of the religion of the carpenter's son with the fate of the working classes provided the essential elements of the new religion of reform. The irrelevance of the traditional churches was total. That conclusion led J.S. Woodsworth to democratic socialism, A.E. Smith to Marxism, Frances Beynon to pacifism and exile, and Alice Chown to rural communalism. There was more than one road to the Kingdom.

Some of this Protestant reform zeal was channelled into wartime fervour after 1914. Only a minority—J.S. Woodsworth and Frances Beynon among them—adopted pacifism as a necessary part of the social gospel. More representative was Salem Bland, who had social views as radical as Woodsworth's but was prepared to stand as a Union government supporter in 1917. Like many others, he hoped that a government of righteousness, elected on a franchise that eliminated much of the "foreign" vote and included part of the female population and on a platform of conscription that ensured French Canadian opposition, would cleanse the Augean stables. In a sense he was right. The Union government attacked patronage, enforced prohibition, placed part of the railway system under public ownership, restricted immigration, advanced the suffragist cause, promoted Canada's national status and won membership in the League of Nations.

J.S. Woodsworth

For the more radical proponents of social Christianity these piecemeal reforms were only a beginning. The Presbyterian General Assembly and especially the Methodist Conference adopted programs for social action that called for fundamental change since, as the Methodists resolved, "the undying ethics of Jesus...demand nothing less than a transference of the whole economic life from a basis of competition and profits to one of co-operation and service." Two new movements of social protest erupted, both of which included radical clergy among their leaders: a radicalized labour movement and the agrarian Progressive movement that captured a large part of rural Ontario and nearly all of the prairie west in the federal election of 1921. Both labour and farm papers regularly carried "sermons for the unsatisfied," as Woodsworth called his *Grain Growers' Guide* column. At the peak of the Winnipeg conflict Woodsworth, following an outdoor meeting of the Labour Church, exulted, "The atmosphere was a great religious revival. The movement is a religious revival."

Yet the spirit of the Methodist camp meeting was not to last. With the failure of the Winnipeg strike, labour radicalism quickly subsided. The farmers' revolt swept all before it between 1919 and 1921, than collapsed into dissension and disunity. The women's movement, fresh from winning the vote in every province except Quebec, likewise lapsed into lethargy and domesticity. While prohibition lingered on, its enforcement proved problematic as the wartime spirit of sacrifice dissipated. And Methodists, so recently radical, proved little different from other employers when faced with a printers' strike at their book publishing company in 1921.

Those social gospellers for whom the fire of prewar optimism still burned shifted their attention to politics. As in so much else, J.S. Woodsworth typified the movement in its drift away from organized religion into secular activities, though he would not have made that distinction. After leaving the ministry and participating in the exciting events of Winnipeg, there seemed only one place for him to go in 1919 and that was politics. The rest of his life was spent building an alternative to the church, a political party devoted to social regeneration. The trajectory was increasingly secular. The movement that had set out to make Christianity relevant passed into the secular city.

The war years had been the testing time for liberal theology and its social gospel offspring. Hopes for the long march of humanity towards a just social order ran high as patriotism and righteousness joined forces. But the triumph never came. The failure of the social gospel's noble dream stemmed from its overly generous assessment of both human beings and society. But that was a failure shared with much else at the end of the Edwardian age. The Great War did not usher in a new era for Canada or the world but instead destroyed the very assumptions on which those fervent hopes were founded.

Historian **Ramsay Cook** served as general editor of the *Dictionary of Canadian Biography*. His books include *The Regenerators: Social Criticism in Late Victorian Canada* (1985).

W.L. Grant, the son of Principal Grant of Queen's University, was one of the few who recognized in 1914 that "the war gives the lie to the believer in the upward march of mankind. We asked for righteousness, and behold oppression, for justice, and behold—the cry from butchered Louvain." Building the Kingdom in the face of that harsh reality was beyond the power of Christian sociology.

Filling the Gap on the Homefront

by Kori Street

W hen war broke out in Europe in August 1914, few in Canada were prepared for the profound impact that it would have on Canadian society. By war's end, one out of every ten men of the Canadian Expeditionary Force (CEF) had been killed and at least twice that number had been maimed or disabled. But the Great War also left its mark on those who did not serve on the battlefield.

When Britain's declaration of war reached Ottawa on August 6, 1914, the Imperial Order of the Daughters of the Empire had already mobilized for the war effort. They were prepared—independently of Sam Hughes, the minister of militia—to organize the women of Canada. As young men volunteered for military service, women rushed to join the war effort in other capacities. Women were as enthusiastic as men about the prospect of war.

As it became distressingly clear that the war would not be over by Christmas, the homefront became increasingly important to its prosecution, and as Canadian casualty lists lengthened and an ever growing number of men were mobilized, the need for women to fill the gap on the homefront became urgent. To meet the demands of the war economy, women were required to perform a wide variety of often unfamiliar tasks. Most of these tasks fell well within the realm of what was seen at the time as appropriate work for a woman or could be rationalized as being necessary because of the war emergency.

The highest proportion of women served the war effort in a volunteer capacity. Women gathered to knit socks and scarves for the soldiers in the trenches, to roll bandages, and to provide welfare services for families of soldiers. Women's volunteer organizations dedicated to supporting the war effort were to be found in every corner of Canada.

The task of conserving resources crucial to the war effort, such as meat, tin or petroleum products, also became women's responsibility. Thus, Canadian women were the target of the Toronto Women's Wartime Thrift Committee's "Waste Not, Want Not" campaign of 1917, which resulted in the publication of a practical guide for housewives on how to be thrifty. "Instead of one beefless day, why not try for six, to make up for the other people less patriotic," was just one of the tips the book offered housewives.

Much of the burden of supplying the Allied war effort fell to Canada and the government found it increasingly difficult to balance the manpower needs of the CEF with the labour needs of the war economy. Encouraging women's increased participation in the paid labour force was a strategy to alleviate labour shortages. In 1916 the munitions industry began to recruit women actively and by 1917 the Imperial Munitions Board could report that despite long hours and dangerous conditions, between 35,000 and 37,000 women in Toronto and Montreal were employed on the assembly lines producing shells. Other women were put to work as welders, packers and inspectors in airplane and ship factories. Other occupations were also opened to women, many of which had been the exclusive preserve of men before the war. Thus in 1917, in Kingston, Ontario, Maude Chart became Canada's first "conducterette."

Farmers were also affected by the labour shortage. As the war intensified, so too did the demand for Canadian produce, and despite the pressure for high output, the farm community came under fire for not releasing or encouraging its men to enlist. One solution that was successful in Ontario, British Columbia, Alberta and Saskatchewan was the employment of young women, especially students and teachers from the cities, as work crews during the summer months. The Young Women's Christian Association took on the responsibility of organizing, transporting and housing these "farmerettes."

In their enthusiasm for the war effort, some women felt constrained by the civilian opportunities for both paid and unpaid service and sought a more direct involvement in the military side of the war. The Nursing Sisters of the Canadian Army Medical Corps offered women the most acceptable opportunity to be in uniform and in direct contact with soldiers both in Canada and overseas. By November 1918, 3,141 women had served as nursing sisters, 2,504 of them overseas.

Other women concentrated on recruiting young men for duty in the CEF. They organized events such as concerts and picnics at which recruiting appeals could be made. They also wrote letters to the newspapers urging young men to join up. One woman in Berlin (soon to be Kitchener), Ontario, wrote in response to a young man's advertisement for room and board that she thought "a nice suit of khaki with board and lodging free will suit you better than a cosy room with board." Another equally humiliating tactic was the handing out of white feathers to unenlisted men. A woman would walk up to a young, able-bodied man not in uniform and, with the intent of publicly branding him a coward, pin the feather to his lapel.

A small group of women were not concerned merely to assist with recruiting men but desired military training for themselves, believing that they could assume the responsibility of home defence. This would release men for duty overseas but not leave Canada unprotected. The women's paramilitary movement had its greatest success in Toronto, where 800 women signed up for training with Jessica McNab's Women's Home Guard of Canada. Such corps were also started in Hamilton and Montreal.

Not all Canadian women shared this enthusiasm for the war. Some women demonstrated their objection by refusing to sign the consent forms releasing their husbands and sons to fight. Other women, such as Laura Hughes of Toronto, Frances Marion Beynon of Winnipeg and Violet McNaughton of Saskatchewan, actively opposed the war and sought its end through peaceful negotiation. Unfortunately they did not realize their goal before 60,661 Canadians had died.

Before 1914, the suffrage movement had been very active in Canada. With the outbreak of hostilities, most suffragists decided to turn their efforts to supporting the war effort. When Prime Minister Robert Borden passed the Wartime Elections Act in 1917, extending the franchise to wives, widows, mothers, sisters and daughters of men who had served or were serving in the Canadian or British military or naval forces, it appeared that women's war service had resulted in a victory for women's rights. The legislation, however, was also a very astute political move on Borden's part, for it gave the vote to the women most likely to reelect his government and support the Conscription Bill of 1917.

Some commentators claim the Great War was emancipatory for Canadian women, citing their entry into the paid labour force and their enfranchisement as proof. Women workers, however, were paid less than their male counterparts even though they did the same work and put in the same hours. In the case of the munitions industry, women received anywhere from 50 to 83 per cent of men's wages. Women's employment was also seen as temporary, regarded not as a woman's right but as a necessary sacrifice for the war. This became clear in 1919 when, in a recession-bound Canada, job opportunities for women sharply constricted and women were strongly encouraged to return to the home. The expanded federal franchise awarded women in 1918, however, can perhaps be seen as recognition of women's wartime service. One thing is certain: Canadian women deserve a greater remembrance than as simply the mothers of the dead or the stoic knitters of socks.

Women's military historian **Kori Street** served three years in the armed forces, and at the time of writing was completing her MA at the Ontario Institute for Studies in Education in Toronto.

A Strike with an Elusive Meaning

by Doug Smith

In the decades since the Winnipeg General Strike, the passions surrounding the strike have never completely died down. Thus, in the summer of 1969, when the United Steelworkers of America presented the city of Winnipeg with a plaque to commemorate the fiftieth anniversary of the strike, many city councillors reacted like new homeowners who had been given a particularly ugly housewarming gift. Robert Taft, a former Winnipeg police chief, said the strike had been a near-insurrection and a disgrace to the city's good name, and there was no way he would let the plaque be displayed on city property. Taft's position did not carry the day and the plaque now hangs outside the city council chamber.

In 1983, a group of labour historians met in Winnipeg to debate the significance of the strike, although debate is probably too genteel a term for what took place. Personal attacks quickly became the order of the day, as scholars accused one another of using the strike to advance their own contemporary political agendas. Was the strike a glorious moment in working-class history? Or was it a failure, a setback that sent the Winnipeg working class scampering into the arms of social democracy and business unionism with its revolutionary pretensions tucked between its legs? It seems that not even time will tell, and the strike's meaning remains elusive.

The basic facts are clear enough. For six weeks during the spring of 1919, tens of thousands of Winnipeg workers, many of whom were not members of any union, went out on strike. Most of them were striking not for personal gain but for an idea: that workers had the right to form unions and that employers had a responsibility to negotiate with those unions. This idea seems almost commonplace now, but in 1919 it provoked a bitter reaction from both employers and the government. Strikers were fired en masse; special laws were rushed through Parliament in a matter of minutes; most significantly, troops were called out. Winnipeg's business elite, horrified by what it saw as a potential revolution, organized itself into a committee of self-defence, better known as the Citizen's Committee of One

THEIR SENTENCE
IS OUR SENTENCE

THOSE WHO ARE
NOT WITH US

Thousand, and set about the hiring of what amounted to a private police force.

Anyone who watched the television news from Beijing during the spring of 1989 has a good idea of how the strike ended. The strike leaders had opposed any violent demonstrations—for six weeks the strikers did nothing more than gather in the city's squares and parks and listen to speakers. But when they held a silent parade down Main Street to oppose the midnight raids that had sent their leaders to Stony Mountain Penitentiary, the strikers were charged by Mounted Police officers, who were in turn backed up by vigilantes and the militia. By the end of what came to be known as Bloody Saturday, one striker was dead, the jails were full, and the streets were patrolled by soldiers armed with machine guns.

The crushing of the Winnipeg General Strike, then, is part of a long and bloody tradition, played out seven decades later in Tiananmen Square. But the movement that led to the strike was as breathtaking and inspirational as the pro-democracy movement that rallied the Chinese students, and it deserves remembering for the same reasons.

The General Strike pitted one Winnipeg, South Winnipeg, against another—the working-class Winnipeg that was growing up on both sides of the Canadian Pacific railyards. There newly arrived immigrants were

Tens of thousands of Winnipeg workers went on strike for an idea: that workers had the right to form unions.

crammed into poorly built rooming houses on tiny lots. Bosses ruled by divine right. The city's raw and rough industries turned those immigrants into class-conscious workers, and in the face of discrimination and exploitation they began to organize themselves. They adopted the values of the labour movement, principally sacrifice and solidarity, and they extended those values from their individual workplaces to their industries to the world of politics. This was no simple accomplishment—to do it they had to develop their own sense of mission and of what constitutes the common good. Moreover, at every step of this journey they were denounced for threatening the civic, provincial or national interest.

In the 1990s the strike seems distant and incomprehensible. Not only do most people apparently not view themselves as workers with primary class loyalties, but they are encouraged to see themselves as consumers rather than as citizens. In a consumer society we look for personal solutions to public problems. In such a culture, sacrifice and solidarity have been made to seem irrelevant and absurd.

The Winnipeg General Strike failed to accomplish its immediate goals; some would argue that by going too far too fast it in fact helped to set the union movement back. And certainly, despite the strides organized labour has taken since 1919, labour has not, as one of the strike organizers defiantly predicted, "come into its own."

But the strike reminds us that so-called ordinary people can make their own history and be actors on the world stage. The labour movement's greatest triumphs have not been improvements in wages and working conditions, as important as such victories are, but the victories of the human spirit that the movement has won when it inspired its members to dream of what might be. Only when people cease to dream such dreams can the Winnipeg General Strike be considered a failure. Ultimately the debate over the meaning of the strike is a debate over the value of those dreams. Or to accept, momentarily, the terms of the strike's critics, it was a failure, but one that, in the words of Samuel Beckett, calls on us to "try again, fail again, fail better."

Doug Smith is a Winnipeg writer and labour historian whose books include *Let Us Rise!: An Illustrated History of the Manitoba Labour Movement* (1985).

Ontario's Bitter Language Fight

by Robert Choquette

Two basic reasons explain the unprecedented explosion of linguistic and racial tensions between French- and English-speaking Canadians from 1911 to 1921. The first reason is the dramatic and rapid change in the linguistic demography of the country in the decades preceding the First World War. This was a time not only of heavy immigration into Canada but also of extensive migration of French Canadians out of Quebec. As a result, the number and proportion of French-speaking Canadians in Ontario grew exponentially, from 26,000 and less than 3 per cent of the Ontario population in 1851 to almost a quarter million and more than 8 per cent of the population in 1911. Although French-speaking Canadians were losing ground in western Canada, the Acadians of the Maritimes were flexing their cultural and linguistic muscles for the first time since their tragic deportation by the British in the eighteenth century. In sum, the French Canada that had appeared in 1867 to be reduced to a Quebec reservation (where most English-speaking Canadians felt it belonged) seemed in 1911 to be changing into an expanding empire.

The second basic reason for the French-English fights of 1911–1921 was the cultural ideology prevalent in English-speaking Canada, made up of various threads including British imperialism, English Canadian nationalism, Anglo-Saxon racism, Protestant bigotry and no-popery, xenophobia and Francophobia. This complex web of values and prejudices reared its ugly head in various countries, albeit with different faces—anti-black policies in the United States, antisemitism in France, the colonial complex of superiority in Britain. What the bigots had in common was the belief that their language and culture were superior to all others. In Canada, bitter and divisive fights had already taken place on the issues of the Red River insurrection (1869–70), the hanging of Louis Riel (1885), Quebec's Jesuit Estates bill (1888), Manitoba's abolition of confessional schools and the official status of French (1890), and the school clauses of the statutes creating the provinces of Alberta and Saskatchewan (1905). Racial and religious prejudice combined to put the migrating French Canadians in their place. With the latter just as determined to preserve their cherished language and culture, the battle was joined.

In 1911 Sir Wilfrid Laurier's Liberal government was defeated at the polls by an alliance between Robert Borden's Conservatives and Henri Bourassa's Quebec nationalist forces. The alliance having served its purpose, it soon unravelled. The Ontario Conservative government of Sir James Whitney was freed to proceed with its policies of repression of Ontario's French-speaking people. While the conscription crisis of 1917–18, with its attendant riots, was perhaps the bitterest conflict of the era between French and English Canadians, the stage for it was set by the Ontario school question that erupted in 1912. Why should French Canadians go to Europe to bleed and die when freedom was refused them in Ontario?

Since the 1850s, Ontario's English-speaking majority had assumed that the province's small French minority would inevitably assimilate into the mainstream. However, the Ontario French refused to do so, and beginning in the 1880s the majority showed increasing concern over the growing importance of the French fact in what they considered Canada's foremost bastion of the English fact. Attention focused on the growing number of French schools in the province. Aided and abetted by the Liberal opposition, Whitney's government decided to adopt drastic measures aimed at enforcing Anglicization.

Since 1890, Ontario had required that beyond the first two years of elementary schooling, English needed to be the language of communications and instruction in the schools of the province, "unless the pupil did not understand English." French schools simply availed themselves of this exception, and in 1912 Whitney's government decided to remove the loophole in the law. The Department of Education implemented the new policy through its Circular of Instructions Number 17, issued on June 25, 1912. In addition to imposing English as the sole language of instruction and communication, the regulation made all French-speaking school inspectors subject to an English-speaking "alter-ego" and ensured that there would be no future development of any new French schools. This was the infamous "Regulation 17" that the Franco-Ontarians resisted for fifteen years, finally obtaining its amendment in their favour in 1927. The fight over Regulation 17 was bitter, painful and ugly. All of French Canada's leaders entered the fray, which served to weld the formerly scattered Franco-Ontarians into a collective unit.

When the Ottawa Separate School Board informed the government that it would not abide by Regulation 17, the government issued another directive making individual teachers responsible for obeying the law under pain of immediate dismissal. In October 1913, the government cut off all subsidies to the rebellious Ottawa board. When the board endeavored to issue bonds to finance its schools, a group of English-speaking Ottawa Catholics obtained a court injunction in 1914 forbidding the board to issue bonds because it was refusing to obey Regulation 17. The Ottawa Separate School Board was driven to close all its schools, being unable to finance them. The Ontario government struck back in April 1915 by legislating the board out of existence and replacing it with a three-person commission appointed by Toronto. In 1916, the courts upheld the government's right to legislate on the language used in schools (Regulation 17) but countermanded its decision to abolish the Ottawa Separate School Board.

While these decisions may have clarified the law, they did not solve the problem. Determined to maintain their longstanding right to French schooling (albeit including the learning of English), teachers went without pay and pupils studied in broken-down firetraps and did without basic equipment and services so that they could learn in their cherished French language.

Some of the bitterest and most persistent opponents of Franco-Ontarian school rights were the English-speaking Catholic clergy, largely of Irish origin. These people belonged to the same linguistic and cultural common front as Ontario's Anglo-Saxon Protestant majority, a mindset that took precedence over religious values. They were also engaged in a petty power struggle with their French Canadian coreligionists over various church appointments throughout Canada. While Orange lodges directed the forces of bigotry in the Protestant camp, Bishop Michael Fallon of London, Bishop David Joseph Scollard of Sault Sainte-Marie and Fr. M.J. Whelan of Ottawa led the English-speaking Catholic fight against "French aggression."

By 1921, both French-and English-speaking Canadians were licking their wounds. Two encyclical letters on the Ontario school question by Pope Benedict XV in 1916 and 1918 helped calm the spirits of Catholic crusaders, Bishop Fallon in particular. The defeat of the Ontario Tory government in 1919, followed two years later by the election of the Liberal Prime Minister Mackenzie King, also helped, as did the death of several leading French-English pugilists and the end of the First World War. The number of Francophones migrating from Quebec seemed to have stabilized; the cauldron of war had expunged some of the bigotry from public opinion; people were tired of constant conflict and bickering; and a series of unimpeachable studies showed that all Franco-Ontarian children not only learned English but wanted to learn it. The stage was set for reconciliation.

One avenue of reconciliation would be the amendment of Regulation 17 in 1927, when the Ontario government authorized bilingual schools. But justice had not come easily.

Robert Choquette is the author of *Language and Religion: A History of English-French Conflict in Ontario* (1975).

Influenza: Disease of the Wind

by Eileen Pettigrew

Canada, with a population of only eight million, suffered 60,000 deaths in the First World War. The Spanish influenza epidemic, which followed on the heels of the war, added 30,000 to 50,000 more deaths, nearly doubling the country's losses.

This epidemic of worldwide proportion probably began in China in the early months of 1918. It was dubbed Spanish influenza by Britain's Royal College of Physicians and Surgeons because Spain, neutral in the war, had no press censorship and made the first public announcement in a cable to London: "A strange form of disease of epidemic character has appeared in Madrid."

Unlike most respiratory complaints, whose chief victims are the very old and the very young, the flu struck hardest at young adults, the same age group so affected by the war, Men who had survived four years in the trenches could not fight this new enemy. It may even have shortened the war; in May 1918 the British fleet, with more than 10,000 sailors sick, couldn't leave port, and in October of that year the German army reported 180,000 cases.

The first reports of the disease in Canada followed the arrival of the hospital ship *Araguaya*, which sailed from England in June, carrying servicemen already ill with flu. The first major civilian outbreak occurred at Victoriaville College in Quebec when two students became ill on September 8, followed immediately by 398 more. In that same month, nine sailors from American ships died at Quebec City and the Polish Infantry Camp at Niagara, Ontario, was infected. By December more than 10,000 cases of influenza were reported among servicemen in Canada.

From central Canada it swept the country. It was carried partly by troops returning to their homes east and west at the rate of 3,400 a month from their disembarkation points, as well as by harvesters responding to a call for 40,000 helpers in the prairie provinces. The Persians called this dread malady the Disease of the Wind, and so it was in Canada. There seemed no easily tracked pattern. Every house but one in a city block might be stricken, and sometimes one person in a household caught the disease while the rest escaped. Survivors remember never knowing where it would hit next and experiencing "fear so thick that even a child could feel it."

What began like a cold often turned to pneumonia, with temperatures as high as 104 degrees Fahrenheit; with no antibiotics to fight it, the pneumonia was almost always fatal. Sometimes it struck so fast that people who were perfectly healthy in the morning were dead by night.

Parliament had prorogued in May 1918 and did not sit again until February 1919. There was no federal health department, hence no central source of information or advice. Local authorities, working in the dark, had to make their own decisions. Some, like Saskatoon's medical health officer, tried to avoid panic by downplaying the seriousness of the situation: "This epidemic is nothing but the old form of influenza, or grippe." In some western communities stringent quarantines were instituted. Spitting on the street was punishable by fines and in many places people wore masks. Schools and theatres closed.

Vaccines were developed in Canada and imported from the United States, and cures and preventives from brandy to garlic had their enthusiasts, but in truth no one knew what to do. Doctors and nurses worked inhuman hours, as did the volunteers who supplied stricken households with food and firewood or moved right in to nurse sick people.

A Prince Edward Island woman has a poignant memory of the day the war's end was announced. Her older sister and four brothers were all ill with flu and her mother, only forty years old, had died of the pneumonia that followed the flu: "My father and I attended her funeral at four o'clock on November 11, 1918, to the sound of bells ringing for the Armistice."

Eileen Pettigrew is author of *The Silent Enemy* (1983), a study of the effect of the 1918 flu epidemic on Canada.

T.E. Lawrence: Military Hero, Anguished Searcher

by Dennis Duffy

In the summer of 1921 T.E. Lawrence, by then the celebrated Lawrence of Arabia, informed his former Oxford tutor, L.C. Jane, that he had recently refused "the rectorship of McGill University in Montreal." According to McGill's archivist, the position of rector has never appeared in the structure of things at that institution. Nor does the name of T.E. Lawrence crop up in either the minute books or the correspondence files of the Board of Governors during the period 1917–24. In this incident, based on undoubted fame and doubtful factual precision, we find a microcosm of Lawrence's public career.

To his own world, he proved the one ground-war hero to emerge from the global disaster that was the Great War. Like the ace pilots, he seemed to embody a more individualistic, chivalric, heroic kind of warfare. The young Oxford archeologist who turned out to be an instinctive military genius, the white leader-inspirer of native levies, the liberator of the Holy Land: all these popular images, mythologies and historical distortions appeared to come true in T.E. Lawrence. He performed prodigies of effort himself, but it was what we would now call the media, and especially the brilliant American publicist Lowell Thomas, that wrapped him in a heroic halo. Lawrence felt ambivalent about this role, often firmly backing into the limelight (as his friend and supporter George Bernard Shaw was to note).

Other confusions beset him too. In terms of his historical influence, he simultaneously worked for the political independence of (some of) the Arab peoples and served as an important agent in their transfer from one empire, the Ottoman, to his own British version. This was to cause him no end of guilt, and guilt-inspired rationalization, as both his letters and his personal memoir, *Seven Pillars of Wisdom*, attest. Finally, the wartime intimation of his sexual ambivalence undermined his sense of his own integrity

T.E. Lawrence

as well. Here is a man of considerable complexity.

These drawbacks to his own era's sense of his heroism, then largely un-noticed or concealed, in fact enthrone him in the pantheon of our own time. The psychiatrist John Mack's 1976 biographical study of Lawrence, *A Prince of Our Disorder*, presented a thoroughly modern hero. Public triumph at the price of private anguish, a self-consciousness that leads to self-hatred: these engage us. In their epic 1962 film, the brilliant trio of director David Lean, screenwriter Robert Bolt and actor Peter O'Toole combined to present exactly that breed of hero; *Lawrence of Arabia*'s enduring popularity proves how intriguing its subject remains.

Lawrence surfaced again in 1989 in Jeremy Wilson's thousand-page au-thorized biography. A biographer writing at this late date had to bring out both sides of his subject, and Wilson did so, though the military man tended to overshadow the existential searcher. But while Wilson told us far more than most readers would ever want to know about British imperial doings in the Middle East (although he unaccountably omitted some incidents that cast Lawrence in an unfavourable light, which Lawrence himself reported in

Seven Pillars of Wisdom), he seemed closest to his subject in following an anguished Lawrence as he sought release among the "other ranks" after the war.

Part of the man's endearing foolishness lay in supposing that he could pass as a private soldier despite friendships that ran throughout the ruling class and despite erudition and brilliance that terrified his immediate military superiors. A squaddie who occupied his spare time translating Homer was an anomoly, and Lawrence was shifted about from service to service and place to place as the newspapers discovered his identity. Yet even amid this he cannot be seen as studiously avoiding the publicity that plagued him. Wilson displayed an affinity with this period of his subject's life. But whichever portion of Wilson's volume you prefer, the fact remains that no single volume on Lawrence has quite captured the whole man.

Writing this article at the time of Canadian involvement in the 1991 Persian Excursion, I cannot think about Lawrence without reflecting on some questions posed by his career. Have any of the imperial reorderings of the Middle East—from Alexander to George Bush—worked? Has any reshuffling given a greater sense of balance to the region? Has any imperial system ever seriously considered leaving control of the region to its indigenous peoples? Has it not always been easier to focus on what seems the "natural" anarchy of the area? Lawrence took credit for the idea of controlling anti-British activity in the new state of Iraq through aerial bombardment. Have contemporary versions of such policies worked any better? Can a region that has always held such geographic and spiritual importance—three world religions began there—survive the addition of the cruel burden of wealth in energy sources as well? Whose interests are best served by continuing the paradox of opulence in nonrenewable resources and abject poverty in political stability?

At the time of writing, I have been thinking and writing about Lawrence, off and on, for some thirty years. I have been driven not by obsession but by my conviction that he stands at a crossroads of history and mythology. Our mythologies about his life and role lie entwined in our fantasies about a region we refuse to view realistically and historically. Others—and now ultimately we—pay for those fantasies.

Dennis Duffy is professor of English literature at Innis College, University of Toronto.

Russia: Power Was in the Streets

by Mary McAuley

The mood among Russian intellectuals in 1910 was one of apprehension. Yet few dreamt that by the end of the decade their world would have changed so utterly. Though the immediate cause of the changes was the Revolution of 1917, the catalyst that set them in motion, in a society whose future was already uncertain, was the First World War.

In 1910, it is true, a stratum of better-off peasant households was emerging, industrial growth rates were substantial, and a new middle class was making its appearance. The tsar had weathered the 1905 revolution and had granted a Duma, or consultative assembly, on a limited franchise. But the demands of the huge and often poverty-stricken peasantry for land and for an end to the tax burden remained unsatisfied, and a brutal regime prevailed in the big industrial plants where peasant boys met skilled workers still smarting from the repression that had followed the strikes of 1905. In 1911 Pyotr Stolypin, the minister responsible for land reforms, was assassinated, and in 1912 tsarist troops responded with violence when the workers at the Lena goldfields came out in protest against barbaric working conditions. The tsar remained an intolerant and inflexible autocrat, concerned only with preserving his rule unchanged.

Still, when war came in 1914, popular support was forthcoming. Peasants were called up, and the factories turned to munitions. But as victories failed to materialize, as soldiers shivered in their trenches without boots or rifles, and as food became scarce in the towns, the mood changed. In the capital, St. Petersburg, discontent grew. Even in court circles, many grumbled about the tsar's inept handling of the war and the influence exerted by his German wife. In February 1917 Cossack soldiers joined a demonstration of women in the bread queues instead of putting it down, and that was the end of tsarism. In Leon Trotsky's words, "Power fell into the streets." The soldiers had abandoned the tsar and no one was willing to defend him. Forced to abdicate, the tsar was held prisoner for more than a year before being executed by Bolsheviks in Ekaterinburg in the Ural Mountains.

V.I. Lenin

Leading members of the Duma, among them Prince Lvov and Alexander Kerensky, formed a Provisional Government with responsibility for waging the war and running the country until a Constituent Assembly could decide Russia's future. Freedom of the press and association was declared. Political parties, trade unions, factory committees and soldiers' committees appeared. *Mitings* were all the rage. In St. Petersburg, factories and regiments sent delegates to a working-class assembly, the soviet. Suppressed after playing a key role in 1905, the soviet now reappeared as the socialist forum in the city. It saw its task not as challenging the government but as defending the revolution. As war dragged on and the economy faltered, however, discontent with the government grew and soviets, springing up across the country, came to be seen as an alternative. Social divisions sharpened— peasant against landowner, worker against factory owner, soldier against officer—and the clamor for peace, bread and land began to batter at the doors of the palaces and government offices.

The Provisional Government could neither satisfy the right, which insisted on the imposition of order at home and the preservation of the Russian Empire (many of whose peoples were now demanding independence), nor meet the radical demands of the poor. In October the Bolsheviks, a working-class socialist party led by a handful of very able intellectuals, seized power in the capital and proclaimed a new Soviet government. Over the next few weeks they established their dominance in the major cities. But while the new government, led by Lenin, had the backing of the factory poor and the peasants in uniform, it could not claim a popular mandate. The Constituent Assembly returns in November gave the Socialist Revolutionaries, the peasant party, an overall majority. The Bolsheviks responded by dissolving the assembly.

It is doubtful that any popularly elected government could have found a peaceful way forward. The peasants simply took the land and turned their backs on the cities, where new battle lines were being drawn. The Bolsheviks and their supporters stood ranged against a variety of opponents: members of the upper classes who saw them as threatening their very existence, and those socialists and workers who considered them dangerous and dictatorial utopians. Russia now faced a bloody civil war. Led by the tsarist generals, "White" armies opposed to the Revolution formed in the south; Britain, France, the United States, Canada and other countries intervened on the White side.

By the summer of 1920 the Bolsheviks had won, but the introduction of socialism looked painfully remote. In October 1917 they had set out to construct a new type of government, where workers ran the affairs of state in a society of social ownership, a workers' militia replaced a standing army, and education and culture became accessible to all. This was the socialist vision. They had believed it would be realized, in backward Russia, with the help of the advanced industrial workers abroad. Day by day the telephonists sat by their machines, waiting for the news that the revolution had begun in Paris or Berlin. In 1918 it was not such a foolish hope, but in 1920 everything was bleaker. The economy was in ruins after seven years of war; peasants' and workers' protests increased. An overblown bureaucracy spilled out of the government's Moscow offices, and power lay in the hands of a Bolshevik party that had grown increasingly quick to use force and silence criticism. In the spring of 1921 the sailors of Kronstadt, "the flower of the revolution," mutinied and demanded free trade and openly elected soviets. The Bolsheviks suppressed the mutiny and denied the validity of the electoral claim.

In their own eyes and those of their supporters abroad, the Bolsheviks were a socialist bulwark in a capitalist world. A decade earlier the socialist movement had looked to Germany to lead the way but the First World War had shattered the hope that workers would refuse to take up arms against one another. Nationalism proved too strong.

With the revolution of 1917, leadership of the international working-class movement passed to Russia, and the stage was set for the authoritarian brand of socialism that has left its mark on the twentieth century. In 1921, however, the remaining intellectuals were preoccupied not with socialism but with a book, *Smena vekh* (Change of landmarks), whose émigré authors saw in the Bolsheviks a national government to save Russia. Was this the significance of 1917, despite the revolutionaries' aims, or did they—as some have argued since—bring ruin to Russia? Whatever the assessment, in its sheer impact on developments throughout the world, the Russian Revolution was probably the most important event of the century.

At the time of writing **Mary McAuley** was tutor in politics at St. Hilda's College, Oxford University.

Ireland: Destructive Adventure

by John Francis Larkin

During 1991 posters displayed in the streets of Dublin invited people to "recreate the Spirit of 1916." Seventy-five years after the Easter Rising, it was difficult to define the "spirit" of that event in a manner that made its celebration seem desirable.

In essence the Rising was a military adventure, promoted by a small group of republican conspirators and crushed by British troops in a week. In the fighting sixty insurgents and 132 soldiers and police were killed; more than 300 civilians died and the centre of Dublin was devastated. Even though minor in comparison to the slaughter on the Western Front, the human and economic cost of the Rising was not inconsiderable.

But what made it the most significant image of the Irish separatist struggle in the twentieth century was the response of the British military authorities. Following trials by courts martial, the leaders of the Rising were executed by firing squad and thereby immortalized as martyrs. The scope for hagiography was greatly increased by the personal decency and integrity many of the leaders were known to possess. Patrick Pearse, Thomas MacDonagh, Joseph Plunkett and James Connolly were people of ability, commitment and passion who had achieved distinction in education, literature and the labour movement. By shooting fifteen leaders of the Rising, the British authorities permitted attention to slide from the destructiveness of the enterprise to the succession of personal dramas embodied in a series of trials, convictions and executions.

At least some of the participants imagined it this way from the beginning. James Connolly may have believed that a capitalist government would not order the shelling of commercial buildings (and therefore would give the insurgents a chance in hand-to-hand fighting), but Pearse entertained a vision of the Irish nation redeemed by blood sacrifice and contemplated death in battle with cool acceptance if not actual eagerness. Apart from the questionable morality of self-sacrifice in favour of an ill-defined abstraction like the "Irish nation" (to say nothing of the whiff of blasphemy given off by the timing of the Rising at Eastertide), a large number of men and women suffered unwillingly to make possible the gesture of Pearse and his comrades.

Perhaps the personal qualities of the leaders of the Rising make it easy to ignore or fail to confront the immorality of their adventure. Only an unrealistically elastic reading of just war theory would deny the objective wrongfulness of a quixotic military exhibition that results in such casualties. But to judge harshly the men who undertook the Rising seems strangely difficult. No doubt the importance of the Rising for the rhetoric of the modern Irish state renders a public moral analysis politically improbable. It is difficult to see how either of the two main parties in the Republic of Ireland could completely disavow the men and the event that both in some way claim as inspiration. What one is less inclined to understand is why the Catholic hierarchy in Ireland has shared this reticence.

The extraordinary harmony that has tended to exist over the public doctrine of the Irish state is one explanation. Another is the use of Patrick Pearse as a model for the youth of Ireland by generations of secondary school teachers, based mainly on the ease with which it was supposed a "man of action" could be presented for admiration and on the complete sexual innocence of the subject. But while it was useful to advise boys to respect the memory of a man apparently free of sexual sin, it is more problematic to choose as a role model a person who writes, as Pearse did on the outbreak of the First World War, that "the old heart of the Earth needed to be warmed with the red wine of the battlefields. Such august homage was never before offered to God as this, the homage of millions of lives given gladly for love of country."

If the problem of uniting the communities that live on the island of Ireland can be tackled with any reasonable prospect of a favourable result, among the tasks that will have to be done is a proper assessment of the damage that Ireland's cherished heroes continue to do from their graves. It is no disrespect to the memory of a dead man that people generally believe that he was wrong. It is a continuing offence to God and humanity that no community in Ireland is yet prepared to confess errors in the interpretation of history.

At the time of writing **John Francis Larkin** was Reid professor of criminal law, criminology and penology at Trinity College, Dublin.

The Twenties

Frans Masereel (1898–1972)

87	The Exuberance and Despair of the 1920s	by Stephanie Vincec
89	Prologue to Our Own Era	by Jean Clair
96	Literary Fistfight in Paris	by Louis Dudek
100	Rocky Road to Church Union	by John Webster Grant
104	No Heroes, No Defeats: A New Era in Canadian Politics	by H. Blair Neatby
109	Agnes Macphail in Parliament	by Terry Crowley
112	Fascism's Mystique of Power	by Alkis Kontos
116	Marcus Garvey: Black Moses	by Robert Hill
119	Ascendancy of the Chiangs	by Mary Rose Donnelly
122	Breath Came and They Lived: The Discovery of Insulin	by Michael Bliss
125	The Public Health Offensive	by Jutta Mason
128	St. Miguel Pro and the Secret Kingdom	by John Matheson

The Exuberance and Despair of the 1920s

by Stephanie Vincec

After the cataclysmic disruption of 1914–18, the world never really returned to "normal." For some this was a cause of despair; for others, optimism. During the 1920s, both groups put much energy into redefining culture, society and world politics, and their decisions strongly influenced the rest of the century.

The breakdown of prewar political structures gave rise to a search for new forms of order. The League of Nations, a cooperative response, proved to be of limited effectiveness, in part because many nations, including the United States, were not members. Another response, totalitarian communism, continued to evolve behind an iron curtain. Interlocked with these developments were attempts to manage the postwar economy, which eventually ended in spectacular failure with the crash of 1929. Social and economic uncertainty throughout the decade, along with fear of Bolshevism, provided a ready climate for fascist movements to grow. Marcus Garvey led a movement among black peoples for African Redemption.

These and other movements were frequently so complex and unfamiliar that it was difficult to say definitively whether they signified world progress or, as Oswald Spengler had predicted, the "decline of the West." In literature, the human journey became more problematic than ever, for the landscape of the mind had become, as T.S. Eliot put it, "a heap of broken images." A Lost Generation of writers and artists frequently expressed an elegiac or guilty mood in their works.

But it was the alternative mood, irrepressible exuberance, that gave the decade its enduring reputation. "Destroy the past and build the future on its ruins!" was George Bernard Shaw's opinion. The studios of Berlin, Paris and New York produced the new and futuristic in great abundance. Painting and sculpture went through a series of "isms" that stretched, distorted and streamlined familiar shapes. Architecture became distinctively modern and cities imitated the New York skyline.

Although hardly at the forefront of international trends, Canada felt their effects and produced its own response. It joined the League and moved towards independent status within the British Commonwealth of Nations. International movements for peace and for women's rights found Canadian followers. The election of MP Agnes Macphail was a small but significant step in women's struggle for equal status. At the same time, ecumenism created an enduring voice by bringing three Protestant denominations together in the United Church of Canada.

Religious life in this decade was marked by Reform theologian Karl Barth's passionate attack on liberal theology and his quest to recover the otherness of God and the priority of revelation. Philosopher-theologian-physician Albert Schweitzer, coming from a Lutheran tradition, proposed "reverence for life" as the key to an ethical civilization.

The loss of a stable European order produced deep ambivalence in the Catholic Church. The church's leaders favoured the status quo. In establishing the feast of Christ the King, however, the church offered a model of genuine authority to a fragmented world and a symbol of hope for a renewed and inclusive human community.

No simple static description fits the 1920s, possibly because many of its ambiguities are still with us. We invite you to reflect with our writers on some of the echoes of that roar from the past.

Stephanie Vincec CSJ was a member of the editorial board of *Compass* magazine and its successor, the board of directors of the Compass Foundation, from 1987 until her death in 1998. She was also a teacher, a literary scholar, and communications director of the Sisters of St. Joseph of Hamilton.

Prologue to Our Own Era

by Jean Clair

The twenties: at what point did we start referring to historical periods by numbers rather than names? The century of Louis XIII, the Regency, the Restoration, the reign of Louis-Philippe, the Empire—all these eras are linked to an individual or a form of government, but they also evoke a particular type of sensibility: a style. To abandon denomination in favour of denumeration is a sign of decadence. Time, once basking in the reflected brilliance of some remarkable individual, suddenly finds itself identified by the banality of a number. The twenties, the thirties, the forties—not only has time become anonymous, its pages seem to flick past more quickly and uniformly, piling one on the other like the layers of silt that fix the ultimate form of a landscape once the major shifts have subsided. The epochs of Pericles, Louis XIV and Franz Josef were all protracted ones. With the twenties, however, began the tyranny of the short term.

The explanation for all of this is not hard to find. The First World War put an end to great empires: sparked by their rivalry, it brought about their ruin. The French, the German, the Hapsburg—all were empires that held sway for a long time. But once they were gone, there commenced the frantic rhythm of falling governments, short-lived republics, endless nationalist squabbles and quarrels that, in their turn, led inexorably to the Second World War. The twenties were in a sense a foretoken of the utterly new world that would emerge when the conflict was finally over.

The twenties: for once arithmetic seems to reflect the events of the real world with perfect precision—or nearly. The year 1919 saw the end of the war and the signing of the Treaty of Versailles, which redefined the borders and, it was thought, the very structure of Europe; 1929 saw the stock market crash and the disintegration of the economic system that had taken root after a fashion during the decade. From a red October to a black one: in ten years there was a shift from east to west, from the upheavals that shook central Europe and its frontiers—soviets in Russia, workers' conferences in Munich, Hamburg and Berlin, Béla Kun's revolution in Hungary—to the financial disaster that brought about the downfall of the new capitalist system in the West.

These years left no one the time to linger, to reflect, to change their mind. The twenties, moreover, marked that moment when automobiles, airplanes, trains and ocean liners more magnificent than any ever seen before or since made travel a commonplace and pulled together the once-distant frontiers of the planet. A finite time, when loves, passions and affections were brief. It was, without a doubt, the decade of *L'Homme pressé*. The literature of the period reflects this feeling of haste: its best novels are written in a style reminiscent of embassy dispatches—curt, clear and often not without a trace of desperate humour. Shifts in moral values, the uncertainty of the future, sudden changes of circumstance, the ambiguity of the sexes (so evident in hair and clothing fashions)—all echoed the steady slipping of currency value, the erosion of the monetary system and regular declines in the stock market. The world of value, both material and spiritual, was clearly a world in crisis; the result was a species of social chaos that a cinema historian, in a reference to one of the key films of the period, made in 1919, was later to call *Caligarism*.

The character of Caligari (so magnificently portrayed by the actor Werner Krauss), the hypnotist, the magician, the asylum director, is the perfect emblematic figure to usher us into the twenties; and the porch we enter as we cross the threshold is constructed of the static Expressionist scenery conceived by Hermann Warm and others. More than simply an urban vision, this scenery, this "set," was the *Kammerspiel* reconstruction of an inner world. The art of cinema had not yet received its modern name: in the countries of northern Europe it was still known by playwright Carl Hauptmann's term "bioscope" and seen as capable of "recording actions, things and beings that come genuinely from the soul."

The twenties were, above all, the years when psychoanalysis evolved from being the secret activity of a sect into an institution that would henceforth hold major international conferences in the great capitals of the western world. If we wish to truly grasp the meaning of the decade, our only possible access is via the mysterious and tortured—Expressionist, to use the term worn so thin in art—*Kammer* of a subjectivity that, following the Apocalypse of 1914, was still struggling to set foot on solid ground.

Precisely halfway through this ten-year period, in 1924, the mobile camera was invented and the practice of high-speed editing became widespread. All was suddenly extraversion and externality, coupled with an ideological activism and dedication to "causes" that would preoccupy creators everywhere. The twisting, gloomy path that had jaggedly mirrored the labyrinth of the soul was supplanted by a brilliantly lit thoroughfare, straining skyward, throbbing with noise, packed with speeding vehicles. Suddenly, we had passed from a world of gargoyles, machicolations and stalactites into one sketched in the pure and aerodynamic lines of a Futurist utopia. It was time to revolutionize the city: to build a city such as had never been seen before, a brand-new city, unlike anything yet imagined. Those postwar architects who, prevented by lack of commissions from actually constructing anything, had sketched on paper a visionary pseudoarchitecture, edifices of crystal and stained glass rising out of inaccessible sites, were thus replaced by others who, while still producing work of a distinctly utopian flavour, rejected dreams in favour of form and actually laid the foundations of that powerful machine that is the modern metropolis: the functional, rational city, the perfect place in which to dwell, to trade, to exchange, maybe even to live, of which, for better or worse, we are the heirs.

Austria's Robert Musil, probably the most lucid writer of his generation, created another emblematic figure of the era in his alter ego Ulrich, the protagonist of *The Man without Qualities*:

Illustrations in this article by Frans Masereel (1898–1972)

Modern man is born in hospital and dies in hospital—hence he should also live in a place like a hospital.—This maxim had just been formulated by a leading architect, and another one, a reformer of interior decoration, demanded movable partition-walls in flats, on the grounds that in living together man must learn to trust man and not shut himself off in a spirit of separatism....He came to the conclusion that he preferred, after all, to take the architectural completion of his personality into his own hands, and he began designing his future furniture himself. But whenever he had just thought out a shape that was solid and impressive, it occurred to him that one could just as easily put a slim, strong, technically functional form in its place; and whenever he designed a reinforced concrete shape looking as though it were emaciated by its own strength, he would recall the thin, vernal lines of a thirteen-year-old girl and sink into reverie instead of making up his mind.

Everything is captured in these lines by Musil: the vacillation between imagination and revolution, apathy and action, commitment to the "avantgarde" and faith in the formulas of days gone by. The passage recalls the figure of Adolf Loos, who saw the plumber as the hero of the contemporary world and, moreover, required of a chair not only that it be comfortable, but that it allow people to seat themselves *quickly*. But scarcely has Ulrich had time to feel the pull of this same rationalism than he begins to be haunted by the fragile forms of slender young girls, and we are plunged back into the morbid and aggressively sexualized world of an Expressionism that refuses to quite die.

As for the house with movable partitions, designed to prevent "separatism" among city dwellers, it reminds us of the amazing building constructed by Pierre Chareau at the very heart of the decade: this house, which included both living and professional quarters, consisted of three storeys that contained not a single opaque or fixed wall, but only movable divisions of perforated steel, grilles that left no corner unit and glass partitions that combined to make it one of the most astonishing panopticons to have been created during our enlightened century. When we recall that the house's owner, a Dr. Dalsace, was a gynecologist in the habit of entertaining a large circle of writers and artists that included Marcel Duchamp, the Jeanneret cousins and Jean Lurçat, we cannot but wonder what secret links exist between this totally transparent building, this "showcase," in the centre of which women revealed themselves utterly to their doctor's gaze, and that other showcase created around the same time—Duchamp's work entitled *Large Glass*. For in the centre of this similarly mechanistic work is displayed "the sexual object" (to use the Freudian vocabulary of the period), denuded, stripped of all sentimentality and drained of all secretion, a cynical and indefatigable device of positively hygienic purity.

Once free of the gloom of Expressionism, the twenties swiftly adopted the vision of the-world-as-showcase, capable of displaying both the incredible profusion of goods manufactured by a now triumphant industry and the associated posturings of this new breed of human being, whose bodies had been transformed by the pencil of Coco Chanel and her like into functional objects with the simple contours of a robot.

The twenties saw the emergence, then, of the machine-house, constructed in the materials of technology and specifically designed, just like a car or a washing machine, to be mass-produced. The word *robot*—a word with an unexpectedly illustrious future—was first coined in 1921 in the play *R.U.R. (Rossum's Universal Robots)* by the Czech writer Capek, who derived it from the verb that in both his own language and in Russian means "to work." At the time, of course, it was a merely fictional term. However, Taylorism was not far off, and as the world awaited the little hero of *Modern Times*, caught up so uncomfortably in his cogwheels, painters of the 1920s gave the dream of a mechanical man a variety of visual embodiments.

Some of the most striking and innovative works of art of the 1920s are actually multiples that exist in at least two identical versions. The most radical innovation of the twenties concerns this concept of reproduction: no longer did the work of art exist exclusively in and for itself, a unique and sacred object, a testament to outstanding genius; it had become a prototype, based on plans and blueprints just like an engineer's and capable of being reproduced and distributed as often and as widely as desired. The theorists of Soviet Productivism pushed this idea to its logical conclusion: the artist-as-artist was to abdicate and take on the new role of engineer in the service of the people, just as easel painting, that quintessential expression of bourgeois subjectivism, was to be abolished and "surpassed" by industrially produced objects of incomparably perfect design.

Less optimistic, even frankly pessimistic, was Walter Benjamin's skeptical Marxism of the early thirties. Benjamin investigated the concept of the work of art in the age of mass production and felt considerable anxiety regarding what he saw as the eradication of our cultural heritage in the face of a rising technology and, ultimately, the halt in human spiritual evolution caused by the loss of what he called *aura*: modern man, he considered, is submerged in images but has himself become an increasingly shadowy presence.

Ulrich, the man without qualities, does not suffer these preoccupations. While he believes in the multiplication of works of art and the development of industrially produced objects—just as other faithful, at other periods, have believed in the multiplication of the loaves—in furnishing his house he remains unmoved by the splendid new possibilities opened up by developments in the decorative arts. He is actually the perfect representative of a revivalist trend that ran through the decade. Wary of innovation, but open-minded enough to feel dissatisfied with styles of the past, Ulrich draws on all the trappings of modernity: neo-Rococo, neo-Cubism, neo-Mannerism.

The twenties: reverie or revolution, refusal or revival, the stark and

frigid realism of the New Objectivity or the uncompromising renovation of social reformers—it was a decade that hesitated and hovered as it faced the ever-recurring prefix, the obsessive syllable that signalled repetition, reprise and effortless mechanical reproduction, but also the repression of a period struggling against the wall of time and the sudden acceleration of its course.

For if there is a watchword that echoed throughout this decade, that made itself heard above all the cries for revolution, it was certainly the "call to order." The decade preceding 1920 had been a tumult of the most astonishing experiments and transgressions. With progress seemingly well under way in all areas of human endeavor, art had become a battlefield on which the formally "advanced"—whether Cubist or Futurist, Fauvist or Expressionist—were constantly gaining ground. Then the Great War, with its real battlefields and its real trenches, dampened enthusiasms; by 1916, midway through the conflict, Apollinaire and even Picasso himself, the demiurge, were beginning to show early symptoms of the great movement towards order and peace. Enough of innovation! It was time to rebuild the world on solid, lasting foundations. So it was back to the past, back to the art of Antiquity, back—it seems clear—in quest of reassurance, comfort and confidence.

Archaism and Neoclassicism thus became the new models, along with the recently discovered art of Rome and the frescos of the first Renaissance. Modernity had started as an adventure led by a handful of guerrillas roaming the fringes of society, poets and painters inhabiting a Bohemia that drifted between Montmartre and Montparnasse, fed by the influx of famished immigrants from eastern Europe. But modernity had now earned full citizenship. On exhibition in the heart of every major metropolis, it even began to be institutionalized: the world's first museums of modern art, its first temples to the new cult, opened their doors during the late twenties. Cubism, Fauvism, Futurism: art's now carefully classified "isms" became formulas—at least in the field of applied arts—to be employed or not according to the taste of the client. What had so recently been a source of scandal now adorned fashionable interiors in the form of tapestries, sculptures and household objects. Modernity, so lately considered primitive, crude, unpredictable, even intolerable, was suddenly invited into drawing rooms, made welcome in the best of circles, officially lauded and applauded, and used to decorate great international express trains and magnificent ocean liners.

The decade was a prologue to an era, an overture played at breakneck speed, rather than a historical period in its own right. And the era that was ushered in was, of course, our own, the very one that is drawing to a close in the 1990s. The sloughing off, in a few short months, of the Soviet veneer revealed to our astonished gaze a Europe that is just as it was before the twenties, with the same particularisms, nationalisms, rivalries and customs; everything is completely intact, as if the Marxist ideology established in 1917 and solidified during the twenties—internally by the New Economic Policy and the beginnings of Stalinism, externally by the International—to become a thick, uniform layer that spread out gradually but relentlessly across the various realities, an intellectual construction we believed eternal, had actually behaved like one of those glaciers that cover parts of the earth but eventually melt and reveal to the incredulous eye of the traveller the fossilized but perfectly preserved remains of animals dead centuries before. In looking at the twenties in all their complexity, we are striving to grasp the central meaning of a period we imagined would endure for thousands of years, but that actually lasted for less than three generations.

Jean Clair, director of the Musée Picasso in Paris, was curator of the exhibit "The 1920s: Age of the Metropolis" at the Montreal Museum of Fine Arts in 1991. A longer version of this essay appeared in the catalogue accompanying that exhibit.

Literary Fistfight in Paris

by Louis Dudek

Canadians are too polite, or too inhibited, to seek out the truth about their own literature. For example, they had a huge drama—or farce—in the relation between Morley Callaghan and John Glassco, but in general have chosen to ignore it.

George Woodcock described *That Summer in Paris* (1963) as "one of Callaghan's most appealing books." And I hailed Glassco's *Memoirs of Montparnasse* (1970) at the moment of its appearance as, artistically, "the best book of prose by a Canadian that I have ever read." Yet no one seems to be aware that these two important books were locked in mortal combat, and that they are the product of a long battle of poisoned pens, stretching from the twenties to the late seventies, in fact up to the demise of Glassco in 1981 and Callaghan in 1990. It is a literary quarrel of some general import. The large currents of our literary and cultural life are involved in the opposition. But that possible realization must follow a review of the history, or gossip, involved in the case.

It all began in 1929, during Morley Callaghan's honeymoon trip to Paris, so fully described in *That Summer in Paris*. Callaghan, already published by Scribners and on the way to big fame, was then twenty-seven, while Glassco was seven years his junior and utterly unknown. And yet, at the age of eighteen Glassco had written a chapter of an autobiography, which had appeared in the Paris magazine *This Quarter*.

There was something very irritating to Callaghan in the superior airs of Glassco and his friend Graeme Taylor, "two boys from Montreal" who seemed absolutely inseparable in their futile sauntering about the Paris cafés. Yet he made friends with them, and they actually found an apartment for him and his wife, over a grocery shop—a great kindness to visitors in Paris.

Glassco, however, kept tittering and sniping in his clever youthful way at all the heroes Callaghan had collected in Paris—Hemingway, Robert

McAlmon, F. Scott Fitzgerald. So when McAlmon spoke well of "that bright little devil" Glassco, while all the while Callaghan knew that behind his back Glassco had ridiculed and laughed outright at McAlmon's verses, Callaghan took a bet with McAlmon, with the editor of *This Quarter* as witness, to see who would write a better story about "the two bright boys" from Montreal.

But Callaghan committed an unwise and dangerous act in writing the story *Now That April's Here*. It is a sad satirical portrait of two lost souls in the Paris of the twenties, two callow provincials on an aimless bohemian adventure ending in futility and desolation. As Brandon Conron points out, the story is "full of clever suggestion and insinuation" (meaning homosexual implication) so that it is not innocent of even deeper malice. It appeared in *This Quarter* as stipulated in the bet (McAlmon produced no story), and then it became the title story in a Callaghan collection published in 1936.

But of course Callaghan should have known that a young man from Montreal who had published in a Paris magazine at nineteen might well develop into an important literary figure. The libellous story might come to haunt Callaghan, although it was simply the result of his principle that one should write from experience. This method inevitably leads to the problem of libel or slander that we are examining.

Callaghan, like Hemingway, belongs to the category of mindless-writers-by-intention, who believe that good writing is best when it is free of ideas or conscious thought. "A writer always got into trouble," Hemingway said, "when he started thinking on the page," and Callaghan fully agreed. Callaghan actually protested that he never began writing with a theme in mind. He just wrote "to tell the truth cleanly." Such a principle can only yield unconscious dreamlike meanings, since the dreamer is occasionally profound, but it would be better, even in Canada, to be more conscious and reflective.

The great event in Callaghan's Paris trip, foolish as it may sound, was his boxing match with Hemingway, in which he knocked down the Great Hunter and War Hero after Scott Fitzgerald forgot to call "time." The result was a permanent estrangement among all three writers, but it was an event that loomed large in Callaghan's imagination. When Hemingway died in 1961 Callaghan was at last free to tell the whole story, and he made this the central episode in *That Summer in Paris*. The subplot of that book, however, was the story of "the two clever little devils...with their bland and distinguished air"—or "Buffy and Graeme," as he actually names them in two places—and how he came to write and publish a rather reprehensible short story about them.

I believe that Callaghan actually intended to apologize, to some degree, for his ill-deed, or at least to explain it away. By 1963, Glassco was emerging as a Canadian literary personality, a very Edwardian-looking gentleman, author of one distinguished book of poetry with another on the way, plus a number of highly artistic pornographic stories, a novel and a successful published sequel to Aubrey Beardsley's *Under the Hill.*

In *That Summer in Paris* Callaghan refers to Glassco and Taylor as "two slender boys in their early twenties...soft spoken with a mocking opinion about everybody." And he speaks of them in a kindly way as "two willowy graceful young men from Montreal whom McAlmon called affectionately 'the clever little devils.'" And yet, at the climactic point, just when he decides that "those two boys...whom I had got to like by this time" were okay, he cannot resist describing Glassco's worst juvenile gaffe. Hemingway had just walked down the street with a very short man carrying boxing gloves. "Does Hemingway bring his butler with him to carry his bag?" Glassco asked of Callaghan, who was sitting at the café table. "No," said Callaghan after a pause. "That's Joan Miró." Callaghan knew that this would "leave them feeling they had committed the most terrible of sins around the Quarter, the sin of unawareness of what was going on."

So Callaghan had simply repeated his unforgivable offence against Glassco. It had to be answered, and the answer was *Memoirs of Montparnasse.*

Glassco had probably written only one chapter of the book in the late twenties, and perhaps a few pages more in the early thirties. But none of that was usable as it stood. Philip Kokotailo has demonstrated clearly in his book *John Glassco's Richer World* that Glassco's book is a reply to Callaghan, by actual word-count against word-count, a passionate rebuttal of Callaghan's view of Paris in the twenties and of Callaghan's portrait of him and his friend Graeme Taylor at that time. This is why Glassco presents an ecstatic, highly coloured picture of the Paris scene, and also why he went to great lengths to pretend that the book had been written on the spot, or nearly so. Actually, as Kokotailo and others have established, the book was written between 1963 and 1965, in Canada.

This is how Glassco depicts Callaghan in *Memoirs of Montparnasse:* "Morley Callaghan was short, dark, and roly-poly, and wore a striped shirt without a collar; with his moon face and little moustache he looked very like Hemingway; he had even the same shrewd little politician's eyes, the same lopsided grin and ingratiating voice. His wife was also short and thickset, and wore a coral dress and a string of beads. Both of them were so friendly and unpretentious that I liked them at once. It was like meeting people from a small town."

The deeper reason for the animosity between Callaghan and Glassco lies in Glassco's affinity with the British esthetic tradition, while Callaghan derives from an American and Canadian tradition of simple realism and directness of style. Oscar Wilde's essay "The Decay of Lying" (1889) defines both sides of the issue.

"That Lying, the telling of beautiful untrue things, is the proper aim of Art," is Wilde's declared principle. It is also that of Glassco in his many fabrications: "I must admit that I was always, though mainly in self-defence, a great practitioner of deceit," he writes in *Memoirs of Montparnasse*. He calls himself "an accomplished liar," and he was, both in his life and in his writing. Yet he revealed a great deal through his subtle fabrications.

The opposite school of fiction, says Wilde, "insists on going directly to life for everything." And, he says, it is "entirely wrong from beginning to end." But this precisely describes Callaghan's position—and incidentally that of many Canadian writers. "As for that great and daily increasing school of novelists," says Wilde, "for whom the sun always rises in the East-End, the only thing that can be said about them is that they find life crude, and leave it raw." Thus, Brandon Conron writes of Callaghan's first novel, "There is an objectivity of treatment which discourages the reader from making any moral judgment, and which made the writing seem 'hard-boiled' at the time when the novel was published."

I have deliberately avoided taking sides in this issue, though I may have presented both contestants as somewhat absurd—as I think they are—because the reader should be left to cogitate the question and debate it in his or her own mind. Such a reader will find it a field for rich speculation, perhaps in the end to discover a "Richer World" than either John Glassco's or Morley Callaghan's. After all, why should we remain provincials or reactionaries forever? Perhaps there is a higher order of being than either of these.

Poet, editor and literary critic **Louis Dudek** taught English at McGill University in Montreal.

Rocky Road to Church Union

by John Webster Grant

The process that would culminate in the formation of the United Church of Canada in 1925 began almost absentmindedly. Following their usual thrifty practice, the Canadian Presbyterians delegated three local ministers to convey greetings to the quadrennial Methodist general conference at Winnipeg in 1902. Principal William Patrick of Manitoba College, the first to speak, suggested on his own initiative that union between the two bodies would be a good thing, and his colleagues backed him up. The Methodists made the obvious response of referring the proposal to a committee, which brought in a favourable report as many delegates were packing to return home or to explore the newly opening prairies at greater leisure.

Obviously this informal initiative would not have borne fruit without prepared minds, and indeed the possibility of union had been talked about for some time both in Canada and elsewhere. Anglicans, who had had "Christian reunion" on their agenda since the first Lambeth Conference in 1867, had actually initiated official conversations with Methodists and Presbyterians in 1886. Their insistence on episcopacy quickly aborted these discussions, but the interest thus stimulated among their proposed partners led to a series of proposals for union or cooperation.

More important in determining the ideology of the union that ultimately took place was an emerging consensus among evangelical Protestants. Initially it laid almost exclusive stress on personal conversion but broadened out to embrace a wide-ranging program of moral and social reform. Thoughts of union naturally followed. A shared pattern of faith and experience constituted a basis that made it thinkable, while the urgency of common action provided practical reasons for it. In this country the inchoate state of the Canadian consciousness was an additional incentive, inviting the churches to fill a moral vacuum left by the politics of expediency. Those who dreamed of a united church envisaged it as an instrument for national renovation that could muster greater resources and command greater credibility than any denomination in isolation.

By the end of the nineteenth century many Protestant leaders had endorsed the idea of union across denominational lines, but suggestions for implementing it had awakened little enthusiasm and union committees had lapsed into inactivity. What happened by 1902 to change the outlook so drastically? The most conspicuous new development was the onset of larger-scale and more cosmopolitan immigration, which strained the resources of individual denominations and threatened a Protestant hegemony that hitherto had been taken for granted. That the decisive initiative took place in Winnipeg may have been significant. It was in the west that denominational competition seemed most wasteful, that many Canadians believed their future lay, and that innovation seemed most plausible. In any case, so much had already been said in favour of union that no serious proposal could easily have been ignored.

Since the rationale of union called for a broad Protestant coalition, an attempt was soon made to include other churches. The small Congregational body was quickly brought into the discussions, and in 1906 invitations were extended to the Anglicans and Baptists. The Baptists, whose congregations were reluctant to surrender autonomy even to their own denominational organizations, lost little time in declining. The response of the Anglicans was equivocal. They expressed willingness to engage in conversation, while pointing out that they were committed to a resolution of the previous Lambeth Conference that included the "historical episcopate" as a necessary constituent of any union in which they might be involved. The joint union committee interpreted this reply as in effect a refusal, although Anglicans insisted that it was not so intended. Reading through a rather muddled correspondence suggests that all parties were rather relieved to be let off the hook.

Meanwhile joint committees of Methodists, Presbyterians and Congregationalists began in 1904 to work on preparing a basis of union, and in 1908 they completed their task. The Basis document unabashedly represented an amalgam of the beliefs and regulations of the uniting churches, on the assumption that these were essentially compatible and that the chief purpose of union was to enable Christians of varying backgrounds but a common loyalty to work together as one. The United Church was to incarnate a consensus that already existed in essentials, not to find a way beyond intractable differences. Failure to include the Anglicans was thus not surprising.

Considering the intensity of controversies that had once separated the negotiating churches, the committees found their task surprisingly easy. The committee on doctrine managed to combine Presbyterian and Congregational emphasis on God's direction of events with Methodist insistence on human free will by asserting both while adding qualifying phrases. The committee on polity, noting that all of the uniting churches operated through mixed bodies of clergy and laity that ranged from the local to the national level, proposed a similar system for the United Church. Some juggling of the functions of these "courts" was necessary, and Congregationalists were asked to surrender their cherished tradition of local independence.

The committees found two matters more difficult than any others. Congregationalists had always objected to the practice, common to Presbyterians and Methodists, of requiring candidates for ordination to subscribe formally to a prescribed doctrinal statement; instead they required a personal statement of belief satisfactory to an examining committee. After threatening to withdraw from the negotiations on this issue, they eventually won their point. The other issue concerned the stationing of ministers. Methodists operated through a committee, while Presbyterians and Congregationalists insisted on the right of congregations to call their ministers. Here the Basis leaned towards Methodist practice, although time would render it practically irrelevant except in placing newly ordained ministers.

Union now had to be sold to the churches. In 1910 every Methodist conference but Newfoundland gave it a decisive majority, and Methodist polity made no provision for local congregations to opt out. Each local Congregational church, being independent, could enter union or not as it chose. Most congregations did, the bulk of the holdouts being ones with a tradition of isolation from their own denomination.

Within Presbyterianism the situation was radically different. Denominational regulations required that any constitutional change should be approved by a majority of regional bodies known as presbyteries, and in the circumstances it was decided to seek the opinions of the entire constituency as well. The process took time, but by 1912 the Basis had been approved by the general assembly, fifty of seventy presbyteries, and about 70 per cent of members and adherents. Instead of proceeding, the assembly determined more than once on delay. Later votes saw the minority only increase, and even when in 1923 the assembly decided to proceed with union "forthwith" it found it necessary to allow individual congregations to make their own decisions. The unfortunate result was to invite campaigning that disrupted congregations, friendships and even families.

Scholars are still debating the reasons for greater opposition among Presbyterians. Some have emphasized class and ethnic prejudices, and undoubtedly these played a part. Keith Clifford has called attention to the affinity of many antiunionist leaders with the highly scholastic Calvinism then dominant at Princeton, and the conservatism of the bulk of the opposition was obvious. Probably the main factors were a general satisfaction with Presbyterianism as it then was and a distrust of the liberalism and social activism that seemed likely to characterize the United Church.

In retrospect one is likely to ask why Presbyterian unionist leaders persisted in the face of such substantial and determined opposition, precipitating local schisms that in many communities outweighed the practical advantages of union. The Presbyterian Church in Canada was itself the result of a series of unions, each of which had been strenuously opposed but eventually proved practically unanimous, and at first the unionists plausibly expected history to repeat itself. The process of union also gathered its own momentum, leading all the negotiating churches to rearrangements that could not readily be undone. By 1923, when the final decision was taken, the die had already been cast.

After a long and painful period of gestation the United Church of Canada was inaugurated on June 10, 1925, at a solemn but enthusiastic service in Toronto's Mutual Street Arena. In many ways the time was not propitious. In *A Christian America,* Robert T. Handy has demonstrated that a long-continued effort by the mainline Protestant churches to mould American society in their image began to fall apart during this decade. The corresponding vision faded a little more slowly in Canada, but a church whose central mandate was the more effective Christianization of Canadian society was inevitably affected by the growth of secularism and religious pluralism and by a general reaction against the strictures of Victorian moralism. In a changing Canada the United Church did not become the invincible engine of moral and social engineering its advocates had desired and its opponents had feared. From the outset it faced financial problems, which mounted during the Depression and forced deep cutbacks. Even more seriously, the gradual disappearance of its anticipated role blunted its sense of direction and left it open to the temptation of latching on to every fashionable cause.

Despite setbacks there were few signs of regret among those who entered the United Church. If it did not become the hoped-for powerhouse of nation-building, it has had—except notably in Francophone Quebec—unmatched resources to operate on a national basis and deal with national issues. It has an indigenous quality that has enabled it to approach Canadian problems untrammelled by commitment to denominational precedents or imported folkways. It has had a freedom to experiment that on occasion might leave it apparently rudderless but often gave it an enhanced purchase on the future. The United Church has not been the radical body its national pronouncements have sometimes suggested, but radicalism has been more at home in it than in most other churches. Beyond these characteristics it has stood as a model of union, demonstrating its capacity to move beyond the stage of experiment and challenging others in their separation. Although designed for a role in Canadian society that is no longer there to play, it has demonstrated considerable resilience, and is likely to continue to do so.

Rev. John Webster Grant taught church history at Emmanuel College, University of Toronto from 1963 to 1984. His books include *The Canadian Experience of Church Union*.

No Heroes, No Defeats: A New Era in Canadian Politics

by H. Blair Neatby

Any decade can be described as decisive but in many ways the decade of the 1920s was more decisive than most in Canada. It was the time when Canadians began to respond to economic and social problems that have dominated the country's politics ever since.

Sir John A. Macdonald's National Policy had been designed to forge a nation out of the scattered British territories north of the United States. Protective tariffs would ensure a captive market for Canadian entrepreneurs. A transcontinental railway would connect the regions and make this market accessible, while also opening up the prairies for settlement. Immigrants would labour in the factories, plough the prairie soil, and buy the products of Canadian industry. Economic interdependence would foster a sense of national identity. Government intervention was intended to be temporary.

By the 1920s the regions were linked by railways, the prairie grasslands were wheatfields and Canadian industries were supplying Canadian customers. Governments, however, did not wither away. The National Policy had fostered a national economy, but it was a vulnerable one. Workers and farmers wanted something free enterprise did not provide: economic security. They looked to governments to provide it.

For the first years of the decade Canada's political system seemed unequal to the task. Third parties and regional protests brought the threat of political deadlock. Prime Minister Mackenzie King's cautious and incremental approach averted major confrontations. It also began the expansion of government activities that would be the central feature of Canadian politics for decades to come.

For those who sought moral reform through government decree, it was a decade of disillusionment. For many Canadians the Great War had been a crusade, an opportunity to accomplish God's work at home as well as abroad. Prohibition and female suffrage were two reforms that held out the promise of a higher level of social morality; in both cases the reformers were betrayed by the political system.

Every province except Quebec had gone "dry" during the war as a gesture of patriotic commitment to the war effort. After the war the "dries" lost ground, and the eventual Canadian compromise was to tax those who drank at home and to segregate other drinkers in austere "licensed premises." Instead of fighting the demon rum, governments turned to selling liquor and pocketing the profits. Female suffrage, too, disappointed its advocates. Nellie McClung had argued that "when the hand that rocks the cradle rules the world it will be a safer cleaner world for the occupants of the cradle." However, women who voted made much the same choices as men, and few women chose to seek election. Agnes Macphail was the only woman elected to the House of Commons during the decade.

A more direct consequence of the war was the thorny question of Canada's status in international affairs. Canadians proudly accepted membership in the League of Nations but few believed that this carried with it any serious international obligations. There was more concern about the nature of Canada's obligations to the British Empire. In the 1920s Canadian leaders played a crucial role in establishing the British Commonwealth of Nations, in which Canada and the other Dominions were "in no way subordinate" to Britain but were expected to work together for the common good.

Another legacy of the war was an embittered French Canada. The promise that there would be no compulsory enlistment had been broken in 1917, when English Canadians formed a Union government to impose conscription. In the 1920s, Mackenzie King tried to restore French Canadian confidence in the federal government by identifying Ernest Lapointe as his preeminent political colleague. In practice this meant that no policies and no appointments of concern to French Canada would be decided without Lapointe's consent. French Canadians saw Lapointe as a co-leader of the Liberal Party and were reassured. There was no formal recognition of French Canadian rights, but it was a pragmatic acknowledgement of Canada's cultural duality.

The Canadian government of the 1920s had to deal with the heritage of the National Policy. The optimism of the Laurier years (1896–1911) had saddled the country with three transcontinental railways, two of them bankrupt, and with more track per capita than any other country in the world. In the 1920s Ottawa began the thankless task of trying to create one efficient railway out of the unprofitable lines it had inherited. The Canadian government was now in the railway business.

The 1920s also saw the integrated national economy of the National Policy threatened by regional economic developments. Economic growth in the decade was associated with pulp and paper and mining, largely financed by American capital to satisfy growing American demand. Because the paper and ore went south, regions of Canada outside Quebec, Ontario and British Columbia, where these industries were concentrated, felt no direct benefits. The other dynamic sector of the economy was automobile manufacturing in tariff-protected branch plants. Here the benefits went to Ontario; people in other regions were painfully aware that they had to pay more for cars than their American neighbours. Closer economic links with the United States and regional rivalries were becoming part of the Canadian pattern.

On top of all this, governments in the 1920s had to grapple with poverty and insecurity. In Canada as elsewhere the "industrial question" seemed to be the crucial social challenge of the postwar era. Workers in the munitions plants had won higher wages but had lost most of the benefits to inflation. Patriotism kept them at work until the war ended, but then came what to many seemed the beginning of a communist revolution with the Winnipeg General Strike of 1919, supported by sympathy strikes across the country. In 1919 more than three million working days were lost to strikes and lockouts and for the next few years industrial strife was the norm.

The federal government did take one small step towards social security with the introduction of old age pensions of $20 a month to needy citizens over the age of seventy. Even this was too generous for the Conservative majority in the Senate, which saw any public assistance as a threat to the moral fibre of the nation; it blocked the bill in 1926 but then allowed it to pass the next year after the Liberal government was reelected. The prosperity of the later years of the decade did more than any government to reduce industrial conflicts, but this proved to be a short-term solution. When the Depression struck, labour still had no right to continued employment, no unemployment insurance and no assurance of welfare payments.

Farmers had their own grievances at the end of the war. Their costs of production had increased with inflation but the prices of their produce had dropped during the postwar depression. They blamed the protective tariffs, which added to their costs without providing them with a protected market. Political action early in the decade produced phenomenal political successes. Less than four years after the war, the United Farmers were in power in Manitoba and Alberta and had formed a government in Ontario with the support of some labour members. In federal politics the Progressives had more seats at Ottawa than the Conservatives.

Political power, unfortunately, did not produce economic remedies.

The prosperity of the last half of the decade passed the farmers by because the recovery in Europe and the protection of European agriculture forced world grain prices even lower. The farmer-labour coalition in Ontario was defeated by the resurgent Conservatives in 1923. The farmer governments in the west survived, but they could not control the price of wheat. In Ottawa, Mackenzie King wooed the Progressives with small reductions in tariffs and freight rates; in 1926 most of the Progressives rejoined the Liberals to keep the high-tariff Conservatives from office.

Mackenzie King

Many prairie farmers, disillusioned with federal politics, turned to self-help. The mid-1920s saw the astonishing growth of the wheat pools with half of the farmers voluntarily pledging to deliver their wheat to a central selling agency. This impressive experiment went sour when a world wheat surplus dragged prices down. In 1928 the agency tried to shore up wheat prices by holding Canada's bumper crop off the world market, but the price continued to drop and the wheat pools averted bankruptcy only by begging Ottawa to bail them out. The lesson of the 1920s was that Ottawa could not avoid being involved in the marketing of Canada's wheat. Economic security for prairie farmers had become a federal responsibility.

The issues discussed at the Dominion-Provincial Conference of 1927 provide a striking illustration of the new era in Canadian politics. The federal government, concerned with Canada's status, proposed to repatriate the British North America Act. This would require a formal procedure for amending the Act in the future and the government accordingly proposed the unanimous consent of the provincial governments in some instances and the consent of two thirds in others. It also suggested Senate reform, including a retirement age for senators and limiting the Senate's power to a suspensive veto. The provincial premiers saw no advantage in changing the constitution and Ottawa did not insist. Repatriation, constitutional amendment and Senate reform were left to future federal-provincial conferences.

The provincial premiers, especially those from the Maritimes and prairies, showed more interest in federal aid for the social programs made necessary by immigration and industrialization. Federal proposals for shared-cost programs were deemed unsatisfactory and the premiers asked instead for exclusive jurisdiction over personal income taxes. King took advantage of special circumstances to offer the Maritime and prairie governments special subsidies, thus recognizing their special need without establishing any binding precedent. The withdrawal of federal claims to water-power developments persuaded Ontario and Quebec to accept this version of equalization grants. Federal-provincial bargaining over programs, subsidies, tax revenues and the constitution was underway.

In retrospect the decade has a surprisingly modern ring. Economic and cultural grievances seemed to call for heroic measures. Mackenzie King's Liberals had nothing heroic to offer. They opted for conciliation and compromise, half-measures and incremental reforms. There was no rolling of the dice as there would be over the Meech Lake Accord in 1990, no talk of a last chance or a new beginning. There were no dramatic victories, but also no drastic defeats or clear losers. There was no confrontation and the country survived. There may be a lesson there.

Historian **H. Blair Neatby** is the author of a biography of Mackenzie King, among other books.

Agnes Macphail in Parliament

by Terry Crowley

Agnes Campbell Macphail emerged onto the national scene in the pivotal federal election of 1921 when she became the first woman elected to the House of Commons. Returned with more than fifty other candidates of the Progressive Party, an alliance of farm and labour interests largely based in western Canada, Macphail was a source of inspiration to those who believed that the end of the First World War would herald a new era in human affairs.

Born in 1890 in Grey County, Ontario, Macphail grew up in a family with a mixed Protestant background. In 1910 she graduated from the Stratford Teachers' College and then taught school for a decade. During her student days she joined the Reorganized Church of Jesus Christ of the Latter Day Saints, which she found more socially conscious than other denominations. Her religious affiliation became a source of controversy during her first election campaign in Grey County, when it was falsely equated with Mormonism and polygamy. Macphail managed to calm that tempest, as well as the one stemming from the notion that there was no place for a woman, especially a single woman, in public life.

While her sex and political affiliation alone made Macphail a threat to the dominant values of her day, she went further and actively attacked those norms. The new MP campaigned for women's right to absolute equality with men, drawing on two great classics: Mary Wollstonecraft's Enlightenment tract, *The Vindication of the Rights of Woman,* and John Stuart Mill's *On the Subjection of Women*. She prophesied a womanhood untrammelled by prevailing stereotypes and unshackled from legal subordination. In 1922 Macphail opposed changes to citizenship laws because they treated women differently from men. In Parliament three years later, she helped make the grounds for divorce more equitable in the western provinces.

As the first woman admitted to debate at the University of Toronto's Hart House, Agnes Macphail roundly denounced marriage ceremonies for forcing women to swear obedience to men. While such views were all essentially liberal, the conservatism of the Liberal Party and of much mainstream religion made her positions seem radical, if not downright incendiary. "When I hear men talking about women being the angel of the home," she noted in the House of Commons, "I always, mentally at least, shrug my shoulders in doubt. I do not want to be the angel of any home. I want for myself what I want for other women, absolute equality. After that is secured, then men and women can take turns being angels."

As the 1920s went on, the country's turbulent politics slowly converted Macphail from radicalism to social democracy. Her experiences in Parliament, particularly with Winnipeg labour MP J.S. Woodsworth (whom she idolized but was not above castigating), led her to abandon the Progressive caucus in 1924 to help create the Ginger Group, a forerunner to the Cooperative Commonwealth Federation (CCF). A 1925 visit to Cape Breton, embittered by pervasive wage slavery and torn by industrial conflict, contributed to this transition in her thought.

While a believer, Macphail did not wear her religious convictions on her sleeve. When she defended temperance in 1926, for instance, she spoke of the dangers of drinking and driving in the automobile age but did not invoke religion or morality. It might be tempting to portray her as a social gospeller who contributed to the disenthronement of Christianity as the moral arbiter of Canadian society early in the century, but this view does not bear close scrutiny. Agnes Macphail never put forward the social mission of the Christian churches as more important than their purely religious function.

Macphail was more concerned with setting a standard for the women who would follow her into public office. While she acknowledged that many women would not adopt the career path she chose for herself, she believed that women's province was as large as men's and that motherhood was only one stage in the life cycle of most women. Macphail advocated meaningful work for women outside the home—if only before and after childrearing—because she felt that women needed to influence society outside their immediate familial surroundings, in the same way men did.

As she believed that the traditions of men should not constrain women, Macphail threw herself into a visible campaign for peace during the 1920s. Her involvement with the Women's International League for Peace and Freedom took her to Washington and Prague where she met American reformer Jane Addams. In Ottawa, Macphail carried on campaigns to have the federal government reduce annual expenses on cadet training to one dollar, create a peace ministry to offset the defence portfolio, and spend as much annually on university chairs and scholarships in international relations as on the military. In 1929 Macphail became the first

Agnes Macphail

Canadian woman to represent the country abroad when she was appointed as a delegate to the League of Nations.

As the new woman for a new age, Agnes Macphail was remarkable not only for her feminist challenge to paternalistic values but also for the tenacity with which she sought to alter outmoded ideas and practices. While her rural background created a certain coarseness of character that was converted into public toughness in the face of massive prejudice against her sex, Agnes Macphail remained wonderfully warm-hearted and generous throughout her career. Her compassion for women and children rendered destitute when men were imprisoned led to her long battle to reform the country's prisons. This struggle also reflected the anti-authoritarianism and distaste for absolute power seen in her peace activities.

Aligning herself with the CCF in the 1930s, she remained in the House of Commons until her defeat in 1940 and later served two terms in the Ontario legislature. By the time Macphail died in 1954, she had become the most important woman in public life that Canada has produced in the twentieth century.

Terry Crowley is the author of *Agnes Macphail and the Politics of Equality* (1990).

Fascism's Mystique of Power

by Alkis Kontos

Fascism's Italian origin is evident in the term itself; it comes from *fasciare,* which means to bind. Its founder, Benito Mussolini, envisioned Fascism as capable of binding the Italian nation into an organic, unified entity that would recapture the glory of the Roman Empire. The Fascist rise to power was a result of a complex web of interacting forces and circumstances. In the epoch of great expectations and unbearable frustrations that followed the Great War, the European context in general, and the Italian in particular, provided fertile soil for Fascism's growth.

Chronic political, social and economic problems had plagued Italy since the time of the *Risorgimento,* the nineteenth-century unification of the country. Political corruption, sociopolitical fragmentation, social unrest, disorder and violence, the absence of a strong parliamentary tradition, the rise of nationalism, and a sense of betrayal of Italy by its allies after the war accentuated existing tensions; the experience and aftermath of the war rendered governmental impotence visible and the collapse of the liberal order inevitable.

With his tactical skill, energy and ruthless ambition, Mussolini masterfully exploited the prevailing mood and conditions. He founded the Italian Fascist Party in 1919, and came to power in 1922 after his famous march on Rome. Fascism had many variants, but the order Mussolini imposed to replace the discredited liberal order stands as a kind of archetype of the phenomenon.

Fascist ideology is neither terribly coherent nor free from contradiction and confusion. It is primarily negative in character: it is hostile to liberalism, democracy and individualism. For the Fascist Mussolini, the prevailing social and cultural decadence, demoralization, disorder and confusion clearly called for renewal and revitalization. But Mussolini was not a philosopher or a systematic, trained thinker; rather, he was a self-taught man of action. Though he was a voracious reader, his reading was neither comprehensive nor meticulous. He took ideas out of context and amalgamated diverse strands of thought, irrespective of accuracy or coherence.

By his own account and that of his friends, Mussolini was influenced primarily by the German philosophers Arthur Schopenhauer and Friedrich Nietzsche, who stressed the idea of the will to power; the French philosopher Henri Bergson, who stressed intuition; Gaetano Mosca and Vilfredo Pareto, two Italian social theorists who articulated an antiparliamentary elitism; Georges Sorel, a French radical syndicalist theorist who advocated the cult of violence and the use of social myth as means of social mobilization; and Niccolò Machiavelli, the famous sixteenth-century Italian political thinker who spoke of the glory of the Roman Empire, the necessity of political violence and the indispensability of the figure of the Prince. From this mixture of past and contemporary thought Mussolini fashioned a doctrinal perspective that provided the fundamentals of Fascist ideology.

Interestingly enough, Karl Marx is not on the list of his intellectual influences even though the young Mussolini was a radical socialist quite well versed in Marxist thought. This is because Fascist ideology stresses the will and asserts voluntarism as against the determinism Marx propounded. The emphasis on the will brings with it a celebration of spontaneity, virility and vitality. Fascists deeply admired and exalted the hero and the warrior and praised action, war, energy and dynamism. In their view, reason is mundane and mediocre, akin to caution and calculation. Weakness is despised; force, strength and power are valued; and violence, veiled in a mystical aura, is creative.

Blending themes from Nietzsche and Sorel with Bergson's intuitionist thinking, Fascism gave prominence to the creative role of irrationalism and dynamism. Yet the goal of energetic action remains unspecified. To navigate the seas of dangerous action is exciting in itself. It is an emotional high. Rational evaluation and intellectual judgement are inadmissible. As it affirmed will and active strength, the fundamental tenets of Fascist doctrine also drew in and significantly transformed the elitism of Mosca and Pareto. The two Italian thinkers argued that societies are ruled by oligarchies, whatever their formal structure. In Pareto's view societies are divided between the ruled class and the more gifted and talented ruling elite. Robert Michels named this the Iron Law of Oligarchy, and Mussolini too saw oligarchy as inflexible and permanent, making Machiavelli's Prince-ruler indispensable. Leadership, discipline and obedience are crucial.

Fascism cast this blend of theories in an organic image of society: the

Benito Mussolini

nation-state is a living organism within which the individual functions as a cell. Without the nation-state the individual is nothing. Rejecting the Marxist notion of class struggle, Fascism sought to remove conflict from the economic sphere through the creation of a corporatist state. In theory, management and labour were to seek unity of purpose in pursuit of greater productivity. In practice the labour unions and associations were stripped of their normal powers, and strikes were outlawed.

Though Fascism claimed that society could and should exist without conflict under its rule by party, state and leader, it insisted on the inevitability and ineradicability of conflict and violence among nation-states. The world is a battlefield and only the nation-state secures, promotes and renders possible a meaningful life for the individual. Thus Mussolini's Fascist regime was expansionist and adopted an imperial policy.

From the ideas of will, power, dynamism and organic unity, Mussolini developed an antimaterialist attitude and embraced a rather mystical spirituality that was severely critical of liberalism and bourgeois life. And beyond the substantive doctrine of Fascism, its ritualized mystique of power —symbols, spectacles, uniforms and parades—was crucial in mobilizing emotions. Mussolini's Fascism was definitely not an intellectual enterprise, yet it drew to its ranks a variety of intellectuals. Individualism and independent thinking are anathema to Fascist doctrine. Intellectuals do not find Fascism appealing on intellectual grounds, but they are attracted to it for other reasons.

Giovanni Gentile, the neo-Hegelian philosopher, served as Mussolini's minister of education and helped articulate the Fascist doctrine of the state. Benedetto Croce, Italy's most illustrious thinker, was favourably disposed towards the movement in its early stages. Luigi Pirandello, the world-renowned writer, enthusiastically supported the Fascists. The poet Filippo Tommaso Marinetti and his group of Futurists, who exalted war, joined the ranks. Arturo Toscanini was with the Fascists in the very early stages of the movement.

Many Italian intellectuals were anticommunists and saw Fascism as the only force capable of stopping the so-called Bolshevik menace. Others were antiliberal and antidemocratic; they found in Fascism the brand of authoritarian conservatism they longed for. Still others did not recognize the true nature of Fascism in its early stages; when they did they turned against it or simply dropped their support.

Fascism also appealed to intellectuals because of its mystique of creativity and its pseudoestheticism. José Antonio Primo de Rivera, the founder of the fascist Falange in Spain, referred to the Falange as a poetic movement, and the Belgian fascist leader, Léon Degrelle, called Mussolini a poet of revolution. Poetry, art and music express the nonrational that the Fascists celebrate so much. Creative intellectuals could be fascinated by Fascism because of its attack on liberal and bourgeois values, believing that the destruction of these values would open the gates of a new creativity. The movement's elitism was also attractive to intellectuals, who saw themselves as special, talented, superior individuals. Their vanity was stroked by their status in Fascism's hierarchical society. Others were mere opportunists, seeking nothing but personal advancement.

But the many and varied reasons for which intellectuals could be attracted to Fascism do not tell the full story. For Fascism has also an inherent appeal in its mystical celebration of the will and power. Power fascinates and intellectuals could easily revel in images of philosopher-kings. More than simply power, Fascism is *unrestrained* power, free of responsibility and accountability. Unlike other ideologies or regimes, Fascism holds the promise of a power orgy: mystical, barbaric and full of vengeance, utterly intolerant and incapable of dialogue. Its vapid moralism is its self-delusion and the opium of the intellectuals.

In their encounters with Fascism, the attraction of which has not yet been extinguished in our tragic epoch, intellectuals need more than ideas: they need character and integrity.

At the time of writing, **Alkis Kontos** taught political science at the University of Toronto.

Marcus Garvey: Black Moses

by Robert Hill

Marcus Garvey, the leader of the largest organized mass movement in black history and progenitor of the modern "black is beautiful" revival, was hailed in the 1920s as a redeemer—"Black Moses." If he failed to realize many of his specific objectives, such as an African return or creation of an African empire, his movement was responsible for an important liberation from the psychological bondage of racial inferiority.

Garvey was born on August 17, 1887, in St. Ann's Bay, Jamaica. He left school at fourteen and spent time in London, England, where he worked with the enigmatic Sudanese-Egyptian nationalist, Dusé Mohamed Ali. Content at first to preach accommodation on his return to Jamaica, Garvey aspired to open an industrial training school modelled on Booker T. Washington's Tuskegee Institute. He came to the United States on Washington's invitation in 1916, but he arrived just after Washington died. His views were soon radically transformed by what he encountered and learned.

Garvey came to the United States at the dawn of the militant "New Negro" era. Black discontent, punctuated by East St. Louis's bloody race riots in 1917 and intensified by postwar disillusionment, reached record heights by the Red Summer of nationwide racial disturbances in 1919. Not long after his arrival, Garvey quietly organized a chapter of the Universal Negro Improvement Association (UNIA), which functioned as a benevolent fraternal organization. Within a few years of this humble beginning, Garvey rose rapidly to become the best-known, most controversial and, for many, most attractive of a new generation of black leaders.

Drawing on a gift for electrifying oratory, Garvey melded Jamaican peasant aspirations for economic and cultural independence with the American gospel of success to create a new gospel of racial pride. "Garveyism" evolved into a religion of success, inspiring millions of blacks worldwide who sought relief from racial dispossession and colonial domination. The UNIA gave this doctrine of racial enterprise a tangible symbol that captured black imaginations when it launched the Black Star shipping line.

By 1920 the UNIA had hundreds of divisions worldwide. It hosted elaborate international conventions and published the *Negro World*, a widely disseminated weekly that was soon banned in many parts of Africa and the Caribbean. The movement's dynamic core was Harlem, which Garvey and the UNIA helped make the cultural capital of the black world. During the 1920s the six-block radius surrounding 135th Street and Lenox Avenue contained the UNIA's international headquarters as well as the cradle of the movement, Liberty Hall, and the offices of all major UNIA-affiliated enterprises. UNIA restaurants, shops and storefront factories spread throughout Harlem, and Garvey and many UNIA officers lived there. During the annual UNIA international conventions, the streets boasted colourful parades led by a regal Garvey, poised in an open car and wearing the plumed hat that became his indelible trademark.

Nearly 1,000 UNIA divisions formed throughout North and Central America, the Caribbean, Africa and Britain, with a lone division in Australia. Many divisions still met as late as the 1950s; a few remain active even today. By the late 1920s, however, the movement had begun to unravel under the strains of internal dissension, opposition from black critics and government harassment. Fiscal irregularities in the shipping line gave the U.S. government—spurred on by a young J. Edgar Hoover—the basis for an indictment that sent Garvey to prison. The government later commuted Garvey's sentence, but only to deport him to Jamaica in November 1927.

Back in Jamaica, Garvey reconstituted the UNIA and held conventions there and in Canada, but the heart of his movement stumbled on in the U.S. without him. While dabbling in Jamaican politics, he remained a keen observer of world events, writing voluminously in a series of his own periodicals. His final move was to London, where he settled in 1935. In his last years he slid into isolation, suffering the final indignity of reading his own obituaries a month before his death on June 10, 1940.

African Redemption, the political program of the UNIA, encompassed the territorial redemption of Africa from colonial rule and the spiritual redemption of the black race. Garvey saw Africa as having fallen from a past greatness that had to be restored for peoples of African descent to resume their rightful place in the world. Such redemption could only be achieved by black peoples themselves.

The impact of Garveyism in Africa was considerable. Garvey himself never set foot in Africa, but for many budding nationalist leaders, it was Garvey who first implanted notions of black self-sufficiency and independence. Garveyism had a special tie with Liberia, the black-ruled country created by freed American slaves in the early nineteenth century and the pri-

Marcus Garvey

Historian **Robert Hill** edited
*The Marcus Garvey and UNIA
Papers* and was guest curator
of the Marcus Garvey centennial
exhibition sponsored by the
Schomburg Center for Research
in Black Culture of the New
York Public Library.

mary objective of Garvey's "back to Africa" campaign. A few Garveyites independently emigrated to Liberia, but the grand UNIA emigration schemes all aborted in the end. Garveyism also flourished in the Caribbean. More than any other early-twentieth-century political phenomenon, it gave expression to a pan-Caribbean consciousness that crossed insular and political boundaries.

Garvey's teachings functioned as a powerful catalyst for diverse religious interpretations deriving from the notion of black divinity as the spiritual mirror of racial sovereignty. The UNIA program of African Redemption was popularly communicated through the oft-repeated prophecy: "Princes shall come out of Egypt; Ethiopia shall soon stretch out her hands unto God" (Ps 68:31). At the August 1924 UNIA convention, Bishop George Alexander McGuire, founder of the African Orthodox Church, enunciated the doctrine of a Black God and unveiled the Black Madonna in Liberty Hall. Various sects proliferated and expanded on the fringes of the Garvey movement or arose from within its fold, such as Black Islam and Rastafarianism, and a major part of Garvey's legacy was transplanted to the religious sphere.

His legacy has also been manifest in the careers of leaders ranging from Kwame Nkrumah of Ghana to Malcolm X in the United States. Borne along on the tide of black popular culture, Garvey's memory has attained the status of a folk myth. He is daily celebrated and recreated as a hero through the storytelling faculty of the black oral tradition. As the embodiment of that oral tradition transmuted into musical performance, Jamaica's reggae music exhibits an amazing fixation with the memory of Garvey. Re-evoking spiritual exile and the historic experience of black dispossession, the music of such performers as Bob Marley and Burning Spear presents a Garvey who speaks from the past directly to the present. The Garvey legend today functions as an icon of universal black pride.

Ascendancy of the Chiangs

by Mary Rose Donnelly

The announcement in late 1991 that Soong Mei-ling was moving to New York from Taiwan, frail and ninety-four years old, was too inconsequential for most news gatherers to report. Sixty-four years earlier, though, when she married Chiang Kai-shek, Soong Mei-ling became the most influential woman in China.

For two decades the Chiangs would dominate China's political life. Madame Chiang was interpreter and adviser to her husband the Generalissimo; as a U.S.-educated woman she swept American public opinion with her charm and poise. She was the first Chinese person and the second woman to address a joint session of the U.S. Congress, and for nearly twenty-five years the beautiful Madame Chiang was on American lists of the ten most admired women in the world.

Madame Chiang was the youngest daughter among six children born to Charlie Jones Soong, who was taken to the United States at the age of twelve and later returned to China as a Methodist missionary. Of Rev. Soong's three daughters, it was said that one loved wealth, another loved China and the third loved power. The first married H.H. Kung, the country's finance minister and a prominent banker; the second eloped with Dr. Sun Yat-sen, the republic's first legitimate president; and the last married Chiang Kai-shek after he first promised to convert to Christianity.

The Chiangs' Christianity played no small part in the U.S.'s continued support of the Generalissimo's Nationalist dictatorship long after it proved indifferent to or incapable of bringing peace to China. The couple cultivated the missionary community in China, taking the more flamboyant and influential missionaries into the inner sanctum of their family. Long abused or ignored by Chinese society, the missionaries were flattered by this attention. Fired by their optimism at seeing Christians in power in China, they or their children, like Time-Life Inc. publisher Henry Luce, sculpted American public opinion. The Chiangs were undoubtedly astute enough to recognize that in the 1920s missionaries were the first and most effective interpreters of other cultures back home in North America.

China had emerged from the First World War disillusioned with the West's claim to moral ascendancy. For a brief time Christianity had been equated with modernity and progress, yet the war had been fought among Christian European peoples. Furthermore, having badgered China into declaring war on Germany, the Allied nations had then turned around and granted Japan full control over the land and industry formerly owned by Germany in China's Shantung province. It was a slap in the face to Chinese nationalism and prompted China's delegation at the Versailles Conference to refuse to sign the treaty.

Into this wave of nationalism and disillusionment with the West's democratic doubletalk came an offer from the newly consolidated government of the Soviet Union in 1920. The Soviets offered to relinquish all rights that they, along with most European countries, had exacted from China over fifty years of military superiority. In the coastal cities, the French, British, Germans and Japanese had wrested "concessions" from China—regions that were protected by their own police and from which they conducted their commerce and affairs with immunity from Chinese law. The Soviet overture to relinquish foreign privilege, calculating in its symbolic value, could not have been more effective in gaining praise from China's political and intellectual circles. For half a century the western powers had been carving up the Chinese watermelon, and the last thing they wanted was a unified China that would reassert its right to dignity and sovereignty.

Sun Yat-sen's appeals to the United States and Britain for recognition of his democratic government were flatly rejected or ignored. China seemed a troublesome backwater of no political consequence; it was valuable for exploitation, not investment. Into that vacuum, the Soviets stepped with friendship, money and arms. In 1921, Sun met with the first of many Soviet advisers, Adolph Joffe. Joffe offered him aid and the support of the fledgling Chinese Communist Party, which had just been founded under its first leader Ch'en Tu-hsiu, a professor at the Peking National University, where Mao Zedong (Mao Tse-tung) was then a library assistant.

Following Sun's death in 1925, his Kuomintang party, with both left and right wings, prepared an assault on the warlords in the north. The northern expedition began in 1926 under the leadership of General Chiang Kai-shek, who had been close to Sun and emerged as his heir apparent. Its intent was to unify China by ferreting out the ragtag armies of the powerful regional warlords and establishing one power centre. Trained in Japan and Moscow, Chiang seemed sympathetic to communism for a time, but began to lean towards the right wing of the Kuomintang.

Chiang Kai-shek and Soong Mei-ling

As his armies swept towards Shanghai, Chiang made a treacherous pact with the business elite and underground gangs and turned on the communists, destroying nearly their entire force. The massacre pushed the remaining Chinese communists underground. There they began a twenty-year struggle in the countryside to build a base of support among China's peasantry, an activity that would lead to their eventual success and relegate the Chiangs, and old China, to the pages of history.

Mary Rose Donnelly, an associate editor of *Compass* from 1991 to 1997 and subsequently a director of the Compass Foundation, is coauthor with Heather Dau of *Katharine: A Biography of Dr. Katharine Boehner Hockin* (1992).

Breath Came and They Lived: The Discovery of Insulin

by Michael Bliss

A few points of light sparkled in the darkness of the early postwar world. The scientists at the University of Toronto who sacrificed dog after dog in arcane experiments through the summer and autumn of 1921 paid no attention to the broad social and political forces reshaping their country and the globe. The only questions on their minds were: Where will we get more dogs? What should we try next? When can we have a clinical trial? Will it work?

The answer they gave the world in 1922 amounted to one of history's most spectacular demonstrations of the power of research to work miracles. The discovery of insulin at Toronto meant salvation for hundreds, thousands, eventually millions of dying diabetics. Virtually overnight, the question of their disease was no longer the speed of death but the quality of life.

This adventure began when Frederick Grant Banting, a young physician in London, Ontario, who enjoyed dabbling in research, approached J.J.R. Macleod, the professor of physiology at the University of Toronto, with a proposal to spend a summer trying to isolate the internal secretion of the pancreas. For many years scientists had hypothesized that some such secretion must control the body's ability to metabolize its food and thus prevent the development of diabetes mellitus. But no one had been able to find the substance, and the ghastly prognosis for people suffering from type I or juvenile diabetes was rapid decline and death within months of onset. The misery could perhaps be prolonged a year or two by reducing food intake and slowly starving to death.

Macleod did not believe Banting's idea would amount to much, but had unused facilities and willing students to lend to the enthusiastic doctor. One of the students, Charles Best, won a coin toss to be Banting's first helper. On May 17, 1921, Banting and Best began experimenting on dogs —producing diabetes by removing the pancreas, and trying to treat it by administering pancreas extracts.

Macleod gave Banting and Best the benefit of his expertise ("We followed your directions in preparing the extract," Best wrote him after the first successful experiment) and when they reported promising results at the end of the summer he insisted that they refine what had been fairly crude procedures. In December Banting and Macleod agreed to add a fourth member to the team, a visiting biochemist from the University of Alberta named J.B. Collip.

In January 1922, the Toronto researchers administered their extract of animal pancreas to a dying diabetic fourteen-year-old boy, Leonard Thompson, in Toronto General Hospital. On the second attempt, a preparation of the extract developed by Collip proved effective in eliminating Thompson's symptoms. For the first time in the history of the world doctors were able to treat severe diabetes. They named their extract "insulin" because it is produced in the "islet" cells of the pancreas.

We now understand that the Toronto group's success depended on their pooling of expertise, the nearly unlimited resources that a world-class university was able to provide, and recent advances others had made in measuring the physiological effects of administration of extract. At the time there was considerable controversy over credit, leading to intense bitterness between Banting and Best on the one hand and Macleod and Collip on the other. In 1923 the Nobel Prize for physiology and medicine was awarded to Banting and Macleod. Banting split his prize money with Best; Macleod split his with Collip.

A wise physician at the university's dinner to honour its Nobel laureates commented that "in insulin there is glory enough for all." The essence of the insulin story was not feuding researchers but the amazing recoveries insulin wrought in dying children. Starved and sometimes comatose sufferers came back to health and nearly normal lives. Two of the first group of emaciated children who were given insulin in Toronto in the summer of 1922 outlived all of its discoverers. One of those patients, Ted Ryder, is alive and flourishing as this is written in 1991, nearly seventy years later. The lives of some ten million diabetics around the world depend on insulin injections.

Even case-hardened physicians were awestruck by the power of insulin to conquer disease and death. Many of them drew on their spiritual heritage for imagery to describe the event. The great American diabetes doctor, Elliott Joslin, said that by Christmas of 1922 he "had witnessed so many near resurrections" as a result of insulin that he realized he was seeing Ezekiel's vision of the valley of dry bones enacted before his eyes:

And behold, there were very many in the open valley; and, lo,

Historian **Michael Bliss**'s books include *The Discovery of Insulin* (1982) and *William Osler: A Life in Medicine* (1999).

they were very dry....Then said he unto me, "Prophesy unto the wind, prophesy, Son of Man, and say to the wind, 'Thus saith the Lord God: Come from the four winds, O breath, and breathe upon these slain, that they may live.'" So I prophesied as he commanded me, and the breath came into them, and they lived, and stood up upon their feet, an exceeding great army.

The Public Health Offensive

by Jutta Mason

In nineteenth-century rural Canada, childbirth, illness and death were events that generally occurred within a person's own house, but quite a few people outside the family were drawn in. Women helped one another in childbirth, and often would sit with a labouring woman until the baby was born, talking and eating together and perhaps working on some "knitties" for the family. Afterwards, some neighbours would help in the house and the barn while others brought the meals. When someone was dying or a child was sick, it was often the same. The activities of looking after the young or the sick or women giving birth linked people.

After the First World War these diverse customs, which varied from place to place and expressed local history, came under attack. In the farm journals and the women's magazines, at the Women's Institute meetings and the missionary societies, the same thing was being said: the war had killed so many; now it was time to take some positive new actions to preserve life. This impulse, combined with expanding unemployment among nurses because of hospital hiring policies, resulted in strong pressure on governments to start up public health departments across the country. In the twenties, large numbers of public health nurses went out into the communities with the mission of saving lives that might otherwise be lost through "ignorance." Paradoxically, their activities drove a wedge between neighbours and between mothers and their children by constantly encouraging people to look to outside authority rather than to one another.

Early on, the nurses often described what they were doing in military terms. In 1920 the Red Cross in Nova Scotia "covered the province with a flank attack," moving public health caravans from village to village. The doctors took out all the children's tonsils and the nurses introduced the people to modern ideas of child welfare and preventive medicine, using the novelty of moving picture shows to illustrate their points. They sought to contrast local customs with the "right" ways of looking after young children or sick people or pregnant women, ways meant to be universal in their application.

The nurse who took on the work of teaching these new ideas was not a neighbour. Her house and her people were often far away from where she worked, and besides, they didn't really matter. She was not tied to any particular place. She had been trained to be interchangeable with all other nurses, and she was said to be able to prevent illness in a whole region, not just to look after one person. She went to church halls and schools and right into people's houses, examining everything, and she told people that their houses were rather dangerous and that their old-fashioned practices were liable to make them sick, or worse.

Red Cross volunteers handed copies of the federal government's advice booklet *The Canadian Mother and Child* (more than a million copies were printed of the 1927 edition, before it was revised in 1940) to all immigrants as they came off the ships in Halifax. The public health nurses distributed such books from house to house or passed them out at the clinics they set up. People were urged to stop feeding their babies at irregular intervals or at night, to stop singing lullabies to them or rocking them in rocking chairs, to stop sleeping in the same bed with them, to stop using their traditional remedies, to stop going to their neighbours' births.

The nurses' counsels were supported by articles in magazines (in 1928 *Chatelaine* advised no more than fifteen minutes of "cuddling" a day), by the missionaries who preached the same things to the Native people on the reserves, by the teachers who held "health drills" in their classrooms, by public health doctors, and by the foundations, newly and richly endowed after major changes in the American income tax laws.

In the past two decades, feminist reworkings of medical history have tended to discover men, or women under the orders of men, as the originators of every instance of violence done in the name of medicine. But in the twenties, the denigration of ordinary women for their customs of child-rearing and neighbourly counsel was a collaborative effort of the public health workers—mainly women—and the organized women's movement. Women's organizations flowered in the twenties, and many of them made the support and promotion of public health nurses a central part of their activity. Through these groups the universal ideas of the right way to do things were taken into the farmhouse parlours where the meetings were held, and in this way local customs were gradually broken.

Mortality statistics were used to justify this work of discrediting local customs. By the time governments began keeping systematic records of births and deaths of their whole populations after the First World War, mortality rates in the West were dropping steadily. These numbers seemed to provide glowing proof of the rightness of public health teachings.

But there were odd details that didn't fit. Several small studies that took a closer look in Saskatchewan and Manitoba showed that many more mothers died in childbirth in the "medically best served districts" than in areas where there were no doctors and nurses at all. And women who went to prenatal care clinics turned out to have more trouble than those who stayed with the old ways. Nor could public health teaching be causally linked to better survival of small children. In a very large study in Chicago in 1924–25, there was less than a quarter the mortality in an immigrant area where the old customs persisted than in the rest of Chicago, where mothers were better off and more compliant with public health instructions.

Such studies were more than disturbing to public health workers: they made no sense at all. And so they were ignored. The pressure to replace neighbourly counsels and practices with medical rules that could be neatly applied everywhere—giving so much work to so many new people, most of them women—was too strong. In the decades that followed, good counsel and mutual help among neighbours moved towards the edge of extinction.

Now that the achievements of science, including medicine, no longer seem so unequivocally glorious, it is a good time to summon up what is left of the stories of ordinary women and see what they did for their children and one another at times of birth and sickness. Condemned for their backwardness, they may have known and done things that are puzzling, mysterious and important to us now.

At the time of writing, Toronto writer **Jutta Mason** had been collecting women's stories from her neighbours and from archival sources for fifteen years.

St. Miguel Pro and the Secret Kingdom

by John Matheson

Among my memories of childhood in the 1930s are some extremely dramatic radio reenactments of the "lives of the saints" and Catholic heroes. Martyrs' lives, of course, were especially favoured. Among the most dramatic moments was the death by firing squad of Miguel Agustín Pro Juárez, the thirty-seven-year-old Jesuit priest accused of banditry and executed in Mexico City on November 23, 1927. Padre Pro's mighty shout of "Long Live Christ the King!" was followed by a volley of rifle shots, and then triumphant music ended the program.

In reality, it seems, there was no triumphant shout. Miguel Pro simply made a quiet statement that affirmed the popular slogan "Viva Cristo Rey!" To Miguel Pro, such greetings (or farewells, if you will) seemed to be road signs pointing to what he once termed "the Secret Kingdom," the "pearl of great price" for which everything of lesser worth must be bartered.

It was not only Miguel's final hour that the radio programmers found so dramatically appealing. The segment quite accurately presented the life of a young Jesuit who was appreciated by fellow Christians for his spontaneity, sense of humour and surprising ability to don a hundred disguises as he bicycled about Mexico City on his priestly ministry. Miguel found the more pious types of parishioners especially mirth-provoking. After receiving his superior's permission to come out of temporary hiding, Miguel noted:

> I quit this isolation and began giving retreats right and left, a heroic ministry which somewhat frightened me as I had no practice in it. By way of rehearsal, I commenced with six-and-a-half dozen old *beatas* [pious ladies] whose moans and groans, sighs and sobs showed me that if I had managed to strike the key to their sentiments, I had also touched that of my own mirth; for such was the laughter that bubbled in my body at the sight of all this bawling and these compunctious faces, that I cut [the retreat] short.

Like earlier Jesuit recusants, such as Edmund Campion, the Mexican

Jesuits began their clandestine apostolate in a time of persecution: the Catholic Church was attacked by one General Carranza and the famous bandit Pancho Villa. By the time Miguel was ordained, in 1925, the president of Mexico was the violently anti-Catholic Plutarco Elías Calles. In July 1926, the government suppressed all public worship. Padre Pro established clandestine communion stations throughout Mexico City and hid out in various residences, including his own family's. He was assisted by two of his brothers, Humberto and Roberto. The three also distributed propaganda for the Religious Defence League. Friends of the league released six hundred balloons over the city, which let loose a brightly coloured shower of leaflets and so caught the attention of the public, the media and the furious President Calles, who ordered the police to track down the instigators of the "balloon affair." In his correspondence, Miguel Pro delights in the Keystone Cops aspect of the police chase.

St. Miguel Pro

A more serious incident, an assassination attempt on the life of General Obregon, led to the arrest of the Pro brothers. The small Essex car used in the attempt had been owned only the week before by one of the Pros. A police search led to the discovery of Religious Defence League materials and, eventually, to the hiding place of the Pro family. Although the mastermind behind the assassination attempt, Luís Segura, confessed his involvement, Calles chose to make an example of Padre Pro.

Needless to say, it is not impossible to discover ambiguities in such movements as the Religious Defence League. The media accused the league of both "anarchy" and "fascism." I leave it to reputable historians to explore in depth the political nuances of Mexican church history of the late twenties.

Several days before his execution, Miguel Pro was joined in his prison cell by another victim of Calles's hunt. The new prisoner's report shows both the confidence and simplicity of Padre Pro's spirit: "The dungeon was narrow, dark and unventilated. In spite of all this, Padre Pro demonstrated patience, resignation, contentment, and even joy. He told us that we should be happy to suffer something for Jesus Christ, and that if worse evils, or even the firing squad, lay ahead for us, we ought to be proud to suffer and die for Christ."

After the execution of Miguel and Humberto Pro, their aged father claimed their bodies and held a wake in his house. Thousands upon thousands of all social classes, including soldiers, filed past to pay their respects. This time, we are told, the cry "Viva Cristo Rey!" echoed throughout the square.

At the time of writing, **John Matheson SJ** taught film studies at Campion College at the University of Regina.

Glenbow Archives, Calgary, Canada. NC-6-12955 (b)

The Thirties

131 Why Do the 1930s Seem So Familiar?   by Martin Royackers
133 From Stock Market Crash to Phony War   by Lukin Robinson
141 Desperate Canadians Turned to Political Messiahs   by Allan Levine
146 On the Prairies, You Had to Learn to Peel a Nickel   by Gail Burns
150 Latin America's Response to the Depression   by Liisa North
153 Education and Economic Democracy:
       The Antigonish Movement   by Greg MacLeod
158 Emmanuel Mounier: Catalyst for a Generation   by John Hellman
160 Norman Bethune: Driven to Be
       an Actor on the World Stage   by Andrée Lévesque
163 Grey Owl's Masquerade for Conservation   by Donald B. Smith
165 The Soviet Union's Literary Underground   by Ioan Davies
168 Guernica: Icon of the Century   by Peter Larisey

Why Do the 1930s Seem So Familiar?

by Martin Royackers

We know the pictures, and some of us still have the memories. The dilapidated wooden house and barn on the prairie, a family standing in front in workworn clothes and careworn faces, watching the soil blow away. Welcome to the 1930s.

There is much about the 1930s that does not seem unfamiliar to us in the 1990s. The dustbowl was a massive ecological and human disaster. Human beings simply did not know, and maybe did not care about, how to accomplish human purposes within the constraints and demands of the natural world. The Great Depression revealed that we really did not know how the economy worked either—or if any did know, they did not succeed in getting it to do what it should. Around the world millions on millions of unemployed, working poor, hoboes and homeless were victims of an economic system whose taste for human sacrifice seemed insatiable.

There were wars, revolutions, massacres and the like going on all over the world, but they did not really lie heavy on Canadian minds. The only exception, perhaps, was Spain, where young idealists (including Dr. Norman Bethune with his mobile blood transfusion unit) challenged the American and Canadian governments' tacit support of a right-wing regime.

This was the decade of Hitler and Mussolini, who gained immense popularity in their countries and beyond with the conviction that their states and their peoples had a manifest destiny, which justified militarism, expansionism and a rather distasteful self-righteousness in their quest to impose their version of a "New World Order."

The familiarity of all these aspects of the thirties is a bit discouraging. And even facing the stark lack of real change and progress in our world over the past sixty years, our society's structures and rhetoric seem to presume that our living standards are going to get better and better, that our economy can continue to expand, that we have within our reach a new world order of peace and harmony, and that our relentless pursuit of technology, control and power will allow us to solve our problems. Perhaps as we look at a rather unhappy decade in our past, we might recognize these illusions that we still carry for what they are.

Moments of progress in the 1930s were not writ as large as the decade's catastrophes, but they were genuine nonetheles: possible sources of hope and guidance for the pursuit of real progress today. Moses Coady and Jimmy Tompkins proposed to the fishers and farmers of eastern Nova Scotia a program of education, self-help and cooperation. The Antigonish Movement allowed hundreds of impoverished communities to take "mastery of their own destiny." Dorothy Day and Peter Maurin opened houses of hospitality for the homeless and started a radical Catholic paper in New York. Emmanuel Mounier assembled a movement that developed a progressive Catholic alternative to both capitalism and communism.

Many of the problems faced in the 1930s were solved, or at least shelved for a while, by the outbreak of the Second World War. In our decade, facing similarly intractable difficulties in creating a just, peaceful and sustainable human world, we might hope for a less drastic resolution. Moses Coady, Dorothy Day and other figures of commitment, faith and integrity may yet prove the more enduring legacy of the dirty thirties.

Martin Royackers SJ was an associate editor of *Compass* and *Compass*'s managing editor until 1994, and continued to write a column for *Compass* from his new posting in Jamaica until the magazine's suspension in 1997.

From Stock Market Crash to Phony War

by Lukin Robinson

For millions of people, the 1930s were mainly years of pain, suffering and turmoil. They were bitter years not only because of the misery of the Great Depression but also because of what they led to: the unprecedented scale of death and destruction in the Second World War. Six developments dominated the decade, at least in the northern half of the world:

- the Great Depression;
- Roosevelt's New Deal in the United States;
- the rise of Nazi Germany;
- the accelerated industrialization of the Soviet Union and the consolidation of Stalin's tyranny, culminating in the massive purges;
- Japanese economic penetration and military expansion in Asia;
- the march to the Second World War.

The Great Depression and the New Deal

The Great Depression began with the stock market crash of 1929. It got worse in Europe when several big banks failed. Production and prices in all countries fell, and unemployment soared. Factory gates closed. There were bread lines, soup kitchens and widespread hunger while at the same time, for want of markets, farmers burned their crops or ploughed them under. The United States and Germany were hit the worst. Most families had only one breadwinner, and neither the U.S. nor Canada had any unemployment insurance. Municipalities, with some help from the provinces and states (which soon ran out of money), were responsible for such welfare as there was. People were ashamed of needing welfare, and the means test the welfare administrators required them to undergo was intrusive and humiliating. Unemployment at 15 to 20 per cent or more and lasting for year after year meant something quite different in terms of poverty and despair from anything we have known since.

The outcome in the U.S. was the New Deal. Franklin Roosevelt became president of a stricken nation in March 1933, just when hundreds of

Franklin D. Roosevelt

banks had failed and, to save the rest, all were closed. It had been a terrible winter. President Hoover kept repeating that prosperity was just around the corner and that the way to recovery was to restore confidence by cutting government spending (then only 6 per cent of GNP compared to 23 per cent at the time of writing in 1992) and balancing the budget. When nominated in July 1932, Roosevelt had said, "I pledge you, I pledge myself, to a New Deal for the American people." At his inauguration, his voice rang out, "The only thing we have to fear is fear itself."

Once the banking system had been saved, recovery and reform got under way. First of all came relief—not generous, but less stingy than before. Then came the National Recovery Act for industry and the Agricultural Adjustment Act to rescue farmers. The Civilian Conservation Corps gave young unemployed men fresh country air, plenty to eat and useful work in conservation, reforestation and other projects. A public works program was begun, under which bridges, tunnels and dams that became American landmarks were built. The Tennessee Valley Authority was established and began its work of reclamation, building dams and supplying cheap electricity under public ownership.

The National Youth Administration helped thousands of students continue their education. Later came public housing, a first in North America although by then commonplace in Europe, and the Works Progress Administration, which built schools, libraries and health clinics and gave work and opportunity to artists, writers, actors and teachers. The Homeowners Loan Corporation gave mortgage relief to more than a million homeowners, the Securities and Exchange Commission reformed and regulated the stock market, and the Social Security Act brought unemployment insurance and old age pensions.

By 1936, production was up by one third, employment by 30 per cent and payrolls by 45 per cent, and Roosevelt was triumphantly reelected. But the next four years were more difficult. The Supreme Court, with a majority of conservative old-timers, had declared many New Deal measures unconstitutional. Roosevelt responded with the idea of appointing up to six new judges. This "court packing plan" tied up the Congress in a long and bitter fight, which Roosevelt eventually lost. However, some of the old-timers retired and the court soon had a liberal majority. Nevertheless, it was a costly interlude which broke the New Deal's momentum.

Under the militant leadership of the Congress of Industrial Organizations, labour began to organize in mass-production industries. The Wagner Act required employers to bargain collectively with unions of the workers' choice. But industry ignored the act. In 1937, sit-down strikes forced Ford, General Motors and U.S. Steel to give in, but others continued to resist

with arms and goons. Labour organized in Canada also, but it was several years into the war before we had an equivalent of the Wagner Act.

Also in 1937, recovery unexpectedly came to a halt. There was a sharp recession, from which recovery was slow and fitful. Unemployment at the end of the decade was still around 15 per cent and GNP no larger than in 1929. Only the war lifted the economy out of the Depression. Nevertheless, the New Deal's achievements were immense. It changed the face and spirit of the country, laid the basis for the welfare state, and gave Roosevelt the popular support that enabled him to run for an unprecedented third term and lead the country in the struggle against Nazi Germany.

Hitler vs. Stalin

Hitler rode to power on the Depression. In May 1928, the Nazis got 2.6 per cent of the vote; in September 1930, they got 18.3 per cent; and in July 1932, 37.1 per cent. They never won a majority in a free election. Hitler was appointed chancellor because the leaders of the political establishment were stupid, pig-headed and incompetent. They quarrelled over the sharing of power, were utterly unable to cope with the Depression and needed the Nazis to smash the left. On the evening of his appointment, January 30, 1933, Nazi storm troopers, their jackboots resounding on the pavement, paraded by torchlight beneath the Chancellery where Hitler stood at a window to celebrate the occasion. Thus began the "midnight of the century." It ended twelve years later in utter defeat and infinite shame.

Elections to the Reichstag, the German parliament, were immediately called. A few days before the election, the Nazis set fire to the Reichstag

Adolf Hitler

building. They then used the fire as an excuse for a nationwide crackdown. All freedom of expression and later of worship was suppressed. First the Communists, then the Social Democrats and then the trade unions were outlawed. Piles of books were burned in the streets; persecution and outrages against Jews became government policy; men and women of the highest culture and renown, including Albert Einstein, fled the country. What were people to think when the head of the government screamed abuse and vilification, and the official press carried the most obscene cartoons and columns of lies, insults and applause for every act of brutality and lawlessness, all this in a country hitherto considered among the most civilized?

At the same time, vigorous measures of economic recovery were undertaken. All notions of orthodox finance were swept aside. The drilled work brigades, the famous autobahns and the Olympic Games of 1936 became symbols of Nazi success. Rearmament was at first hidden; later it was publicly celebrated. Hitler was said to have restored German pride after the humiliation of defeat and the trauma of inflation that had wiped out middle-class savings. He certainly appealed to racism, chauvinism and the thirst for revenge.

Facing Germany was Soviet Russia. Throughout the Cold War and since, Hitler and Stalin have been branded as two of a kind, with both their regimes defined as totalitarian. No doubt they were in many dreadful ways the same. But in the 1930s there were heated debates and differences of view. Conservatives considered Stalin and the example of socialism in Russia the main danger, and consequently favoured Nazi Germany. Liberals and the left increasingly saw Hitler as the enemy, and overlooked the facts of Stalin's tyranny. Hitler eventually settled the issue by one act of aggression after another, while the Soviet government called unceasingly for collective resistance.

Soviet industrialization went forward at an extraordinary pace, as one five-year plan followed another. With enormous effort, untold sacrifice, constant trial and error and a great deal of waste, the Soviet Union achieved in years what in other industrial countries had taken decades. Millions moved from the country to bursting towns and cities, where they came under the discipline of factory labour. A new managerial elite was formed, which ruthlessly enforced its orders. There was compulsory military service, and a powerful defence industry was built up. It would be tested to the limit.

Agriculture was collectivized. It was a disaster. Farm output fell, millions of animals were slaughtered and there was widespread famine. The facts were officially denied, and few observers dared to tell the truth. No help was offered from the West, and it might have been refused if it had been. Instead, grain exports were continued, at fire-sale prices, in order to buy machinery and equipment and hire foreign experts. Collectivization imposed without mercy permanently hardened the regime; it became more repressive and relied increasingly on fear, coercion and the secret police.

The show trials and purges of 1936–38 were the culmination of this process. Paranoia gripped the country, and Stalin most of all. Everyone was under suspicion; no one felt secure. Since the government refused to acknowledge mistakes and failures, they had to be blamed on "enemies of the people." There was also growing fear of war, and—not without cause—of spies and hostile agents from abroad.

The trials and purges liquidated the remaining revolutionaries from Lenin's day who did not agree with Stalin's policies and methods, as well as hundreds of thousands of others who for one reason or another or no reason at all were thought to have allowed even a flicker of doubt to cross their minds. By sacrificing countless energetic and dedicated people, many of whom were beginning at last to master their jobs, they set back the country's progress and weakened the army. And they did grave damage to the country's reputation abroad. Hitler and his supporters made the most of this, and appeasement gained ground.

The March to War

The 1930s began with Japan's invasion of Manchuria in 1931. The League of Nations expressed disapproval but did nothing, thereby showing its impotence. In 1935 Germany decreed conscription, in defiance of the Treaty of Versailles. A few months later, the British government signed a naval agreement with Germany, foolishly believing that Hitler, having just broken one treaty, would respect another. That summer, Italy invaded Abyssinia. The League imposed economic sanctions but stopped short of including oil, which might have made the sanctions effective. In 1936, Hitler sent his army into the Rhineland, again in defiance of Versailles. France and Britain did nothing.

The Spanish Civil War broke out in August. Britain refused to sell arms to the democratically elected Republican government; France, with a Popular Front government and a socialist as prime minister, did likewise. Hitler and Mussolini sent troops and weapons in abundance to the rebel armies under Franco, including pilots and planes. The bombing of Guernica, made famous by Picasso, was a milestone in terror from the air. But Madrid held out. The international brigades, including 1,400 Canadians in the Mackenzie-Papineau battalion, fought for the Republic and suffered terrible casualties. Dr. Norman Bethune broke new ground and saved many lives by taking his mobile blood transfusion units to the wounded at the front. Soviet Russia gave what help it could.

Josef Stalin

In 1937, Japan invaded China. Shanghai was bombed. The printed picture of a crying child with shredded clothes sitting in the street was seen by millions. Roosevelt made his famous Quarantine speech, but public opinion overwhelmingly favoured American neutrality. Only later did people in the outside world learn of another event that was to have great consequences: the Long March of the Communists under Mao to the northwest of China in 1934–36.

In March 1938, Hitler occupied Austria and threatened Czechoslovakia. The capitulation at Munich followed in September. Neville Chamberlain, who with his umbrella was the symbol of appeasement, proclaimed "peace in our time." Winston Churchill said, "We have sustained a total and unmitigated defeat." Five weeks later, the Nazis celebrated their triumph with the *Kristallnacht*, in which ninety-one Jews were killed, more than 30,000 were sent to concentration camps where many died, Jewish shops were smashed and almost 200 synagogues were destroyed. It did not, as has so often been said, initiate the persecution of the Jews; there had been outrages from the beginning. But it was a clear warning of what was to come.

In 1939, Hitler took what was left of Czechoslovakia and turned his attention to Poland. After three years of civil war, republican Spain was finally defeated.

The German-Soviet nonaggression pact was the final blow. All its proposals for collective resistance having been rejected, the Soviet government switched sides. Hitler invaded Poland; Britain and France declared war; and Stalin became the great appeaser.

Thus began the Second World War. However, there was little fighting in the west; the first six months were known as the phony war. For the western allies, the real war began in the spring of 1940 with the occupation of Denmark and Norway, the invasion of Belgium and Holland and the collapse of France. England held out, the Battle of Britain was won, and the United States slowly became "the arsenal of democracy" on the allied side.

At each of these steps in the march to war, Hitler could have been stopped. We now know that he could not have held the Rhineland in 1936 if the French, as was their right and duty, had sent in troops. Hitler knew it too. We know that the German army could not have vanquished Czechoslovakia in 1938; again Hitler knew it, as did the German generals, who were prepared to overthrow him if he ordered an attack. Only the surrender at Munich saved him, and indeed consolidated his power.

A French journalist summed it up: nothing, she wrote, gives one a better idea of infinity than human stupidity. In spite of the accumulating evidence, most people in North America and what remained of civilized Europe preferred not to believe what was happening. Politicians, including

Canada's prime minister, fawned on Hitler and praised his government as a bulwark against communism. It was only after Munich that appeasement became a dirty word.

Why was Nazi Germany not stopped before it was too late? This is a question that haunts the memory and conscience of every liberal and thoughtful person who grew up in the 1930s and before. It is a question that George Bush and his advisers should have asked themselves instead of giving aid and comfort to Saddam Hussein.

The Shape of the Decade

The Great Depression affected everything in the 1930s. There had been depressions before, but none had been so deep or caused so much desolation. Unemployment had never been so high, business had never been so discredited and the established order had never been so widely questioned and assailed. Thus, the Great Depression explains the upsurge of militancy among working people in Canada and the United States, the demonstrations and hunger marches, the union organizing drives. It explains the crushing defeat in 1935 of the Conservative government under R.B. Bennett (known as Richard Bughouse Bennett because of the bug-infested bunkhouses in the forests where unemployed men were sent to work). It explains the founding of the CCF and the flowering of left-wing literature and art.

It explains the New Deal and why it repudiated orthodox finance, balanced budgets, "sound" money and the overriding need to restore business confidence as the means of recovery—ideas and policies that by the nineties were again in high favour, as if we had learned nothing in the meantime. It explains the Keynesian revolution in economics, which overturned the ruling dogma that mass unemployment and depression were theoretically impossible. It explains the rise to power of Hitler, not only because he appealed directly to the prevailing misery and fear but also because the Depression showed how utterly incapable the governing parties were of doing anything about it.

It explains the comparison made between capitalist failure and socialist promise, illustrated as many people believed by the Soviet example. In one case, the anarchy of private enterprise and production for profit and all the suffering of depression. In the other, social ownership of farm and factory, planning for the common good, giant strides in industrialization, and impressive progress in education, culture and living standards. This was the idealized picture. One-sided and distorted though it was, it nevertheless inspired millions to immense exertions and gave hope to millions more. However difficult it may be to give retrospective credit to this picture to-

Economist **Lukin Robinson** grew up in Switzerland during the 1930s. He served as Canadian research director for the International Union of Mine, Mill and Smelter Workers, vice-president of an economic consulting firm and an economist with the Ontario Public Service Employees Union.

day, its power and influence on public opinion at the time is a fact that history cannot gainsay.

Thus, on the one hand the 1930s produced the menace of Hitler and a resurgent Germany. On the other hand, the 1930s also produced Roosevelt and the New Deal, Stalin and the buildup of the Soviet Union, and finally, in Churchill, the leading opponent of appeasement and, as of 1940, British prime minister. In this way, the conflicts arising out of the Great Depression gave shape to the principal warring states and their leaders in the great collision of the first half of the 1940s, at the end of which nations and peoples were determined that depression and world war must not be allowed to happen again.

Desperate Canadians Turned to Political Messiahs

by Allan Levine

For eight terrible years, from 1930 to 1938, Canadians were anxious, scared, despondent and desperate. It was only natural that they turned for salvation to their politicians, the leaders who had guided them through the Great War and offered them hope and prosperity in the years that followed. But like many in Canada, the country's political leaders were not only surprised by the economic upheaval that gripped the world after 1929 but also unprepared to adapt their age-old policies and seek new and unconventional solutions. In Ottawa, practical politics then meant balancing the budget and paying off the huge debt incurred by the Canadian National Railways. It did not mean assuming more responsibility for the unemployed, which under the British North America Act fell into the jurisdiction of the provinces and municipalities.

Curiously, Canadians first turned to R.B. Bennett, an arrogant and dour wealthy corporate lawyer, who had become leader of the Conservative Party in 1927. During the federal election campaign of 1930, which he ultimately won, Bennett told voters that he could save them from the imminent economic disaster. Singlehandedly R.B. Bennett was going to end the Depression. He intended to solve the crisis with protective tariffs and "blast" his way into world markets. Such traditional policies, however, did not work and Bennett grew frustrated, bitter and very unpopular. His futile attempt in 1934 to implement his "New Deal" reforms—including minimum wage laws and unemployment insurance—was too late. William Lyon Mackenzie King and the Liberals were returned to power in the election of 1935, which marked the start of twenty-two years of Liberal rule.

It was the same story across the country. The despair of the Depression demanded change, and provincial governments, the majority of which were Conservative, were deemed expendable. The only provincial administration to survive from 1930 to the end of the decade was John Bracken's

William Aberhart

Progressive government in Manitoba, and Bracken was forced to form a coalition with the Liberals. Psychologically defeated, people wanted a saviour, not only to provide new economic answers but more significantly to reassure them that they were not to blame for their hardships and troubles. In short, Canadians were searching for political messiahs who could give them hope for the future.

Around the world, the response was similar. The 1930s witnessed the rise of leaders as different as Hitler and Mussolini in Europe, Franklin Roosevelt in the United States, and Duff Pattullo, Mitchell Hepburn, William Aberhart and Maurice Duplessis in Canada. Their ideologies and policies may have spanned the political spectrum, but they possessed in common that special and difficult-to-define trait called charisma, first identified by the German sociologist Max Weber: the perception that some "higher power" had bestowed on them a unique and "inimitable quality." Politicians of extraordinary personality and ego, they offered their followers deliverance and scapegoats, dazzling crowds with oratory and promises for a better future. Using powerful words and religious images, they appealed for, and demanded, a new moral order.

As "men of the people," they railed against the enemies, real and imagined, of their downtrodden flock: business establishments, elites, "special interests," bankers, Jews and Communists. They promised redistribution of wealth and alleviation of debt. Salvation, however, had a heavy price. With few exceptions, once in power these populists showed their true colours as authoritarian demagogues who were determined to do whatever it took, including trampling civil liberties, to achieve their personal destinies.

Socialism was one viable solution in Canada, yet the birth of the Co-operative Commonwealth Federation (CCF) in Regina in 1933 with its stated intention "to eradicate capitalism" proved too much for the vast majority of middle-class Canadians fearful of anything resembling Communism. Despite the credibility of its soft-spoken leader, Rev. J.S. Woodsworth, the CCF was initially generally regarded with disdain and perceived as no less subversive than the "Red Menace." One Catholic journal in Saskatchewan, where the CCF was later to have its greatest electoral success, described the party's platform as "inspired by the old Jew Karl Marx, the father and author of the Communist Manifesto."

Nevertheless, the CCF's demands for reform and social justice could not be entirely ignored. In British Columbia, the stylish sixty-year old leader of the provincial Liberal Party, Duff Pattullo, rode to power in November 1933 with a promise of "Work and Wages." Pattullo's vision of "socialized capitalism," in which the state would deal more effectively with social and economic development, was inspired by the example of President Roosevelt's New Deal. Unlike FDR, however, Pattullo did not have the money or resources to implement innovative unemployment relief and social programs, and neither R.B. Bennett nor Mackenzie King was anxious to surrender control of tax revenues for such schemes. His grand reforms were put on hold. Impatient, Pattullo pushed through a "Special Powers Act" in 1934 that effectively made the premier a dictator. Though the act was never invoked, Pattullo's reputation as an authoritarian leader, perhaps not entirely deserved, was confirmed.

Another Liberal with a mind of his own was the brash and erratic Mitchell Hepburn. Only the desperation of the Depression could have enabled such an inconsistent and impulsive personality (not to mention, an alcoholic and a notorious womanizer) to gain power in Ontario. Hepburn talked like a left-wing liberal reformer and attracted wide support. A brilliant campaigner, he was never too specific about how he planned to solve the Depression; he just said he could do it. And in 1934, the vast majority of Ontarians believed and trusted him. As even Mackenzie King (the two Liberal leaders detested each other) was later forced to concede, "People believe [Hepburn] is honest; know he is fearless and regard him as efficient in Administration. His manner, evidently, as well, catches the man on the street. It is the 'fellows' that count & he is one of them in language and spirit."

Hepburn managed to institute a few reforms, but the real economic problems of the day were beyond his capacity and control. In the end, he was not the radical or the social reformer he had pretended to be. Indeed, when it counted, as it did in 1937 during the General Motors strike in Oshawa, the man who had identified himself with the "little fellow," the unemployed workman and the struggling farmer, turned out to be nothing but an advocate for big business.

Across the country in Alberta, politics was being transformed with equal drama by William Aberhart, whom popular historian Pierre Berton has described as "the most electrifying political figure the country has ever produced." On August 22, 1935, Aberhart and his newly formed Social Credit Party defeated the reigning United Farmers of Alberta and assumed control of the province, the beginning of thirty-six straight years of Social Credit rule. A teacher by training, Aberhart was the prime example of the 1930s political prophet and his victory was nothing less than sensational. Revered by his loyal followers as a "Man of God," he mesmerized an entire province with his promises for a glorious and prosperous future.

Struggling with debt and unemployment, dejected Albertans needed to be rescued. They needed to be reassured that the harsh economic times were not of their making but the fault of those who had victimized them in

Maurice Duplessis

the past, eastern Canadian bankers and international financiers—the "Fifty Big Shots" as Aberhart labelled them. Using radio like no other Canadian politician before or since to spread his peculiar Social Credit gospel, Aberhart convinced Albertans that his unorthodox plan for restructuring the economy (developed by the British engineer Major C.H. Douglas in the 1920s) was their only answer. He explained to them why there was "poverty in the midst of plenty," to quote a popular Social Credit slogan, and dangled before them dividends of $25 a month and "just" prices.

Psychologically, this mixture of economics, religious fervour and political passion was irresistible. But the federal government prevented Aberhart from implementing his Social Credit platform by disallowing every piece of financial legislation he passed. By the end of the decade, the Social Credit government's economic policies were not much different from those of any Conservative administration.

In office, Aberhart initially proved to be a tyrant. When journalists criticized him, he tried to censor them; when a former cabinet minister threatened to bring out a book exposing him as a fraud, he blackmailed the publisher to halt publication; and when he tired of debates in the Legislature he stopped answering the opposition's questions, choosing instead to speak to the people directly on the radio. None of this made a difference to his army of supporters. Social Credit, observes historian Blair Neatby, "remained an ideal, a faith, an abstraction," and William Aberhart was still "the champion" who defended Alberta's interests against eastern domination.

Finally, in Quebec there was the political phenomenon of Maurice Duplessis, as much a product of the Depression as Hepburn and Aberhart but even more dishonest about his intentions. During the 1935 Quebec election campaign, Duplessis, the leader of the provincial Conservatives, who had been out of office since 1897, united with a group of dissident left-leaning nationalist Liberals led by Paul Gouin to form a new party called the Union Nationale. Promising to end the corruption practised by a generation of Liberal administrations, reform capitalism and regulate the "trusts" and English bankers who controlled the province, Duplessis came close to defeating the Liberals. In a second election held in August 1936, the Union Nationale won a major victory.

Gouin had left the coalition over a disagreement with the outspoken Duplessis, but his Liberal supporters believed that the new premier would indeed institute the economic reforms he had pledged himself to. They were wrong. Duplessis was as partisan as the Liberals he replaced and had no intention of bothering capitalists with state regulations. Instead, using his infamous "Padlock law," he turned the full force of the government and the police on any individual, group or movement he suspected of having socialist sympathies. In a province where a fascist leader like Adrien Arcand was attracting a considerable following, where support in the Spanish Civil War was on the side of the right and General Franco, and where anti-semitism was regarded as an acceptable credo, Duplessis's dictatorial actions met with little opposition. Except for a defeat in the election of 1939, mainly due to the intervention of federal Liberals, Duplessis's hold on Quebec remained firm until his death in 1959.

By the early 1990s, as the country struggled with economic problems similar to those faced by Canadians in the thirties, resentment and cynicism against elected politicians reached unprecedented levels. (A poll showed that the public regard politicians with less respect than car dealers and rock musicians.) Canadians demanded change and the times seemed ripe again for the coming of a new political prophet. The popularity of such self-declared saviours as Lucien Bouchard and Preston Manning appeared all too familiar. But if there is one lesson to be learned from the political history of the 1930s, it is that those who proclaim themselves to be the tribunes of the people may turn out be something very different indeed.

Allan Levine teaches at St. John's Ravenscourt School in Winnipeg and is the author of several books on Canadian political history, most recently *Scrum Wars: The Prime Ministers and the Media.*

On the Prairies, You Had to Learn to Peel a Nickel

by Gail Burns

The word my parents used to describe the task of rearing a family during the 1930s was *tough*. "Things were really tough"; "you had to learn to peel a nickel"; "you had to make your own fun"; "you had to help one another." There was a sense of everyone being in the same boat struggling against unknown hostile forces. Some endured more hardship than others but no one got through the thirties unscathed.

We grew up hearing Depression survival stories and like all war stories they contained sadness, gratitude, pride, relief and humour. In November 1929 my mother, Deane Doody, married a well-to-do up-and-comer whose very next paycheque was cut in half without notice. "And that was just the start of it!" After a few more cuts, my father's company consolidated its western division and transferred him, but not his pregnant wife, to Vancouver. My mother moved back to her parents' home. "Lots of people did that in those days," she claimed. Indeed, my grandparents' spacious house soon sheltered two returned daughters with families as well as a bachelor son. Everyone moved over a little more and my grandmother began to take in roomers. Lots of people did that too. Grandma's workload was eased when Sophie knocked on the door one day and stayed for fifteen years. She had come in from the farm with no job and no money and went from door to door offering to work for room and board. Yes, lots of people did that too.

C. Rhodes Smith, who went on to a distinguished career as a cabinet minister and judge in Manitoba, had already been practising law in Winnipeg for eight years when the stock market crashed in October 1929. "Thousands of people were out of work immediately and everyone who had investments was adversely affected," he remembered:

> A number of our [Winnipeg's] businesses suffered—a number of people lost jobs. Banks and real estate businesses collapsed. Real

estate was the biggest business in Winnipeg then except for the railroads—and they laid off a lot of people too. Enrolment at universities was way down. The first year I taught law in 1925 there were twenty-five first-year students. By the mid-thirties it was down to twelve. One year it was eight.

In 1935, Smith was elected to Winnipeg city council: "That year there were 8,300 families on relief and 5,000 single men. And that was after a lot had gone east or west." The population of Winnipeg at the time was 221,242. Smith was made chair of a special commission to examine the problems of single men on relief because many complaints had been received about their poor living conditions:

> You should have seen the places they lived in. Conditions were awful. I saw bedbugs crawling up the walls. Hotel owners divided the rooms—maybe three out of one, just room for a single bed and a washstand. Single men ate in soup kitchens. They fed 4,000 every day. One day there was a disturbance. A man in the line broke open a loaf of bread and the interior of the loaves was green. They were being fed moldy food.

Many people converted their homes to rooming houses and predictably some became rundown and overcrowded: "I met one fellow living in a basement on a cot with springs but no mattress—no bedclothes. There were lots like that." In the early years of the Depression, "The Salvation Army was the closest thing to relief. But very soon, the Salvation Army couldn't handle it, the city couldn't and the province couldn't." People drifted—from farms into the cities, from east to west or west to east: "People came to the cities to get jobs. If they stayed for a year they got unemployment relief. Most wanted to work—a great many gave up in despair."

If conditions were bad in Manitoba, they were worse in Saskatchewan, with its farm-based economy faced with sagging world wheat prices and prolonged drought. "My wife and I took our boys west one summer—twenty-five miles into Saskatchewan we saw empty fields, miles and miles of nothing," Smith recalled. "Finally we saw a green field in the distance. It was a solid mass of Russian thistle. That's what happens when a farm's deserted. There was no sign of crops until we got to northern Alberta."

Mildred Hetlelid, who taught in Saskatchewan then, remembered her grade 11 and 12 boys riding the rails for the summer: "There was a rush east to get work, because there were no crops and so there was no work. Some of them had terrible experiences. These young kids had never been away from home before." She remembered Saskatchewan farmers abandoning their homes and walking north or east with just the baby buggy and the

clothes on their backs.

Hetlelid recalled that wells dried up and cattle died. When she began her teaching career at Lafleche, Saskatchewan, in 1926, her starting salary was $1,200, "pretty good money then." However, "In 1929, I was getting $1,000. And at that time I was principal of a two-room school and had three teachers under me." To keep her expenses down, Hetlelid lived with farm families who boarded teachers as a way of working their taxes. "If the farmer's taxes were paid up at the end of six weeks, I moved on," she said. "I did that for three years. It helped them, they got their taxes paid, and it helped me."

When she later married another teacher, their combined annual salary, as principal and vice-principal, was $1,700. "But we never got paid," she laughed. "We might get $25 a month. We'd get a note saying they owed it to us." The *they* in this instance was the local school board. The province and municipalities had no money because the tax base was depleted. No one had money—not farmers, not teachers, not shopkeepers, not municipalities. "Nobody knew how to deal with a depression," Hetlelid said.

Maybe, but Hetlelid and her ilk devised some very clever ways of dealing with a cashless economy. The Hetlelids moved to Congress, Saskatchewan, and Mildred stopped teaching. A niece who was also a teacher lived with them. "We didn't get any money and there were three of us," Hetlelid said. "So the storekeeper was a bachelor and he boarded with us for dinner and supper. And I did his washing and ironing. Then I took the money he paid us back to him to buy more groceries. And I don't know what we'd have done if we hadn't had this extra money." By paying her father's property taxes, Hetlelid found another way to generate cash: "Because the municipality owed me money, I paid his taxes with my notes, and he gave me the cash. You had to do these things." This work for promissory notes continued until the end of the decade—after Saskatchewan produced a couple of successful crops and after Gordon Hetlelid had given up teaching: "They wrote and asked us, 'Will you take 25 per cent off?' By that time we'd had ten no-crop years and so we took it. No, it wasn't fair, but there was no money around."

But Hetlelid insisted that "we had a lot of fun in those years too." Some of that fun was found in community relief projects: "I was on the committee distributing a carload of clothes that had come from eastern Canada. And one lady had sent a sample-size box of Lux soapflakes and a note explaining how to use it. We also got high-heeled slippers and a long dress with leg-of-mutton sleeves. We kept them for our home talent plays." Carloads of fruit and vegetables were put to good use, but prairie people didn't know quite what to do with a boxcar full of salt cod: "One fellow took his slab of salted codfish, printed his name on it and put it on his gate."

She said, "The only thing I couldn't live through again was the dust." Hetlelid described waking up each morning to clear weather. Then it would cloud over as though it might rain. But it was always another dust storm:

> And your house would just be littered with the finest dust—through closed windows and doors. If you had food out it would be covered. It was in your hair, in your skin, your eyes and mouth. I just couldn't go through it again. It's a nightmare to me.

For Mildred Hetlelid it was the sweet smell of rain and two good crop years that signalled the end of bad times. Rhodes Smith pointed out that misery was much alleviated once relief systems were in place. Inevitably, however, the end of the Depression is connected with the launching of the Second World War. "By 1941, there was work and good money for everyone," said Smith. "I don't think it takes a war, but that's what happened then."

The comparison of the present sluggish economy with the dirty thirties just wouldn't wash with those who survived these years. Smith was categorical:

> It's nothing like as bad. The unemployed are not walking the streets. No marches—like the freight train from the west. People climbed on at every stop intent on marching on Ottawa. When they reached Regina they were stopped by the Mounted Police. There were 2,000. How many thousands more would have joined before they reached Ottawa?

He maintained that social programs have made a difference: "Unemployment Insurance has helped a great deal. The vast majority use it well. They've earned it. There shouldn't be resentment."

While most would not want Canada to abandon its social safety net, people who lived through the Depression have expressed a niggling worry that society is perhaps getting softer. As Hetlelid put it, "There's something very fine about surmounting these difficulties. You get a feeling of accomplishment that some people never get." But if the young people of the nineties had to make the sacrifices and adjustments that were required of people during the Depression, she said, they would rise to the challenge.

Writer **Gail Burns** served as an associate editor of *Compass* from 1984 to 1987 before returning to her native Winnipeg.

Latin America's Response to the Depression

by Liisa North

The 1930s opened with a burst of political violence and ruthless repression over great parts of Latin America. The decade ended on a note of hope, as reform movements arose to challenge the rule of tightly knit oligarchies and even gained the political initiative in a few countries. The immediate cause of the political explosion was, of course, the Great Depression. The reason why its impact was nothing short of catastrophic, however, cannot be fully grasped without looking at Latin America's pre-Depression development pattern.

Several decades of rapid economic growth preceded the Depression, but that growth was almost entirely based on the export of primary products. Since domestic markets remained underdeveloped as dependence on international trade increased, the region was particularly vulnerable to the economic crisis that originated in the great centres of capitalist production. Most Latin Americans, moreover, never benefited from the export expansion, which took place under the aegis of landlord oligarchies that usurped the remaining lands of the peasantry. The most fertile areas were converted to the production of coffee, cotton, meat and sugar for foreign markets. Meanwhile, U.S.-based corporations took charge of mineral production and repatriated their profits instead of investing them locally.

As Latin America's export proceeds plummeted with the onset of the Depression—their value in 1930–34 was only about half the 1925–29 average—the great estate owners and mining corporations tried to cut their losses by reducing wages and dismissing workers. Governments, almost entirely dependent on export and import taxes, lost their income and cut back public-sector jobs and services.

All over Latin America, labourers turned to agitation and strikes, the unemployed to mass demonstrations, and dispossessed peasants to rebellion. The response of the elites was brutal. In El Salvador, up to 30,000 peasants may have been killed in the *matanza* of 1932; sugar workers were mowed down by the military in the "Trujillo Rebellion" of the same year in Peru. In short, the privileged classes, including most of the middle class, which had prospered during the previous export boom years, dug in to defend their interests. They united in support of despotic regimes—some headed by military figures, others by civilians—which resorted to systematic repression to maintain "public order" in the face of popular protest.

As the first shock waves of the Depression receded, middle-class reformers, backed by fledgeling working-class organizations, managed to gain the political initiative in a few of the larger and more economically developed countries. In the small Central American and Caribbean nations, however, reactionary dictatorships consolidated their hold with military force, while in the continent's giant, Brazil, a militant radical coalition was ruthlessly suppressed.

Whether or not the reform movements achieved national power in the 1930s, they did become major players on the Latin American political stage and had a profound impact on public policy well into the 1960s and beyond. These movements included the Socialist Party of Chile (Salvador Allende was among its founding members); the PRI, which still rules Mexico; and the Apra party of Peru whose head occupied the presidency of that country from 1985 to 1990.

These parties traced the causes of the region's crisis to oligarchic rule and excessive dependence on world markets and foreign investors. They advocated state-promoted industrialization to diversify the economy and expand work opportunities; nationalization and regulation of foreign investment to keep a greater share of export profits at home; expansion of educational opportunities to improve skills and promote social mobility; and political freedoms to guarantee movement towards democracy. Some of them even favoured thoroughgoing agrarian reform.

In the second half of the 1930s, Chile and Mexico began to pursue these policies. Under a Popular Front government that included the Radical, Socialist and Communist parties, Chile increased taxation of foreign-owned copper enterprises and established a state development corporation to direct investment towards industrial diversification. In Mexico, during the presidency of Lázaro Cárdenas, foreign-owned oil companies were nationalized and agrarian reform benefited a large segment of the peasantry.

During the following decades, similar policies were adopted in most Latin American countries, but their emphasis was the modernization of urban society and the diversification of industry behind protectionist barriers. Agrarian reform, when attempted, remained truncated as a consequence of elite opposition. Meanwhile, the so-called "Indian problem" was left to assimilation—that is, cultural genocide.

The development model that emerged from the 1930s came to be known as Import Substitution Industrialization (ISI). Its basic flaw lay in its reliance on increasing the size of the economic pie to improve mass welfare. Counting on the trickle-down effects of growth, most Latin American governments avoided redistributive reforms. Even in Mexico, large estates kept much of the best land and, worse yet, it was those estates rather than peasant agriculture that secured most public credit and infrastructure such as irrigation works. Only in democratic Costa Rica was the power of the large landlord class effectively curbed.

In the 1980s and 1990s, international financial institutions such as the World Bank and the International Monetary Fund, together with Washington, have spearheaded the critique of the ISI model, inveighing against inflation, inefficient industries and wasteful public bureaucracies that inhibit private initiative. But their recipe for renewed growth does not hold much promise.

Liisa North is the author of *Bitter Grounds: Roots of Revolt in El Salvador* (1985).

The policy package sponsored by the international financial institutions demands export promotion, foreign investment, the dismantling of protectionist barriers and the withdrawal of the state from economic management. Ignoring the continent's historic maldistribution of land and income, it bears a strong resemblance to the oligarchically sponsored export economy model that led Latin America to the catastrophic economic crisis and political repression of the 1930s. Indeed, it seems that the region is being forced to come full circle to repeat the errors of its tragic past instead of advancing towards a democratic future based on social justice.

Education and Economic Democracy: The Antigonish Movement

by Greg MacLeod

During the 1930s, a remarkable movement for social and economic reform took hold in Atlantic Canada. Today, more than ever, the basic insights of the Antigonish Movement, as it was called, are applicable and deeply needed.

Fundamentally, the Antigonish Movement was a program to gain control of a percentage of the economy so as to transform it. Through kitchen meetings and public assemblies, groups were organized to form cooperative fish plants, grocery stores and credit unions. Especially in the coal-mining towns, the accent was on the education of labour leaders. It was a "people's school," educating people to own and manage their own businesses.

Most of the organization took place during the Depression years and the benefits were easily understood. Fishermen could sell to the cooperative instead of to the local fish baron. Workers could borrow from the credit union instead of paying usurious interest rates. Housewives could avoid the oppressive "company store" by joining the cooperative store. The Catholic priests who led the movement, Dr. Jimmy Tompkins and Dr. Moses Coady, thought that these examples of a just economic approach would spread to the whole economy as people "learned a lesson." Their new approaches to education were recognized when Harvard University granted Tompkins an honorary doctorate.

This was not an exclusively Catholic movement, nor a clerical movement, nor simply a product of the Antigonish diocese or St. Francis Xavier University. Despite its name, most of the activity took place in Cape Breton and was led by Cape Breton natives. It encompassed Acadian priests such as Fr. G.A. Belcourt of Prince Edward Island, who in the nineteenth century had formed the Farmer's Bank of Rustico for the good of farmers and fishermen. There were United Church leaders such as J.D.N. MacDonald of credit union fame. It involved country pastors throughout the region and many laypeople who led in both the labour movement and the cooperative movement out of a sense of religious commitment. All of them would have agreed with the words of the leader of another cooperative movement, Don José María of Mondragon, Spain: "If the Gospel does not apply to the economy, to what does it apply?"

The most fascinating part of this tradition in the Atlantic is not the institutions it spawned but the thinking behind those institutions. As Dr. Alex Laidlaw, onetime assistant to Dr. Coady and one of the best thinkers to come out of the movement, said much later, "Behind it is the power of a universal truth." Laidlaw was referring to some shared insights about human reality that have inspired and guided the movement. The Antigonish Movement was summarized in six principles outlined by Harry Johnston in 1944:

- primacy of the person;
- social and economic reform through education;
- change through group action;
- education begins with the economic;
- personal change requires institutional change;
- a full and abundant life for all.

It was Dr. Jimmy Tompkins who crystallized the new ideas on reform that kindled the Antigonish Movement in the 1930s. Tompkins's first interest was education for all people, and he closely followed the growth of the contemporary movement for universal and comprehensive education in Europe and America. He brought these forces together with the movement for economic democracy expressed in the growth of cooperatives. Tompkins taught regular university courses at St. Francis Xavier from 1902 on, but in 1922 he was fired as vice-president of St. FX. It was then, at the age of fifty-two, that he started working on cooperatives in Canso.

In the booklet *Knowledge for the People* (1921), Tompkins expressed his admiration for the Workers' Educational Association set up in Oxford in 1903, with its great emphasis on economic education: "Educational Extension is one of the terms used to describe numerous ventures to meet the growing demand among the multitudes for knowledge and training." He was inspired by the University of Wisconsin, which devoted one fifth of its budget to extension education, and admired the University of Saskatchewan, where out of 1,481 students in 1920, 999 were in extension programs.

What Tompkins and Coady added to the traditional notion of workers' control over the economy is the broader notion of education. Education begins with the economic, but the goal is development of the total person. Furthermore, since one becomes a person only through the sharing relationship, a person cannot be educated as an individual unit but only as part of the group. The modern American notion of individualistic empowerment as the lever of economic change is something quite different. Today's educational movements of empowerment are designed to enable an individual to compete; the Tompkins strategy was designed to enable persons to cooperate.

At meetings Dr. Tompkins would take a match and break it; then he would take a stack of matches and try to break them but could not. The message was always: alone you are weak and can be broken; together you are strong. Authentic education involves group action in the economic institutions of society and this action should have as its result not only the personal growth of the organizers but also the good of the whole community. Leaders in the movement saw both cooperatives and labour unions as institutional frameworks through which education and economic change could be achieved.

The original concept of the Extension movement was that the university was the centre for scientific and general intellectual leadership. Tompkins said that we should be using our best brains to solve our worst problems. He believed the role of the university was essential for any serious social and economic reform and was appalled at the proliferation of small sectarian universities competing with one another in one of the poorest regions of the country. Tompkins eventually obtained the collaboration of the Carnegie Foundation in an attempt to federate the universities in the area. Coady also attacked the educational system as a trap-door that allowed the brightest of the children of poor communities to escape to a richer life while forgetting the people left behind.

Since social and personal values were the driving force behind the reforming organizations of the 1930s, it is not surprising that church people played a leading role. However, the involvement of religion had some negative effects. The clergy's penchant for dogmatism and demand for blind fidelity made it difficult for people to offer constructive criticism. Also, the clergy tended to place great value on moral qualities while undervaluing competence. Perhaps because of their liberal and classical education, many of the clergy regarded business as an inferior activity, something of a necessary evil. Some of the cooperatives' business failures may have been the result of undue clerical influence.

The positive side, however, is that the institutions are still here and they are commercially viable. The potential for new future roles is still strong. Indeed, discussions at meetings of the major cooperative institutions indicate that there is a growing interest in a restoration of the original motivation.

Originally, institutions were not seen as ends in themselves; rather, they were very much subject to change and evolution. The end purpose was considered to be development of people and the community. However, these distinctions were frequently forgotten. In his book *Search for Community*, George Melnyk points out that cooperatives go through stages: from movement to institutionalization. The cooperative movement in the Atlantic has followed that pattern. The failure of the cooperative movement to respond to the needs of more recent decades is related to rigid institutionalization and a tendency to downplay the importance of vision and values.

Some of the strongest criticisms have come from within the movement itself. On the occasion of the fiftieth anniversary of the St. FX Extension Department in 1978, Alex Laidlaw suggested that the movement was becoming sterile and institutionalized. He advised that there should be less rhetoric and more attention paid to empirical reality. Dr. Laidlaw pointed out that it is a popular misconception that people in the Atlantic flocked to the cooperatives. Even though it has roots going back to the turn of the last century, the Atlantic cooperative movement controls very little of the local economy. Economically, the movement failed—unemployment in Cape Breton in 1978 was about 20 per cent; in 1992 it ranged around 25 or 30 per cent.

Leaders such as Laidlaw have been open in chiding traditional reformers for distortions of the original vision. These distortions include:

- the belief that "everyone can do everything." This kind of populism is a hindrance in a modern technocratic system and downplays the importance of management.
- the belief that "right spirit can move mountains." It is dangerous to rely on enthusiasm instead of technical organization and strategy.
- the idea that "each group should maintain its autonomy." Hyperautonomy has encouraged limitation of the movement to single-function cooperative entities that have little economic weight. The result is a lot of isolated and independent groups in many communities. They miss out on opportunities for development and growth because they do not want to work together with other community groups out of fear of losing some autonomy.
- antagonism towards business and labour unions. Many cooperative organizations began in rural areas and incorporated some of the traditional antipathy of rural people to industrial systems. Frequently leaders offered a blanket criticism of business with inadequate distinctions.

At a meeting of community activists in Wolfville, N.S., in 1975, Laidlaw said:

> If credit unions and cooperatives are not a distinctly different kind of business, if they are not a reform movement, a social movement oriented to change, then perhaps the poor and those who are left outside the mainstream of our society will have to build a separate movement of their own, maybe with community development corporations, to serve their needs and exert leverage on the power structures.

The question is whether anything can be salvaged from the impressive reform movements of the thirties or whether they will remain simply occasions for nostalgic speeches. Most of the institutions that flowered in the thirties have cast aside the old visions and values. As Kropotin warned, "Cooperatives are fast becoming exercises in collective egotism." But it is not the original ideas that are at fault. It is something like the truths of the Judeo-Christian tradition—the ideas were right but they were never really tried.

Nevertheless, as someone who is attempting to marry the old inspirations with the hard realities of the postindustrial world, I believe that much of value remains. I see three very important lessons from the thirties, incorporated in challenges for renewed leadership by three sectors. The first challenge is to the church, to recognize that change comes only through the promotion of values and moral commitment rather than institutional loyalty and ideologies. The second is to social activists, to realize that moral commitment can be tested only through setting up new value-based commercial institutions that are flexible and adaptable—conferences and seminars are not enough. And finally, universities must take their proper role, for without the best of science and technology, social and economic reform is ephemeral.

Fr. Greg MacLeod, professor of philosophy at the University College of Cape Breton in Sydney, N.S., is a longtime activist in and writer about the cooperative movement. He is the author of *From Mondragon to America: Experiments in Community Economic Development* (1997).

Emmanuel Mounier:
Catalyst for a Generation

by John Hellman

Like his hero, the pre–First World War left-Catholic writer Charles Péguy, Emmanuel Mounier abandoned a French academic career to direct a politically radical review. With the help of a galaxy of talented, rebellious young intellectuals—and the support of a few well-known elders such as Jacques Maritain, Nicholas Berdyaev and Gabriel Marcel—he founded *Esprit* in 1932. The Russian exile Berdyaev's startling essay on the common ideals of Christianity and communism quickly established the review's notoriety and originality. Under Mounier, the review attacked what it called the "established disorder" of western capitalism in the name of humanistic values and, while opposing Stalinism, insisted that humanity needed some of the values defended by socialism to live.

While Mounier and several of his closest comrades were serious Catholics, his review soon attracted brilliant young Protestants, Jews and even nonbelievers who wanted to explore the place of the spiritual dimension in the debates of the 1930s. Mounier led the *Esprit* group in establishing a new philosophical and political stance of its own, personalism—an approach to thinking and living that would fight for the human person against the wounding forces of both capitalism and communism. The personalists described, and lived, a new style of Christian (or humanist) experience, which involved radically transcending materialism and embracing a spirit of poverty, fraternity, simplicity and solidarity with the poor and oppressed.

Personalism was quickly denounced as a "red-Christian" phenomenon by the anti-communist right and as a cryptofascist initiative by Communist intellectuals. But after Mounier led *Esprit* in supporting the radical social reforms proposed by the French Popular Front, in denouncing Franco's Christian crusader stance in the Spanish Civil War, and in opposing the Munich agreements, he became known as one of France's, and the world's, most prominent progressive Catholic intellectuals.

Since the militantly reactionary Action Française had great influence over the French Catholic hierarchy and intelligentsia, even after its condemnation by Rome in the late 1920s, his high-profile role as a young Catholic of the left was courageous, innovative and controversial. Young writers, artists, teachers and priests who were sympathetic to religion or the spiritual dimension of life but had progressive political instincts became committed readers of *Esprit* and members of the various *Esprit* groups established in major European cities, several Latin American countries, and Quebec. Mounier, who set the highest literary and intellectual standards, also showed great personal openness, generosity and warmth at the various *Esprit* lectures, congresses, discussion groups and summer camps.

The personalist movement provided inspiration and ties of friendship for philosophers, historians, theologians, poets and playwrights. The *Esprit* inspiration would strongly mark Peter Maurin and Dorothy Day of the *Catholic Worker* in the United States, and in Canada Gérard Pelletier and Pierre Trudeau, the founders of *Cité Libre*, and the philosopher Charles Taylor. *Esprit* was able to express the spirit of the times in a remarkable way and to precipitate a common effort that effected an important change in the intellectual generation that came into its own in the 1930s.

Mounier's relatively small-circulation review, although erudite and difficult to read, became the most influential French review of the decade. Its personalist language spread and became popularized in a host of other publications, and it would be the only new intellectual review of the interwar period to survive the war. Mounier's personal influence was due less to the power and originality of his writings than to his role as assembler and leader of a movement decisive for an intellectual generation. Although he did author an important philosophical description of the communitarian dimension of personalism, the *Personalist Manifesto* (1936), this tract was in fact a communal effort.

With the rise of Hitler and the Munich crisis, and the mobilization of many of *Esprit*'s regulars, Mounier declared that France could survive confrontation with the fascist powers only by submitting to a vigorous, total, internal revolution. *Esprit* held to this line until the defeat and occupation of 1940. After the collapse of the Third Republic and the advent of the Pétain regime, Mounier would play a decisive role in establishing the famous École Nationale des Cadres d'Uriage, in the alpine Château Bayard above Grenoble, to train new young leaders for his country.

Historian **John Hellman** is the author of *The Knight-Monks of Vichy France: Uriage, 1940–1945* (1993).

Norman Bethune: Driven to Be an Actor on the World Stage

by Andrée Lévesque

Heroes make us uneasy. Twentieth-century cults of personality have cured us of the exaltation of individuals. Yet what is one to do when the personality of an individual stands out from the surrounding dreariness of life, when one person rises above the crowd and leaves his or her mark on the times? What circumstances turn a strong personality into a hero and a myth? What, in the case of Norman Bethune, constituted the transition from the rebel doctor to the committed revolutionary?

Bethune's role in setting up a blood transfusion unit during the Spanish Civil War and his participation in Mao Zedong's Eighth Army have been well documented; his Montreal years and the events that led to his political commitment remain less well known. Yet these eight years, 1928 to 1936, witnessed his personal transformation just as the country was turning from the roaring twenties to the grumbling thirties.

Bethune arrived in Montreal at thirty-eight, having just released himself from the Trudeau Sanatorium in Saranac Lake, N.Y., where he was treated for tuberculosis for two years. Eager to specialize in thoracic surgery, he joined Dr. Edward Archibald at the Royal Victoria Hospital from 1928 to 1932. During these years, he earned himself a reputation for nonconformity, devotion to his patients, and the speed with which he operated. His bold surgical practice was controversial and earned him accusations of recklessness, which led to his departure. In early 1933 he was appointed chief of pulmonary surgery and bronchoscopy at the Hôpital du Sacré-Coeur, in a Montreal suburb, and he held this position until his resignation in 1936.

By 1933 Montreal was in the depths of the Depression. Bethune's ethnic background, affiliation with the Royal Victoria and residence in the western part of the city identified him as a member of the Anglo-Saxon elite, but at Sacré-Coeur, a Catholic Francophone hospital, he was in daily contact with people who were experiencing serious physical and economic hardship.

Even before the crash, the Montreal working class was plagued with irregular work, employment in labour-intensive low-wage sectors, and a high rate of unemployment. Soon, close to a third of the labour force was unemployed. By 1934, 125,000 people out of a population of 819,000 were on welfare.

Montreal was one of the unhealthiest cities for workers to live in. Infant mortality was above 100 per thousand live births, and much higher in working-class districts in the eastern part of the city and along the Lachine Canal. The incidence of tuberculosis in Montreal was three times as high as in Toronto. Although the rate had been dropping, it rose again in the mid-thirties. Late diagnosis and a shortage of beds, partly due to budgetary restraints, worsened the situation. In a city where one quarter of households had less than one room per person and where 18,000 people lived in what the authorities defined as slums, the risk of contagion was always high. One would have had to be totally insensitive to ignore this reality.

Norman Bethune

Until 1935, the picture we have of Bethune is that of a compassionate, gifted doctor, impatient, creative (could he not paint frescos and invent surgical instruments?), endowed with a very large ego. An iconoclast who fancied shocking people; an epicurean who liked to eat and drink well; in short, a "bohemian" closer to the world of artists and poets than to that of the medical profession. A rebel, surely, but not a revolutionary. But all that would soon change.

In August 1935, Bethune attended the International Physiological Congress in Leningrad and Moscow. This trip proved a turning point in his life. Back in Canada, he joined a Marxist study group, started reading the great Marxist texts, and made new friends among militants, especially artists on the left. At the time, when the Depression seemed to herald the collapse of capitalism, Communism was proposing an alternative to a society based on profit and competition. The appeal of the Marxist analysis for anyone seriously concerned with social justice and economic democracy cannot be underestimated. Bethune chose the most radical trend and joined the Communist Party of Canada in November 1935. The party was then embarking on its United Front period, calling on a broad coalition to oppose fascism. It was a most propitious time to join.

Bethune was not sectarian, and at the urging of a CCF member from the Verdun YMCA he opened a clinic for the unemployed in Pointe-St-Charles. He became increasingly interested in health care and soon presented to his friends a model city for tuberculosis patients, complete with clinics, therapy, recreation and rehabilitation centres. In a period of financial restraint, such a utopian project did not gather much support.

Starting in the fall of 1935, Bethune lived in a state of high effervescence. He presented papers at professional conferences, particularly on health care in the Soviet Union; attended party meetings; set up art classes for children with his artist friends Fritz Brandtner and Marion Scott; painted and wrote poetry; kept up his clinic for the unemployed; and started meeting with other health professionals to study health care systems in various countries. What began as a study group composed of doctors, nurses, social workers and a dentist soon turned to a concrete project: to develop a blueprint for socialized medicine in Quebec and present it to doctors, politicians and candidates in the upcoming provincial election of August 1936.

What was known until then as the Bethune Group had to find a name. Not to frighten people, the title avoided the word socialized or socialist and settled for "the Montreal Group for the Security of the People's Health," with Norman Bethune as secretary. State responsibility in social welfare was then very limited. Institutions could get government subsidies for their destitute patients; state-supported public health units took care of vaccination, contagious diseases and sanitation; and just two months before the election the city of Montreal set up a medical relief committee for the unemployed.

The Montreal Group proposed a variety of medical plans. One was municipal medicine accessible to everyone, with an expansion of the public health units to include doctors, nurses and dentists on salary working on preventing and curing diseases. Compulsory health insurance constituted a second plan, and voluntary health and hospital insurance was a third. A fourth plan was to cover only the unemployed for the whole province. Although the press commented favourably, the plans were ignored by politicians, and after the election of Maurice Duplessis's Union Nationale government, an increasingly disillusioned Bethune became more concerned with the march of fascism in Spain.

The chaos of the Depression, the ideal of collective care and the rise of fascism galvanized Norman Bethune and propelled him onto the world stage, from the Canadian Blood Transfusion Unit in Spain with Hazen Sise in 1936–37 to the International Peace Hospital on the Shansi border behind the Japanese lines in 1938–39 where, having cut himself with his scalpel, he died of blood poisoning for lack of proper medication.

While the Depression left many bewildered, it drove Bethune to action. As the flamboyant Montreal surgeon, the ambulance driver on the Guadalajara Front, or the emaciated doctor with his makeshift operating table in the midst of a guerrilla army, Bethune was always characterized by a passionate temper, a sense of justice, and the capacity to engage in action for a collective cause. Unlike W.H. Auden's disillusioned drinker, "uncertain and afraid," Bethune was assured and unafraid, and did not see "the clever hopes expire of a low dishonest decade."

Historian **Andrée Lévesque**'s publications have focused on the 1930s and the left in Quebec, among other subjects.

Grey Owl's Masquerade for Conservation

by Donald B. Smith

Grey Owl

The tall, hawk-faced man stood proudly before his audience of nearly 3,000 in Toronto's Massey Hall on March 26, 1938, the final stop in a six-month lecture tour of Britain, Canada and the United States. Since October 1937 he had addressed more than a quarter of a million people, including the Royal Family in a command performance at Buckingham Palace. Grey Owl, the "Modern Hiawatha," spoke of the north, of its forests and animals, and of his people, the North American Indians.

Through his four books, his lectures and his half-dozen films with the beaver, Grey Owl had become one of the best known Canadians of the day. When he spoke in Toronto in 1936, the event's organizers estimated that 800 people would attend his talk in the King Edward Hotel's Crystal Ballroom. Instead 1,700 crowded in, and another 500 had to be turned away.

Grey Owl published his first book, *Men of the Last Frontier*, a collection of tales in honour of the life of the "wilderness man," in 1931. *Pilgrims of the Wild*, which appeared three years later, became a runaway bestseller. In *Pilgrims* he told of his transformation from trapper to conservationist. He completed it and his subsequent two books, *The Adventures of Sajo and Her Beaver People* (1935) and *Tales of an Empty Cabin* (1936) at Prince Albert National Park in Saskatchewan, where he looked after a beaver conservation program. He lived at Beaver Lodge, a small cabin at best six by seven metres in extent. The beaver had built their lodge outside, and partially inside, his home, appropriating a quarter of his living space.

Who was Grey Owl? In *The Canadian Who's Who* of 1936–37, Sir Charles G.D. Roberts, one of Canada's most distinguished literary figures, obtained and printed Grey Owl's full story. The entry reads: "Born encampment, State of Sonora, Mexico; son of George, a native of Scotland, and Kathrine (Cochise) Belaney; a half-breed Apache Indian...adopted as blood-brother by Ojibway tribe, 1920...speaks Ojibway but has forgotten Apache."

Grey Owl gave one of the best talks of his career that evening at Massey Hall. The overriding theme throughout his lectures was simple: "Remember you belong to Nature, not it to you." For more than six months he had devoted all of his physical and emotional strength to his crusade for conservation. He returned to Beaver Lodge in early April 1938, totally exhausted and run down. Only three days later he had to be rushed to hospital, and he died in Prince Albert on April 13. Then came the bombshell.

Swift detective work on both sides of the Atlantic in the week after his death allowed reporters to discover Grey Owl's real identity. Canada's most popular Indian was really one Archie Belaney, born and raised in Hastings, England, who had left home in 1906 at the age of seventeen to live in northern Canada. Belaney had so admired the Indians for their ability to live in the wilderness that he created a new identity for himself in Canada as a North American Indian. Although taken by surprise, few Canadian newspapers condemned him for his masquerade. They recognized his attainments as a writer and a spokesperson for conservation.

A new generation of readers discovered his books in the 1960s and 1970s when the environment became a popular concern. In 1988 Edwin and Margery Wilder, an American couple, became so influenced by Grey Owl's conservationist philosophy that they donated $750,000 to ensure the preservation of Beaver Lodge and the wilderness canoe routes in Prince Albert National Park.

Donald B. Smith is the author of *From the Land of Shadows: The Making of Grey Owl* (1990).

The Soviet Union's Literary Underground

by Ioan Davies

Intellectuals in the USSR lived out the thirties by a series of stratagems. "Every day I find it harder to breathe," wrote the Leningrad-born Jewish poet Osip Mandelshtam in 1930. He had been denied living quarters in Leningrad by a literary party functionary who declared that "Mandelshtam shall not live in Leningrad because we won't give him a room." His transition to Moscow ("stagnant, sterile, Stalinized") and thence to Voronezh in south-central Russia marked the beginning of Soviet *samizdat* or underground publishing, though in Mandelshtam's case the poetry was spoken aloud and transmitted from memory by his wife Nadezhda and other friends.

Mandelshtam's poem on Stalin ("He rolls the executions on his tongue like berries") and his parables based on Egyptian motifs ("Thinks with bone, feels with forehead/Strives to recall its human image") conditioned his final sentence to a concentration camp in 1938, and hence his death. Thanks to the Writers' Union, which the Stalinist bureaucracy had established in 1932 as both a home for compliant writers and a monitor of deviance, Mandelshtam's reputation was henceforth entirely in *samizdat*.

Anna Akhmatova, another poet who was harassed by the bureaucracy ("One Lesson we shall not forget/Blood smells of blood alone") had no poetry published officially in Russia between 1923 and 1940, though the first poem of her cycle on Soviet terror, *Requiem*, was distributed in *samizdat* in 1934. (The complete poems were published in Munich in 1963.) Isaak Babel, whose major stories, written as a cavalry officer in the 1920s, were hailed by Maxim Gorky (novelist, Stalin's literary adviser and apologist for the gulags) and others as the very stuff of the new Soviet literature, silenced himself after 1930 when he was denounced as a renegade, and wrote virtually nothing until his death in a gulag in 1940. Even after his "rehabilitation" in the 1950s, his work appeared only in *samizdat*.

Boris Pasternak, who in 1958 would win the Nobel Prize for literature and be obliged to turn it down, and Mikhail Bakhtin, the most important Russian literary critic of this century, present, in many ways, the ultimate

Boris Pasternak

symbols of the 1930s. Though they both survived into the post-Stalin era, they did so at great cost. Both struggled to make sense of the period through camouflage. Throughout the 1930s Pasternak turned his talents to translation (Goethe, Shelley, Byron, Keats and especially Shakespeare) and spreading rumors about conversations with Stalin that never took place. Only later did the *Hamlet Poems* and *Doctor Zhivago* appear, but both in *samizdat* and in editions published abroad.

Bakhtin, writing on Dostoevski, Rabelais, Freud and Goethe, and also probably under the names of some of his students, produced a corpus of work that created something of an underground university in Russia, where *samizdat* and books that were officially issued and then instantly withdrawn from circulation created a carnivalesque theoretical alternative to the bludgeoning of Stalinist imperial ideology. Only after the 1960s has his work been available in the West.

With the collapse of Communism in Russia, these authors should have enjoyed their finest hour. But alas, apart from a few brief months in the late eighties and early nineties, none of them was available in Russia at the time of writing in 1992. The idea that the Russian intelligentsia should be seen as the hidden voice of God, the invisible government, was shown as something of a fraud. The Bakhtin Centre in Moscow, having been denied any government support, was appealing for money to finally publish Bakhtin's complete works. The works of Mandelshtam, Babel and Pasternak had not been around for months. According to many Russians, the 1990s are the 1930s all over again. The twin terrors of the 1930s—an economic blind alley coupled with Slavic revanchism—were with us again. This time, however, the blind alley was an unbridled market economy, while Slavic fascism waited in the wings. The only *samizdat* was pornography.

The real problem is that Stalin effectively put his boot into any sense of cultural continuity. The ongoing discourse among the different segments of Russian society was frozen by a few, decisive chops. As the institutions (the theatres, the museums, the Academies of Science, the publishing houses, the film industry) that struggled to maintain continuity, in however constricted a form, were dismantled or strapped for funds, it was difficult for Russians to know what constituted a tradition. Nor could a new *samizdat* emerge, because it was unclear what tradition it would draw on, or indeed what was the opposition.

One of the most literate societies in the world (at least Stalin achieved that!) should, at worst, have had access to my library, where many Russians sit alphabetically beside one another, displaying a richness of Russian culture that is available in Russia itself only in decaying memories. Akhmatova sits next to Akhmadula; Bakhtin next to Babel, Blok, Biely and Berda'ev;

Gorky next to Gumilev, Gogol and Gellman; Marx next to Mandelshtam and Malevich; Pushkin next to Paustovsky and Pasternak, Trotsky next to Tolstoy, Tolstaya and Turgenev. Either in *samizdat* or in the sanctioned press they should all have been available. The tragedy was that the debate that might take place among all these divergent views of Russian society and culture was happening not in Russia but in North American universities. In Russia, simply listing those names read like a litany of the dead.

Ioan Davies is the author of *Writers in Prison* (1990).

Guernica: Icon of the Century

by Peter Larisey

The thirties were a troubled, darkening decade, lurching towards explosion. Each year created new horrors, new attacks on commonly held feelings for human life, and hinted at worse. But no event before the opening of the Second World War so outraged and dismayed the world as the deliberate bombing and strafing of the civilian population of the small Spanish Basque town of Guernica on April 26, 1937. The agents were Hitler's war planes; their commander and strategist was General Francisco Franco, leader of the fascist Falangist party of Spain.

Pablo Picasso, by 1937 already an internationally famous artist, belonged to Franco's Republican opponents, who for a while governed Spain. In 1936 this government had appointed Picasso the director of Madrid's Prado Museum, and in January 1937 it asked him to paint a mural for the Spanish Pavilion at the Paris World's Fair, scheduled to open in June. With the bombing of Guernica, Picasso had the subject of his mural.

Guernica is perhaps the best known painting of our century, transcending the event it commemorates and its decade. But it does not transcend human suffering. Picasso's capacity for deep feeling, his stylistic innovations, his contemplative renditions of violence in bullfights, his sensual depictions of lovemaking—all these contributed to the power of this vast, near-colourless painting. To interpret the destruction of morality in his *Guernica*, Picasso had to destroy painting as well. Gone are colours, even of blood. Gone are beauty of form, realism of space, pride in subtle techniques. What is left is a subjective and perhaps universal image that embodies the horror and chaos of the experience of extreme suffering.

Amid all the distortions of shapes, we see highly sensitive parts of bodies articulated: palms of hands and soles of feet; open, screaming mouths with their daggerlike, misshapen tongues; the erect nipples of two of the women. The figures also suffer from claustrophobia in this all but spaceless world. The twisting body of the horse, collapsing from a spear through its body, is about to crush the dying man sprawled on the ground; under the

impassive head of the bull, the screaming woman experiences the limpness of her dead infant.

The emotional power of the distortions and the reminders of sensual pain help us to experience these sufferings. Perhaps the impact of *Guernica* has something to do with the prolonged grieving we experience as we count off the subsequent deliberate military targetings of civilians: London and Coventry; Stalingrad and Dresden; Hiroshima and Nagasaki; the villages of Vietnam and Cambodia; and now the wreckage of what was Yugoslavia. Guernica was only the first. Through Picasso's outrage and pain, we are linked to the horrors of the darkness we struggle against.

Pablo Picasso (1881–1973), *Guernica*, 1937. Oil on canvas, 3.4 x 7.8 m. Madrid, Museo Reina Sofía. © Succession Pablo Picasso/SODRAC (Montreal) 1999

Art historian **Peter Larisey** teaches about art and religion at Regis College in Toronto and is the author of *Light for a Cold Land: Lawren Harris's Work and Life—an Interpretation* (1993). He was an associate editor of *Compass* from 1992 to 1997 and subsequently secretary of the Compass Foundation.

The Forties

DND/PL144274

171 **The Second World War's Long Shadow** by Robert Chodos

173 **Are We Losing Sight of the Trees?** by Gil Drolet

176 **The Lasting Trauma of the Holocaust** by Michael Lerner

180 **The Atomic Bomb: Face to Face
with Infinite Destruction** by Robert Jay Lifton

184 **Connections to the War Still Vibrate** by Brian McKenna

189 **Country Girl at Intelligence HQ** by Imogen Ryan

192 **In the Movies, Even Lassie Went to War** by Marc Gervais

196 **In Canada, a Legacy of Welfare and Political Division** by Eric Kierans

200 **An Ambiguous International Role for Canada** by Denis Smith

204 **Postwar Social Life Stressed Conformity** by Mary Louise Adams

208 **Alfred Pellan and the Quebec Painters' Quiet Revolution** by Malcolm Reid

The Second World War's Long Shadow

by Robert Chodos

Although I was born two years after the end of the Second World War, as a young child I was not fully convinced that the war was over. Radio bulletins from Korea, one of my earliest memories of the outside world, were one source of confusion: to a four-year-old, war was war, and it was easy to confound this faraway conflict with the bigger war grownups never seemed to stop talking about. More broadly, the war didn't appear to be over because the shadow cast by the events of 1939–45 was omnipresent in those early postwar years.

The shadow has not completely lifted even today. Brian McKenna evokes the extent to which deeply embedded memories of the war still affect us. And the effort to shape the postwar world in the half-decade after 1945 created the context for events that are still the stuff of newspaper headlines in the 1990s. The steps towards reconciliation between Israelis and Palestinians in this decade are an attempt to deal with an injustice that arose out of the establishment of the state of Israel in 1948. That same year, the election of the National Party in South Africa set the stage for the institutionalization of the apartheid system that has been dramatically dismantled in the nineties. The threat of nuclear proliferation? The role of the United Nations in collective security? Moves towards European unity? International monetary instability? Free trade? While all these issues have antecedents that go back centuries, their modern history begins in the 1940s.

In Canada too, issues that run through our history start to take on their current form in the 1940s. As Eric Kierans argues, it was the federal government's attempt to establish the agenda for postwar Canada in 1945–46, and provincial governments' resistance to that attempt, that set in motion a sequence of constitutional disputes to which there is still no end in sight. It was also in the immediate postwar period that Canada seriously embarked on a course of economic integration with the United States, whose implications we continue to grapple with. Economic growth and migration from both the countryside and city cores to the burgeoning suburbs created a new framework for daily life, described here by Mary Louise Adams. And the physical shape of Canada itself was established in 1949, as Prime Minister Louis Saint-Laurent helped solve a British colonial problem by welcoming a somewhat hesitant Newfoundland.

For myself as a Jew, to be born in 1947 meant to begin life at the crux of the modern history of my people. The rich Jewish life of central and eastern Europe had been destroyed in the ghettos and gas ovens; we were about to experience a new beginning in our ancient homeland. Catholics had to wait another two decades for their own crucial turning point. The currents that would lead to the Second Vatican Council were already flowing in the work of theologians of the 1940s; however, they received no encouragement from the church's institutional leaders of the time.

In his introduction to the section on the 1930s, Martin Royackers notes that the problems of the Depression were solved by the outbreak of the Second World War, and hopes that the problems of our own decade will be subject to "a less drastic resolution." Indeed, the new methods of warmaking introduced in the 1940s have made that hope a necessity. We are again faced with the challenge of reshaping the world, but we cannot repeat the 1940s experience of tearing it all down and rebuilding it. Is there another way? That is perhaps the most urgent question that our contemplation of the 1940s poses to us.

Robert Chodos is president of the Compass Foundation and editor of the *Canadian Forum*. He was editor of *Compass* from 1987 to 1997.

Are We Losing Sight of the Trees?

by Gil Drolet

As the Second World War moves imperceptibly away from us in the rear-view mirror of passing time, many can no longer see the trees for the forest. Yet it is the trees that make up the forest, and for more than half a century a whole system of facts and beliefs has been scrutinized by pundits, not all of them well-informed or well-intentioned, with the result that villains and heroes have changed places in the minds of an increasingly susceptible public perversely attracted to the cynicism of those bent on finding fault even when it means inventing it.

No doubt the Nuremberg trials dispensed a victor's justice, and the Russian presence was an embarrassment in the light of their own "crimes against humanity" and their politically motivated deviousness (evidenced in their blaming the Germans for the murder of 15,000 Polish officers in Katyn Forest when—as came out after the dissolution of the Soviet Union—they in fact had done the deed). No doubt the United States and Canada revealed a reprehensible paranoia in interning their citizens of Japanese ancestry immediately following Pearl Harbor. Once again the "yellow peril" brought forth white racism, as those of German or Italian extraction were allowed their freedom provided local security forces were assured of their loyalty.

And it is true that war assumes its own Hegelian-Darwinian imperative, that it becomes a "driverless train" carrying its passengers to a fate beyond the control of any human agency, and that therefore it is difficult to write about it without vitiating its impact on the individual and society. But the consensus emerging from the historiography of the Second World War is that it was a struggle against the virulent evil of Hitler's Germany and Japan's brutal expansionism. Dwight Eisenhower called his memoir *Crusade in Europe* and, in a sense, that is what the war was.

In another sense, Kurt Vonnegut, a survivor of the bombing of Dresden (where he was held as an American POW), was also right when he subtitled his *Slaughterhouse Five* the "Children's Crusade," for once again it

Hermann Göring, Rudolf Hess and Joachim von Ribbentrop at the Nuremburg Trials.

was the young men who had to do the fighting though the dying was certainly not limited to them. In 1914–18, 5 per cent of fatalities were civilians; more than 50 per cent were civilians twenty-five years later. This fact forces on us the uncomfortable admission succinctly described by Lecomte du Nouy concerning saturation bombing: "The most heinous crime of the totalitarian states was to impose on Western civilization this dilemma: to refrain from borrowing their methods of warfare and resign themselves to extinction, or to use them and revert to brutishness."

Regrettably, we have increasingly been exposed of late to the quodlibets of charlatans whose powers of persuasion are enhanced by the medium of television and film so that there is a blurring of truth that bears out Orwell's prophecies. These "experts" enjoy a popularity that is as insidious as it is undeserved. The problem is compounded by the fact that the general public watches and listens much more than it reads, and even those who do read must practise great discernment for good history flows from the quality of the author's data, methodology and, above all, ethics.

Verifiable cataclysms are now said never to have taken place while oppressors and those they oppressed are made to share the scales of victimization equally. This was demonstrated in Berlin on the National Day of Mourning in November 1993, when the *Neue Wache* memorial was rededicated and the victims of fascism were derided by linking them to those responsible for it.

In 1945, the Germans indulged in limitless self-pity, and their perceptible refusal to accept responsibility for the barbarity of the Third Reich spawned a revisionism that is now enjoying unwarranted acceptance all over the world. In 1974, the prominent historian Ernst Nolte wrote a massive and sophisticated apology for modern Germany that sought to humanize Nazism's misdeeds by comparing them with the crimes of others. This same agenda provided the foundation for his *Die Vergangeheit die nicht vergehen wird* (The past that will never go away), which gave birth to the "Historians' Dispute" of 1986–87, in which the "so-called annihilation of the Jews" was relativized with the claim that the "gulag" antedated Auschwitz and that Bolshevik "class murder" was the antecedent of Nazi "race murder."

Such insensitivity is not limited to contemporary Germans. Ronald Reagan's visit as U.S. president to the *Soldatenfriedhof* at Bitburg where SS men are buried, despite the pleas of Holocaust survivors, showed callous contempt for innocent victims. His visit to Bergen-Belsen, as an afterthought, hardly helped matters.

In England, David Irving's brand of "history" makes him a worthy successor to Sir Oswald Mosley and his British Union of Fascists. In Canada, Holocaust deniers such as Jim Keegstra and Ernst Zundel follow in the footsteps of Adrien Arcand and his pro-Nazi Parti National Social Chrétien. In France, the United States and elsewhere, the ghosts of fascists past have not been laid to rest and have found their contemporary seconders.

All manner of absurdities have cropped up since 1945 and we are increasingly victims of convenient moral relativism. We have seen Klaus Barbie, member of the master race, Butcher of Lyon, killer of Jews and torturer of *résistants*, being defended by a black man, an Arab, a Bolivian and an Asian, all of whom would have been candidates for Zyklon-B in the 1940s. I have also heard a Canadian history teacher in a prominent English-Catholic high school admit that Hitler had burned "a few Jews," and I read some time ago about a young university student in the United States wearing a T-shirt proclaiming that "Belsen was a gas!" Moral relativism leads to comparative trivialization, which in turn leads to insensitivity to the historical record. With the passage of time, history is being distorted and denied.

Gil Drolet taught literature at the Collège Militaire Royal in Saint-Jean, Quebec.

The Lasting Trauma of the Holocaust

by Michael Lerner

Six million Jews were murdered by the Nazis in the 1940s. But the most important lessons of the Holocaust come from looking not at the forties but at the thirties and earlier, and from asking the question: What made it possible in the first place? In the immediate sense, what made it possible was the triumph of fascism throughout Europe. So the question gets thrown further back: Why did fascism triumph? And to answer that question it is necessary to look at the painful transition to the modern world.

Although the free marketplace offered people an opportunity to advance economically, it simultaneously undermined traditional forms of support and ways of life that had provided a degree of stability and continuity. So not everyone welcomed the triumph of the marketplace over feudal economies. Many people suffered considerable dislocation, not only physically but also psychologically, and those people tended to idealize some previously existing circumstance in which there had been a greater degree of family and community support and institutions, most importantly the church, that had provided some degree of caring. To some extent this was an idealization of the past, and it papered over the degree to which the feudal order itself had been oppressive. But as the bourgeois revolution developed in Europe, it became clearer and clearer, at least to the less successful sectors of the population, that this revolution was a mixed blessing at best.

These sectors of the population saw the Jews as one of the main elements in the triumph of the marketplace. Jews were unequivocally on the side of the bourgeois revolution and the disintegration of older feudal ties, which were deeply enmeshed in Catholic and Protestant antisemitism. For Jews, the old order had produced a life in which they felt constantly at the mercy of mobs stirred up by local clergy every Good Friday. Whatever its problems, the new order seemed to offer them equality and, in its most secular form, anonymity. If the new order could eliminate religion from the public sphere, then Jews would not be subject to any special restrictions. But many non-Jews felt that the absence of any ethical or religious or spiritual values in public life was creating a situation in which there was no barrier between them and the most severely exploitative aspects of the capitalist market. And so non-Jews were very resentful of the weakening of national or religious forms in society, and they saw the Jews as an important element in fostering these tendencies.

In a society that was being emptied of any meaning and purpose, regimes based on authority and fear came forward and said, "We can provide you with a sense of meaning and purpose by connecting you with the most reactionary forms of nationalism or the most reactionary forms of religion." The socialist left, meanwhile, did not understand that people craved a sense of meaning and purpose. All the left offered, in essence, was a better deal in the market. It pooh-poohed issues of meaning and purpose, so that people were attracted to the right.

The leap from support for reactionary and authoritarian regimes out of a sense of spiritual and psychological dislocation to mass murder is not as great as it might appear. There is an enormous amount of rage and anger in people, even in American society today, and all the more so in societies where economic conditions have been degraded as well as spiritual conditions. American society deals with its rage in a number of ways: a very high level of consumption of drugs and alcohol, and television, another drug that works to keep rage and pain contained. Not all societies have such effective forms of suppression of rage.

In addition, the Holocaust took place in the midst of a war, so that death and killing were in the air. Another factor was the long history in Europe of murdering Jews, largely attributable to Christian antisemitism. For centuries Christian churches had been teaching terrible things about the Jewish people, inculcating hatred of Jews in the population, and carrying out that teaching by promoting restrictions on Jewish rights. Over those centuries the church's language of love had very little to do with its actual practice. To be sure, there were constant attempts to renew the church and get it back to its original loving and caring message. But the church was not a force whose main impact was bringing people to a higher level of love and caring and sensitivity to neighbour. And insofar as it did, it never extended that love and caring to the Jews, who were to be at best tolerated and at worst oppressed.

That the church's legacy of hate towards Jews persisted was demonstrated by the virtual absence of any serious stand against Nazi antisemitism by people in the organized church. There was no debate throughout the church in Europe about whether to take such a stand. There was no European-wide movement, say, to call together a conference in 1937 of all pro-Jewish Catholics to figure out how to fight antisemitism. There was no organization of Catholics comparable to the organization of religious Jews in Israel today who are opposed to the dominant position towards the Palestinians.

To prevent something like the Holocaust from happening again, it is important to understand that people who are drawn to reactionary nationalism or fascism or reactionary forms of religion are not evil people, but they have legitimate needs that market society cannot fulfil and that the left does not try to fulfil. So they go to the right because they are looking for some framework of meaning and purpose, some way of dealing with the dislocations of the capitalist world and connecting to a community that has been undermined by the dynamics of the market. To head off fascism in the future, the task is to recreate alternative forms of community and of meaning and purpose that do not require reactionary, racist, sexist and homophobic connections.

However, these are not the main lessons that have been drawn from the Holocaust. Instead of focusing on the reasons why the Holocaust happened, the Jewish world has focused on the end product. One kind of reaction this has produced has been theological. Any notion that there is a God who intervenes in history or indeed that there is a God at all has been put into severe question. The conclusion that has been drawn from the Holocaust about the difficulty of sustaining religious faith has caused tremendous trauma for many Jews.

Another main approach has focused not on God but on humanity, saying that what we learn from the Holocaust is that the fantasies of the Enlightenment have been shown to be fatally flawed: all of the theories about human perfectibility and progress have been disproved. In this view, there is an inherent evil in the world that is much more powerful than we had ever been willing to believe. In particular, the views of left-wing optimists that manifested themselves either in liberal or in socialist movements have all been falsified by reality.

Others have argued that nobody who believed in human perfectibility maintained that it would happen by 1939 or that there would not be any struggle involved in human transformation towards the good. Furthermore, if the triumph of the Nazis is to be attributed to the forces of evil and lack of progress, then how does one account for the defeat of the Nazis by Communists and by the West? Perhaps that outcome actually represented a triumph of the Enlightenment, whose ideals were upheld by the West and often explicitly repudiated by Nazi Germany.

These are the kinds of arguments that go on in the Jewish world, and it has been the more pessimistic views that have triumphed, even though the arguments don't necessarily lead to their triumph. "What we've learned," many Jews have concluded, "is that we can rely only on force. We can't rely on God, we can't rely on human ideals, we can't rely on brotherhood or sisterhood. The nations of the world turned their backs on us and betrayed us and so we have no option but to focus inward, to repudiate all of the internationalist and other-regarding tendencies in Jewish consciousness, and instead to focus entirely on our own needs. We must protect our own interests, understanding that nobody else will, and make ourselves as strong as possible."

In the state of Israel, which came into being in the wake of the Holocaust in 1948, these arguments were used by, and gave credence to, the political right. They were invoked from the start by the right-wing leader Menachem Begin, but he remained a rather peripheral figure until the Six-Day War in 1967, when the Jewish people felt the trauma of the possible destruction of Israel and a new destruction of Jews. After 1967, more people began to pay attention to Begin, and by 1977 he was elected prime minister. In regard to Palestinians, who were seen as the further embodiment of the Nazis, these ideas became a justification for policies that were insensitive at best and immoral at worst. Similarly, it was after 1967 that these same ideas began to gain a foothold in American Jewry, where they became the dominant ideas by the end of the 1970s, resulting in an increasing sense that what was appropriate for Jews to do was to focus on their own interests at the expense of other-regarding energies and tendencies.

However, these ideas have a delusional character. Israel is a tiny little state that can't be strong in itself, so its strength depended on its relationship with the United States. As a result, Israel became a client state of the United States, doing dirty work for the United States around the world. This put Israel into the position of winning for itself the very enemies that it had feared it would have. A self-perpetuating cycle was set in motion in which Israel became more and more isolated by performing activities that it would not have engaged in had it not been traumatized by the Holocaust. Had it been able to look at its own objective interests in terms of what it was facing directly, it would have been able to work out a much more rational position for itself in the Middle East.

With the mutual recognition agreement between Israel and the Palestine Liberation Organization in September 1993, we caught a glimpse of an Israel, and a Jewish people, that are no longer traumatized by the Holocaust. At the time of writing the peace process was stalled, Israel had reverted to older patterns of behaviour, and the promise of that moment remained unfulfilled. Nevertheless, an Israel that no longer feels it has to be strong and self-interested to the exclusion of older and deeper Jewish values is now, finally, a real possibility.

Rabbi Michael Lerner is editor of *Tikkun* magazine, a bimonthly Jewish critique of politics, culture and society published in New York and San Francisco. This article is taken from an interview conducted in New York in December 1993.

The Atomic Bomb: Face to Face
with Infinite Destruction

by Robert Jay Lifton

W hen American planes dropped nuclear bombs on the Japanese cities of Hiroshima and Nagasaki in August 1945, the world had to
confront the possibility of destruction without limit.

People exposed to the atomic bomb in Hiroshima and Nagasaki became involved in a lifelong immersion in death. This immersion took place
in various stages: the sea of death around them at the time of the bomb,
then the appearance of grotesque symptoms of acute radiation effects soon
afterwards, then the appearance of later radiation effects (various kinds of
leukemia, cancer and other fatal conditions) years or decades after the weapon was used, and finally the recognition that the effects of radiation can
extend to subsequent generations in ways that are still not fully understood.
Victims of the weapon had the sense that it kills on a newly massive scale
and that its effects can be sustained into infinity.

Being the victims of the first use of nuclear weapons also gave the people of Hiroshima the profoundly unsettling sense of being human guinea
pigs—not without reason, since the scientific and military impulse to find
out what this weapon that so much special effort had been put into making
would finally accomplish was one of the motivations for American deci-
sion-makers in using it.

But they were not to be the only human guinea pigs. In the early 1990s
it was revealed that the Soviet Union had released radiation on various
populations, particularly on soldiers whom they had march right into it, because they wanted to study battlefield effects of radiation. Americans shook
their heads sadly at this unscrupulous and immoral behaviour on the part of
an evil regime. And then a short time later they read about American authorities having done the very same thing. Just as nuclear weapons stand for
destruction on an infinite level, the release of radiation on one's own population suggests the infinite human evil associated with the weapons.

By about 1950, before the weapons were actually big enough or numerous enough to destroy the world, the end of the world was suggested in nuclear-related films: the weapon created a sense of ultimate destruction even before it could physically bring about that situation, although the reality would catch up soon enough. As a result of the bomb, every single conflict of any size in the world is potentially a total one and can potentially bring about the most extreme consequences.

During the first half of the twentieth century the technological escalation of killing was precipitous. The First World War remains virtually unmatched for direct mass slaughter, and it led Sigmund Freud to speculate about our capacity to destroy ourselves completely. But for most people, the idea of total destruction was a post-bomb image. From the introduction of atomic bombs and their use, the idea of the world coming to an end, of our destroying ourselves with our own technology, became the property of everyone.

Radiation, the grotesque dimension of the bomb that renders it radically different from other weapons, is a crucial dimension of its psychological effect. Films of the early fifties were very focused on the issue of radiation. A weapon that can destroy on a scale a thousand times greater than previous weapons may be horrible to imagine, but somehow the human mind can take it in as still within the same discourse. Radiation effects, however, add a more than natural dimension: the idea of leaving behind in your bones a deadly substance that can strike you down and kill you at any moment unpredictably. The existence of this dimension was revealed in the grotesque symptoms that radiation caused in people exposed not only to the atomic bombs but also to nuclear accidents, to the making of the weapons, or to the intentional release of radiation into the atmosphere by our own authorities.

Once the bomb was developed, it would have taken great courage and foresight not to have used it in wartime. Indeed, it is sometimes claimed that there was an advantage in using it: we can appreciate its destructiveness in a way that we could not without its having been used. That is a serious argument that can't be lightly dismissed. But I must reject the argument and devoutly wish that the bomb had not been used, because the use of the weapon released it from any taboo. The minority of scientists who opposed its use wanted to render it taboo because they recognized its revolutionary destructiveness. As it was, the bomb entered the world as a usable weapon, or to put it another way, the genocidal device became a usable weapon, rather than remaining a genocidal device and not being confused with a weapon.

It is also argued that use of the bomb actually saved lives because without it the United States would have had to invade Japan at a cost of up to a million lives. However, there seems little doubt that the war could have been brought to an end in a rather short time without any use of the weapons. The Japanese were suing for surrender in the months prior to the use of the bomb, and although there were struggles within the Japanese government about whether to surrender and under what conditions, there was a very powerful impulse towards it.

Nor is it clear where the estimates of the large number of lives that an invasion might have cost came from. The early figure put forward by the military was that an invasion might cost twenty or thirty thousand lives. Indeed, many have since pointed out that no invasion would have been necessary. So the war could well have been ended with a considerable saving of lives by not using the weapon.

Soon after Hiroshima, a cultural crisis occurred in the United States, characterized by a variety of fears: that others would use the weapons against *us*, and that the world wouldn't last very long. We in the United States dealt with that crisis by embracing the very agent of our terror, so that nuclear weapons became a pseudoreligion. We virtually deified them, with exaggerated dependence on them for maintaining the peace, saving the world, keeping the world going. This pattern of "nuclearism"—in both American and Soviet leaders—became a genocidal ideology, with significant parallels to Nazism: the misuse and distortion of science, the enlistment of scientists, and the creation of a potentially genocidal bureaucracy, genocidal institutions and bureaucratic momentum in which the threshold into genocide could be crossed at any time. Of course, nuclear weapons designers and strategists can be perfectly decent people, and they are not Nazis. However, otherwise decent people can readily become involved in genocide if they embrace a genocidal ideology or become socialized into a genocidal environment.

The role of nuclear weapons in preventing war since Hiroshima has been too uncritically assumed. We quickly forget the atmosphere during the Cold War, but it was a very dangerous era in which much of the warlike sentiment coming from both the United States and the Soviet Union emerged in conjunction with the nuclear buildup. With the weapons and the accompanying "deterrence" policy—which as a policy really meant the willingness on the part of either country to destroy the other, and the world into the bargain, as a response to a threat to national security—the world came close to nuclear war on at least four or five occasions.

One of the unfortunate byproducts of the end of the Cold War was a loss of appropriate responses to the danger of nuclear weapons. During the latter phases of the Cold War, as both American and Soviet leadership became increasingly irresponsible, nuclear fear intensified. My view of nuclear fear was never that it was something we should try to overcome. I saw nuclear fear, at least in adults, as a valuable response, more or less appropriate to the danger, so that it was a wrong and immoral use of psychiatrists and psychologists to diminish it. A better use was to diminish nuclear numbing and allow in the nuclear fear.

In the nineties we have had considerably less nuclear fear, as a study we did at the Center on Violence and Human Survival showed. We found that nuclear fear was becoming less a matter of awareness and more a background shadow, while fear of environmental destruction was becoming more prominent. At the same time, the danger posed by nuclear weapons has not diminished. It may be greater, because of less control over many of the weapons, the chaos in the former Soviet Union and the deeply intensified risk of nuclear proliferation. But we no longer have the advantage of an appropriate response to the weapons and to the danger that they actually represent.

Yet the end of the Cold War, despite all the chaos and pain and danger that have followed upon it, was a liberating and deeply desirable historical event. It permitted more minds to be free from distorting polarizations and to give thought to the real problems that exist in the world, which are formidable. There is a cast of mind now taking shape in all of us that I call the protean self, after Proteus, a Greek god who was many-sided and a shape-shifter. We are more fluid in our sense of self and we have the capacity for certain forms of imagination that allow for transformation, the avoidance of intellectual and moral dead ends, and transcendence of the narrow, self-defeating directions that we've been immersed in for too long.

The protean self has been produced by larger historical forces than the end of the Cold War: indeed, our late-twentieth-century technological capacity to annihilate ourselves as a species is one of those forces. But the end of the Cold War gives us a chance to put the protean self into more creative forms of expression and to move towards species consciousness, which means not just a lovely distant ideal but a nitty-gritty sense of ourselves as human beings related to all other human beings on the planet.

Psychiatrist **Robert Jay Lifton**'s books include *Death in Life: Survivors of Hiroshima* and *The Protean Self: Human Resilience in an Age of Fragmentation* (1993). This article is taken from an interview conducted in New York in December 1993.

Connections to the War Still Vibrate

by Brian McKenna

> *I am beginning to believe that we know everything, that all history, includ-*
> *ing the history of each family, is part of us, such that when we hear any se-*
> *cret revealed, a secret about a grandfather, or an uncle, or a secret about the*
> *battle of Dresden in 1945, our lives are made suddenly clearer to us, as the*
> *unnatural heaviness of an unspoken truth is dispersed. For perhaps we are*
> *like stones, our own history and the history of the world imbedded in us,*
> *we hold a sorrow deep within and cannot weep until that history is sung.*
> —Susan Griffin, *A Chorus of Stones*

O n August 9, 1945, within hours of my birth in Montreal, one of my grandfather's sisters was on the other side of the Pacific Ocean, about to be engulfed in an event so horrible that the full reality would be suppressed for decades.

Sister Regina McKenna of Montreal's Order of the Sacred Heart had been teaching at the order's convent school in Japan when war was de-clared. She and the other Canadian nuns were interned. That morning in 1945, the Japanese guards allowed her to climb a hill to gather grass for the camp cow. The hills encircled the city of Nagasaki. She described Nagasaki as Japan's largest Catholic city, and was always somehow reassured by the many church spires. On that clear August morning, she heard the approach of a single Allied aircraft. In a letter home on September 12, my Aunt Reggie, as the family called her, described what happened next:

> I think the approach of a solitary plane deceived the Japanese....I
> looked up to see if it were visible, but quickly decided that it
> would be wiser to hurry back to the camp....I began to run. I had
> gone only a few steps when suddenly there was a fearful explosion
> and everything was golden yellow. It seemed as though the sun
> had burst and I was lost in its midst....All the first day and night the
> mountains were on fire for miles and miles.

Two thirds of the population of Nagasaki are dead. The city itself is a mass of ruins. They are still burning the dead. The hospitals having been destroyed, the wounded are not properly attended to. Some patients apparently recover, then suddenly die from haemorrhages.

The imprint of that explosion was like the effect of a gigantic X-ray, left on her body and her mind for a lifetime. In the end it comes as no surprise that Aunt Reggie eventually succumbed to cancer. Her mind seemed deeply affected. Her friends said "she was never quite right" after experiencing that cataclysm. Now we can give it a name. After Vietnam it came to be known as post-traumatic stress syndrome. Three out of four people who experience war first-hand suffer from it. After the Second World War this syndrome was given no name, and in most cases no treatment was offered.

From my earliest days, I was aware of that letter from my great aunt. The family treated it as an heirloom. But despite its power and the coincidence of my birth, I did not believe it was connected to my life as a student, son and brother—nor, later, as a husband and father, journalist and filmmaker. But sometimes if you don't take the first hint, there are others.

On Remembrance Day 1987, I visited the cenotaph in Westmount, the Montreal suburb where I lived at the time. I was with my family as silence fell on the eleventh hour of the eleventh day of the eleventh month, marking the armistice that ended the First World War and laid the ground for the second. When the Remembrance Day ceremony ended, my family and I approached the cenotaph and saw engraved on a stone tablet, among many others, the name Adrian Harold McKenna. I had heard vague stories of long-dead Westmount relatives, but when my daughter Robin ran her twelve-year-old fingers over the name and asked exactly how we were related and how Adrian died, I couldn't answer. So we started digging, and in uncovering the story took one step into a new type of war reporting.

Our search took us to the Ottawa government office of National Personnel Records. There, amid hundreds of thousands of files on every man and woman who has served Canada through all its wars, was a dossier on Adrian Harold McKenna. He turned out to be my grandfather's—and my Aunt Reggie's—younger brother.

Official forms in the file told how when he signed up to go to war, Adrian McKenna lived on a certain street in Westmount. Two generations later I had unknowingly moved to the same one-block street. He had graduated from Loyola College at the age of twenty-one. So had I. The documents showed that he joined a Montreal regiment and was shipped to France in 1915 to fight Germany in the Great War. The war diary of Adrian's battalion describes how early in the new year of 1916, while carrying shells across No Man's Land in the darkness, Corporal Adrian McKenna was hit. His chums tried to rescue him, but they were presumably pinned down by sniper fire from the German lines.

In 1988, after a long search through the Flemish countryside, my brother and I found the small Commonwealth Military Cemetery where Adrian is buried. It is called La Laiterie for a dairy that was once nearby. His plot, marked by a beautiful pale rose, lay at the back, beside an old wall of crumbling red brick. When Terry and I found Adrian's white headstone, engraved with the maple leaf and our family name, it was unexpectedly searing. In a space-time continuum, the shock was as if we had just opened one of those terrible telegrams to discover Adrian had been killed yesterday.

I tried to picture his death. They say in battle you fight first for the friends you have forged in war, the ones with whom you have drilled and fought and suffered. So he died first for his friends, for love. Emily Dickinson wrote that "flags vex a dying face," but it is my deep sense that Adrian also died for another kind of love, *pro patria*, for his country.

We continued a voyage into the dangerous landscape of the past, visiting the killing fields of the First World War. We became convinced that we should use our journalistic and film skills to communicate the story of those battles. Together we made a 100-minute documentary, *The Killing Ground*, the fruit of our effort to travel down the tunnel of years and discover the story of the 60,661 Canadians like Adrian who died in the Great War. When that project was completed, we turned our attention to the Second World War. We knew there would be controversy, but we had no inkling that it would become a bench-clearing brawl.

Again, we were determined to apply our experience covering war and revolution to a story fifty years old. We launched the investigation in the spirit of free historical inquiry, which is in the air everywhere, and sometimes embarrassing to the once-powerful. Three films, collectively entitled *The Valour and the Horror*, eventually took shape: the first on the 1941 battle of Hong Kong, the second on Bomber Command, and the third on Normandy.

In all three films we strove to present the kind of personal detail that makes military history come alive. Hong Kong, the subject of the first film, was Canada's first major battle of the Second World War. For nine days 2,000 green Canadian troops, thrown for political reasons into a situation for which they were totally unprepared, fought so bravely and so savagely that Thucydides should have been present to record their valour. Throughout the struggle, they also had to fight the incompetence and arrogance of the British command. A revealing story was told to me by Lionel Speller, a dispatch rider from Victoria, B.C., who was given the particularly perilous mission of racing through Japanese lines to deliver a crucial parcel to one of the British commanders. Speller watched transfixed as this colonel opened the package to reveal two tins of dog food for the officer's pet Scottie. When Speller began to question whether this was worth the risk he just took, he was threatened with a court-martial by this British officer.

The Valour and the Horror seized a huge audience and provoked an immense reaction. Though acclaimed as a "celebration of valour and a condemnation of war," the films also drew fierce attacks, especially from Canada's professional veterans' organizations. Upset at criticism of some generals, politicians and other wartime commanders, the veterans' groups successfully triggered an investigation by the Canadian Radio-television and Telecommunications Commission and, most theatrically, a series of hearings by the Senate. While the CRTC would ultimately reject the veterans' complaints, the Senate Subcommittee on Veterans Affairs forged ahead, claiming that the hearings were designed to provide a forum for deeply held grievances against the films and the filmmakers.

For me, one of the most memorable moments in the Senate hearings came during the testimony of Maurice Tugwell, president of the Mackenzie Institute for the Study of Terrorism, Revolution and Propaganda in Victoria, B.C. Tugwell described himself as a recent British immigrant, and his CV revealed that he was a newly retired British general. He told the committee that his long experience with terrorism, revolution and propaganda led him to conclude that this six-hour series on Canada in the Second World War was quite possibly an Irish Republican Army plot, produced "by Irish Catholic Canadians, perhaps loyal to the Republican cause.

"There seems no doubt that the McKennas are fighters," concluded Tugwell with a rhetorical flourish, "but would they fight for Canada?"

Tugwell's name rang a bell. Some years ago I did a film study on torture. The investigation took us to Northern Ireland, where the British army tortured a dozen men wrongly suspected of being members of the IRA. In January 1972, Maurice Tugwell was the senior operations officer responsible for "Bloody Sunday" in Derry, Northern Ireland. British army paratroops ambushed a Catholic civil rights march on January 30, 1972, shooting dead thirteen civilians who were unarmed—but Irish, Catholic and probably loyal to the Republican cause. None of them turned out to be IRA.

General Tugwell well symbolizes the caste of military officer who seeks to make official an interpretation of what happened in the Second World War that must not vary from the image created by British and Canadian propaganda films made in those years and for many years afterward. It is a simple picture. We wore white hats, were valorous, treated prisoners respectfully and fought always from the high moral ground. They wore black hats, were evil, took no prisoners and fought from an ethical sewer.

May I rise to the challenge and answer General Tugwell's question: Would we fight for Canada? I would first answer this way. By making these films, General Tugwell, we believe we are fighting for a Canada that one day will be free of your racist and ultimately fascist ideology. The second part of my answer to General Tugwell deals with the implicit question in his utterance. Would I take up arms to defend my country? This is a serious question at the end of the twentieth century.

St. Augustine and the *City of God* still provide the most compelling answer. As evil as is war ultimately, some foes are so evil that it is the greater good to fight. The Just War. That was clearly the case in the Second World War against the racist and totalitarian regimes that took power in Japan, Germany and fascist Italy. But a just cause does not justify everything done in its name.

Some critics of the films have accused us of what is called presentism —judging the leaders and policies of the Second World War by today's different standards—especially in our criticism of Bomber Command's deliberate bombing of German civilians.

I believe that what the Allied command did in Germany was wrong even by the standards of the time. The same questions we posed in *The Valour and the Horror* were asked then. But there is also a deeper question here, a question about what history is. To quote the brilliant English historian Edward Hallet Carr, "All history is contemporary history: History consists essentially in seeing the past through the eyes of the present and in the light of its problems." This is especially true of an event that remains as vividly alive in the minds of many Canadians, that cuts as close to the bone, as the Second World War.

Montreal-based filmmaker and journalist **Brian McKenna** won a 1992 Gemini Award for *The Valour and the Horror*, his series about the Second World War.

The past vibrates in the present, and if we understand from where the vibration comes, from what atomic explosion, from what festering psychic wound, then maybe we can, with our children's help, avoid the next wound and the final explosion.

Country Girl at Intelligence HQ

by Imogen Ryan

When the war broke out in 1939 I was twenty-one and in my final year of university, where I was reading modern languages: French and German with some Italian. Our home was nine miles from Harwich, Essex, where the Stour and Orwell rivers reach the sea, and where there was a naval base. Within a few days of returning home from university I enlisted in the Women's Royal Naval Service, the "Wrens."

The first job I had was on a "degaussing" range in the port. Degaussing was a process to demagnetize ships, making them less vulnerable to the magnetic mines that the enemy had started to lay. Once demagnetized, the vessels would pass over an electrical installation in the harbour that registered the ship's magnetic force, and this was photographed instantaneously on cameras installed in our office. The Wrens' specific job was to develop the photographs quickly and to report what adjustments were needed. It was not a very arduous task. We also made the tea and swept and tidied the place.

In the summer of 1940 the Wrens "Special Duties" category was set up, with the object of intercepting German radio telegraphing (R/T) traffic. After a short training course in how to pass on information quickly and accurately and in German procedures and naval vocabulary, I was posted back to Harwich. The R/T traffic that we kept watch for was mostly either from aircraft or from enemy torpedo boats, which would prey on the coastal convoys. As most convoys travelled at night with escorting vessels, most of the intercepted traffic was at night too, and we had to keep a twenty-four-hour watch. Once we had picked up the signs of this traffic beginning, we worked at speed: the listener taking down the conversations verbatim and another telephoning the signals through to the base (either in translation or in German) where the duty officer could contact the convoy escort and they could go into action.

That winter it was decided that some of the Special Duties Wrens should learn teleprinting so that people at different naval bases could get into instant contact about enemy activity in the area. I was sent back to

Greenwich on a fortnight's course. All this time I had never been issued with a uniform. I am very short and nothing small enough could be found. There was talk of having one made specially small, but nothing happened and I continued happily to wear my own clothes. Presumably the authorities had more pressing things to think about.

Nemesis, though, overtook me on that course in the form of Dame Vera Laughton Matthews, head of the WRNS. She visited Greenwich, and came to meet us all. She asked me why I was not properly dressed. I explained that everything was too big. She said nothing to me, but two weeks later I was fully kitted-out. Actually, wearing a uniform was no hardship, particularly when clothes rationing was brought in and civilian clothes in any tolerable shape or form were immensely hard to find and used a frightening number of one's precious coupons.

Next I was posted to the naval base at Plymouth to work the teleprinter next to the plotting room. There was no traffic there, however, because the western coastline and convoy routes were too long a trip for German motor torpedo boats based in France to be effective. As a result, as far as work was concerned, the chief excitement was comparing notes on the daily crossword. Excitement of a different kind came our way after we had been in Plymouth about a week. The Germans decided to bomb the place and within another week had reduced the centre of the town to heaps of rubble. Our quarters were not completely destroyed but were too unsafe to be used.

Eight months later I was posted to Norfolk, where I remained for the year. After two or three months in another quiet posting in Wales, I was posted to Bletchley Park, the government intelligence headquarters. This meant a complete change of work and of living conditions. Several thousand people worked at Bletchley: professors, mathematicians, chess players and civil servants, as well as members of all three armed forces. The Germans never learned that their "ULTRA" codes had been broken, and continued to use them up to the very end of the war. That an organization of such complexity, employing so many people, never let its secret be discovered seems almost miraculous.

With great foresight, the Wrens had taken the back half of Woburn Abbey as their living quarters. We were in the north-facing servants rooms, behind the parapet on the roof. Our bathrooms housed huge porcelain tubs fed by taps the size of hydrants, the lavatories had wallpaper covered with palm trees, and the petty officers' sitting room was the Duchess of Bedford's bedroom. Woburn was by far the grandest of our Wren quarters, but they were nearly all in beautiful and historic houses.

After a third training course in Greenwich, this time to become an officer, I returned to Bletchley and was delighted to be transferred to the research department in the Naval Section, where my knowledge of German was needed. The department existed largely to clarify the exact meaning of technical terms that appeared in German signals. We had a very good library of reference books and technical dictionaries to refer to on such subjects as gunnery, mechanical engineering, electricity, torpedoes, mines and so on.

A Third Officer's pay was £150 a year. We were free of living expenses, except for mess bills, and even transport to and from work was free. We were picked up by a station wagon, and the names of the four Wren drivers were Kitcat, Winterbotham, Pinecoffin and Westerdick. They were all charming.

The greatest source of enjoyment in working at Bletchley was in the people I met there. A lot of the most brilliant and senior were on another plane altogether, but the average level of intelligence and attainment was high, and this made for very good company indeed. Even at the time, I was conscious of how lucky I was to be there, living with people whose view of the world and understanding of events was opening my own mind. I was a pretty simple country girl, not very widely read, not particularly interested in current events, whose main loves were the countryside, nature and horses. Bletchley educated me and I never cease to be thankful for this.

Victory in Europe came in May 1945. I had been in the Wrens for five years. Rather than take secretarial training, which seemed to offer a life of being somebody else's personal assistant at the best, and something considerably more humdrum at the worst, I was now determined to train for a profession. I had made many lasting friendships, and perhaps it sounds unfeeling to say that I enjoyed life during such a terrible war when so many people were suffering horribly, but I did. What is saddening is that after five years of bloody conflict, during which six million Jews were slaughtered in concentration camps as part of a carefully planned campaign of genocide and countless millions of Russians as well as people in western Europe, the Far East and elsewhere suffered and died, we have not learned to live together more harmoniously or less determined to defend our own selfish interests.

After the war **Imogen Ryan** raised four children, and at the time of writing lived in Donhead St. Mary, Dorset, England.

In the Movies, Even Lassie Went to War

by Marc Gervais

It is the early 1940s, and the United States is genuinely part of the Second World War. All of Hollywood is mobilized for the war effort. There are of course the incomparable newsreels, the Frank Capra "Why We Fight" series and others, which Canadians, like everyone else, gobble up. Better still, John Grierson has established the National Film Board, which means that Canadians are allowed to see their own wonderful newsreels as well, along with NFB series of the magnitude of *Canada Carries On* and *The World in Action*. But for movies (those fiction works of the imagination), Washington and Ottawa have long decided that Canadians must turn to Hollywood. And we are only too glad to do so.

There is a little boy in Sherbrooke (myself) going to the Granada Theatre in the afternoon with his grandmother, learning about the war and, as a byproduct, about "America's" amazing superiority morally and in every other way. Even Lassie has joined the war effort and has cannily managed to find her way into Norway. Her master, Peter Lawford, a pilot, has been shot down and is trying to escape from the Nazi occupation forces. I can still thrill to the sight of Lassie streaking across the cliffs of the Norwegian fjords to the sound of Grieg's piano concerto, fooling the Nazis, saving Peter Lawford, and thereby guaranteeing the survival of civilization as we know it.

It is not, of course, always that simple and naïve and childlike. But it is consistently blatant and devastatingly effective. War releases certain mechanisms that seem to be inherent to people living in social groupings—call it the tribal mystique in all its manifestations, from the noblest to the most ignoble. Restraint, reason, decency—these have no place in the cultural war context. Xenophobic reflexes, always more or less latently there, find expression in the most outlandish, even surrealistic, incarnations. At the same time, an idealized, benign image of the home country is at least an underlying assumption, though generally it also finds some kind of overt and ritualized manifestation.

All of this appears most skilfully in the movie that has come to symbolize Hollywood in the forties: a romantic film noir called *Casablanca*. Undeniably sharp and witty, *Casablanca* unhappily also serves as an outstanding example of gross racial stereotyping. The arrogant, evil Nazi, the clever, lecherous Frenchman, the blustering, emotional Italian, the totally corrupt, oily "Arabs"—these are only a few in a long list. The Norwegians (Ilsa and the underground agent) and the east Europeans (the heroic Czech Victor and a young Bulgarian couple) come off rather nicely; but then, the film is directed by Michael Curtiz, one of Hollywood's "Hungarian Mafia."

Then there is Rick. He is rather sombre, and he may lead a somewhat shady life, but he *is* Humphrey Bogart and he *is* American—and therefore, deep down, eminently decent. Above all, he it is, in his manifest superiority, who determines each one's fate. That superiority reveals some well-accepted attitudes. Sam, the noble, wise, warm-hearted black man, is musical and knows his place, existing strictly in terms of Boss (Rick), and we love him for it. Ilsa is nothing short of breathtaking: never has Ingrid Bergman glowed so glowingly. She never complicates things by thinking for herself, by acting from her own convictions. Rick and Victor take care of that, and Ilsa does *her* job: she is *beautiful*, the heart companion for her men, the catalyst for male sacrifice and heroism.

Somehow, while other films undergo radical reappraisal, *Casablanca*, to all intents and purposes, continues to escape any serious analysis from today's politically correct standpoint. Maybe that is because, as Umberto Eco has pointed out, *Casablanca* is the most cliché-ridden good movie ever made, a veritable treasure trove of clichés, cinematic and otherwise, furnishing limitless delights for the contemporary postmodern sensibility. We cannot take it terribly seriously; instead we consciously exult in the cinematic self-referential game. It is fun, it touches us, but it is only a game of signs quite divorced from "reality" (assuming that such a reality does exist).

But that is today. In 1943, if there is a touch of that having-our-cake-and-eating-it-too sophistication in the response to *Casablanca*, it is surely minimal. The movie's context is the Second World War, and it is truly appealing to the heart, to romance, to sacrifice, to the cause, to an implied vision of America. Precisely because of all those clichés, it represents a most comfortable and reassuring "text," enriched (if that is the word) by a plethora of subtexts growing out of cultural attitudes many of which can be described as rather reprehensible.

So film noir, too, marches to the common Hollywood drumbeat. From its very roots (Germany), film noir stood for a dark incarnation of the human condition, growing out of psychological and social and even ontological pessimism. But now, thanks to wartime cultural simplification, these shadowy, ill-defined and elusive concerns are displaced, reduced to one source and one target, the hated Axis Powers. Do away with these patently evil forces and life will indeed be wonderful, as America is wonderful. Who needs existential anguish anyway?

It is interesting to note that when the outstanding incarnation of film noir in the forties, the Private Eye genre, turns inward on America, much of the menace is softened. For all their world-weary cynical talk, those "slumming angels" Philip Marlowe and Sam Spade are relative pussycats when stacked up against the semipsychotic thirties hoodlums played by James Cagney and Edward G. Robinson.

More sentiment, more softness, more romance—this is how Hollywood pictures America (or, by extension, some of its allies, particularly England) in the wartime forties. The brilliant and brittle comedies of manners of the thirties, for example, lose much of their edge; and the same can be said of musicals. Fred Astaire's sophistication and the relative toughness of Ginger Rogers and of those wisecracking chorus hoofers give way to the much lusher and more sentimental MGM offerings served up by the Arthur Free Unit: think of Gene Kelly, of Judy Garland, of those mellifluous MGM strings. And above all, in film after film, melodrama presents images of a Middle America eminently worth fighting for.

Anyone familiar with the Hollywood product of the forties knows how partial, in its attempt to capture what was specific to a certain cultural period, this bird's-eye view has been. To be sure, in this world-dominating industry, huge numbers of movies were churned out, many reflecting not the war but rather enduring Hollywood filmmaking patterns. Besides, there were some major *artistic* creations, free to explore, expand, extend well beyond the recipes—as art works will do. And so, in 1941, *Citizen Kane*, an extraordinary film that may well be the most overpraised movie of all time, became a testament to the genius and uncompromising individuality of its wonder-boy director, Orson Welles. These qualities, plus Welles's wild lack of discipline, would eventually exile him from Hollywood.

And there were other fine artists, none more eminent than those two relatively staid great masters who knew the secret of how to combine art and popular appeal, John Ford and Alfred Hitchcock. They continued to use Hollywood for their own ends, creating some of their finest work. Ford actually became a fifty-year-old war hero. But before he left for war he bequeathed us *The Grapes of Wrath* and *The Long Voyage Home*, and when he returned, he inaugurated the greatest period of the western with *My Darling Clementine, Fort Apache* and *She Wore A Yellow Ribbon*. Hitchcock, the Englishman ever true to himself and true to Hollywood, excelled with *Shadow of a Doubt* and *Notorious*, among many others.

I have been dealing mostly with the wartime forties, but postwar films witnessed no appreciable decline: one could compile lists of good, solid, popular movies. During this period, Hollywood was preeminent in every way, totally dominating the filmmaking world, and thereby further extending the cultural dominance of the American myth across the world. But these proved to be the last days of the Golden Era. And the dominant Hollywood myth, that of the American Dream, was coming to an end—and perhaps not only in Hollywood.

With the defeat of evil-over-there, Hollywood began to turn its critical eye on America. Racism began to be explored (*Crossfire, Pinky, Home of the Brave*). The hopes for peace and joy everafter turned cynical as the Cold War bred national paranoia: the Red Menace, and above all the reaction to it, testified to a rot from within. The Hollywood purges were beginning, setting the tone for the fifties.

As a matter of fact, everything in Hollywood seemed to be changing; and that in itself was threatening enough. With improved film stock and other advances, a legacy from the war, films—and not only westerns—were beginning to move out of doors, away from the mammoth sound stages of the big studios. The existence of the studio system itself was threatened by antitrust laws. The Hollywood quasimonopoly was also menaced, as films from the "outside world" began to appear: the French and especially the British were experiencing a renaissance, and Italian Neo-Realism was ushering in a whole new era in cultural filmmaking. And as if that were not enough, television and wide screens, those phenomena of the fifties that threw everything off balance, were just around the corner. An age of innocence that never was really innocent was coming to an end.

Marc Gervais teaches film in the communications department at Concordia University in Montreal. He was a member of *Compass*'s publishing policy committee in the 1980s and a contributing editor of *Compass* from 1993 to 1997.

In Canada, a Legacy of Welfare and Political Division

by Eric Kierans

Despite the suffering of the Depression and 20 per cent unemployment, the 1930s had been a period of "the less government, the better." Even such instruments of government economic intervention as were set up did not fully realize their potential until later. Thus the Bank of Canada, although established in 1934, could be considered an institution whose time had not yet come. Graham Towers, the first governor, did not believe in deficits or unnecessary expansion of the money supply (what he considered to be necessary was never made clear).

Meanwhile, the Royal Commission on Dominion-Provincial Relations (Rowell-Sirois), created in 1937 "to provide for a reexamination of the economic and financial basis of Confederation and of the distribution of legislative powers in the light of the economic and social developments of the last seventy years," did not present its report until May 1940.

With the outbreak of the Second World War, however, the federal government came alive and Canada suddenly became a command economy. There was no need to argue over goals or to determine priorities. There was only one objective—to win the war.

This objective defined the goods and services to be produced and determined the allocation of the country's human and material resources. Authority took over in the form of centralized decision-making and through direct price and wage controls organized the economy for all-out war. Individual freedom and civil liberties were limited, although not severely so. The hard part of economic policy, the fair distribution of incomes, was put on the back burner. After ten years of heavy unemployment, the easy availability of work made redistribution a nonissue.

Indeed, one could say that employment was over-full, with unemployment declining from 11.4 per cent in 1939 to 1.4 per cent in 1944 and averaging less than 3 per cent throughout the decade. Women joined the labour force in large numbers, retirees were called back, overtime increased and work itself had a purpose.

By 1944, the Gross National Product had more than doubled from $5.6 billion to $11.8 billion. The transformation of the Canadian economy from a state of continuing depression to a driving industrial powerhouse was as extraordinary as it was unexpected. Given the sluggish and unimaginative performance of governments in the thirties, few could have foreseen the virtually faultless performance of the war years.

On the fiscal side, there was no problem of demand. Government expenditures on goods and services rose year after year. The problem was money. How to pay for the war? There were three main sources: taxes, borrowing and cautious expansion of the money supply while a careful eye was kept on inflationary prices. Comparing 1939 to 1945, personal income taxes rose from $143 million to $938 million; corporate income taxes increased from $115 million to $599 million. As far as possible, it was pay as you go.

On the borrowing side, all-out campaigns for War Bonds and Victory Loans raised a net $12.5 billion from the savings of Canadians. The federal debt rose from $5.2 billion in 1940 to $16 billion in 1946, through bonds sold entirely in Canada. The wartime government even reduced the amount of public debt held by nonresidents from $1.3 billion to $1.1 billion during the same period. In financing the war effort, Canada depended on no one outside its borders. We were truly an independent country.

Meanwhile, a combination of the work of the Wartime Prices and Trade Board under Donald Gordon, Bank of Canada policy in keeping interest rates low, and exchange controls kept inflation to reasonable levels during the war years.

On the political front, however, relations between the federal and provincial governments deteriorated. Federal government expenditures on goods and services increased from $566 million in 1939 to $3.6 billion in

Eric Aldwinckle, *It's Our War*. Colour offset lithograph, 79.1 x 53.2 cm. National Archives of Canada, Second World War Collection.

1942. To finance the increased expenditures, Ottawa turned to the main recommendations of the 1940 Rowell-Sirois Report, which urged that the federal government be given a monopoly on income taxes and succession duties. A Dominion-provincial conference to seek acceptance of these proposals in January 1941 failed utterly. Eventually, given the needs of wartime financing, an agreement was reached to rent these fields of taxation to the Dominion for the duration of the war plus one year after the cessation of hostilities. An act of Parliament, the Dominion-Provincial Taxation Agreement Act of 1942, formalized the arrangement.

In the spring of 1941, the federal government established a Committee on Postwar Reconstruction and appointed Cyril James, the principal of McGill University, as its chair. With his customary initiative and energy, James set to work. He promptly hired Professor Leonard Marsh, former director of a ten-year McGill social science project that had been financed by the Rockefeller Foundation. Marsh's Report on Social Security for Canada of March 1943, along with the James Committee report six months later, laid the foundations for welfare and reconstruction policies in Canada for the rest of the forties.

Parallels with the Sir William Beveridge's 1942 report on "Social Insurance and Allied Services" in Britain were quickly drawn, as both James and Marsh were graduates of the University of London, Beveridge's university, and both knew Sir William well. Their success, however, aroused the ire and hostility of the Ottawa mandarins, reasonably proud of their own successful management of the war effort and hostile to "interlopers." Graham Towers, Donald Gordon and the deputy minister of finance, Clifford Clark, quickly arranged to reduce the studies of the James Committee to the status of advisory and background material.

Ottawa mandarins had their own fish to fry. They were now in control of 76 per cent of the revenues of all governments; provinces collected 11 per cent of total government revenues—less than the municipalities and school boards, which collected 12 per cent. Ottawa was in complete command of the Canadian economy and intended to keep things that way. With the Germans driven out of North Africa, Russian victories on the eastern front and the Allies poised for the invasion of Europe, the end of the war was in sight and the mandarins were concerned that their monopoly of income taxes and succession duties would, by the agreement of 1942, also come to an end.

New needs and reasons to retain control of income taxes had to be found. The federal government had already taken over responsibility for unemployment through an amendment to the British North America Act in 1940. The need to guard against postwar depression and unemployment, plus a set of far-reaching social programs, became the new goals.

In 1944, Parliament passed seven bills of major social significance in quick succession—the Family Allowance Act, the Agricultural and Fisheries Price Support acts, the National Housing Act, the Industrial Development Bank Act, the Farm Improvement Loans Act and the Export Credits Insurance Act. The famous White Paper on Employment and Income was tabled the following year, committing the government to the stable levels of employment and income that Beveridge, James and Marsh had proposed. Ottawa had found the rationale for a continuing centralized state.

The agenda of the 1945–46 Dominion-Provincial Conference on Reconstruction outlined the steps to be taken to turn Canada into a centralized state in peacetime. It turned out to be, in Harvey Perry's words, "one of the political miscalculations of the century." The Dominion government's proposal that the "provincial governments should, by agreement, forego the imposition of personal income taxes, corporation taxes and succession duties" in exchange for subsidies was turned back and the conference failed.

Finance Minister J.L. Ilsley refused to seek a constitutional amendment, and the demands of Quebec Premier Maurice Duplessis that Ottawa live up to the terms of the BNA Act were ignored. Ottawa's insensitivity to calls for respect for provincial autonomy was manifest throughout the conference. As the premier of Nova Scotia, Angus L. Macdonald, put it, "Provincial governments will become mere annuitants of Ottawa."

The Liberal government won the June 1945 election, called after the victory in Europe, with only a small majority, but it pursued its centralizing course. In 1947 it persuaded all provinces except Ontario and Quebec to give up their tax rights for increased subsidies, and ensuing agreements eventually brought in Ontario. This left only Quebec insisting that the BNA Act and Confederation with it had been "wrecked" by the unilateral, illegal and unconstitutional actions of the federal government.

The heritage of the forties is Beveridge welfarism and the political and constitutional divisions in Canada arising from Ottawa's unilateral and illegal repudiation of its own agreement with the provinces, the Dominion-Provincial Taxation Agreement Act of 1942. Canadians have been paying for this deliberate occupation of provincial powers and jurisdiction ever since.

Economist **Eric Kierans** was a cabinet minister in the Quebec government of Jean Lesage from 1963 to 1966 and in the federal government of Pierre Elliott Trudeau from 1968 to 1971. He was a contributing editor of *Compass* from 1993 to 1997.

An Ambiguous International Role for Canada

by Denis Smith

anada found confidence and renewed prosperity in the Second World War. Its military and industrial contribution to victory had been disproportionate to its size, and it emerged from war as a leading industrial country. Prime Minister Mackenzie King's canny management of domestic conflict had kept the country more united than it had been in the First World War; and Canadians had absorbed expectations about the postwar world that were widely shared in the United States and Britain as well. A brave new world, glimpsed and then lost after 1919, might yet be born.

At home, all parties were determined to maintain employment and prosperity. Abroad, the government intended to act in concert with its allies to build a postwar system of economic and political cooperation aimed at preventing another catastrophic world war. Given a free hand, the prime minister might have preferred a return to semi-isolation, but King knew that was not possible. To prevent war and assure prosperity, Britain and especially the United States would have to play leading roles in the new system, and Canada, as their historic partner, would have to assist them.

As long as King had his way, it would do so cautiously. But within his own administration there were bolder, more ambitious minds at work. In the Department of External Affairs, the young recruits of the late 1920s and 1930s were just reaching their peak years. They were both nationalists and internationalists, confident that Canada could play an independent role in the world and certain that international cooperation was necessary. Geoffrey Pearson has written:

> Most Canadian historians had trained their students to believe in the progress of "colony to nation," and it was as nation-builders that Canadian diplomats saw themselves, shaping the profile of a new actor on the world stage. If they could also be builders of a

new world order, so much the better. They were fortunate that a more or less united public opinion stood behind them.

In Ottawa, Washington and London, Canadian diplomats worked hard to assure Canada a place in postwar councils as the leading "middle power." Canada and other smaller countries, they insisted, should possess international status on the basis of the "functional principle": influence should vary from issue to issue, according to variations in resources, knowledge and experience. The point was conceded, and Canada found ample outlet for its diplomatic skills in the early postwar years. Canadian delegates were active participants in designing new international monetary institutions at Bretton Woods, in drawing up plans for international civil aviation at Chicago, in creating the new United Nations organization at San Francisco, in providing postwar relief through UNRRA, and in efforts to negotiate peacetime control of atomic weapons at the United Nations.

Canada's hope was that the United Nations would preserve the peace through a worldwide regime of collective security. It was encouraged by the provisions for peace enforcement in the UN Charter, which were stronger than the provisions in the old League of Nations charter, and above all by the commitment of the United States to an active role in the new institution, in contrast to its refusal to join the League. But developments in the first few years after the war would frustrate the hope of collective security and in the process cause Canada's international role to take an unanticipated turn.

The UN system depended on maintaining cooperation among the Grand Alliance of Britain, the United States and the Soviet Union. Within a few months of war's end that prospect was fading. The West's understanding of the Soviet Union had been muddled by its own wartime propaganda, which treated the USSR not just as an ally of necessity but as a reformed tyranny, moving steadily towards democracy under the inspired leadership of that good patriot "Uncle Joe" Stalin. However, the Soviets made brutally clear in 1946 and 1947 their intention to protect themselves with compliant puppet governments in the countries along their western frontiers that they had occupied in wartime and to prevent the reemergence of a powerful and independent Germany. For the Soviets, wartime occupation of eastern and central Europe offered security from a hostile world, and they had no intention of giving up this security in the postwar era. The motive was conservative rather than aggressive, and at first the West gave signs of accepting such a protective sphere.

But Stalin conducted his early postwar diplomacy disastrously and soon lost western trust. He pressed the boundaries of Soviet influence too far and reawakened old fears of Communist plotting, subversion and war. The European nations, only recently shattered by one tyranny, could easily imagine the terrible prospect of another one. The Americans, still struggling to understand their place in the postwar balance of power and burdened with the image of a friendly Soviet Union, justified their new role of world leadership by demonizing the Soviets. The Soviets, Americans were now told, had discarded their mask. Not only was the regime a harsh dictatorship (which was true), but its beliefs required it to engage in a campaign of world domination (which was more doubtful). Stalinism was the new Nazism, and it would have to be resisted everywhere. That became the American mission, the justification for generous foreign aid (notably the Marshall Plan), a new web of alliances, rearmament and an era of domestic intolerance.

The Soviet Union was clearly unfriendly, pathologically intolerant and suspicious; it was also shattered by war, cautious and generally unadventurous. But its own diplomatic ineptitude and American image-making turned it into a Cold War enemy of the West.

From mid-1947, easy oversimplifications—which would govern policy for the next forty years—filled the vacuum of western confusion about the shape of the postwar world. There was once again one foe, and all foreign policy would flow from that assumption. In an inexorable play of move and countermove, attitudes hardened on the Soviet side as well. Each side saw its own acts as defensive and the other's as aggressive. Each contributed to a forty-year binge of horrific arms development. And each, fortunately, came to recognize that direct conflict between the two alliances would be intolerable.

Canada was caught in the middle. When Mackenzie King learned, in September 1945, of spy rings operating out of the Soviet embassy in Ottawa and extending to the U.S. and Britain, he feared that their exposure might bring on war. Polar projection maps also made him see that an all-out war might be fought in Canadian skies. So there were fresh reasons why Canada should work for peace. Canadians no longer lived in a "fire-proof house," as their country had once been characterized, and no one in Ottawa doubted that the country's security would rest primarily on closer links with the United States (with the mother country close in the background).

By mid-1948, when Mackenzie King was about to be replaced by his chosen successor Louis Saint-Laurent, Canada was already engaged in negotiations to create the North Atlantic Treaty Organization (NATO). The initiative for talks came from Britain, but the most zealous advocates of the alliance were in Canada's Department of External Affairs. Since the United Nations had failed to provide the security it briefly promised, Canada would seek it in the more familiar surroundings of the family. In April 1949 the treaty was signed in Washington, and the postwar system took on its essential form. The Warsaw Pact became NATO's eastern counterpart a few years later.

On the whole this was a comfortable and reassuring system for Canada, giving it a multilateral association where it could accept, and within limits influence, American leadership. After 1950, NATO offered Canada the chance to develop and display its peacetime military skills as well, through its substantial contributions to combined forces in Europe.

But Canada's role in the middle was always slightly ambiguous. The initial desire of 1945 for independence remained, and Canadian politicians could never give total commitment to one side in the Cold War. This was a matter of conscience, temperament, historical judgement and geographic interest. Canadians preferred negotiation to arms, and the country's diplomats—led by Lester Pearson—were skilled in the trade. Thus, while bipolar conflict typified the world for almost half a century after 1950, Canadians remained prominent in the efforts to contain and diminish it. It was probably good fortune that when a Canadian prime minister, Brian Mulroney, eventually abandoned Canada's principled ambiguity for outright advocacy of American policy, he chose to do so at the very moment when the whole Cold War system became irrelevant.

Political scientist **Denis Smith**'s books include *Diplomacy of Fear: Canada and the Cold War, 1941–1948* and *Rogue Tory: The Life and Legend of John G. Diefenbaker* (1995).

Postwar Social Life Stressed Conformity

by Mary Louise Adams

The end of the Second World War signalled a new beginning for many Canadians. But after the material deprivation of the Depression and the emotional turmoil of the war, not all Canadians were ready to throw their faith behind either the nascent peace or the "modern," prosperous future that seemed to be at their doorstep. The war had led to significant changes on the social landscape, changes some thought could lead to instability. And, of course, the end of the Second World War passed quickly to the beginning of the Cold War, further fuelling the uncertainty of the times.

That this uncertainty persisted in the face of considerable economic improvement is one of the significant features of the immediate postwar period. Canadian manufacturing wages doubled between 1945 and 1956 while prices rose only slightly. Unemployment remained between 2.8 and 5.9 per cent, depending on the region, until the mid-1950s. In contrast, the 1933 national unemployment rate had been 20 per cent. Clearly, many Canadians were better off than they had been. Still, speechmakers and journalists spoke often of a collective distrust of the future. They wrote of such things as "outside turmoil" and "external threats" to Canada's stability—loose references to the Cold War.

In Canada, Cold War rhetoric and the activities that followed from it were subtler than they were in the United States. Nevertheless, American attitudes had a big impact in this country. Certainly, few Canadians could have escaped the prevailing anticommunism that infused the popular culture of the era. At the very least, Canadians and Americans shared a fear of, and a fascination with, the bomb. In 1946, the Toronto Board of Education proclaimed the theme of Education Week to be "Education for the Atomic Age," marking the bomb and nuclear energy as the harbingers of a new era. Four years later, a *Chatelaine* editorial identified the bomb as the "biggest thing in our new half century." The magazine encouraged its readers to have faith in the "experts, and the scientists."

Canada's version of the Cold War started in 1945 when Igor Gou-

zenko, a cipher clerk in the Soviet embassy in Ottawa, defected and claimed that the Soviets had been running a spy ring in Canada. Investigations
into his allegations focused national attention on the need for internal
defences against Communism. An unsuccessful search for spy rings gave
way to efforts to track "domestic dissidents." Those who were most likely
to be put under surveillance included labour organizers, members of Communist and socialist organizations, peace activists and homosexuals and others, like single mothers, whose morals were "weak."

Deviance from any number of mainstream norms was suspect in the
early years of the Cold War. Deviance challenged the homogeneity that was
seen to be central to Canada's strength as a nation. The conformity that is so
often identified as a primary aspect of postwar social life wasn't simply a characteristic of increased consumerism or the centralization of popular culture
and entertainment industries. It was also produced by an approach to citizenship that demanded of Canadians a willingness to help create a smooth social
fabric and adopt a shared set of behavioural standards and mores.

In this context, having a family was an important marker of social belonging and conformity to prevailing standards. It was a sign of maturity, of
one's ability to take on responsibility. As a psychiatrist argued in *Chatelaine*,
raising children was, at root, a patriotic obligation. Thus the family became a
symbol of safety—not just on the individual level but on the national level as
well. Families would help the West win the Cold War, and expert voices
were greeted with anxiety when they claimed that "the family" was threatened in the postwar world. The fact that families were being formed by more
people more often than at any other time in this century did little to counter
a pervasive sense that "the family," as a social institution, was under threat.

In 1941, the average age of first marriage for women was 25.4 years of
age. By 1961 that figure had dropped to 22 years of age. Between 1937 and
1954, the marriage rate for women between the ages of fifteen and nineteen doubled from 30 per 1000 to 62 per 1000. Once married, these
women had more children, more quickly, than their mothers did. Between
1937 and 1947, the number of births per 1000 of the population rose from
20.1 to 28.9 and it continued to rise until 1956. Most of this increase was
accounted for by mothers under twenty-five years of age and by families
with three or more children.

Commentators explained the baby boom in a number of ways: larger
families provided security in an insecure world; the baby bonus (established
in 1945) and widespread prosperity made children easier to afford; improvements in maternal and child health made pregnancy a less risky proposition. What few mentioned was the tremendous pressure applied to anyone who failed to follow the trend, as evidenced by the RCMP crackdown

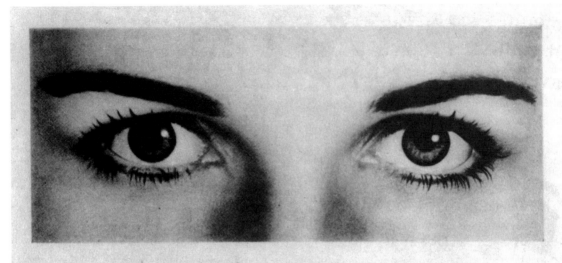

"Trust my EYES to make thrifty buys"

As the war ended, advertisers trained their sights on the civilian population

on "deviants."

To demonstrate the family's alleged decline, social critics called up divorce statistics. At the end of the Second World War, the divorce rate in Canada tripled. After 1946, the rate fell off, but then it rose steadily from 1951 to 1968. Most of the early rise was attributable to poorly considered wartime weddings, although increasing economic opportunities for women may also have been an important factor.

Inevitably, discussions about the family touched on debates about the state of postwar youth. For many adolescents, wartime had meant that their precarious "transitional years" were spent without a lot of adult supervision. Teenage girls and boys were among those who kept the war industries operating. Educators, civic officials and journalists all claimed that the wartime climate had set teenagers on the path of trouble. The emergence of rock and roll and a specific "teenaged" culture did nothing to quell their fears.

In part, the uproar over youth and delinquency was played out on the backs of mothers. After the war there was a concerted effort by government agencies, business and many civic organizations to push women out of the paid workforce and back into the home. Working women were told it was their patriotic duty to give up their positions to returning soldiers. They were also told that their children suffered as they worked, and that a mother's absence could transform a "normal" youth into a delinquent.

Nevertheless, women's labour force participation failed to return to its prewar levels, and large numbers of married women in particular continued to work. To some, these changes suggested that the difference between gender roles was diminishing, a trend that could only lead to the demasculinization of men.

While both women and men were under a tremendous strain to build what *Chatelaine* called "modern marriages"—"a new kind of joint-ownership marriage…which may beat any earlier model back to Adam and Eve"—most of this task fell to women. The popular assumption was that gender roles were relaxing. But expectations remained that women would be responsible for domestic life and men for "breadwinning."

While present-day nostalgia connects the postwar "Ozzie and Harriet"–type family back to earlier decades and pegs it as exemplifying so-called "traditional" values, some historians argue that the postwar version of the family was, in fact, something new. Postwar families were units of consumption rather than production. For the first time the "ideal" family was expected not just to meet the economic and physical needs of its members but all their emotional needs as well. In part, these heightened expectations were a consequence of the economic changes and prosperity that favoured consumerism over mutual dependence and bungalows over farms and crowded downtown apartments. But the phenomenon and experience of the nuclear-family-as-island was also related to postwar desires for individual satisfaction and to the need for social stability.

To see that such desires were too great to be satisfied by the family on its own, we need only look to feminism and the other social movements that developed out of the late 1950s and early 1960s. To say that such desires should be satisfied by families in the 1990s is to ignore the lessons of hindsight.

Sociologist **Mary Louise Adams** wrote her dissertation on teenagers and sexuality in postwar Toronto at the Ontario Institute on Studies in Education.

Alfred Pellan and the Quebec Painters' Quiet Revolution

by Malcolm Reid

When France fell to the Nazis in 1940 and Alfred Pellan came back to Canada, he was thirty-four years old and not very well known. But he had been painting since he was a teenager. He had a firm black line of his own, a way with colours, a love of people. He had the Paris of the twenties and thirties in his blood, and believed in most of its radicalisms.

He set to work remaking the world of painting in Montreal. All through the Second World War and the immediate postwar years, Pellan painted and organized. With a rival group led by Paul-Émile Borduas, and in symbiosis with groups in Toronto, Winnipeg and Vancouver, he and his friends made Canadian painting modern.

Quebec's Quiet Revolution thus began twenty years earlier in painting than in other fields of life. And it placed Montreal in the leadership role for all of Canada. The revolution of Pellan and his colleagues was little concerned with politics and social structures. All their sympathies were with a loosening of traditional bonds, yes. But they were astride many of the divisions that made for political quarrels. Religion was no real problem for them, as it was for the writers of the time. And class? The painters were from the common people, but they knew their buyers would be the rich and the government. Most of all, they did not live by being English or French. English Canada admired them, and they were in contact with English Canadian painters.

And are painters not the rebels who worry least about language? Their language speaks straight to the eyes. It can be read by small children and others who don't really possess language. I know this, for I was moved by Pellan in magazines and art books (which were just being invented in 1945) before I entered school. Leafing through *Canadian Art*, to which my family subscribed in their suburb in Ontario, I followed lines, shapes, turns, twists, energies, reds, greens, patchworks it seemed would never end. My eye could never get enough of Alfred Pellan.

Looking back, we can see now that the Montreal of the forties was a wonderfully receptive city for the art of painting. Montreal was French, and while the French city may have been puritanical in most things, Frenchness and painting went together. The city's galleries spread west along Sherbrooke Street. Artists who hadn't yet won their way into these galleries held their own events, in their studios farther east, near the art schools, near the night life.

Pellan had never been a Montrealer before. He was a son of the Quebec City working-class district of Limoilou, and had studied at the École des Beaux-Arts in that city. Alfred Pelland, Sr., was a locomotive engineer, a widower and a man who encouraged his son in painting from the time the boy was fourteen. Born in 1906, the younger Alfred Pelland had often been sick in bed and uninterested in school until his father bought him a paint kit and painting came into his life. His mother had died when he was a baby.

In France, where he had been sent to discover modern art on a provincial scholarship, Pellan had dropped the unpronounced *d* from the end of his name. "I found the new spelling more *plastic*," he said, and there it is, lettered in capital letters on every painting from 1930 on. PELLAN.

What Pellan painted in those years grew wilder and wilder.

From still-lifes and portraits in which pots and pans and faces were slightly bent, he moved on to huge canvases and panels of wood in which wild plants, and humans, and animals undulated out in all directions, and faces gazed sideways, forward and upward within the same painting. All was clearly stated with black lines, and all was injected with colours from an afternoon of autumn sunlight in the Laurentian Shield.

While in Paris, he was clearly influenced by Fernand Léger and the Swiss painter Paul Klee. And on his rediscovering Canada, Haida totem poles became an influence. But to me, Pellan is Pellan. The only really haunting affinity I see is with the work of Robert Lapalme, a Quebec artist of the same generation, but one who worked more often in little black-and-white newspaper cartoons than in oils or canvas. Lapalme drew a beautiful caricature of Pellan when Pellan was doing battle with the director of the École des Beaux-Arts de Montréal, where he taught. Pellan's long but notably flattened-down nose and curly black hair were stressed in the cartoon.

Was Pellan as pugnacious a man as this made him look? Certainly he was combative for modern art. But Pellan's own art has a cartoon quality to it, and its good humour explodes. Its invention of new and strange worlds goes on and on and on. I cannot believe he was not a happy man when I look at it.

Pellan was a teacher, and he was articulate about what he was doing in downtown Montreal as the war, and then the industrialization of pious Quebec, charged forward. But the key words here came from another

Alfred Pellan (1906–1988), *Quatre Femmes* (*Four Women*), 1943–1947. Oil on canvas, 208.4 x 167.8 cm. Montreal, Collection Musée d'art contemporain de Montréal/The Musée d'art contemporain de Montréal Collection. Photo: MACM

painter, Jacques de Tonnancour, who wrote *Prisme d'Yeux*, the manifesto of Pellan's group. (This name suggests the filtering of reality through the prism of the human eye, but perhaps it also hints at God, or the gods, being involved: *d'Yeux = Dieu*.)

"We do not adhere to any bright new esthetic," says *Prisme d'Yeux*, "but try to stay within the oldest esthetic on the earth, the one that was present in the people who painted in the caves, and which opens out in every direction there is."

This may be aimed at Paul-Émile Borduas and his group of *automatistes*. Pellan and Borduas quarrelled over what seems, as I look back on it as a Québécois of the nineties, like nothing much. "Borduas wasn't a good friend, because he wanted to be worshipped," Pellan said years later. "I'd have liked to work in comradeship with him and not in conflict, but he wouldn't let that be."

Prisme d'Yeux concentrates on painting itself. It pleads for art, and implies that art's liberation will be good for society. By contrast, the Borduas group's manifesto, *Refus Global*, published a few months later, speaks in terms of anarchy and politics and sociology, and is a document of the Quebec revolution.

Well before the *Refus*, a young writer named Rémi-Paul Forgues came from a seminar by Borduas and wrote, "We place our faith in Borduas, he is our compensation for the absurd age in which we live." So perhaps Borduas knew the time would be right for his manifesto, with its famous socially-oriented opening, "Born of modest working-class or petit-bourgeois families…," and its closing promise that "within a foreseeable future, people will be able to develop, untrammelled, their own individual skills, through impassioned, impulsive action and glorious independence.

Meanwhile we must work without respite, hand in hand with those who long for a better life; together we must persevere, regardless of praise or persecution, towards the joyful fulfilment of our fierce desire for freedom."

Borduas had a flair for the social debate that Pellan never had. The book of the era was Gabrielle Roy's *The Tin Flute*, and a year later (1949) the Asbestos Strike would break out. It was a period in which social debate would be in the air.

The year of those manifestos, 1948, was an important year for Alfred Pellan. His first faithful backer, his railwayman father, died, shortly after retiring from the Canadian Pacific. And Pellan, turned forty, married Madeleine Polisena, a handsome round-faced young woman who had studied art. She was surprised at the painter's falling in love with her, but she responded, and she became a very strong partner. Not long after getting married they bought a house in the village of Auteuil near Montreal. In 1988, the last year of Pellan's life, a friend and I took a bus out to Auteuil in what proved to be a vain attempt to meet the wiry old painter. Still, Pellan has always been an important part of my life. He opened my eyes. He opened the window.

Quebec City writer **Malcolm Reid** is a former Quebec correspondent of the Toronto *Globe and Mail* and the author of *The Shouting Signpainters*, a study of Quebec left-wing movements in the 1960s. His articles have appeared in the *Last Post, This Magazine, Canadian Dimension* and other magazines, in addition to *Compass*.

The Fifties

213   A Sense of Time Standing Still   by Curtis Fahey
215   The Cold War Masked a Geopolitical Agenda   by Anatol Rapoport
220   Power, Confusion and Corporate Interests:
      McCarthy and Hoover   by Peter Dale Scott
225   The Fifties Look: Selling a Self-Image   by Philip Street
228   My Adventures in Darkest Suburbia   by Miriam Blair
231   Maire-Alain Couturier: The Priest Who
      Championed Modern Art   by Peter Larisey
235   A Peasant Pope Breathed New Life into the Church   by Romeo Maione
238   The Federal Institution that United Quebecers   by Louis Balthazar
241   TV Hard-Wired Canada into Two Solitudes   by Mark Starowicz
244   We Created an Elvis to Meet Our Need   by Malcolm Reid
248   Beckett's Poetic Rendering of Faith and Doubt   by Craig Stewart Walker
251   Tony Walsh: A Gentle Man Who Challenged Others   by Stephen Hagarty

A Sense of Time Standing Still

by Curtis Fahey

I should first declare a conflict of interest. Born in 1951, I cannot think of the 1950s without thinking of my childhood, and so my perspective on that decade is tinged by nostalgia. What I see is partly determined by my memories of growing up.

In the early 1950s my family embarked on an odyssey typical of the time: like millions of other North Americans, we moved from an apartment into our first house. The house, located in Montreal North, was not palatial by any means, but in the eyes of a toddler it was almost unimaginably large and fascinating. Another memory concerns the almost magical place of television in our lives; Dragnet, Disney, Hopalong Cassidy, Zorro, Perry Mason, Howdy Doody, Ed Sullivan (my family was glued to the set the first time Elvis swivelled his hips), Lassie and Hockey Night in Canada were some of the programs that captivated us. It is hard to understand now, but television inspired in me—and likely many others—a sense of wonder that has not been duplicated since.

When I was not watching TV, I engaged in other pastimes that now seem typical of the 1950s: flicking my yo-yo, spinning a hula-hoop, playing cowboys and Indians or, sometimes, reliving the heroic life of Davy Crockett, aided by my very own coonskin cap. As with most other families in the 1950s, my mother stayed at home while my father went to work. And like most other Catholics of the time, we took our faith seriously, attending Mass regularly, confessing our sins (privately, in the quiet of the confessional) before receiving Communion, and reciting the rosary frequently.

All of these memories conform to the almost stereotypical view of the 1950s. But is that all there was to the decade? Hardly. For one thing, our image of the 1950s as a decade of universal economic prosperity is misleading. Not everyone lived the good life; the poor were still with us, home ownership was a dream that many could still not realize, and gadgets such as automatic washing machines and televisions came into universal use only in the following decade.

The standard view that the 1950s were somehow unique can also lead us astray. To a greater extent than other decades, the 1950s were an extension of the decade that had come before. The mass consumerism of the 1950s—deftly analysed here by Philip Street—was rooted in the economic growth that had begun in the late 1940s on the heels of the Second World War. Similarly, while the war itself was a forties event, its legacy survived into the 1950s, shaping our view of the world throughout the decade and bequeathing to us in the person of Adolf Hitler a symbol of evil that is only now beginning to lose its power.

Then there was the Cold War. It too had begun in the 1940s and, as Anatol Rapoport reminds us, it would continue through the 1950s and beyond. We lived under the threat of a nuclear war whose horrors had first been glimpsed in 1945. Intellectually, the ideological self-righteousness and conformism so characteristic of the 1950s were products both of the Allied victory in 1945 and of the Cold War that followed. The Cold War—a conflict that long seemed ordained to last forever—was central to the continuity that strikes us when we look back at the 1950s, a continuity that leaves us with the curious sense of time standing still.

We attempt to convey a sense of the richness of life in the 1950s and of that decade's relevance to Canada in the 1990s.

Historian and editor **Curtis Fahey** was an associate editor of *Compass* from 1990 to 1997 and subsequently a director of the Compass Foundation.

The Cold War Masked a Geopolitical Agenda

by Anatol Rapoport

Our habit of partitioning history into decades, centuries and millennia is a manifestation of a biological accident. We have ten fingers; hence the decimal system. To some extent, to be sure, historical epochs fit, albeit very roughly, into centuries. I think of the nineteenth century as beginning in 1789 and ending in 1914, and the twentieth as ending in 1989: dates that mark momentous events, identified as the milestones of history. Similarly, decades are not always neat ten-year periods.

The fifties could be said to have begun as early as March 5, 1946, the date of Winston Churchill's famous pronouncement: "From Stettin in the Baltic to Trieste in the Adriatic, an iron curtain has descended across the Continent." This was in effect the declaration of the Cold War.

Reality soon matched Churchill's description as the Soviet Union installed regimes sympathetic to it in eastern Europe while western Europe concluded a military alliance with the United States. But the first campaign of the Cold War was waged within America by the political right against an "internal enemy." The House Un-American Activities Committee, charged back in 1938 with probing all varieties of political extremism and having nothing to show for its efforts, found an ideal target too big to miss: everything that could be connected with the political left, ranging from the enthusiasts for the New Deal to "dupes of the Communists" (as Albert Einstein was once called in *Life* magazine) to Soviet spies.

At first the committee generated considerable opposition, especially after its 1947 hearings on "subversion" in the motion picture industry. But the campaign gathered momentum during the headline-spawning espionage trial of Alger Hiss, a highly respected State Department official. Finally, the hitherto obscure Senator Joseph McCarthy unleashed mass hysteria when in a speech delivered on February 9, 1950, he declared that he had in his wallet a list of 205 card-carrying Communists employed by

Nikita Khrushchev

the State Department.

The public response was overwhelming. Subversion became the top issue in the presidential campaign of 1952. Even Dwight Eisenhower, the Republican candidate for president, felt obliged to enlist McCarthy's support. Eventually McCarthy overreached himself by attacking the military in the person of its highest-ranking personage, five-star general and Nobel Peace Prize laureate George Marshall, who had been Harry Truman's secretary of state. The military hit back and knocked McCarthy out. He was censured by the Senate in December 1954.

The witch hunt in the Soviet Union coincided roughly with the McCarthy carnival. It ended abruptly in 1953 with the death of Joseph Stalin. The target was western culture in all its aspects—science, literature, the arts, not to speak of political ideas. Understandably, the Soviet version was incomparably more severe. Victims were not only expelled from their jobs and professions but also incarcerated in forced labour camps and sometimes shot.

The witch hunts were the high-water mark of the "ideological struggle," which was the way the Cold War was sold to the respective publics by the power elites of the combatants. Underlying this intensely publicized struggle of good vs. evil was another, fuelled by geopolitical considerations. American interests in that struggle are revealed in a 1948 internal State Department document, classified at the time but now available:

"We have about 50% of the world's wealth, but only 6.3% of its population. In this situation we cannot fail to be the object of envy and resentment. Our real task in the coming period is to devise a pattern of relationships which will permit us to maintain this position of disparity without positive detriment to our national security."

The author was George F. Kennan, who under the pseudonym "Mr. X" published the famous paper on the "policy of containment." The fundamental assumption underlying that policy was that Communism is by its nature expansionist and unless this "flood" is energetically stemmed, it will seep through every weak spot in the frontier of the "free world." The power behind this expansionist pressure was obviously the Soviet Union. The historic mission of the United States was to supply the power behind the resistance.

Interventionism—or counterinsurgency, as it was called in the fifties—was essentially the implementation of the containment policy. Its ideological rationalization was based on the belief that the United States was the ordained leader of the Free World and so must give the Russians to understand that no "spread of Communism" would be tolerated. Further, Americans nurtured a conviction that the policy promoted the rule of law as against that of force.

Of course some American actions, such as the overthrow of an elected government in Iran in 1953 and in Guatemala in 1954, were difficult to reconcile with the image of law versus force. It was reasoned, however, that this was done according to the American definition of "legitimate government." To qualify as legitimate, a government had to be not only non-Communist but also anti-Communist. In his book *Counter-Insurgency Warfare*, J.S. Pustay went a step further. Defining counterinsurgency warfare as defence of incumbent governments against subversion, he identified anti-Communist governments as "incumbent" whether they were in power or not. Thus, according to Pustay's definition the "incumbent" governments of Iran and Guatemala were the anti-Communist governments installed by the U.S., not the elected governments they replaced.

If the fifties began as early as 1946, they lasted until the culminating event of the first phase of the Cold War: the Cuban Missile Crisis of 1962. In the U.S., that first phase was marked by supreme confidence in both the righteousness and the invulnerability of American leadership.

The Cuban Missile Crisis was a vivid demonstration of "brinkmanship," as the assertion of American political will in the implementation of the containment policy came to be called. The term stems from the boast of John Foster Dulles, secretary of state under Eisenhower in the fifties, that he had deliberately brought the country to the "brink of war" to convince the Soviets that America meant what it threatened. Specifically, Dulles declared in effect that the United States would hold the Soviet Union responsible for any political event anywhere in the world that the United States chose to interpret as "Communist aggression," and that a nuclear attack on the Soviet Union could be expected as a retaliatory measure if the United States chose to administer it. The installation of missiles with nuclear warheads in Cuba was evidently regarded as an event of this type.

Possibly we owe our survival to Soviet leader Nikita Khrushchev, who was the first to step back from the brink. "Some comrades abroad," he remarked, "claim that Khrushchev is making a mess of things and is afraid of war. Let me say once again that I should like to see the kind of bloody fool who is genuinely not afraid of war." John F. Kennedy also deserves some credit for passing up the opportunity to gloat over the humiliation of the USSR. It was probably the close brush with irreversible catastrophe that ended the foolhardy cockiness of the American establishment in the first phase of the Cold War and provided the main impetus to the turbulent sixties.

Another symptom of a change of mood at the end of the (extended)

Dwight D. Eisenhower

fifties was President Eisenhower's often quoted pejorative reference in his farewell address (1961) to the "military-industrial complex." The gloomy prophecy of the dominance of war-oriented preoccupations and commitments in the economic and political life of the U.S. was fully realized. The "intellectualization" of war played a prominent part in this process.

It seems paradoxical at first that the U.S., traditionally the least militarized of the major powers, has become the most militarized. I think the explanation lies in the particular adaptation of war mentality to American libidinal commitments—technolatry (worship of technology) and identification of prosperity with vigorous business enterprise regardless of what it produces. Both fit in admirably with American experience in the two world wars. It has been said that the First World War was the chemists' war (high explosives, poison gas), the Second World War was the physicists' war (radar, atomic bomb), and the Third World War would be the mathematicians' war (the design of complex strategies). Thus, preparation for the Third World War was experienced in the fifties as flexing newly developed intellectual muscles.

Scientists, academics and other intellectuals, now welcomed as advisers, nurtured that image. A theory of "limited war" was developed to accommodate the idea that a war could be conducted in a way that would serve some of the common interests of the combatants. Henry Kissinger, who would later be secretary of state under Richard Nixon, wrote in 1957:

> It is possible to conceive of a pattern of limited nuclear war with its own appropriate tactics and with limitation as to targets, areas, and the size of weapons used....If the Soviet leadership is clear about our intentions, a framework of war limitation may be established by the operation of self-interest—by the fear of all-out nuclear war and by the fact that new tactics make many of the targets of traditional warfare less profitable.

Finally, the invigorating effect on the American economy of the Second World War and the arms race that occurred in its wake should not be overlooked. Unlike the people of Europe and Asia, Americans experienced the Second World War not as a disaster but as an economic windfall. The Great Depression was dissipated. Moreover, the short depression of the early fifties was aborted by the Korean War. Finally, the war machine came to be perceived as a pump, keeping the economy going in somewhat the same way as the heart keeps us alive by pumping blood.

This addiction to a perpetual war economy has outlived the Cold War.

It remains the most formidable obstacle to turning attention away from ideological hangups and geopolitical ambitions towards the genuine threats to civilization and perhaps to humanity: the continued menace of total destruction as long as stockpiles of genocidal weapons exist, irreversible degradation of the environment, and the growing disparity between the affluent and destitute worlds—the disparity whose perpetuation Kennan suggested was in America's cardinal interest.

In the United States, the Cold War was depicted in public pronouncements, political campaigns and mass media as a struggle of democracy against dictatorship, freedom against tyranny, at times Judeo-Christian ethics against godless power lust. One is tempted to view these depictions as camouflage cast over a hidden agenda that Kennan described clearly and forthrightly. However, this interpretation would hardly be fair to the vast majority of Americans who sincerely believed in the missionary role of the United States as the "leader of the free world," just as the Crusaders believed they were serving God and the architects of internal terror in the Soviet Union believed they were facilitating the march of humanity towards a humane and glorious future. If there is a component of human nature that is universal and independent of culture, education or intellectual level, it is the propensity to rationalize, especially actions that in others appear reprehensible.

Longtime peace activist and scholar **Anatol Rapoport** has taught peace and conflict studies at University College, University of Toronto, and written numerous books on peace issues.

Power, Confusion and Corporate Interests: McCarthy and Hoover

by Peter Dale Scott

At the time of the televised hearings that pitted Senator Joseph McCarthy against the United States Army in 1954, I was a young Canadian in the United States. I watched in the Junior Common Room of Eliott House at Harvard University, surrounded by the best and the brightest young Americans. In the hearings the Army's counsel, Joseph Welch, destroyed McCarthy, and the people around me cheered. It seemed as if the clouds were being dispelled, and the forces that wanted to make America a know-nothing country were being abolished. At the time, that was my impression as well. But even if McCarthy himself was finished, McCarthyism was part of a larger set of phenomena, some of which survived the 1950s and have continued into our own time.

The United States went into the postwar era with more power than any other country had ever had in the history of the world. But despite this power, America behaved in a desperate way in the early fifties, acting as if its very survival was threatened. I was astonished at how frightened Americans were, but their paranoid responses had an element of sincerity to them. It was a time of paranoia, which was connected with its being simultaneously a time where visions of a rational order for the world were possible. I went into the Canadian foreign service in the 1950s believing that there were benign forces at work in government that had the chance to fulfil the promise of peace made at the end of the Second World War, strengthen the United Nations, and make for a more orderly and peaceful world. And yet the very possibility of reasonable, peaceful solutions accelerated the desire on all sides to seize various high grounds before that began.

The United States had no real tradition of experience for the power it enjoyed. America isn't a nation in the same sense as, say, France, where over the centuries a national structure has been successfully superimposed on regional differences. So while there is a great deal of power in Washington, there is also confusion and disarray, which undermines that power and helps explain the paranoia that accompanied its exercise in the 1950s. America did not yet know how it was going to fulfil its new role of being a world leader. To fill the vacuum, a number of competing power centres emerged.

One of these was the Federal Bureau of Investigation and its head, J. Edgar Hoover, who sincerely believed, and had believed since about 1921, that the Communists were out to destroy the United States, and therefore his top responsibility was to penetrate the Communist Party and any other Soviet apparatus. He committed enormous resources to this task, to the point that eventually one Communist in six in the United States was on the FBI payroll. Senator McCarthy's lists of Communists in the State Department very likely came from Hoover.

The name "McCarthyism" has generally been given to the paranoid anti-Communism of the early 1950s and the domestic repression of people in the United States, many of them quite innocent of anything. But what was going on was much bigger than one rather dumb senator from Wisconsin could be responsible for. "Hooverism" would be a better term, since Hoover was the central figure in this phenomenon, but in fact it was an institutional phenomenon and not a personal one. Hoover was much too smart, too much of a political animal, to put himself out in the forefront, and McCarthy was the perfect person to act as the public face of Hooverism because he had no such instinct of self-preservation. McCarthy behaved like a man on drugs from the beginning, and he really was on drugs at the end. Hoover ultimately dropped McCarthy, but that was when he saw that McCarthy was becoming more of a political liability than a political asset.

One of the people who advised McCarthy to take on anti-Communism as an issue was a Catholic priest, Fr. Edmund Walsh of Georgetown University. Catholics in eastern Europe felt a sense of anger and betrayal at the Yalta agreement, arrived at between the Protestants Roosevelt and Churchill and the Communist Stalin at the end of the Second World War. Yalta in effect gave Catholic eastern Europe away in the name of a peaceful new order that never occurred. Stalin had his own legitimate interests for security in eastern Europe, but to give him Poland was an excessive act of generosity on the part of people for whom it was not theirs to give. One of the things that moved Fr. Walsh to encourage McCarthy appears to have been the hope of undoing Yalta, and McCarthy's attack on the State Department was an attack on the architects of Yalta to establish that Yalta was some kind of treasonous act. There was much wrong with Yalta. But labelling it an act of sedition or subversion by Communist agents in the State Department was the wrong way to attack it. This attack did not achieve the goal of undoing Yalta, and only muddied the political waters.

Senator Joseph McCarthy

J. Edgar Hoover

Another power centre focused on the newly created Central Intelligence Agency, whose origin was in part connected to the separate peace negotiated with the Germans in Italy in 1945 by Allen Dulles, later CIA director. As part of this deal, the United States took on a whole apparatus of anti-Communist operatives allied to the Nazis in eastern Europe, and the creation of the CIA was part of the plan for using these people. When Congress authorized the CIA in 1947, it was presented as an intelligence agency in the traditional sense, an espionage agency collecting information. But from the very beginning, a different role was foreseen for it, whose origins were partly in the assets of German totalitarianism: covert operations, which included toppling governments and building secret armies.

In its public language, the National Security Act, under which the CIA was established, was absolutely devoid of any hint of what was to come. The act contained a clause, "Such other activities as the National Security Council shall from time to time direct," but that was a rather shaky statutory basis for covert operations. So the National Security Council fleshed it out somewhat with a secret directive called NSC-68 in 1950, which was a decision to resort to dirty tricks to stop what was perceived as the menace of the Communist enemy. The CIA overthrew the governments of Mohammed Mossadegh in Iran in 1953 and Jacobo Arbenz in Guatemala in 1954, and later in the decade turned its attention to Cuba and Indochina.

J. Edgar Hoover resisted the creation of the CIA. He wanted centralized intelligence, but he did not want it in some other body: he wanted it only in the FBI. When the CIA was set up despite the FBI's opposition, the relationship between the two agencies became one of infighting and internal paranoia. The CIA was worried about Hoover's power in Congress, which was real because Hoover had blackmailed many senators and congressmen. There were former FBI agents in the CIA, which created paranoia in the CIA that some of them were still reporting to Hoover, which was probably the case. The CIA was also one of McCarthy's targets, although not publicly, and this was part of the same struggle.

Hoover's high point was the first half of the 1950s. In the early fifties, it was very risky for a congressman to oppose a budgetary request from J. Edgar Hoover. Towards the end of the decade, however, Hoover was clearly losing the battle for status in Washington, and his position declined even further with the election of John F. Kennedy as president in 1960. After Stalin died in 1953 and the Soviet face changed, Hoover's paranoia became harder and harder to justify. Increasingly, the actions he wanted to take against the Communists were not being backed up, and the Supreme Court declared much of the repressive legislation Hoover had forced through unconstitutional. So while Hoover's domestic repression was centre-stage in the early 1950s, by the end of the decade what the CIA was doing overseas was becoming much more important.

Hoover and McCarthy enjoyed broad public support in the early 1950s, but the same was not true of the CIA's covert operations later in the decade, especially its activities in Indochina. Its operations had to be conducted secretly because it was almost certain that they would not be popular. However, the CIA's power was greatly enhanced by its alliance with multinational corporate forces. Its predecessor, the wartime Office of Strategic Services, was created out of segments of private intelligence networks, maintained by the United Fruit Company, the oil companies, banks and other corporations. These ties were further cemented by the fact that people do a stint in the CIA, as they do in the FBI or Justice or the State Department, and then work for private industry in their full maturity. One of the reasons private corporations can push the government around is that they recruit veterans of the government who know how it works and have friends on the inside.

The Communist menace in practice was the threat that some country under its own constitution would nationalize an American company. That's what led to the CIA interventions in Iran and Guatemala: neither Mossadegh nor Arbenz was a Communist. The oil companies lobbied heavily for the Iran intervention, and United Fruit for the operation in Guatemala; in fact, United Fruit also lobbied for the CIA to do something in Iran to create a precedent for Guatemala. Mobil Corporation was the chief corporate lobbyist for intervention in Indochina, because among the major oil companies it was the one with the fewest sources of oil in the ground. It needed more, and it knew that the South China Sea was an area of potential—a prediction that has been amply proven true.

McCarthyism was a disease, a kind of social mental illness, that America has largely healed itself from. But the CIA and its activities in international politics have done great and continuing damage to the American political system. The world has not made the adjustment of developing institutions to adequately reconcile national interests on the global level. And so there is no countervailing power to multinational corporate interests, which have probably been more thoroughly in control in the 1990s than ever before. The postwar era has generated enormous multinational wealth. That wealth finds its way into American elections and dominates them. No one can be elected against the determined opposition of multinational interests. I don't know of anyone who has criticized the CIA in Congress and then been reelected.

I resigned from the Canadian foreign service in 1961, aware that the international power game was much more complex than I had suspected. I continue to be an optimist about the long drift of time towards a better era, but the American constitutional system may never really recover from the damage done to it by the elevation of the United States to international superpower status. I don't believe that democratic forces will ever unseat the multinational forces. That's a done deal now, and it happened in the 1950s.

Peter Dale Scott is a poet, a former Canadian diplomat, former professor of English at the University of California at Berkeley, and the author of several books on the American political system, including *Cocaine Politics* (1992) and *Deep Politics and the Assassination of JFK* (1993). This article is taken from an interview conducted in Berkeley in December 1994.

The Fifties Look: Selling a Self-Image

by Philip Street

In the mid-fifties America was enjoying the zenith of its affluence and influence. McCarthyism was in remission and the future looked bright: with the help of scientific progress, American wealth (and democracy) could spread out to bless the world.

This exuberant optimism found expression in, among other things, the designs of automobiles, clothes, appliances and the ads calculated to sell them. Despite many divergent trends, the phrase "1950s design" conjures up images that form, in retrospect, a cohesive picture of that cultural moment—a *moment* because it was really outside a sense of history. The upward curve seemed to have no end.

In the title of his 1986 book, Thomas Hine dubbed the look of that cultural moment "Populuxe." The word embodies the paradoxical claim of the new affluence: popular luxury, "fantasy on an assembly line." (In his explication of the word, Hine notes that it ends with "a thoroughly unnecessary 'e' to give it class.") Populuxe was Betty Crocker Moms and grey-flannel Dads in the new suburban space. It was plastic dinnerware, bulky sofas on spindly legs, starburst clocks, cars with tailfins—all in two-tone pastels. It could be called the "low modern" style. There was a "high modern" style, influenced by prewar European art and boosted in America by refugees from the Bauhaus and such homegrown proponents as Paul Rand, the designer of the IBM logo. The difference between high and low was the difference between a Mies van der Rohe skyscraper and a Las Vegas casino.

Some design elements found their way into both these styles. The free-form ameboid shapes seen in Miró paintings and Matisse cutouts show up as palette-shaped blobs in advertising designs (high and low) and in coffee tables, formica patterns and kidney-shaped swimming pools. Hine suggests that this blob may have been a precursor of the popular boomerang motif. He disqualifies the boomerang itself as a source of the motif, however: "The form had the aura of infinite forward movement. The idea of

going back where you came from never entered into it."

It took a few years for the fantasy assembly line to get rolling. The post-war boom was largely a matter of satisfying demand. But by the mid-fifties, ever-increasing productivity was threatening to outstrip consumer spending. Americans were apparently too easily satisfied with the cars, TV sets, clothes and other goods that they already had. Thus, marketing for consumption was the pressing problem, and manufacturers enlisted the aid of advertising agencies. One ad executive summed up the spirit of the new age: "What makes this country great is the creation of wants and desires, the creation of dissatisfaction with the old and outmoded." Just as car manufacturers strove to make everyone ashamed to drive a car more than two or three years old, makers of kitchen appliances promoted "psychological obsolescence" by managing colour trends.

Advertising had always tried to play on people's insecurities and desires, but many campaigns had depended on reasoned arguments. Now it was dawning on advertisers that people rarely made spending choices rationally. The answers that consumers gave in surveys and focus groups had little bearing on how they would behave in the marketplace, as the Chrysler Corporation learned the hard way. In 1953 Chrysler decided, on the basis of market surveys, that Americans wanted a simpler, smaller car. Chrysler launched the new line in 1954 and watched its market share plunge from 26 to 13 per cent. Reversing itself immediately, Chrysler introduced the longest car in the low-price range and the first car with a three-colour exterior—and bounced back substantially in 1955.

In this climate motivational research came into its own. Psychologists became consultants to industry, and their insights were augmented by further tests and focus groups. Subjects in these groups would be probed indirectly, in the manner of Rorschach tests, to uncover fears and desires that they were likely not aware of and wouldn't divulge if they were. These methods were the subject of Vance Packard's 1957 book *The Hidden Persuaders*. Not surprisingly, ads that made a subtle pitch to sex, power and status became the norm. Or not so subtle: the Chrysler ad heralding the return to "longer, lower, leaner lines" promises "new personal power and personal pride that the ordinary motorist cannot even imagine!"

When it became clear that the consumer wasn't really buying a product but rather a self-image, it was much easier for manufacturers to profile their products to elicit the desired result. One brand of beer was distinguished and conservative, and the man who drank it incidentally smoked distinguished cigarettes and used distinguished hair oil rather than the sportier brands of these products, which were different mainly by way of the label.

Marshall McLuhan put his finger on the manipulations of advertising in his very enjoyable 1951 book *The Mechanical Bride*. One reproduced ad for nylon stockings shows a demure young woman looking off to her left while a stallion rears in the background. McLuhan analyses the sexual suggestion and concludes, "Effective advertising gains its ends partly by distracting the attention of the reader from its presuppositions and by its quiet fusion with other levels of experience. And in this respect it is the supreme form of cynical demagogic flattery." The rise of manipulative advertising did not go unnoticed by the larger public; standup comics and *MAD* magazine had a field day lampooning ads. But these were conscious objections, and the ads were designed to slip past the watchdog of consciousness.

When he turned his attention to the subject again in 1964 in *Understanding Media*, McLuhan wrote almost reverentially that "historians and archeologists will one day discover that the ads of our time are the richest and most faithful daily reflections that any society ever made of its entire range of activities."

In selling the American Dream to Americans, Populuxe reflected the aspirations as well as the activities of its society.

As a style it fell out of favour in the mid-sixties, but it has returned since the late seventies in graphic design, quoted with irony and nostalgia. The "Memphis" style of the early eighties—kidney-shaped sofas, ziggurat lamps—appropriated the exuberance of Populuxe. The design elements are used to evoke a myth, now of a postwar paradise lost, when convertibles were big and gas was cheap and the future looked bright. The boomerang has come home to rest.

Philip Street, art director of *Compass* from 1990 to 1997, a director of the Compass Foundation and the designer of this book, works in the animation department of the Canadian Broadcasting Corporation. His cartoon strip *Fisher* appears in the Toronto *Globe and Mail*.

My Adventures in Darkest Suburbia

by Miriam Blair

I got married in 1951 at the age of twenty, when I was in the middle of an arts course at McGill University. I was enjoying the course immensely, but it never occurred to anyone that I should defer the wedding until I got my degree. My parents, having paid for my expensive education, positively encouraged me to abandon it to get married. In their view, and mine, education was just a stopgap until I could be handed over safely into the care of a reliable man.

I started life as a housewife in Chicago. I can remember leafing anxiously through *The Joy of Cooking* before putting on my hat and gloves and going out to buy the exact ingredients for the evening meal. I felt very lonely, insecure and young, and was very nervous lest the butcher find out that I didn't know the difference between a chop and a steak. Happily I soon found a clerical job downtown. I enjoyed the job, but I looked on it as a temporary expedient until I could get on with my real life's work as the mother of a large family.

We then moved to England, where we lived for two and a half years and where my first two children were born. The war was still very much in evidence there. Allison was born in a large shabby hospital with the end of the corridor boarded off where it had received a direct hit. There was no bathroom for the patients as it too had been bombed, so we used the sluice room. There was still rationing, and a very spartan attitude to life prevailed. People didn't have central heating and claimed it was unhealthy, you only ate food that was in season, and you mended and repaired and "made do." I carried this attitude with me back to Quebec City, my husband's home town, where we lived for the rest of the decade and where our next two children were born.

We did make improvements to our split-level home, which like most new suburban houses had no fences or hedges, only a lawn hastily spread by the developers. We planted hedges, made fences, planted unsuitable trees (which later invaded the drains) and dug up a paved parking area to plant a vegetable garden, which was so unusual that it became one of the tourist sights of the neighbourhood. Inside the house we built a whole wall of bookshelves. After we sold the house and moved to England again, the new occupant took out the bookshelves, cut down the fences and paved over the vegetable garden.

My husband was not unusual at the time in being still the very image of the Victorian paterfamilias. My mother-in-law once told me that she didn't teach her sons how to cook because she didn't want her future daughters-in-law to take advantage of them. So the domestic arrangements were entirely my responsibility, as was anything pertaining to the children. Ronnie would read to me while I washed the dishes, until one magical Christmas when a dishwasher arrived.

The children came home for lunch at twelve, and my husband at one. I would eat lunch with the children, send the oldest ones off to school again as Ronnie was arriving, serve him his lunch and go to bed for an hour, with Ronnie there to cope with any emergencies. This saved my life. Thursday was my day with the car. I would bundle up the little ones, put them in the car and drag them around the A&P supermarket at the brand new shopping centre, the first we had ever seen.

Every year, just after the New Year celebrations had died down, Ronnie went off on a six-week business trip to South America and the Caribbean. I can still remember the despair I felt seeing him go, knowing that I would be alone with the children and the snow for what seemed like an eternity.

The first year he went we had only just moved to Quebec City, so I didn't know many people. A few days before he left I came down with mononucleosis. I had two very small children and was too sick to get out of bed. Ronnie arranged for a babysitter and waved goodbye. The sitter didn't speak any English and the children refused to have anything to do with her, so she left. My parents-in-law were out on the west coast for the winter. Fortunately our new doctor and his wife, who lived on our street, took pity on me and arranged for the children to go into foster care and for me to move in with another neighbour. So I spent the next few weeks on her sofa until my in-laws came home, retrieved the children and took me in.

In subsequent years, these times alone weren't so bad if the children were well enough to go outside and play. I made a strict rule always to take the little ones out for a walk if it was humanly possible. My father-in-law had made us a beautiful red sleigh big enough to tuck the babies into. There were no sidewalks, so I just pushed them along the streets past people peering through their curtains wondering who this crazy woman was taking her babies out in subzero weather where no pedestrian had ever been seen before.

I didn't know one working mother. It was just not a possibility. There was no day care or kindergarten for the children, so they were all at home until they started primary school. My eldest was one month short of seven when she was finally allowed to start school, so she was my unpaid nanny, babysitter, nurse and right-hand man.

I don't think I was a characteristic housewife of the fifties. Looking back on it I feel as if I was fighting the growing consumerism all the way. I made all my own bread and most of the children's clothes (my poor children were emotionally scarred for life by my attempts) as well as all of my own. I smocked dresses and knitted sweaters and socks, and I insisted on breastfeeding my babies when it was almost unheard of in Quebec. I was considered old-fashioned before all that became fashionable again. We were also the only people we knew who didn't have a television set. I didn't listen to the radio much and certainly didn't have time to read the newspapers, so the world events of the fifties passed me by completely.

All this seems very tame with the knowledge I now have about how most of the world has to live. Granted I was all but imprisoned by the snow and cold and lack of car in the winter, but now young mothers are almost equally imprisoned by their cars and spend hours ferrying their children hither and to. I didn't have nearly so many choices, so we just had to get on with it.

Miriam Blair and her husband Ron recently returned to Quebec City after living for more than three decades in Ivy Hatch, Kent, England.

Maire-Alain Couturier: The Priest Who Championed Modern Art

by Peter Larisey

To the French Dominican priest Marie-Alain Couturier (1897–1954), the gap separating the church and modern creative art was intolerable. One of the most daring of his attempts at bridge-building between great modern artists and the church came to fruition in the early 1950s.

Couturier was that rare combination: profoundly contemporary in culture and profoundly Christian. In his personal life, the reconciliation of the church and the modern world was well advanced decades before the Second Vatican Council saw that this task was necessary. Couturier agreed with Pope Pius XI that "the great scandal of the nineteenth century is that the Church lost the working class," whom Couturier described as "the poor, those among whom Christ would have lived." But Couturier also regretted that the church lost "philosophers, poets and artists." It was in creating and implementing his synthesis of poverty, creative imagination and a theology of hope that Couturier made his great contributions to the development of a modern religious art.

Couturier was a modern artist himself and a priest with deep religious feeling for and understanding of the importance of culture and the imagination. One of his important links with the modernist tradition was through his teacher, Maurice Denis, who during the late 1880s and the early 1890s had been a young and very articulate member of the group of Symbolist artists gathered around Paul Gauguin at Pont-Aven in Brittany.

When Couturier began his artistic and theological struggles, almost all Catholic works of art being produced were timid and sentimental variations on the officially sanctioned, classically derived and backward-looking productions of the art schools and the academic exhibitions. The Catholic

Fernand Léger, *The Virgin of the Litany*, 1949. Mosaic, 10 x 20.6 m. Notre-Dame-de-Toute-Grâce, Plateau d'Assy, France. Photo by the author.

preference was for an art that strove to escape the modern world, mainly by prolonging the nineteenth-century revival of Renaissance art. So bad had things become, thanks to "the academic imperialism of the Art Schools," that over the years the "visual habits" of the faithful had been corrupted and "imprisoned in conformism."

To accomplish the needed liberation of both art and church, Couturier developed a strategy. Since there were no real Christian artists able to create the great modern art the Christian community needed, Couturier argued, "It would be safer to turn to geniuses without faith than to believers without talent."

It was a radical statement, especially for the many Catholics who attempted to hold themselves aloof from the modern world and its art. But Couturier had had personal experience of the power of great modern art to function as a link with the human spirit, with deep, sacred feelings for creativity and life. He claimed that only through such living modern art could the church's long-moribund artistic traditions hope to be revitalized.

Couturier's ideas had their most startling and controversial expression in the church of Notre-Dame-de-Toute-Grâce. Consecrated in 1950, it stands on the Plateau d'Assy, high in the French Alps. The church and its square tower form the centrepiece of a village composed mainly of tuberculosis patients and their caregivers. The wide, overhanging eaves of the church's shallow pitched roof echo the alpine style of the regional domestic architecture.

Looking over the cluster of artists Couturier sought out for the Assy church, we can see that they were not geniuses without any faith but rather artists without an active Christian faith. Marc Chagall and Jacques Lipchitz were both Jewish. Fernand Léger and Jean Lurçat were Communists. Pierre Bonnard was an agnostic and Germaine Richier an atheist. Henri Matisse, although apparently not otherwise interested in Christianity, was already deeply involved with a Christian art project at Vence. Georges Rouault was a well-known Catholic artist, but not an academic one. For this reason he was almost seventy and had never had a commission for a church. These are the artists whose works made the church at Assy a significant—some said "notorious"—moment in the history of modern liturgical art. We will look at two of these works.

The first work to greet the visitor is Fernand Léger's mosaic on the church's façade, *The Virgin of the Litany*. Large, very flat areas of red, blue, yellow and green are organized in an abstract design around a simplified head of the virgin in a large medallion. This brightly coloured flat wall is screened from the viewer by heavily rusticated granite columns. The visitor sees the flat simplified black and white presentations of the objects that form the metaphors of the litany—"Morning Star", "Ark of the Covenant", "Tower of Ivory", "Mystical Rose" and so on—as well as the words themselves. It is an important piece of liturgical art because it is excellent in conception and execution, encouraging to parishioners in its bright, simple colours, and immediately readable by all.

Why would the Communist Léger consider such a commission? Several factors were involved. The mural project gave the artist a long-desired opportunity to create a work that was both architectural in its setting and communal in its intentions: an art for the people. Thus, as Couturier understood very well, there was a convergence of interests between the church's liturgical needs and the Communists'.

Another very persuasive factor for the artist was his personal friendship with the energetic modernist priest. Although Couturier had admired the famous painter's work for years, they met only during their exile in North America during the Second World War (part of which Couturier spent in Montreal, helping to catalyse the development of modern art in Quebec). Their common support for the French Resistance during the war helped cement their friendship. Léger would always remain outside the official church, but with the mediation of Fr. Couturier he would undertake other specifically Christian liturgical projects.

On the right in the narthex area as the visitor walks into the church is

Jacob Lipchitz, *Notre-Dame-de-Liesse*, 1955, bronze. Notre-Dame-de-Toute-Grâce, Plateau d'Assy, France. Photograph © Vis-Art.

Art historian **Peter Larisey** teaches about art and religion at Regis College in Toronto and is the author of *Light for a Cold Land: Lawren Harris's Work and Life—an Interpretation* (1993). He was an associate editor of *Compass* from 1992 to 1997 and subsequently secretary of the Compass Foundation.

Jacques Lipchitz's bronze sculpture, *Notre-Dame-de-Liesse*, completed and installed in 1955, after Couturier's death. The germination of this work took almost ten years. At an exhibition of the artist's work in 1946, someone from the Assy church asked Lipchitz to sculpt a Madonna for them. "Do you know that I am a Jew?" the artist asked. "If it doesn't bother you, it doesn't bother us," was the reply.

In 1947, Lipchitz and Couturier established the commission while the priest was visiting New York. The artist, who admired the whole Assy project and felt he wanted to do the work, agreed with conditions. One of these was that he could place an inscription on the back of the sculpture. It reads, in French: "Jacob Lipchitz, Jew, faithful to the religion of his ancestors, has made this Virgin to foster understanding between people on earth so that the life of the spirit may reign." Part of the reason the work took so long was that Lipchitz did not wish to take money for his sculpture and had to fit it in between other commissions.

Starting from a teardrop shape, the sculptor's image of Notre-Dame-de-Liesse grew over the years, eventually acquiring flower forms, a sacrificial lamb and Mary's gown, which suggests both gynecological forms and the cosmos replete with stars of David. The whole is supported by angels and seemingly held suspended by the dove of the Spirit.

Lipchitz, who was and remained a religious Jew, saw Christianity as belonging to "one Judeo-Christian western tradition…a kind of direct continuation" of Judaism, not a completely separate faith. It was fortunate for religious art that he could see so deeply and so participate in Fr. Couturier's quest.

It was because Couturier too saw so deeply into art and into Christianity that he was a person of hope. Intensely alive in the church and in the life of modern art, he was well positioned to foster the reanimation of Christian art. He had a deep respect and trust for artists. He believed that "every true artist is an inspired person, prepared and predisposed by nature and temperament for spiritual intuitions: why not for the coming of the Spirit himself, who blows, after all, where he wills?" The freedom of Couturier's intelligence enabled him to perceive the deep intuitions of his artist associates and to understand how their insights converged towards an as yet undefined modernist Catholic tradition.

A Peasant Pope Breathed New Life into the Church

by Romeo Maione

The spirit of humanity in the 1950s was at a very low ebb; the horren-dous events of the previous decade had etched despair on our souls. This same despair was affecting religious life. How could evil have run rampant during the 1940s? Had not the major religions of our world preached the message of love and human solidarity for centuries? Had all their efforts been futile?

Adding further to the prevailing darkness in church circles was a new phenomenon that was sweeping the West: the loss of workers to the faith. Meanwhile, the Roman Catholic Church in the 1950s did its best to ignore reality, concentrating instead on institutional problems and viewing with suspicion the efforts of elements in the French church to reevangelize workers. And when the real problems were faced, they were buttered up with "cheap grace." To win back the masses, the Catholic Church brought St. Joseph out of the fog of history and made him the patron of workers. More incredible still, an inane discussion then ensued on whether Joseph was the patron of workers or of artisans; the left wanted the word "worker" while the right insisted on the word "artisan."

All of this was happening when Pope Pius XII was ailing. A seriously ill pope invariably triggers intense political manoeuvring in the Curia, and by the late 1950s the battle lines had been drawn between the "feudalists" of the south and the churches of the industrial north. At the 1958 conclave following Pius's death, the opposing forces each tried but failed to elect one of their own men, and so began looking for an older cardinal who could serve as a compromise candidate. At length they settled on seventy-six-year-old Cardinal Angelo Roncalli from Venice, who became Pope John XXIII. Of peasant origin, Roncalli was seen as a transitional pope who could keep the chair of Peter warm for a few years until other arrangements could be made. No one imagined that in a few years this pope, through the

Pope John XXIII

Second Vatican Council that he convened and continued to inspire even after his death in 1963, would propel the church out of its feudal cocoon and into the modern world.

I remember well my first meeting with Pope John a week after he was elected. As part of traditional protocol, a new pope meets with the various government delegations that attended the enthronement ceremonies. Pope John insisted that he also meet with a delegation of lay leaders in the church. As the international president of the Young Christian Workers, an organization dedicated to the education of working people, I was asked to be part of this small group.

At that time, I was suffering from a serious attack of sciatica; not to put too fine a point on it, I was leaning like the Tower of Pisa. As was the custom of the day, one was expected to genuflect when introduced to the pope. Because of my back, I told the papal secretary that I could not kneel. When the pope entered, he gave his usual commentary on a Gospel passage and then had a personal word with each person. He came to me and then, gazing at my formidable size, said, "I suppose that you are the man that cannot kneel down; you better not—who would be able to pick you up?" The assembly erupted in laughter; the gift of humour had descended on the once-dour Vatican.

Pope John XXIII was a master of "one-liners." A few months after our first encounter, I met him again as a member of the Catholic International Organizations executive. Once more, he moved around the room and talked to each of us. A woman from France who was international president of Catholic Women Organizations excitedly showed the pope a relic of Pope John XXII—one of the less distinguished figures in the history of the papacy, to put it mildly. (An Avignon pope, John XXII chewed gold and silver with his food as an aid to "munching" it thoroughly.) The new John told her, "Take good care of it but I can assure you that I will not die rich like him."

My next audience with the pope occurred in the company of Monsignor Joseph Cardijn, the Belgian founder of the Young Christian Workers. Cardijn, who was to be made a cardinal by Pope Paul VI in 1964, had made an annual tour of the Curia since 1925. This time, however, he was ill at ease; it would be his first meeting with John and he didn't know what to expect. Could he persuade the pope to give his support to the Young Christian Workers? He asked everyone he met about the new pope; most people advised him that John loved to talk and so he should get his business done quickly and then strike up a conversation about other matters.

When the pope himself came into the room—it was more customary for a secretary to summon guests into a chamber where the pope waited—he embraced Cardijn and said, "You sure are an important person; one has to become pope to be able to meet you."

He escorted us into his office and immediately moved to pick up a rather heavy chair. I tried to help but John waved me away: "No, I can carry it. It is much lighter to carry than the Church." Cardijn then started on his business agenda—the need for chaplains to train workers' leaders, for a new social encyclical, and so on. The pope took notes all the while and eventually said, "Now that the business is over we can talk." He asked how the press in Brussels was covering his trips outside the Vatican. "Front-page news every time," we reported. "Good to hear that," he replied, adding, "They are not very happy around here, but then all that I am doing is visiting my flock." With his travels, John became the first pope to stop being a "prisoner" of the Vatican.

The pope asked us:

> Could I ask that you get your vast membership to pray for the Council? It is very important that we bring the Christian churches together. It is a shame that we remain so divided. At our religious services we read the same Gospels and when we leave the church we fall into hatred of each other. This must end and we must take the leadership. We always say that we have the fullness of truth. What is truth but love, so if we have the fullness of truth, then we must be the first to put forward our hand in friendship.

Up to this point we had been speaking in French, but now the pope asked me, "Maione is an Italian name. Do you speak Italian?" Yes, I said, but my brand of Italian was a dialect the pope was likely not familiar with. "Speak and let me try to place your dialect." So I spoke Italian and, after a few moments, the pope said, "Your parents are from Campobassa." I hesitated. How does one tell the pope that he is wrong? "No, they are from the Marches." John was unabashed. "Well, I was only 100 kilometres south; in these things I am not exactly infallible." Like a peasant he loved to talk and always went to the heart of things. He represented the great values of peasant culture even as that culture was disappearing.

Pope John brought the church into the modern world, freed the papacy to travel and, I think, was well on the way to developing a new "job description" for the pope, as Bishop of Rome whose major task would be less to govern and more to be the point of unity of all Christians. "Life is difficult but it can be won," he told me at the launch of his social encyclical *Mater et Magistra* in 1961, the seventieth anniversary of Pope Leo XIII's landmark *Rerum Novarum*. He certainly had triumphed in his own life. One can only wonder what he would have achieved both for his church and for all of humanity had he lived longer.

A pioneering lay Catholic activist, **Romeo Maione** was international president of the Young Catholic Workers in the 1950s. He lives in Ottawa.

The Federal Institution that United Quebecers

by Louis Balthazar

For French Canadians in Quebec, the 1950s were an unprecedented era of prosperity. The postwar economic recovery had especially beneficial effects on this small population that had just begun to see itself as part of the modern world. The social mobilization of Francophone Quebecers took place rapidly and dramatically in the 1950s; in other words, the frequency and variety of communications that characterize modern urban society came to Quebec. One of the most remarkable tools of this social mobilization was television. Starting in 1952, Francophone Quebecers, perhaps even more than other Canadians, became avid television viewers, and the new medium had special significance for them.

For obvious linguistic reasons, the Canadian Broadcasting Corporation had to establish not one but two television networks. And because Canada's French-speaking population was overwhelmingly concentrated in Quebec, the CBC's French network has long served as a kind of Quebec network. This was a de facto recognition of Canadian duality.

In addition, while the CBC English network broadcast many American programs, the French network had no outside sources of programming (there was little dubbing of American programs and almost nothing was yet being done in France in 1952) and so had to produce all its own programs. Overnight, Montreal became one of the world's major centres of live television production. This was an extraordinary outlet for French Canadian writers, directors, actors and artists of all kinds. To a large extent, the burst of cultural dynamism associated with the Quiet Revolution of the 1960s had its roots in this feverish activity that took place in the early years of television.

All of a sudden, an artist could earn a living and reach large audiences all over Quebec. And for the first time in French Canadian history, cultural production could take place in a secular context. The CBC French network was the first major French Canadian cultural institution that was not controlled by the Catholic Church.

Production had to be concentrated in Montreal. There was little possibility of producing programs in other places, and Montreal had already established itself as Canada's French-language cultural centre. In 1952, Montreal was still largely dominated by English-speaking economic elites. The west end was the most desirable area of downtown Montreal, and there was nothing French about it. Here, for all practical purposes English was the only language of communication—even though Francophones made up 70 per cent of the population of the city as a whole.

The streets of Quebec literally emptied for programs such as *La Famille Plouffe*. English audiences enjoyed it too. CBC Still Photo Collection, Toronto.

The paradox was accentuated when the CBC's studios were established in the Ford Hotel, an old Anglophone hotel on Dorchester Boulevard West (now renamed René-Lévesque Boulevard) between Mackay and Bishop streets. Imagine the reaction of these proud artists, writers and broadcasters—people who made their living using the French language—when they went to neighbourhood restaurants, bars and stores where no one had ever considered that any language except English could be used for public communication in a major city. And imagine the explosive possibilities of this situation, and its potential for generating a strong nationalist current.

A strike called by Francophone producers in late 1958 intensified this antagonism. The producers struck initially over union recognition demands, but the strike soon took on a nationalist character. Most of the other employees supported the producers, so that production was paralysed for the whole winter. But there was no support from the English network in Toronto, and even less from the federal government. René Lévesque, the French network's most popular journalist at the time, was one of many who came to the conclusion that the French network hardly mattered to Canada's Anglophone majority and the CBC could carry on without its French network.

In this way, influential cultural elites turned towards nationalism within an institution controlled by the federal government. Later on, there would be frequent accusations that the French network was infested with Quebec nationalists and even separatists. Not much progress would be made in correcting this situation, which has a lot more to do with the mood of Quebec's cultural circles than with a deliberate plot.

While television encouraged the blossoming of nationalist sentiment among Quebec's cultural elites, it also had an effect on the population as a whole. Rural and urban Quebecers alike quickly tuned into television and were completely captivated and fascinated by this new form of entertainment. While it took a number of years before virtually every household had a television set, almost everyone wanted to see the first hit shows—at home or at a friend's house. The streets literally emptied for *téléromans* (TV serials) such as *La Famille Plouffe* and *Le Survenant*. And because people had access to only one French-language station, everybody was watching the same program at the same time. Even public affairs programs attracted large audiences. Journalists such as André Laurendeau and especially René Lévesque, the host of *Point de Mire* (1956–59), became stars. They opened a window on the world and made Quebecers aware of international realities.

All this contributed considerably towards bringing Francophone Quebecers closer to one another. The same image of themselves and the world was projected daily to all Francophone Quebecers; watching these images, Quebecers experienced an unprecedented feeling of cohesion.

Later, when Hydro-Quebec used the slogan *"On est six millions, faut se parler!"* (We are six million, let's talk to one another!), it was an instant success because it corresponded to a feeling that had been strengthened by television.

Unfortunately, Quebec's Anglophones by and large did not take advantage of this opportunity to become integrated into Quebec's Francophone cultural life or at least to become more familiar with the language of the majority in their province. They stayed tuned to the English network, and they were less attracted to French programs than Francophone viewers were to English ones. Nor did the French minorities in the other provinces benefit from this cultural explosion in Quebec. With the exception of the border regions of Ontario and New Brunswick, it took more than ten years before the other provinces very gradually began to join the French network.

The coming of television thus resulted in a paradox. A federal institution, whose primary purpose was to bring all Canadians closer together, contributed greatly to strengthening Quebec nationalism and the feeling of belonging to a Francophone Quebec collectivity. It has never been possible to entrench Canadian duality in official documents, but television entrenched it on the ground. This is still true today.

A former Jesuit, **Louis Balthazar** has taught political science at Laval University in Quebec City for more than thirty years. His books include *Le Québec dans l'espace américain*, written in collaboration with Alfred O. Hero, Jr. (1999).

TV Hard-Wired Canada into Two Solitudes

by Mark Starowicz

In the early 1980s, at a friend's wedding reception, three hundred guests, most of them in publishing, media, law or business, gathered in a Toronto garden. The bride came from a theatre family, so there were several actors as well. Then a murmur rippled through the garden, and guests excitedly rushed to one corner.

"What's going on?" I asked the man next to me.

"Clarabelle!" he said. He said it in the same tone one might say "Jane Fonda!"—and dashed off to join the crowd. And so did I.

It was Alfie Scopp, the actor who had played Clarabelle the clown in *The Canadian Howdy Doody Show* in the 1950s. And for the next hour, all these reporters, producers, lawyers and writers of my generation—myself included—fell over one another to get a glimpse of him and shake his hand.

It was a reminder of an early, innocent sense of Canadian community on television.

Our family came to Canada in 1953, the year after CBC television started. One chose one's friends carefully. At least a couple of them had to have TVs, or one wouldn't get invited to watch *Howdy Doody* or *Uncle Chichimus* or *Hockey Night in Canada*.

But after Clarabelle, and Percy Saltzman's chalk, infidelity set in. Most of us lived in apartments. But some friends—the well-off ones—lived in houses, although that's not how we saw the equation. They were "well off" because they had *antennas* and it just happened that their parents needed to own a house to hold one up. They could catch (and the voice would drop a bit here) "American stations."

Not that the CBC didn't carry American programs. It carried *Roy Rogers, Wild Bill Hickock, Our Miss Brooks* and *Disneyland*. But for the less wholesome diet, the slightly "wicked" stuff, like *Highway Patrol* and the other crime shows, you had to go to the source. American shows seemed more metropolitan, and funnier. They also had more people like us—Ital-

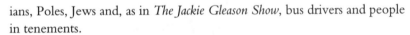

ians, Poles, Jews and, as in *The Jackie Gleason Show*, bus drivers and people in tenements.

I went though the *CBC Times* program listings from 1952 to 1959 for this article, and I feel a little ashamed about what I've just described. The drama special I skipped for *Highway Patrol* was *Sunshine Sketches* with John Drainie and Timothy Findley. The pianist I ignored was Glenn Gould. *The Big Revue* was directed by Norman Jewison. I was only eight, and rarely watched *Fighting Words* with Nathan Cohen.

Reading those program schedules stirs my admiration for the majesty of the enterprise, for the commitment to teleplays and anthology drama. And also a sense of anger, lost opportunity and paradox.

Anger because it's obvious from the schedules that we undernourished the dawn of the television age in English Canada. The best writers and performers had been assembled, but they weren't given the capacity to develop the volume and the production values to compete.

Lost opportunity because we let the popular culture slip to the United States. Canadian television kept us together in childhood: we all knew Clarabelle. But soon after that, when we needed adventure, family comedies, characters to follow and identify with—stories about growing up, about being twelve, about teenage crushes, about having loud immigrant uncles—we had so few that we turned to the American channels.

The paradox is the different impact the advent of television had in

English Canada and in Quebec.

Whenever I'm asked to speak about television at a high school or university, one set portion of my "seminar" always reduces the room to complete silence. It's a sad little interlude, and it starts like this: "Think of all the Canadian channels, public or private or specialty, that you've watched. All the thousands of hours. Now name me one, just *one* French Canadian who appeared outside a newscast, a public affairs show, or a sporting event. A character in a drama perhaps? Or in a sitcom? Or in a series? Name one."

It gets them every time. Of course there are answers—*Scoop* or *Emilie* on CBC—but they're so scarce they obviously haven't left an impact. The look in the students' eyes seems to say, "I never even thought about that."

I could not have asked the same question about blacks in South Africa in the apartheid era. There were black characters on the South African Broadcasting Corporation. We have, unwittingly perhaps, developed an almost airtight cultural apartheid. In fact, there are more American Hispanics than French Canadians on English Canadian television stations.

One could probably reverse the situation and ask a Quebec audience when they last saw an English Canadian outside of a newscast, with broadly similar results.

Television, the great homogenizer that is supposed to wipe out national identity and regional distinction, did not have the same effect in French Canada as in English Canada. In Quebec, it's now generally apparent, television was an empowering force that gave French Canadians an enhanced sense of themselves, their own community. In English Canada, though television created unifying experiences, it was also an instrument of the continental flood. The Canadian electronic brain was never wired so it could carry French cultural currents into English Canada, and English currents into Quebec. Except for *The Plouffe Family* and a bilingual show called *Handyman*, it was hard-wired in solitudes.

The English lost their sitcom and serial ground, for lack of resources and perhaps even will. The French eventually won their popular battle with home-grown sitcoms and *téléromans*. The question that nags is: could we have won both battles together?

Mark Starowicz created CBC radio's *Sunday Morning* and CBC television's *The Journal*, and now heads the Canadian history project, which is producing a series of films that will air on CBC television beginning in the fall of 2000.

We Created an Elvis to Meet Our Need

by Malcolm Reid

> *Weep for Adonais—he is dead!*
>
> —Percy Bysshe Shelley

I was fifteen, in grade ten at Nepean High School in the suburbs of Ottawa, when Elvis came along. Did he come along, or did I bring him along? Did all of us bring him along, all of us who were around fifteen in the autumn of 1956? I believe there is a sense in which we did. We made him; we created an Elvis to our need.

But that autumn, I didn't know that I wanted to create such a thing as Elvis Presley. I thought I was declining to participate. I was television critic for my neighbourhood weekly newspaper, and television had played the main role in bringing Elvis before the people. I saw those performances on *Stage Show*, the Dorsey brothers' TV show on Saturday nights: the lean young man in the tweed sports jacket, with the clipped polite southern words, the little carefully written kidding remarks ("Here's our latest RCA Victor escape—uh, release") and the pounding song "Heartbreak Hotel." But in my writing I minimized the excitement the new singer was creating. I called him "The Groaner."

Of course, this was really not an insult. Much of the appeal was in the groaning quality of the voice, and the voice was central to what was happening. It was the groan of feeling lost, as well as the groan of love. The body was important too. The face. Beyond the stock tales of how much his sensuous moves scared the TV companies and the parents, Elvis was a natural dancer.

And I too yearned to see the overthrow of the conventionalized attitudes of swing-era elegance exemplified by Tommy and Jimmy Dorsey, with their horns and their suits, and vibrate with something a little more rebellious. But I had another need as well.

In the preceding five years I'd been captured by such songs as "Unchained Melody," a prison ballad sung by Al Hibbler; "Sixteen Tons," a

miners' protest delivered by Tennessee Ernie Ford; and "How Were They to Know it was the Kid's Last Fight?", a boxing tale recounted by Frankie Laine. These songs had a narrative quality, a social quality. Because Elvis's erotic appeal was so direct, because of the *séducteur* in him, I didn't see at first that he had that quality. The troubadour, the chronicler, was more visible for me in Harry Belafonte, also a *séducteur*, also emerging at this time, and also a profound influence on fifties popular culture.

It's only now, with the succeeding decades to enlighten me, that I've come to see an Elvis that satisfies me. Then, there was only one hint of the Elvis I needed:

> *Well, if your baby leaves you*
> *You'll find a new place to dwell:*
> *Way down at the end of Lonely Street*
> *In Heartbreak Hotel.*

The hint was the archaic word *dwell*. Elvis probably didn't write it (he is cocredited on the disk), but he sang it with the ease with which he entered all the texts created for him or borrowed by him. That word, and the pale brown wood of the guitar.

Elvis Presley, from the start, was known to all as a former truck driver, the son of a poor southern family. His menacing-yet-attracting quality came from the erotic, but also from this working-class aura. Rock was a music of the poor as well as a music of youth. This has always seemed to me more important than a claim of Africanity, of black soul, for the pale-skin-ned handsome man. Many white singers before Elvis had had a portion of Afro in their art. In getting close to the African beat they were getting close to love, yes, but also to the explosiveness of oppressed life, the need to call up a lot of emotion and humanity to compensate for the lack of worldly goods.

Elvis was doing this anew. He was defining the American working class after the Second World War: nerves taut, but without much question-ing of society.

> *Well bless my soul*
> *What's wrong with me?*
> *I'm itchy as a man*
> *On a fuzzy tree....*

That was written for Presley by Otis Blackwell, a black New York composer of great wit; the star learned much from Blackwell's manner of singing on his demos. It was Elvis's *"ugh"* before the refrain *I'm All Shook Up* that began to win me. Then my liking was consolidated by:

> *Everybody in the whole cell block*
> *Was dancin' to the jailhouse rock*

"Jailhouse Rock" was written by Lieber and Stoller, Elvis's most faith-ful song suppliers. Here a little bit of conventionalization, or turning-it-into-a-joke, was creeping in. And all Presleyans seem to agree that the taut nerves of that first period, 1956–58, were lost soon, with Elvis's tame entry into the U.S. Army, with the haircut, with the affection (even before the Army called) for the word *sir*, with the song by Blackwell containing the words *teddy bear*.

I'm one of those dreamers who dreams of an Elvis who could have de-veloped artistically, pulled the potential out of his midcentury cry, said more, understood more. Couldn't he have worked with Ray Charles in song? With Tennessee Williams in film? But his handler, Colonel Tom Parker, a Dutch immigrant from the world of the circus, was not interested in this kind of development. Parker felt Elvis's selling point was his all-alone-and-unique quality, not his oneness with an American or a youth tradition. So he kept him in strictly-Elvis projects and places: the Las Vegas shows, the likeable-comedy films.

This produced one superb work in the later years, the song "In the Ghetto," by Mac Davis, which Elvis delivered as if he indeed felt what was happening in the black districts of the northern U.S. cities in the late sixties: *People, doncha understand?* In those years the youth-culture world paid little attention to *l'Elvis actuel*. No one wondered at his absence at Woodstock. It was with his death in 1977, in great unhappiness, that the honouring of *l'Elvis historique* soared again.

L'Elvis historique! He is the one who grew and grew after that first moment, that first sensation at the end of the fifties. He is the one who is growing still. His growth began even *before* that autumn when Nepean High School felt his impact, and there are ways of seeking out those early moments. *The Sun Collection*, the recordings Elvis made for Sun Records in Memphis before RCA Victor called, is such a way. Ah, the beauty of

Train I ride—
Sixteen coaches long....

Now that's the kind of stuff he could have sung with Ray Charles! The link with the American tradition was there. Phil Ochs, the thoughtful and melodic folksinger of the sixties, was very captured by the historic Elvis. He had a gold suit of the kind Elvis wore at Las Vegas made for himself, and performed a concert at Carnegie Hall in it. Ochs was trying to show the continuity from the hedonistic rockers of Elvis's era to the social-philosopher rockers of the youth movement he was part of in 1970. He implied that the protesters couldn't have done it without Elvis.

"The thing we've got to try to do," Ochs said, "is to get Elvis Presley to be Che Guevara. Because if you don't do that, you're just banging your head against the wall." This is surely a wishful juggling of charismatic names in the arts and social revolution. But just as surely, it contains this kernel: social change needs emotion and desire as well as reasoning and dialectic. A similar thought floats up at me from the compact disc of an Amerindian poet-singer from the American west, John Trudell. "Elvis was our baby-boom Che," he chants.

Change was not the keynote in Baby Boom North America, so those who helped us change are precious. They began to lead us out of Lonely Street.

Change *is* the keynote now. Phil Ochs says it, in a song he composed on a night walk through Toronto ten years after Elvis had come forth:

A race around the stars,
A journey through the universe ablaze
With changes.

Quebec City writer **Malcolm Reid** is a former Quebec correspondent of the Toronto *Globe and Mail* and the author of *The Shouting Signpainters*, a study of Quebec left-wing movements in the 1960s. His articles have appeared in the *Last Post, This Magazine, Canadian Dimension* and other magazines, in addition to *Compass*.

Beckett's Poetic Rendering of Faith and Doubt

by Craig Stewart Walker

What looks increasingly like the most important play of the twentieth century entered public life fairly quietly with its French publication in late 1952, becoming a minor *succès de scandale* with its premiere production several months later in a small Parisian theatre.

However, the private life of *Waiting for Godot* began several years earlier. Samuel Beckett, as a member of the French Resistance, had fled Paris in 1942 to escape the Gestapo. When he returned after the war, he found the city haunted and humiliated, no longer the glamorous beauty he had known. In its bosom, euphoria mingled with moral despair and gloomy introspection competed with fatuous diversion. It was in this atmosphere that *Waiting for Godot* began to take shape.

This paternity does not in itself make *Waiting for Godot* valuable or profound. After all, much of this century's literature has arisen from grim ruminations about our civilization's propensity for self-destruction and evil; indeed, Saul Bellow has decried the "dangerous wasteland myth" recklessly perpetuated throughout modernity. But if, like T.S. Eliot, Beckett seemed to echo Dante's wonder "that death had undone so many," he also earnestly shared Dante's attempt to make sense of the moral cosmos within which we endeavor, with uncertain success, to act as custodians of our own souls.

Nothing has served to obscure Beckett's work so much as the "absurdist" label that was affixed to him along with playwrights such as Eugène Ionesco. Ionesco's response to modern life was a celebration of absurdity, and as such was perhaps, as Susan Sontag once argued, symptomatic of a depressing anti-intellectual decay. Beckett, however, remained deeply troubled by the absurd elements of the modern human condition. His work challenges the tyranny of existential despair by seeking a coherent artistic form for it: the fearful is not transcended through denial, but only through creative transformation. In this light, just as Dante was able to create a co-

herent poetic representation of the spiritual crisis of his age in
The Divine Comedy, so *Waiting for Godot* may be the closest our
century has come to achieving such a representation of our
own spiritual crisis.

The Divine Comedy expresses a certainty born of reawakened faith, and so provides a specific and convincing imagina-
tive framework for that faith. But what framework is appropriate for a community of souls whose faith has been irrevocably
shaken free of such certainty? Where religious experience reflects a theology like Paul Tillich's, in which doubt is not denied as the opposite of faith but absorbed as its informing principle, what would a poetic rendering of this experience look
like? The short answer is that it would look a lot like *Waiting
for Godot*.

Beckett deflected attempts at conventional Christian read-
ings of the play. Asked whether he meant to write a Christian
allegory, he irritably replied, "I meant what I said." Though
Beckett's motto was, "No symbols where none intended," he
also issued the caveat that "the danger is in the neatness of identifications." In other words, there are two pitfalls we need to
avoid: presumption on one side, and negligence on the other.
Vladimir's allusion to the two thieves crucified with Christ, for
instance, is not mere coincidence, but this does not mean that
he and Estragon *are* the two thieves.

Like Dante, Beckett begins with humanity *in medias res*,
somewhere along the road of human destiny. As Vladimir declares, "At this place, at this moment of time, all mankind is us,

Samuel Beckett

whether we like it or not." The historical moment and geographic location
are unspecified: Beckett's tramps exist in a state of suspension between uncertain memories and inchoate expectations, just as the two crucified thieves
to whom they allude are suspended between damnation and redemption.
Despite repeated *dis*appointment, they attempt to keep their appointment to
meet Godot. The play depicts what they do *en attendant Godot*, as the original
French title had it—"while awaiting Godot."

Who is Godot? Here our wariness of "the neatness of identifications"
must begin. It happens that "Godo" is spoken Irish for God, but Beckett
warned, "If Godot was God, that's what I'd have called him." So Godot is
not God—or, at least, not God in the form in which God actually ever ar-
rives. Rather, the name Godot may be an instance of the literary figure
"preterition," in which summary mention is made of something while pro-
fessing to omit it. In other words, the name indicates that the unseen char-

acter is in certain respects Godlike but is, ultimately, "not-God." The *-ot* may be a diminutive (Charlie Chaplin is "Charlot" in France), suggesting that the character expected is more endearing than the true God. If Godot evokes the French word *godillot*, he is as familiar and even as despised as an old boot.

The main point is that, notoriously, Godot doesn't come. *Waiting for Godot* has been described as a play in which "nothing happens—twice." Actually, what happens is that instead of the expected Godot, Vladimir and Estragon twice get Pozzo (who is mistaken for Godot) and his man, Lucky. In place of the hoped-for message—perhaps a new covenant—they get Lucky's famous and apparently incoherent speech.

The speech is often treated as a piece of Carrollian nonsense, but it does contain a specific message, whose very obscurity reflects the difficulty of attaining coherence in such a matter—a concept Beckett picked up from James Joyce. Lucky acknowledges that an apparently apathetic divinity ("a personal God quaquaquaqua with white beard quaquaquaqua outside time without extension who from the heights of divine apathia divine athambia divine aphasia loves us dearly with some exceptions for reasons unknown but time will tell") and an indifferent nature ("heaven so blue still and calm so calm"; one thinks of the cloudless skies over Auschwitz) offer little comfort to those who sense that humanity is spiritually dwindling. However, he insists on defiant persistence. Doubt and disappointment must be acknowledged, yet humanity must nevertheless prevail in the struggle for spiritual truth. He ends the speech incoherently muttering "the skull, the skull," which may, without straining, invoke Golgotha (that is, Calvary), and thus lend to Lucky's "unfinished" a sense of correcting Jesus' "It is finished" (Jn 19:30).

Christianity posed a question to Judaism: what if the Messiah has already come? From one point of view, *Waiting for Godot* poses a question to Christianity: what if the Second Coming has already taken place? In other words, suppose we have been made the *permanent* custodians of our own souls? How then can we occupy ourselves fruitfully when eschatology becomes so dubious? Yet the play is by no means nihilist. Rather, it prompts us to ask ourselves: how exactly will we recognize, as Tillich put it, "the God who appears when God has disappeared in the anxiety of doubt?"

Craig Stewart Walker teaches in the drama department at Queen's University in Kingston, Ontario.

Tony Walsh: A Gentle Man Who Challenged Others

by Stephen Hagarty

In the early 1950s in Montreal, Tony Walsh and a few of his friends founded Benedict Labre House to feed, clothe and shelter homeless, transient men. In health and sickness, day in and day out, sometimes with much help, sometimes with none, Tony personally made meals for the men who came to the door, washed their dishes, cleaned their soiled linen, and led his volunteer workers, lay and religious, by an example that both inspired and unsettled.

Over the years, Labre House broadened its work to include the needs of poor families in the neighbourhood, as well as others who were referred from around the city. Guided by Tony and assisted by several extremely devoted companions who led mostly hidden lives, Labre House volunteers collected and distributed food, ran a clothing depot, visited the sick and those in prison, and held evenings focused on the discussion of social issues or the prayerful strengthening of their commitment. During these days too, Tony himself was constantly called on to meet with people who were sent to him for spiritual advice and emotional healing.

Who was Tony Walsh? Born in Paris in 1898, he was raised mostly in Ireland. Describing his youth, Tony said, "I was given a very unusual opportunity of sharing for a time the lives lived by shepherds, crofters, fishermen, grooms and fishwives—people who were illiterate but poets at heart....They were my tutors who opened a life to me that is unknown to most people."

Not yet eighteen, he joined the Irish Guards, served in the trenches of the First World War and was awarded the Military Medal. Later he immigrated to Canada, worked his way across the country on fox farms and cattle ranches, and settled finally in the Okanagan Valley of British Columbia. There, on the encouragement of a missionary priest, he became a schoolteacher on the Inkameep Indian Reserve. The Native stories, songs and dances that filled him with ecstasy became the motivational theme for his life as a teacher. He encouraged Native heritage through its traditional stories, art, songs and dances. In the words of one of his pupils years later, "He helped the children and the adults to rediscover their own culture, realize a pride in their own race, and a sense of their own self-worth."

After more than ten years of teaching, he went to work for the Canadian Legion War Services in Port Alberni and Gordon Head on Vancouver Island. Again his skills as a compassionate communicator through drama, dance and art were called on, this time as a rehabilitation counsellor for soldiers who were emotionally damaged by their experiences in the Second World War.

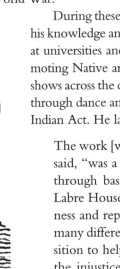

Tony Walsh

During these years in western Canada, he continually developed his knowledge and sponsorship of Native culture, studying part-time at universities and museums in Canada and the United States, promoting Native artists at home and in Europe, performing one-man shows across the continent that interpreted Native myths and legends through dance and pantomime, and contributing to a revision of the Indian Act. He later reflected on this period in his life:

> The work [with Native people] done in great solitude," he said, "was a kind of novitiate which enabled me to think through basic things and prepared me for the work of Labre House....The base of my commitment is thankfulness and reparation; thankfulness for sensing beauty in so many different forms, for friendship, and for being in a position to help and to heal; reparation to make amends for the injustice and callousness that the western world has caused primitive peoples.

Tony came to live in Montreal in 1948. Writing about the emergence of this charismatic individual in the English-speaking world of Montreal, Murray Ballantyne, a former editor of the Catholic newspaper *The Ensign*, observed:

> Tony Walsh is surely one of the gentlest men ever to have arrived in this city. Yet this quiet man challenged us. He took the counsels of perfection literally. He seemed to carry no weight, yet he changed the lives of so many. In a world that worshipped bigness, he chose littleness; in a world that struggled for wealth, he chose a life of voluntary poverty.

After his retirement from Labre House in 1967, Tony Walsh dedicated himself to what he called "channelling," continuing the supportive relationships he had made with people throughout and the world, linking them with one another to create an ongoing community of shared concern for the world's vulnerable people. Meanwhile, the work of Labre House continued, entrusted to the hands and hearts of others.

On May 28, 1994, Tony Walsh died at the age of ninety-five. Today, in keeping with his own final request, his body lies buried in an unmarked grave in a Montreal cemetery.

Stephen Hagarty was one of the founders of Benedict Labre House. He lives in Castleton, Ontario.

The Sixties

255   The Multi-Ring Sixties Brought Lasting Change   by Peter Larisey

257   A Generation that Said No to Plastics   by Robert Chodos

262   Vatican II: Outpouring of the Spirit and Human Shift   by Janet Somerville

268   Showing the Maple Leaf in Vietnam   by Victor Levant

272   From Hope to a Hole in the Park: The Columbia Revolt   by Peter Larisey

277   Expo 67: Theme Park for a Happy Future   by David Eley

279   Fit, Young and Casual Were the Trinity   by Margaret Visser

281   Hockey Had Not Yet Lost Its Soul   by Curtis Fahey

284   Three Sixties Stories

       ❀   The Jungle Collided with Rochdale College   by Ray Bennett

       ❀   My Discovery of Bob Dylan   by Robert Morgan

       ❀   Changing The World with My Guitar   by Bob Bossin

288   Taking the Longer View   by Judy MacDonald

290   Georges and Pauline Vanier: The Vice-Regal Couple Who Inspired Canadians   by Jacques Monet

The Multi-Ring Sixties Brought Lasting Change

by Peter Larisey

The 1960s were an important time for me, and I am not alone. Everybody has opinions about that watershed decade. As I reflect on it, aspects of the decade poke, slide and jostle their way into my conscious memory.

Early on, the 1960s generated an enormous and pervasive optimism. Pope John XXIII was so attractive a religious leader that even skeptics wondered if there might not be some mysterious good in the church after all. Ecumenism flourished: Christians of all denominations and people of other faiths felt encouraged by this chubby peasant pope. Janet Somerville captures the excitement that surrounded John XXIII's inspired summoning of the Second Vatican Council. This risky, tradition-defying and brave papal action was of a pattern with the resistance to blindly held traditions that marked the decade.

Political events are as vivid a memory as the religious ones. Quebec's *Révolution Tranquille*, evoked here by Robert Chodos, began in 1960 with the election of Jean Lesage as premier; as historian René Durocher put it, "Everything came under scrutiny, everything was discussed." In the eyes of many, politics became for a time an attractive and honourable profession when the youthful John F. Kennedy was inaugurated as president of the United States in 1961. The tragedy of his murder in 1963 underlined the pain of the struggle for justice and, until cynicism reasserted itself, inspired some to risk heroism.

For some others, political and religious motivations were combined. Hunted and frequently jailed, American Jesuit Dan Berrigan and his brother were among the ultimately successful leaders in the nonviolent struggle to end their country's tragic involvement in the Vietnam War. Victor Levant gives us a glimpse of Canada's role in that conflict.

An important part of my own experience had to do with that combination of politics and education dubbed "student unrest." At universities from Montreal to Berkeley to Paris and Tokyo, and notably at Columbia University in New York, where I was studying art history, students started revolutions—or rioted, depending on who is writing the history.

Even more pervasive was the "sexual revolution," helped along by the emergence of "the pill." The diminishing of family structures and values and the emergence of gay activism were among the decade's other challenges to the procreative model of human sexuality.

People who have grown up since the sixties have often expressed an acute distrust of comfortable baby-boom consumers continuing to recall their supposed heroic social justice struggles during this decade. In this skeptical view, many of the 1960s changes have not survived the conversion of baby boomers away from social idealism towards security and affluence.

But in politics, efforts to reverse gains in civil rights have not been completely successful. And in the Catholic Church, the Second Vatican Council still troubles conservatives. They now have to cope with energetic factions that are no longer inhibited from pressing for reform on issues like the requirement for clerical celibacy or silent about the second-class status of women in the church. At least some of the events and values in the multi-ring 1960s arena have had lasting effects.

Art historian **Peter Larisey** teaches about art and religion at Regis College in Toronto and is the author of *Light for a Cold Land: Lawren Harris's Work and Life—an Interpretation* (1993). He was an associate editor of *Compass* from 1992 to 1997 and subsequently secretary of the Compass Foundation.

A Generation that Said No to Plastics

by Robert Chodos

There was a decade called the sixties, which began in January 1960 and ended in December 1969, but there was also something called The Sixties, of which rock music, hippies, drugs, sex, student protest and radical politics were some of the outward signs. Not everyone who lived through the sixties fully experienced The Sixties, but there were few who were not affected in some way. The Sixties didn't begin until the sixties were about half over; as for when, or indeed whether, The Sixties ended, there are probably as many answers as there are people who went through them.

Why did The Sixties happen in the sixties? Historian Modris Eksteins suggests in this book (p. 49) that something very like The Sixties was taking shape in the 1910s when it was cut short by the First World War. The war was followed by the failed attempt to return to "normalcy" in the 1920s, the Great Depression, the Second World War and the paranoid Cold War of the 1950s. By the 1960s the tragic cycle of the early and mid–twentieth century had finally run its course.

At the same time, post–Second World War prosperity was still at its height, fuelling the optimism that underlay The Sixties. There were also the sheer demographics of the era: the accession of the first wave of the baby boom to young adulthood. The powerful experiences of that stage of life were made even more powerful by the circumstance that so many of us were undergoing these experiences all at once—and larger numbers of us were congregated on university campuses than ever before.

Nor would the sixties have become The Sixties without the war in Vietnam. For people seeking evidence of the corrupt nature of the System, the Vietnam War was the smoking gun. I'm not sure whether it was because Vietnam was uncommonly foolish and futile as wars go, whether war appeared less palatable as television showed us more of it, or whether a generation had simply arisen that decided to take Isaiah seriously and Just Say No to war. In any case, one of the slogans of the antiwar movement was "What if they gave a war and nobody came?" In unprecedented numbers, people—young people especially—declined the invitation to participate in or support the Vietnam War.

The images that The Sixties most commonly evoke are American ones (Haight-Ashbury, Students for a Democratic Society, Woodstock), perhaps with a few British rock groups and Paris street marches thrown in. I spent most of the decade in Quebec, which had its own Sixties, intertwined with the American Sixties but not identical to them. As the name of a magazine of the time had it, Quebec was almost America: *Presqu'Amérique*.

The 1960s began in Quebec with the defeat of the hidebound Union Nationale provincial government, the election of Jean Lesage's Liberals, and the burst of energy that became known as the Quiet Revolution. In retrospect, many of the reforms of the Quiet Revolution were part of a wave of provincial affirmation that swept Canada at the time—in Ontario very similar reforms occurred in the name of Tory continuity under John Robarts. But as with most things, this affirmation had an extra dimension in Quebec, a dimension that was provided by nationalism.

The Quiet Revolution was already on the wane and conservative forces in the Lesage government had gained the upper hand by the time Quebec's Sixties really got underway in 1964. A number of things happened within a few months that signalled the start of a new era. One such event in Quebec was the confrontation between demonstrators and police during a visit by Queen Elizabeth that became known as "Nightstick Saturday." Another sign was the formation of the Union Génerale des Étudiants du Québec (UGEQ), the Quebec student union that split off from the Canadian Union of Students. UGEQ adopted a Paris-inspired philosophy of student unionism, according to which students were young intellectual workers whose proper role was to be in solidarity with fellow members of the working class. Almost at the same time, in Berkeley, the Free Speech Movement was mobilizing students at the University of California. And a few months later, President Lyndon Johnson began the long journey up the escalator in Vietnam, touching off the first student protests and teach-ins.

The atmosphere in Quebec heated up after the 1966 election unexpectedly led to the narrow defeat of the Lesage Liberals and the return of the Union Nationale. In a foretaste of what was to come, the votes the Liberals needed to win were siphoned off by two small parties favouring Quebec independence. The new premier, Daniel Johnson (whose sons Pierre-Marc and Daniel, Jr., both later served brief terms as premier), was a skilled politician who managed to keep the lid on for two years, despite Charles de Gaulle's "Vive le Québec libre" speech and René Lévesque's departure from the Liberal Party to found the sovereignty-association movement—

which became the Parti Québécois.

If Quebec was *Presqu'Amérique*, as a student at the province's most prestigious Anglophone educational institution, McGill University, I inhabited a kind of *Presque Québec*. For a small but not insignificant group of Anglophone students—of which the *McGill Daily*, in whose offices I spent most of my time, was one of the bastions—identification with Quebec held a powerful attraction. A debate raged at McGill on whether to join UGEQ, and we threw ourselves into the pro-UGEQ cause. In 1967, on our third try, we finally gathered enough support to win a student referendum, and McGill joined UGEQ shortly afterwards.

Our attraction to Quebec student politics was based partly on its sheer verve and zest, but also on the prevailing sense that Quebec nationalism was anti-imperialist and of a piece with anti-imperialist movements elsewhere in the world. Canada, by contrast, was irredeemably enmeshed in the American Empire, as well as being insufferably dull. Demonstrating against the Vietnam War in Montreal, we could shout in the same breath, "*Le Vietnam aux Vietnamiens—le Québec aux Québécois!*" Another image for the Quebec struggle was posited by Pierre Vallières in *Nègres blancs d'Amérique* (White Niggers of America), the massive book he wrote in a New York jail after he was arrested for his participation in the terrorist Front de Libération du Québec. We found this image appealing as well: we had absorbed Jerry Farber's essay "The Student as Nigger" and so the circle of identification was complete.

The idea that these various struggles might be separated by more than nuance came later. In particular, it took English Canadian sympathizers a long time (perhaps until the free trade election of 1988) to realize fully that the mainstream of the Quebec nationalist movement, embodied in the Parti Québécois, envisioned Quebec as a modern, capitalist, North American society, albeit a French-speaking one. When this realization finally hit, many English Canadians felt betrayed by the Francophone Quebecers whose cause they had once championed. But what happened was not so much betrayal as the intrusion of reality into the romanticized view of Quebec that they had long entertained.

Daniel Johnson *père* died in 1968, and his successor, Jean-Jacques Bertrand, lacked his political talents. Quebec activists moved into the streets. In the fall of 1968 it was the cégeps, the new junior colleges established as part of Quebec's educational reform, that exploded. The next spring, Quebec radicals turned their attention to that fortress of Anglophone privilege, McGill University, demanding that it be converted into a French-language institution. A fifth column of McGill students—again centred on the

McGill Daily—agreed. A few days before the large *McGill Français* demonstration of March 1969, with tension in Montreal running high, a taxi I was in was stopped by police for having four people in its front seat. In the back seat were 100,000 copies of a propaganda leaflet members of the *Daily* staff had helped publish. We were held in a downtown police station for a couple of hours and then released without charge.

After *McGill Français*, we demonstrated for the release from prison of revolutionary leaders Pierre Vallières and Charles Gagnon, then in support of taxi drivers fighting an airport limousine monopoly, and then against the Bertrand government's lenient language legislation. In the fall hardly a week went by without a demonstration of some kind. Finally the authoritarian city government of Mayor Jean Drapeau passed an anti-demonstration bylaw, and except for a group of brave women who defied the ban in November, the demonstrations stopped.

Meanwhile, UGEQ was dissolving in a morass of ideological contradictions. The group of McGill students also fell apart, a casualty of internal tensions, especially between its male and female members. I had also been involved in discussions with some of my *Daily* friends and other student journalists about starting a radical newsmagazine, and this became my primary interest. The first issue of the *Last Post* came out in December 1969, but this was a Canadian project, and essentially one of the seventies. For me The Sixties and the sixties ended more or less simultaneously.

Were The Sixties a blip in time or have they had lasting effects? There is certainly evidence for the first hypothesis. Optimism turned to cynicism. The call to order was heard from Richard Nixon ("the silent majority") and Pierre Trudeau (*"fini les folies"*). Students grew up and made their way in the world.

But none of the reactionaries of subsequent decades, from Margaret Thatcher to Mike Harris, has ever been quite able to reestablish the pre-Sixties synthesis. Sixties radicalism, political and cultural, may have been ephemeral, but the late twentieth century has been marked by movements for change that incorporate the best of the spirit of The Sixties.

Preeminent among these are the feminist and environmental movements. The origins of both are sometimes attributed to books published in the 1960s—Betty Friedan's *The Feminine Mystique* and Rachel Carson's *Silent Spring*—and yet consciousness of the issues they raise was muted before 1970. Only one of the 264 Canadians elected to the House of Commons in 1968 was a woman, Grace McInnis (NDP—Vancouver Kingsway). Newspapers still ran separate "Help Wanted Male" and "Help Wanted Female" ads. Even radical groups were often forums for macho posturing.

But in an era in which questioning established institutions was the order of the day, the institution of patriarchy could not long escape scrutiny. Women's liberation and consciousness raising groups were formed in increasing numbers towards the end of the decade. In 1967, the federal government of Prime Minister Lester Pearson appointed a Royal Commission on the Status of Women, chaired by Florence Bird, but it would be 1970 before it issued its report, which documented systemic discrimination against women. Another dimension of the questioning of received notions of gender was opened up in 1969, when a riot in New York's Greenwich Village marked the beginning of the modern gay/lesbian movement.

The environmental movement, which also took hold in the early 1970s, likewise fed on Sixties skepticism about established institutions, and especially large corporations. Another movement that has had considerable impact in the last decades of the century traces its origins in Canada to 1969, when Native people reacted angrily to a white paper issued by the minister of Indian affairs of the time, Jean Chrétien, suggesting that Indians should disappear into the mainstream of Canadian society. And of course, the modern, nationalist and nettlesome Quebec that became part of the Canadian scene in the 1960s has persisted through subsequent years.

Three decades on, the cracks in the synthesis called modernity that appeared in The Sixties have not been repaired. Instead, they have grown wider and deeper, to the point where many people doubt whether the synthesis can be sustained at all. And while it would be foolhardy to venture a prediction as to what a new synthesis would look like, it is a fair guess that the movements that have arisen out of The Sixties are signs of some of the conditions such a synthesis will need to fulfil if it is to work.

On my twenty-first birthday, in 1968, I was in Baltimore, temporarily separated from the Quebec that sustained me, pursuing a brief and spectacularly unsuccessful attempt to obtain an advanced degree in mathematics. Alone, I took a long walk to a movie theatre, where I saw one of the most popular films of the time, Mike Nichols's *The Graduate*. The protagonist of the film was, like me, a bored recent university graduate with little appetite for the standard options offered by the adult world. In the film's most memorable line, a family friend takes him aside and says, "I have just one word to say to you, my boy. *Plastics*. There's a great future in it!" The word summed up the spiritual emptiness of the world against which so many members of the generation of The Sixties were in revolt. Whatever else we would do with our lives, we weren't going to make plastics. And by and large, we haven't.

Robert Chodos is president of the Compass Foundation and editor of the *Canadian Forum*. He was editor of *Compass* from 1987 to 1997.

Vatican II: Outpouring of the Spirit and Human Shift

by Janet Somerville

When the Second Vatican Council started in 1962, I was living in Holland as a member of an international movement of laywomen called Grail. Although Grail imitated religious life, it never was a religious community canonically, so it was part of the lay apostolate. I had known since I was fifteen that my vocation was to be a lay agent of the church's development and its future. That call hit me as dramatically as other people got hit by their vocation to be a priest or a sister.

Other elements of change in the church were also present in my life. As an undergraduate at St. Michael's College in Toronto in the late 1950s, I took the affirmative side in a debate resolving that the liturgy should be celebrated in the vernacular. I was completely convinced by my arguments, so when the switch to the vernacular came some years later, I felt it was a triumph of something I'd been saying all along. Furthermore, I was in a Catholic subset where enthusiasm for Scripture had already begun, and Catholics were being encouraged to join Scripture study groups.

With Grail I felt I was part of a vanguard, but when the Second Vatican Council began my vanguard started falling apart. Within a few years Grail became a post–Catholic movement with no formal link to the church. I had wanted it to be a life vehicle for me, my clan within the church, but it was no longer the kind of organization where I could make the kind of commitment I sought. I also had a personal reason for returning to Canada: my mother had been badly injured in an accident, and I was needed at home.

Only the year before, the Toronto School of Theology had begun operation, and for the first time in history it was possible for a layperson to do a graduate degree in theology. So during the council's second and third years, I was doing my MA in theology. Gregory Baum, a very gifted interpreter of what the council was doing, went to every session, flew back from Rome and told us what was happening. It was unbelievably exciting. I felt like one of the pioneers of a whole new chapter in church life, extremely lucky to be born in a time when all this could come together and I could enter it and be a lay theologian. I was thrilled at the rising up of Scripture as something that all Catholics were being encouraged to feed themselves on, the rising of ecumenism, and the reconnection of the sacraments with both those sources of reflection.

Mutuality and Hope

In the earlier mood of Catholicism, there was so much emphasis on the teaching authority of the hierarchy that no layperson would have thought of getting a degree in theology: why would you learn all that stuff when it was somebody's else's job to teach? So the message from Vatican II that had the greatest impact was that the church is a people: God communicates not only with the pope and the bishops and the teachers of the church but with everybody, and we have reason to raise our voices up in the church and say what we think as a part of educating one another.

The shape and feeling and colour of the sacraments underwent a transformation. Some of the changes were small, but they hit people viscerally. At communion, for example, the priest would now say, in a language you understood, "This is the body of Christ," and you would say, "Amen!" The change introduced a little bit of mutuality and dialogue and taking personal responsibility for what the sacrament meant.

The switch from the liturgy being in Latin to being in English changed the experience of Catholicism completely, and I understand why some people say the change was a reduction, because it located the acceptance of faith at a whole different point in the brain. When you worship in a language that you don't understand, something quite moving and powerful can happen, but it isn't comprehension. You can't take it into your power and say, "I agree with this part," and "I don't agree with that part." By locating the experience of religion at a different point in the human spectrum of response, the switch into the vernacular represented a huge psychological change.

Another message of Vatican II that broke with the past was that God has high hopes for the world and it is intrinsic to being a Christian to take your life in the world seriously and try to bring about God's hopes through it.

Most Catholics in North America before the Second World War were poor and Irish. They were used to being despised and oppressed, and they did not expect the world to change. However, although my father was poor, he believed that the world could be made a better place by militant combined action, and that the Catholic Church had principles—what we now call Catholic social teaching—that would make the world fairer. In that regard I had already entered a sense of the lay apostolate. I was thrilled to see the council document *Gaudium et Spes* say that we do belong in the world and that God has hope for the world, because I had heard it from my father.

Unfortunately, many of the wonderful insights of Vatican II were translated into legislation and forced on people in a short time frame. Whereas before the mass had to be in Latin, now you weren't *allowed* to celebrate a Latin mass. This approach betrayed the insights themselves.

There were other negative consequences as well. In my theology class, I was one of two laypeople. All the rest were priests or religious, and every one of them left the priesthood and religious life. Many of them encountered a Freudian understanding of how you become an adult, and a whole lot of repressed adolescences that hadn't been lived when people were adolescents came out. My classmates did many things that weren't very ethical by ordinary human standards, like lying to their superiors so they could continue to get their fees paid. I didn't want to stay in that atmosphere for very much longer, and I decided not to go on for a doctorate. At one and the same time I was seeing a dawn that filled me with hope and an abandonment of commitment and seriousness in many that filled me with confusion.

Now that I'm older, I see everything as more ambiguous. The stability and self-transcendence I remember from my childhood also seem like repression, and it had to end. But where in my twenties I thought of the Second Vatican Council as an outpouring of the Spirit in quite absolute terms, I now have learned that there are paradigm shifts that human tribes go through. They are messy and painful but utterly necessary. People lose energy and continuity and stability, but the new stuff coming in is forged by history with all its messiness. Although I still believe that the Spirit of God was noticeably merciful and some wonderful perennial truths of revelation were celebrated during the period of the Second Vatican Council, I see that it was also a perfectly human shift where a paradigm that had worked very well under particular historical circumstances got broken and a lot of people got lost.

I still prefer the set of symbols that the Second Vatican Council celebrated to the previous set and to some of the current offerings, but I recognize that they are a historical combination that holds some aspects of revelation better than others. Notably missing is an understanding of suffering. The popular church music of the time was sentimental, cheerful stuff that couldn't hold the passion and death of Jesus or the passion of any of the prophets. It lied when it told us that with dialogue we would understand one another, and we would all be included, and things would get better all the time. The consumer culture in North America was saying, "Just buy the right things and you'll be fine." We can't help being shaped by that culture, and some of it got into our theological and ecclesiological thinking.

New Challenges

There is much more room for tragic vision in liberation theology, which came along later in the sixties. It has room for martyrdom—for going all the way to your death without seeing what you long to see.

Vatican II's emphasis on the Bible helped open the way for liberation theology. Liberation theology's most important source book is the Bible and especially the Hebrew Scriptures, which the Second Vatican Council celebrated and praised. But the Hebrew prophets were much more tragic characters than is reflected in the optimism of *Gaudium et Spes* and especially its North American interpretation.

The Latin American fathers noticed that *Gaudium et Spes* was far too glib and optimistic and middle-class to fit the lives of the people back home. Gustavo Gutierrez saw that Vatican II had produced a European, and essentially bourgeois, synthesis of the Gospel and culture. To be able to take the experience of the people they were living with seriously, Latin Americans would have to come up with their own synthesis, and this was the project of liberation theology, which in a way was as much a new beginning as Vatican II was.

Another event that dampened the early enthusiasm of Vatican II was Pope Paul VI's 1968 encyclical *Humanae Vitae*, which confirmed the church's opposition to artificial contraception. I was a CBC producer at the time and I heartily wished that Pope Paul VI had just left the question open and let people live with the uncertainty.

Most North American Catholics, after brief flurries of guilt, decided to ignore what *Humanae Vitae* was saying and go with their experience. The North American culture simply won out in that battle. Within ten years, watching the sexual scene, I had begun to think that there is something very problematic about high-tech, large-scale chemical repression of the reproductive side of sex. A whole generation of younger people is growing up without any awareness that having sexual intercourse with someone naturally has consequences that don't fit unless you are ready to share your whole life with that partner. Most young Catholics today don't see any reason to wait until marriage for sexual union, which I think is a huge loss of a sacramental understanding of everyday life.

Vatican II legitimated debate and took lay experience much more seriously as a source of guidance for the church, and I'm delighted it did. Also, it tended to deemphasize any teaching of the church that isn't grounded on Scripture, which the teaching on birth control obviously isn't. In that sense, Vatican II prepared people to say to Paul VI, "Thank you but we'll follow our own conscience." The Vatican II documents opened a door to the North American culture to come in and dictate our response.

According to some thinkers I respect, Vatican II was the church's response to the challenges raised by the Enlightenment and the French Revolution. It was not an attempt to deal with the twentieth century or with socialism and the workers' movement, and certainly not with modern feminism.

But feminism, which didn't even exist at the time of the Second Vatican Council, became the most exciting intellectual movement in ordinary life in North America. Questions relating to feminism have largely superseded those relating to Vatican II. In daily life the really painful issues are between people who love what feminism is doing and people who don't. Progressive Catholics who are feminists are as suspicious of Scripture for feminist reasons as the council helped me to become of church documents. I still love the common ecumenical language that the Second Vatican Council celebrated, which is a biblical language, but many of my friends can't use it because for them it's sexist and classist.

In 1995, the Congregation of the Doctrine of the Faith published its judgement that the teaching in *Ordinatio Sacerdotalis* that the church has no authority whatever to ordain women is infallible. I felt the same anger and embarrassment and pain and resentment over this judgement that I felt over *Humanae Vitae*, and while in later years I began to see that *Humanae Vitae* had an important dialectical function vis à vis our secular culture, I haven't got to that point with this judgement yet. However, it doesn't feel like a fight about the Second Vatican Council. It's a fight about feminism as a vehicle of a transformed understanding of our whole tradition.

Nobody in the Second Vatican Council was thinking of the ordination of women. But the judgement felt like a premature attempt to close a question that is viscerally and vigorously open in the North American church, and it ran sharply against my Vatican II–cultivated sense of the importance of dialogue and the internal ecumenism of the church.

Another part of the Second Vatican Council, however, was a tremendous recognition of the wholeness of being a layperson, and from that point of view I am often offended by the importance that some of my colleagues give to the issue of ordination, of women or of anybody. Furthermore, in our technological juggernaut culture, there is a tendency to see everyone as an economic actor and anything that detracts from unisex economic functionality as regressive. I think modern culture's denial that there is a difference between male and female loses something wonderfully juicy in humanity. But the judgement of the Sacred Congregation for the Doctrine of the Faith didn't say anything very helpful about that problem.

The Vatican II Synthesis

Three decades later, we can see that Vatican II brought about a new synthesis, and I still rejoice in it. The ecumenical dialogue has been a thing of great light, even though it won't have any final resolution in my lifetime. While the overwhelmingly European weight of the Second Vatican Council gave too optimistic a tone to the hope-for-the-world spirituality, it is nevertheless essential for understanding the meaning of everything from Abraham on. I wish that a practical result of the council had been that Catholics regularly met on Wednesday night for Bible study the way Protestants used to, but that didn't happen. I hope that we don't lose the rediscovery of the Bible for everyone, but rather develop it.

Before the Second Vatican Council, many people were held in the church by knee-jerk, frightened, immature conformism, and I am not sure that is better than secularization. There is a lot less frightened conformism to the church now, while many people are frightenedly conforming to the secular world. The church's inevitable withdrawal from ghetto-based tribal authority and strength has favoured the other bully, which is secular public opinion. That other bully is now the tyrant in many people's lives. But if somebody has to be a tyrant, I'm glad it's the world and not the church.

Janet Somerville is general secretary of the Canadian Council of Churches and a former associate editor of *Catholic New Times*. She was a contributing editor of *Compass* from 1993 to 1997. This article is taken from an interview conducted in Toronto in November 1995.

Showing the Maple Leaf in Vietnam

by Victor Levant

For many Canadians, the Vietnam War was an occasion to feel smug. Canada had no troops in Vietnam; it welcomed American draft resisters and even deserters from the U.S. Army. Its medical aid programs and its presence as a member of the International Control Commission (ICC), which was supposed to supervise the 1954 Geneva Accords that had ended France's war in Indochina, seemed innocuous enough, possibly even constructive.

Gradually, however, a different story about Canada's presence in Vietnam emerged. In this version, Canada used its diplomatic and humanitarian position in Vietnam to serve the interests of the United States. The most thorough account of Canada's mutlifaceted service to the American war effort was the book *Quiet Complicity* by Victor Levant of John Abbott College in Montreal (Toronto: Between the Lines, 1986). In this excerpt, Levant dissects the political motives behind Canadian medical aid to South Vietnam.

—Editor

At the height of the National Liberation Front's Tet Offensive in February 1968, Alje Vennema, a Canadian doctor at the Quang Ngai tuberculosis centre, suggested to Ormond Dier, Canadian ambassador to South Vietnam and head of the ICC delegation, that "all voluntary medical personnel be withdrawn from Quang Ngai because they were risking their lives." Vennema later wrote:

> Dier's response was that we must have Canadians at Quang Ngai because it was very important for Canadians to be in Vietnam. Canadians had died for Canada before he said. I asked if it's that important why don't you send a civil servant there from the Department of External Affairs who can just sit there and wave the flag! But he put a lot of things in perspective for me. What was important in Vietnam was Canadian representation—to show we were here.

A similar view of the Canadian aid program in Vietnam was expressed by former External Aid Office adviser Dr. Michael Hall. Testifying before the House of Commons External Affairs Committee in November 1967, he said that "most of the aid given to Vietnam is not given because we want to give them this particular material or these particular people but it is a whole reaction to a demand for involvement." In March 1968, Senior ICC Political Officer Gordon Longmier told medical records librarian Claire Culhane, "Well, our project in Vietnam is 50 per cent humanitarian and 50 per cent political." David Anderson, Liberal MP and former administrator of the Canadian aid program, admitted to the External Affairs Committee in December 1968 that "a good portion of our aid was strictly for political purposes that were of no value to the people in the area concerned."

Conversations between Dr. Hall and the South Vietnamese minister of health about the value of establishing an orthopedic service reveal that this evaluation was shared by the authorities in Saigon. "Dr. Hall," he was told, "you must clearly understand that you are not here as an orthopedic surgeon, you are here as a representative of Canada." U.S. officials concurred that it was neither the precise projects nor the amount of aid that was important, only its existence. "There are many ways of expressing that [support]," submitted Secretary of State Dean Rusk to the U.S. Senate Foreign Relations Committee:

> Some have done it in troops, others have done it in various forms of assistance, but it should be made clear to the authorities in Hanoi by a maximum number of the world community that the independence and future of these smaller countries of Southeast Asia are of great concern to the rest of the world.

In fact, Canadian aid to Saigon was part and parcel of a coordinated and integrated allied counterinsurgency effort in Vietnam, the program developed by the Free World Military Assistance Office. The goals of this program were summarized in the confidential Command History prepared by the Military Assistance Command, Vietnam, as follows:

> Although many forms of assistance are urgently needed in the Republic of Vietnam the most sought-after are support units or individuals that will have major impact on favorable progress in the counter-insurgency effort by:
> 1) Dramatically demonstrating to the government and people of the Republic of Vietnam and to the rest of the world that other free countries are interested in helping the Vietnamese people maintain their freedom and achieve peace.
> 2) Providing assistance, short of direct combat actions, of a form that will have the most immediate and noticeable effect on the counter-insurgency effort in a particular locale.

Thirty-three nations, Canada included, were members of the Free World Assistance Program (FWA), furnishing what were described before the Senate Committee on Foreign Relations as "all kinds of materials and services needed in Vietnam, such as medical supplies, hospital equipment, refugee relief supplies, schools and hospital construction and so forth." Although coordinated by the U.S. State Department, the Free World Assistance Program was sponsored by the Pentagon. Of all the contributions to the Free World Assistance Program from its inception in July 1964 to the height of the war in December 1968, the Canadian contribution of $9,303,508 was the fourth largest.

Canadian pledges of aid to South Vietnam were made through the FWA program, as a March 1965 cable from the U.S. embassy in Saigon to its counterpart in Ottawa reveals. The cable states that an officer in the Canadian embassy had advised that a request from Saigon for aluminum warehouses and roofing material would likely be made against Canada's $500,000 Free World Assistance Program offer. However, conscious of the neutral image necessitated by its role on the ICC, Ottawa would channel its assistance through the Colombo Plan or the Red Cross. Washington was sensitive to Canada's ICC role and had no objection.

In the field, Canadians relied on the United States for logistical and material supplies—specifically on the Agency for International Development (AID), Air America and the Military Assistance Command, Vietnam. "There was nothing we could do in Vietnam without the Americans," wrote Dr. Vennema. "We depended on them for transportation, often for food, for everything." Dr. Hall told the Commons External Affairs Committee in November 1967 that the drugs and supplies available to Vennema "were derived from the Ministry of Health, that is American money, the Medico stocks given at the hospital, also American, and what he could get from local American army units; only recently did he get Canadian supplies." Canadian medical personnel, reported Claire Culhane, "had to register with the CIA-operated Air America to obtain…priority numbers as part of the Free World Assistance Group." Washington never hid these facts. "AID provides the funds and co-ordinates the efforts of 47 Free World medical teams in Vietnam," declared the State Department in November 1968.

It was precisely the humanitarian appearance of Canadian aid, most of it medically related, and the program's ostensible lack of political content that constituted its greatest asset to the counterinsurgency program. "Medicine is an ideal…action program," wrote Colonel Spurgeon Neel of the U.S. army, "because its humanitarian aspects can be raised above the level of political turbulence.…It provides an apolitical avenue through which favorable influence may be maintained and it provides immediate high impact communication."

The campaigns for medical aid in both the United States and Canada assumed a propaganda role designed to mask U.S. responsibility for the deaths and injuries of civilians in South Vietnam. Announcing the establishment of two rehabilitation clinics in Da Nang and Can Tho, Dr. Howard Rusk of the World Rehabilitation Fund said that "never before in history has any nation in the world, including the U.S., established a militarily operational hospital program in wartime to care for injured civilians. This new program could well be called 'Operation Compassion,' for here all civilian casualties who need and seek care will be treated alike." Questioned about the use of napalm in Vietnam, Dr. Rusk declared: "This writer personally saw every burn case in the twenty hospitals he visited. Among them was not a single case of burns due to napalm and but two from phosphorus shells."

Members of the Canadian medical team adopted the same stance. As late as August 16, 1968, one Canadian doctor told the Canadian press that "he had never seen a single case of napalm burns and that the majority of patients he had treated were traffic accidents." Those who chose another path were silenced. When the Toronto *Star* reported that Dr. Vennema said he was handling "20–30 napalm bomb casualties" in the Quang Ngai TB centre, the Canadian ICC delegation received a cable from Ottawa saying: "Better talk to Vennema about this. That type of thing should not be said. The U.S. government says there are no napalm cases in this province."

From Hope to a Hole in the Park:
The Columbia Revolt

by Peter Larisey

No baby boomer, I was already thirty when the 1960s began. As a theology student in the first half of the decade, I was swimming in hope, optimism and hard work, trying to realize in Canada the openness proclaimed in the great documents of the Second Vatican Council. Later in the decade I would be caught in the stress and pain of the inevitable confrontations as pressures for social change reached explosive levels both within and outside the church. And in the raw environment of the student revolution at Columbia University, I would have to take, for the first time in my life, a political decision that risked a great deal.

From 1962 to 1966, I benefited from the hope generated by Pope John XXIII and his summoning of the Second Vatican Council. When the council began, I had spent almost ten years in the Society of Jesus, a group of men that in its training sometimes seemed to be trying hard to leapfrog backwards in time past its dynamic and mystical founder, St. Ignatius, into a monastic lifestyle slightly modified by a nineteenth-century Jesuit mythology about being "Soldiers of Jesus Christ." Like most of the official church, they were out of touch with the modern world and, for the most part, out of sight.

Now the church wanted to relate to the modern world. The council sought a renewed Christian ecumenism, proclaimed affection and respect for the Jews and God's irrevocable saving covenant with them, and expressed the Church's esteem for Islam, Hinduism, Buddhism and other faiths. I felt that the Holy Spirit was vigorously animating the Church—including especially good Pope John but also the more adventuresome among my friends and colleagues.

Even in straight-faced English Canada we were breathing in the optimistic international atmosphere that was hard to resist. Many usually dour church administrators were shifting from their ordinary modes of thinking:

they began to wonder if the presence of the Spirit in the Church shouldn't be trusted after all. And they started asking questions: "Why not some changes?" "Does the church have to behave as though only the elderly and unimaginative could be moved by the Spirit?

Some senior Canadian Jesuits were affected by this optimistic atmosphere. After years of attempts, I finally had a superior, the late Fr. Angus MacDougall, who was willing to allow me to try seriously to understand how art and religion are related, especially in the modern world. Thus my horizons expanded rapidly. With my lifelong but undeveloped interest in religion and art, I could finally see myself as part of the liberating convergence of all that was good and creative.

I was excited. A new attitude towards Christianity and culture was being created, and it was one in which I could discern a role for myself. The Spirit was especially evident, it seemed to me, in the talents and works of contemporary artists whom I valued for themselves and could see as necessary companions for the modern reforming church.

I found I had a lot to learn about art and the world when I worked on an exhibition shown in January 1963 in the spacious suburban buildings in North Toronto that then housed Regis College. Entitled "Canadian Religious Art Today—I," it was helped enormously by the late Alan Jarvis, who recently had been director of the National Gallery of Canada. Through this and a second exhibition (we presented "Canadian Religious Art Today—II" in April 1966 and in June toured it to the Musée du Québec), I had my first experience of close contact with many artists. I saw how basically religious they were, although most of them had long since lost interest in organized churches or synagogues.

It was a happy time because my small world and insignificant energies seemed connected—a part of the whole Church that was meant to be there in the modern world to help mediate God's healing presence.

In the fall of 1967, these enthusiasms brought me to graduate studies in the history of modern art at Columbia University in New York. However, I had lots of insecurities. I had been a less than impressive student in Jesuit programs of theology and philosophy and so the responsible—and perhaps skeptical—Jesuits did not give me carte blanche. I had to prove that I could handle these studies in art history. My first fall term was difficult but rewarding. I settled into the second term—the spring of 1968—needing no extra persuasion to keep mind and energies focused on my main goals and my fascinating studies. I was the very image of determination and concentration and tried to avoid being distracted by any other concerns.

But that changed one morning when I arrived at Columbia's Morningside Heights campus. The night before, the campus was as it had been for a few weeks. Protesting undergraduate students had taken over many of the buildings including Low Memorial Library, which housed the office of the university president, Grayson Kirk, on the big-windowed main floor. One day I had seen a student whom I had gotten to know at Catholic functions on the campus dangling his legs from the open window of the chief executive's office and enjoying a huge presidential cigar.

But that morning the jocularity had ended. At about 2 a.m. during the night, President Kirk, against much advice, called the New York Police Department to raid the campus and retake Low Memorial Library. A large number of faculty members—many of them distinguished, some of them quite elderly and revered—set up a human chain around the building, hoping to protect the students peacefully and dissuade the police from their attack. They failed. Far from respecting the distinguished faculty members, the police shocked onlookers with their rough treatment of them, injuring at least one elderly professor. The police went on to take control of the building, injuring students in their way and enraging everyone else.

When I walked into the university, still very detached from it all, there was blood on the campus, which was crowded with as many police as students. I was disturbed by the intensity of the students' anger and hatred, directed especially towards the police, and their irrational, threatening rhetoric. As a Christian and particularly as a priest, I felt I had to try to mediate a situation that was lurching towards disaster, but first I had to find out what it was all about.

The problem had begun essentially as an issue of social justice. The east edge of the Morningside Heights campus was bordered by a cliff that separated it from Harlem, the main area for New York's mostly powerless black population. At the foot of the cliff was a long, narrow strip of land, Morningside Park, one of the few parks in the whole Harlem area. Columbia, a rich and powerful university, led by its businessman president, exploited its connections in city council and elsewhere and acquired land from this narrow strip, cutting it almost in two. The university wanted the land to build a ten-storey gymnasium, which would not be open to its Harlem neighbors.

After initial protests, the university agreed to let Harlem residents use the bottom floor. This was not enough for the protestors, many of them Columbia undergraduates. In response, President Kirk had a chain-link fence built around the construction site to keep protestors at a distance while shovels, bulldozers and trucks roared.

When students tore down part of the fence, the infuriated Kirk had them arrested by the city police. That was decisive. In retaliation, the students started taking over—the cool word was "liberating"—campus buildings, culminating with Low Memorial Library. The students' level of organization, thanks to Students for a Democratic Society (SDS) and its youthful Columbia leader, Mark Rudd, took the administration off guard.

The crisis was at a standstill that morning after the police bust. The "strike," as the revolution was usually called, was run by a parliament-like legislature called the "Strike Steering Committee" on which SDS had most of the seats. To maintain its position of strength in negotiations with the administration and police, SDS had to close all the buildings on campus that had not been taken over. To do this, it needed the graduate students—a majority at Columbia—to maintain the picket lines.

Graduate students met each morning during the crisis to discuss options, consider proposals and make recommendations. After further discussions and proposals, strategies for dealing with the threatening crisis were worked out. And these were ultimately successful.

In exchange for our support of the strike, the graduate students' organization was given about 50 per cent of the seats on the Strike Steering Committee. This meant that we were able to moderate strike legislation, defeating proposals that were dangerous to persons or threatening to libraries and other property. We kept up these moderating strategies until this 1968 chapter of student unrest was dissipated by the anticlimax of the ending of the school year in May.

Working in this struggle, I could spend whole days in often stressful meetings. Because I was a delegate for the art history students, I met with them in the mornings. Then in the afternoons I would be at meetings with delegates from all the departments. As an alternate delegate to the Strike Steering Committee, I sometimes had to go to that evening meeting so that our vote could be counted.

In addition to the toll in time and energy, everyone involved in this revolution took risks. The first of the risks for me was that I would lose standing in the art history department. I was reminded of this almost daily as a professor from the department went around to picket lines, listing names to report to our department head, who had insisted that in the art history department it would always be "business as usual."

The other risk was more serious: the Jesuits might withdraw their support for my religion and art studies if they didn't interpret my involvement in the "strike" as I had. Skeptical as he was, the good provincial superior, Fr. MacDougall, listened to my detailed account. Then, in a statement that revealed his distaste for the whole thing but left me free to continue my studies, he said carefully, as though weighing each syllable, "Well, I don't think you have done anything *wrong*."

Relieved I was, but too exhausted to rejoice. Especially when I thought of all the papers that I had to postpone because of this involvement, which I then saw and still see as both religious and political.

Grayson Kirk resigned as president of Columbia soon after the crisis. The gym that started it all never got built. It was replaced by the Dodge Fitness Center, a series of facilities under the existing campus that required no new land. And although the narrow strip of Morningside Park has been improved by the city—baseball and soccer fields have been added to the north and south—the hole dug by Columbia near the centre of the park had not been put right at the time of writing. The university negotiated an end to its lease of the land in the early 1980s and, according to a Columbia spokesperson, repairing the damage is now the responsibility of New York City.

The crisis of the gymnasium in Morningside Park made Columbia an arena where important 1960s issues—the injustices of racism and worsening poverty, impassioned opposition to the ideologies that prolonged the Vietnam war, the idealism and heady energies of the arriving baby boomers—came into violent contact with the arrogance, the intransigence and what I see as the blind selfishness of rich, powerful and long-established interests. The hole dug in Morningside Park in 1968 by Columbia University is a wound that still speaks with sad eloquence of the ongoing divisions in our North American society.

Art historian **Peter Larisey** teaches about art and religion at Regis College in Toronto and is the author of *Light for a Cold Land: Lawren Harris's Work and Life—an Interpretation* (1993). He was an associate editor of *Compass* from 1992 to 1997 and subsequently secretary of the Compass Foundation.

Expo 67: Theme Park for a Happy Future

by David Eley

Canada celebrated the hundredth anniversary of Confederation in 1967 with some large projects—the Trans-Canada Highway, the National Arts Centre in Ottawa (delivered later)—and with smaller flag-waving-and-fireworks occasions in every village and city. But the most expansive expression of the centenary was Expo 67, a class A-1 world's fair built on Île Sainte-Hélène and Île Notre-Dame in the St. Lawrence River at Montreal.

While the Trans-Canada Highway endures for our use today, Expo, transitional like the stages of our lives, is long past. But in its year it was a joyous and wondrous festival. We felt we were a young nation, and like a strong youth we hosted the rest of the world. We weren't shy to meet them, and we were embraced by the attention, affection and admiration of the nations.

I had moved to Montreal the summer before and could watch the physical construction of the fair site from a distance. This building process was an important experience for Canada, but more particularly for the province of Quebec and the city of Montreal. The coming of age of the Quiet Revolution was being confirmed in the eyes of the world.

What took shape was a futuristic utopian city of buildings, streets, waterways, parks and public squares. It felt very new. It was the way life could be, or so the designers thought. Some of the individual buildings, such as Bucky Fuller's geodesic dome, were the cutting edge of architectural thinking. The harmony of overall space, water and buildings was the main statement. These islands were to be a microcosm of the world: many nations, many languages, many cultures, but the one great harmony of humanity. The title seemed to sum it up: *Man and His World / Terre des hommes.* (But it would never be used today.)

When the fair finally opened we were not disappointed. The millions from the world came, mainly Americans but many others too. We locals began to take it in stride: "I saw the chairman of the Soviet Union today."

We bought the "passport" that allowed entry for the full six months, studied our maps and lists, and planned our visits as one might plan a European holiday. We wanted to see and hear and smell and taste everything. I still remember a baroque altarpiece in the Belgian pavilion, the Alexander Calder statue in the great square, and the space capsule in the U.S. pavilion. In the Iraqi pavilion I experienced the beauty of Islam for the first time. The world was a wonderful place: at least this microcosm of it told us so. I had never before had an opportunity to take it all in.

But we were younger then. A look back three decades later provides a more critical view of what the theme park for a happy future really relied on: unfailing technology. Our ingenuity would conquer all; "Man in Control," as one of the theme pavilions proclaimed.

Now I feel older and my country seems much older. The island site is still there but it is much stripped down and houses a casino. More important, we seem incapable of making the promised political and social changes as a country and our energy and care are measured out by deficits. Do we care any more what we can offer to the the rest of the world? Can we age so quickly? But this heady remembering of that miraculous summer of 1967 awakens again the hope of global peace, Canada's modest place in the world, and our need for maximum openness to diversity, beauty, the spirit and what is different in the other. Concern for the future is still a human theme.

David Eley is a chaplain at Concordia University and director of the Loyola Peace Institute in Montreal and was chair of *Compass*'s Publishing Policy Committee from 1984 to 1995.

Fit, Young and Casual Were the Trinity

by Margaret Visser

Fashion is almost invariably kind to the powerful. For a start, the rich can afford better clothes. And clothing can be used for the benefit of the group in power to conceal physical faults and lapses—and, where appropriate, beauty.

For example, when everybody wore the white powdered wig, it meant that beautiful hair could simply not be seen: the wig was a triumph of money over bodily giftedness—and most especially over youth. In the nineteenth century, the modern dark tubular business suit was invented largely to disguise the poor physiques of the newly powerful, sedentary rich. The same garment made the muscular working classes look uncomfortable, even foolish, in "proper" dress, especially in cheap versions of it.

Youth, with its recent access to money, became powerful in the 1960s, and its weapon at once was fashion. With a single blow, fashion made looking "proper" intolerably embarrassing. Clothing began to reveal rather than conceal, to the disadvantage of the no-longer-young.

Middle-aged women were forced to wear tight clothes and display their legs in shorter and shorter skirts. If they wore skirts below the knee, or otherwise unfashionable clothing, they risked "not counting" on the social and sexual scene. Men had to grow their hair out even if bald (men have often favoured short hair partly because it makes baldness less obvious). Hats died because they meant formality; they also hide hair.

There were two main codes of dress in the sixties. The simple, hard-edged, angular silhouette of up-to-the-minute clothing was often achieved with new artificial fabrics: dresses were made of plastic, elastic, even "paper" (actually cellulose and rayon). Designers made fortunes by marketing modernity, mass-producing nonconformity, and keeping prices low. For the decade's horror of the old to translate into an addiction to sporting every *dernier cri*, constant changes in fashion had to be affordable.

Alternatively, you wore rags: second-hand clothing, rumpled, ripped, transparent or flapping open to display your youthful body and proclaim your readiness for sex. Accessories included toe-freeing, long-lasting and therefore antimaterialistic sandals; beads; and headbands both to restrain and to draw attention to your long, abundant hair.

Most people, in most places and times, have worn traditional rather than fashionable clothing: each social group had its "costume," which it wore with a few personal twists and decorations added. In the sixties, a "people's uniform" returned, in the form of blue jeans. The middle classes began to wear cheap denim pants to project an informal image, and therefore one of self-confidence, physical and political activity, and youth.

Clothing for the demonstrably young and the fit has to allow for movement, to leave arms and legs free. Work clothes do this, as do clothes for sport and relaxation. Polite behaviour, on the other hand, expresses a willingness to restrain oneself: it requires limbs to be controlled and even hobbled, allowing only small, hesitant movements. People began to discard such rules and signs both in manner and in dress, even when not anticipating very much physical exertion. The effect of such dressing was usually more symbolic than practical: it meant one was standing free, rejecting social structures that might hamper movement, and maintaining a readiness to take the consequences. Fit, young and casual now became the trinity of laws.

Jeans enabled women to dress like men—even as they emphasized the difference between the sexes. Tight jeans flatter the young, exalt the skinny, disqualify the dumpy and the old. They are classically dyed blue, the modern West's favourite, most conservative colour. By wearing jeans, therefore, you could fervently conform on several different levels with society's demands, even as you dressed for the most desperately desired role of the decade, that of Dissident.

The ostensible "comfort" of blue jeans, meanwhile, was severely reduced as people used extreme techniques in the shrinking of their jeans to fit their forms ever more closely, then aged and bleached them to look as though they—and therefore their owners—had experienced life. In any case, denim's roughness and toughness itself underlined the body's softness, and so lent it more sexual allure.

Margaret Visser was a contributing editor of *Compass* from 1995 to 1997. She now lives in Barcelona, Catalonia, Spain and is working on a book about the church of Sant'Agnese fuori le Mura in Rome, scheduled for publication in 2000.

The miniskirt exacted a heavy price for granting women the young, fit, casual, sexually liberated look. True, it left legs bare, with connotations of action; the miniskirt was unthinkable without the marketing of pantyhose, which had previously been designed for acrobats and children. But a grown woman had constantly to watch out. She could not afford to let the tiny tight tube ride up at the back; she sat with legs (often encased in high hot narrow boots) under tighter control than ever before; and she never ever bent over from a standing position. Courtly etiquette has rarely been more demanding.

Hockey Had Not Yet Lost Its Soul

by Curtis Fahey

One night in the 1960s I was in the Montreal Forum watching a National Hockey League game. The details are hazy now: even the identity of the Canadiens' opponents escapes me. But I vividly remember the sheer excitement triggered by the speed of the game, the roars of the crowd, the championship banners hanging from the rafters. And I also remember the moment when the Canadiens' great centre, Jean Béliveau, burst up the ice on a breakaway. He "deked" the goalie so effectively that the fellow was left lying helpless on the ice, then casually reached around him to flick the puck into the net. It was vintage Béliveau.

I have seen many other beautiful goals, but it is only this one that keeps playing itself back in my mind. Why? I suppose it has something to with my being in the Forum in the first place; even in the 1960s, it was virtually impossible for someone without the right corporate connections to get a seat to a Canadiens game. I made it into the temple only twice. Another reason involves Béliveau himself. The Canadiens captain was a giant of the game in the 1960s, because of both his skill and his sheer elegance. He skated in long, smooth strides, stickhandled brilliantly, passed with precision, and was a master playmaker. Novelist Hugh Hood called him "poetry in motion."

Since that night in the Forum, hockey has changed almost beyond recognition. The most obvious change is in the number of teams: the six-team NHL expanded to twelve in 1967, by 1974 there were eighteen teams, and by 1995 there were twenty-six. Another change is all about money. Until the 1960s, most hockey players earned modest salaries. In the nineties the average salary is well in excess of what most people can expect to earn over several years, while the superstars' salaries defy imagination: Wayne Gretzky earned $6.5 million in 1995–96, exclusive of endorsements. Such players, with their retinue of agents, lawyers and accountants, are corporations on skates.

As for the game itself, it is frequently said that the quality of play has been in a downward spiral since the 1960s, the result of excessive expan-

Jean Béliveau

sion. I am not convinced. There were indeed great players in the 1960s, but great players came afterwards too; the likes of Gretzky, Guy Lafleur and Mario Lemieux would have been stars in any era. Further, in the 1960s there were far more gifted players in Canada than the six-team NHL could accommodate. For a few years after the expansion of 1967, hockey did suffer, but the Soviet-Canada clash of 1972 gave the NHL the kick it needed. Following that epic series, Soviet and Canadian hockey each borrowed the best from the other's game. In Canada, the results were apparent with the Canadiens' dynasty of the late 1970s and the Edmonton Oilers' dynasty of the 1980s. Both teams played superb hockey, even by 1960s standards.

Yet there is something wrong with 1990s hockey, which I think can be traced to commercialization run wild. Hockey has always been a business, and we should not romanticize the past. The 1995 film *Net Worth* showed the ugly side of the old six-team league, with greedy owners shamelessly exploiting underpaid players. But in the 1960s, the business part of hockey did not dominate the sport's public face; hockey fans could close their eyes to that side of things and concentrate on the game itself. Today, the millions earned by owners and players have carved a chasm between the sport and ordinary people. Omnipresent advertising—during TV broadcasts, on rink boards and even on the ice itself—makes the message that hockey is a business inescapable. The mere existence of the Anaheim Mighty Ducks, the Disney empire's contribution to the sport, reinforces the point.

Commercialization, moreover, has developed alongside growing Americanization. The NHL had always been American in its structure; four of the six pre-expansion clubs were in U.S. cities, after all. But at least those cities—New York, Boston, Detroit and Chicago—knew something about snow and ice; the current NHL boasts teams in such wintry places as Tampa Bay and San José. Still more grating, the number of Canadian teams is shrinking and may shrink even further, while there seems no end in sight to the proliferation of teams in the United States. In the nineties, the Quebec Nordiques became the Colorado Avalanche, the Winnipeg Jets became the Phoenix Coyotes, and other "small-market" Canadian franchises are similarly endangered. Money talks.

For many of us, hockey has lost its soul in the course of its transformation into big business, and so we cannot help but look back on the 1960s with some nostalgia. In those years players actually seemed to play for the love of the game, the small number of teams gave the sport an intimate feel, and the rivalry of the Toronto Maple Leafs and Montreal Canadiens was part of our national life.

I seldom watch NHL games any more. For the most part, I prefer watching old timers' matches or even kids' shinny on neighbourhood rinks. Whenever I do that, or on those rare occasions when I do watch an NHL game and am treated to a beautiful play, I am reminded what a great game hockey is. For me, such moments conjure up ghosts from the 1960s— Bobby Orr, Gordie Howe, Terry Sawchuk, Johnny Bower, Bobby Hull, Frank Mahovlich, and of course Jean Béliveau.

Historian and editor **Curtis Fahey** was an associate editor of *Compass* from 1990 to 1997 and subsequently a director of the Compass Foundation.

Three Sixties Stories

THE JUNGLE COLLIDED WITH ROCHDALE COLLEGE

by Ray Bennett

On a cold, post-snowfall Saturday in December, I am gingerly circling a grey, eighteen-storey seniors' apartment building on the northern fringe of the University of Toronto campus. This is, or was, Rochdale College. And it is part of my personal history.

Rochdale College, financed by a Central Mortgage and Housing Corporation mortgage, ten floors of conventional co-op housing for conventional U of T and Ryerson students, topped by six floors of radical experiment in alternative education for us unconventional types. "Degrees" sold as fundraisers. Design your own classes. Do your own thing. People came from all over North America in those ever-so-hopeful days of the fall of 1968.

But as the weather did its thing and fall shaded into winter, a snowball was building momentum. The two-block-by-three-block slice of countercultural street life known as "the Yorkville scene" knew a good thing when it saw one and began to move the couple of blocks west to the warmth and nonhierarchical verticality of the grey high-rise. Before long the brutal urban/human jungle blew into the benign vacuum of "do your own thing" and collided with the Rochdale experiment. Grimy questions of power, advantage and privilege reasserted themselves. Could we have expected anything different? Yes, we could. We did.

In 1995, I peek into the management office of these "Senator David A. Croll Apartments"—the office where, in the later stages of Rochdale's history, the enforcers of "Rochdale Security" used dogs to control outsiders' access to an exotic, promising and forbidden interior. Now a garish bust of Elvis sits elevated in one corner, overlooking the business of administering seniors' housing. "The King" presides here in a time of "strange days," a time of confusion, a time of moving forward and backward at once, when the urban seems in danger of becoming the jungle in the worst sense, when might is right, the image commands, profits rule and "security" is a com-

At the time of writing, **Ray Bennett** was completing a master's degree in environmental studies at York University and teaching English as a second language in Toronto.

modity to be purchased by those who can. Another experiment about to spiral out of control?

MY DISCOVERY OF BOB DYLAN

by Robert Morgan

It was the Monday night of the Labour Day weekend and I had just returned to Toronto after being away all summer. Now I was crossing Mount Pleasant Road, coming back from Murray's pool hall with my two best friends. For years we had been the inseparable triumvirate and now we were locked in a silence we had never known and could not understand. I didn't know who they were, these slouching, now softly whiskered boyhood chums, and worse, I had no idea who I was to them. And as we walked this new awkward silence together, on that last day of summer, it seemed that everything was different, that everything had changed. I realized I was going back to a house that had stopped being my home. I was sick at heart.

Stepping onto the curb I saw an older teenager standing under a street lamp. I noticed his long hair, faded jeans and boots with heels, and I suddenly recognized him. He had once been a friend of my sister's, a folksinger who had worn black turtlenecks and sung Kingston Trio hits sitting on the new blue broadloom in our den as my parents smiled their approval. But now he looked so different: the long hair, the boots, the small, knowing grin and slight nod of the head that came in silent response to my "hello." I passed by, and a moment later I heard it. From the transistor radio on the sidewalk beside him came a sudden single shot from a snare drum, followed immediately by an organ, and then the music flowed down the street towards me.

My companions and I walked on, heads down, listening. I stopped. I thought I had heard the strange, unfamiliar voice in the song singing something about the Rolling Stones, so I turned and walked back into the street light. The older teenager's grin had grown into a wide smile. He looked over at me, pointed to the radio on the sidewalk and said a single word. "Dylan!"

I stood listening and then, moving with an authority I didn't know I possessed, I picked up the radio and put it inside the open *Globe and Mail* box on the corner. I had learned as a paper boy that it made sound louder and fuller, and I knelt down in front of the box to listen. My mentor knelt

beside me, then without a word leaned forward and put his head right inside the box. I followed his example and put my head inside next to his.
The rays of the street light slanted in from behind us, turning the inside of
the box golden and beautiful, and he reached in his hand, turned up the
volume of the radio and said to me: "Listen. Just listen to this." And the
voice sang out:

> *You used to be so amused*
> *At Napoleon in rags and the language that he used.*
> *Go to him now, he calls you, you can't refuse.*
> *When you ain't got nothin', you got nothin' to lose.*
> *You're invisible now, you got no secrets to conceal.*

Robert Morgan took performances of "Like a Rolling Stone"
and other Bob Dylan songs from
his bedroom in his parents'
house to the main stage of the
St. Lawrence Centre in Toronto
as part of his show "The Heart
of Mine Tour."

And then that question! That question that was better than a thousand
answers. That question no one had really asked me for such a long, long
time. The right question at exactly the right time.

How does it feel?

And I knew somehow that I had changed. It could not have been otherwise. It was the last night of summer in 1966 and I had just turned sixteen.

CHANGING THE WORLD WITH MY GUITAR

by Bob Bossin

In 1968 Paris blew and so did Columbia University. Vietnam raged.
Tanks entered Prague. In Toronto, Rochdale College opened—O
eighteen-storey palace of sin! I was twenty-two.

It was a great time to be young. We really thought we could change
the world. We were naïve, but in our naïveté we threw ourselves with passion and intensity into the biggest issues of the time. The pictures don't
show the crackle of energy and optimism, of being a part, a *significant* part,
of something real and new and sweeping. What we did mattered.

So did the music. It went everywhere with us. Phil Ochs on the picket
line, *Sergeant Pepper* back home. The Jefferson Airplane sang, "We are all
outlaws in the eyes of Amerika," and we were. We rolled, and sang, our
own.

So I thought, in 1970, if I have a gift, it is to take ideas and give them a
kind of folk expression. I could see (undoubtedly with the aid of drugs) a
useful, socially responsible role for myself: I would take my guitar and make

up songs to sing while changing the world.

And as it turns out, that is precisely what I've done. The world has proved harder to budge than I thought and, as a career, I cannot wholeheartedly recommend folksinging. But the fact is, I have done, and continue to do, what I chose in the sixties. Myth aside, so have many of us. And for all our defeats by the rich and powerful—who are always stronger—the world is the better for our efforts.

Bob Bossin is a folksinger living in the Gulf Islands of British Columbia and one of the founders of Stringband.

Taking the Longer View

by Judy MacDonald

The sixties are nothing if not personal. Mention the sixties and people of a certain age launch into the songs, personal insights and moments that mattered to them—still matter to them. Then there are those of us who sort of missed it. Some of my sixties moments:

- My missionary family leaves Guyana just before independence (just one and a half at the time, I don't remember—but it counts, anyway);
- I walk through our Saskatoon swinging door between the kitchen and dining room to find my brothers taunting their best friend, John-John;
- I get a Jiminy Cricket walking toy and dance to "Who's Afraid of the Big Bad Wolf?" in my friend's basement in Edmonton (we've moved again);
- We travel across the prairies by car to my dad's new church in Windsor. The kids across the street make fun of me until I impress them with my pet mouse. We become the best of friends. I start grade one.

The end of a tumultuous decade.

Most of my peers resist talk about generational experience. Things are just too obviously divided—by race, class, music, clothes, politics, sexual orientation, status and aspirations. I know these divisions were part of the sixties too, but it doesn't seem that there was the same hesitation in the movement to speak *for* someone else. There were more straight middle-class whites confidently telling people what's what. If the sixties have handed down any legacy at all, though, it is a philosophy of openness, whether or not it was always acted out at the time. As a result, we now hear more distinct voices from more places than ever before.

Despite our differences, there are a few things that unite large numbers of post-boomers. In Canada, many of us grew up somewhere other than where we live now—another city, province or country. This leads to a kind of physical dissociation that makes it hard to organize: we all feel like strangers. All of us but the most privileged also share the same huge, yawning question at the end of each day: will I make it?

In a material sense, if "making it" means that we share the same standard of living the previous generation had, the outlook is bleak. But making it does not have to be seen this way. We learned that from the sixties when, coming out of utopian fifties materialism, a lot of people questioned the consumer culture for the first time in a while. It was just unfortunate that some people had to see it all change by the time they were twenty-five or so. They insisted that things had to happen, not just in their lifetime, but in their youth.

What do we want? Change! When do we want it? Now! What do we do when we don't get it when we want it? Get a decent job, settle down, get that car/house/ lifestyle, then wax poetic about our youthful idealism that was, sadly, doomed!

When some sixties revolutionaries found themselves flirting with thirty, they jumped ship. I guess they could afford to. I don't believe this is the case for the most committed activists, who can still be seen slogging it out for whatever they believe in. But with these exceptions, it's even more regrettable that there wasn't an acceptance that change can happen over time—over a *long* time.

A couple of years ago, an older friend questioned a reference to William Morris and his crafts movement, started in the face of the Industrial Revolution, as a model to follow now. From my friend's perspective, Morris had failed because the change he desired did not occur in his lifetime. Well, if there's even one person, a hundred years later, getting strength by this example, to me that's success.

But will *I* make it?

Only if I leave behind the me-generation detritus and the lean-mean-economic-machine dogma presented to us today as a quasi-religion. The question raised in the sixties, then too quickly dropped, was: will *we* make it? That *we* can't mean the young or the old or any one segment of society. It is all of us, including those to come.

Judy MacDonald was a contributing editor of *Compass* from 1995 to 1997, an associate editor in 1997, and subsequently a director of the Compass Foundation. She is a former managing editor of *This Magazine* and currently chair of the editorial board of the *Canadian Forum*. Her first novel, *Jane*, was published in 1999.

Georges and Pauline Vanier: the Vice-Regal Couple Who Inspired Canadians

by Jacques Monet

Georges Vanier

For six years in the 1960s Canadians elected minority governments—the first such extended period of political instability since before Confederation. A difficult recession, the rise of violent separatism in Quebec, militancies that split traditional parties and created Créditistes, strong pressures from nervous allies in Asia, western Europe and the United States—all these put pressure and strain on the Canadian experience. The blessing—for there was one—was in the office of the Governor General.

Georges Vanier was a much decorated war hero turned esteemed diplomat, his wife Pauline a lively, outgoing woman of extraordinary vitality. They won the admiration and affection of Canadians, Georges for his deft handling of problems and his concern for the poor and humble; Pauline for her tremendous spiritual energy and the dazzling smile that gave a heightened sense of self to everyone she met. They were a close-knit couple obviously enjoying and understanding each other. "We always think of them together" became a phrase often repeated by their many friends.

With Lester Pearson, the governor general renewed the dormant constitutional practice of regular scheduled visits to his office by the prime minister. Also, in his gentle but very firm way he often exercised his "right to advise" the prime minister, notably pressing him towards the abolition of capital punishment in 1967.

In June 1964, the Vaniers organized what would become one of their main legacies: the Canadian Conference on the Family, which drew some 300 scholars and experts to Rideau Hall. Out of the deliberation of those specialists, the Vanier Institute of the Family was born. Ever since, it has aided parents in need of counsel and helped deepen our understanding of the vital importance of the quality of family life. "A close look at the family in Canada," Georges observed, "could help more people to find the warmth and delight we found ourselves."

The governor general and his wife impressed by what they did. But much more, they inspired because of who they were.

Compassion was perhaps the main quality they shared. In Georges it went back to experiences as a young officer in the First World War. For Pauline, born to privilege and wealth, compassion went back to an early visit to the Montreal slums and a sharp lesson from her mother that wealth was entrusted to her as a gift for others.

For both the Vaniers, compassion was nurtured by their experience as diplomats during the Second World War. One of Georges's main concerns was to assist refugees, particularly Jewish victims of the Nazis, and find new homes for them in Canada. Pauline's care was to provide immediate aid and sustenance, often in the Vaniers' own quarters. After the liberation of Paris in 1944, she created a haven of comfort and reassurance for tortured *maquisards*, wounded soldiers and orphaned children in the apartment requisitioned for the Canadians in the Hôtel Vendôme. Georges visited Buchenwald and broadcast an indignant and moving reaction back to Canada. "Tonight," commented one reporter, "you put Christ on the airwaves."

Pauline Vanier

The Vaniers' compassion was rooted in a deeply spiritual experience. At the time of their return to Paris in 1944 they began to set aside a daily half hour of prayer together in addition to Mass and Communion. Despite the commitments of a very draining public life, they developed a habit of meditation close to that of monks, martyrs and mystics. Their prayer was the wellspring of Georges's deep sensitivity to the needs of others and his marvellous capacity for passing easily in his conversation from ordinary subjects to profound truths of the spirit. "Have you ever seen the Vaniers at prayer?" asked a noted Canadian journalist in 1967. "They are utterly rapt. Their whole hearts and minds are in a deep communication with God. Some say God is dead. How absurd. If God is dead, with whom are the Vaniers talking?"

Above all, the Vaniers gave the 1960s a vision of hope. In his last public utterance, three days before his death in 1967, Georges summed it up:

> One often hears the cries of distress of those who long for what they call the good old times, but I tell you the good times are now. The best time is always the present time, because it alone offers the opportunity for action, because it is ours, because on God's scale it is apocalyptic.

A year or so later, a student who had been observing Pauline's energy and joy for several days confided, "She shows that being religious can be fun." By the end of the decade the blessing of their moral insight was obvious, and the Vaniers had become, in the words of Michael Valpy, "one of the noblest symbols of the Canadian journey."

Jacques Monet SJ is a historian and has been president of both Regis College in Toronto and the University of Sudbury. He was a member of the *Compass* editorial board from 1990 to 1992.

The Seventies

"FUDDLE DUDDLE"

293   **Watching the 1970s Weave and Unravel**   by Mary Rose Donnelly

295   **From Boom to Economic Crisis**   by Mel Watkins

300   **Christians Made Justice a Vital Concern**   by Michael Czerny

306   **New Horizons for Canada**   by Doug Smith

310   **Canadians Listened to "Ni-wha Judge"**   by Louisa Blair

314   **Nobel Moved Away from the Mainstream**   by Malcolm Reid

317   **Watergate: We Still Don't Know Why**   by Rae Murphy

320   **Woody's World: Beyond Sex and Death**   by Marc Gervais

322   **Finding Feminism, Rediscovering Faith**   by Denise Nadeau

326   **I Came Too Late for Sixties Magic**   by Charlie Angus

328   **Oscar Romero: El Salvador's Archbishop to the Poor**   by Frances Arbour

Watching the 1970s Weave and Unravel

by Mary Rose Donnelly

Only now, in the middle of a lifetime, have I reconciled myself to spiders. So it was with ambivalent fascination that I discovered a nest of perhaps a hundred tiny orphaned babies in the garden, appearing as a comet of gold in a magically woven universe taut along the French lilac. Having joggled the slender branches bracing the web looking for wasted flower bracts to prune, I watched, rapt, as a jumble of dozens of pinhead-sized spiders dropped, fanning out and down like climbers rappelling out over a mountainside. As quickly as they were shaken free, the tiny infantry dragged itself up on invisible scaffolding to quietly reclaim some vestige of its old formation.

In much the same way, I look back in awe at the weaving and unravelling and weaving again of what we know to be the seventies. Was there anything that hadn't been knocked loose, pried apart or turned inside out by then?

Military triumphalism went out with a whimper as the United States limped away from Vietnam. But tempered by the sixties, we looked with skeptical eyes as the U.S. rebuilt its web within Latin America and propped up ruthless dictatorships in Chile, Argentina, El Salvador and Guatemala. In the midst of the slaughter, tiny Nicaragua emerged in momentary defiance of U.S. self-interest.

A little-understood conflict in the Middle East took turns that sent ripples through the oft-oblivious West. Anwar Sadat and Menachem Begin hashed out the first steps of a peace settlement at Camp David. Meanwhile, Arab oil producers pushed us to a sharper understanding of the Middle East conflict with an embargo that sent a shiver through the West, forcing the price of oil to five times its early-seventies value.

As Mel Watkins explains, this "oil shock," combined with Richard Nixon's decision to cut the U.S. dollar loose from its fixed price in relation to gold, set the world economy into the spin of recession. At the end of the day, however, a new consciousness of environmental preservation had settled into countries where consumerism had seemed a divine right. In Canada, this consciousness expressed itself in the unexpected response to the Mackenzie Valley Pipeline Inquiry, described here by Louisa Blair.

The wondrous jostling of the Roman Catholic Church in the Second Vatican Council had finally sifted down to tiny parishes everywhere. Music was transformed by the St. Louis Jesuits; youth groups, Marriage Encounter and the charismatic movement gave a home to Catholics yearning for a spiritual life, but with their feet planted in the world. Gloriously spirited movements like L'Arche and Taizé captured the imagination of people who yearned to weave together their hearts, spirit and work.

In the seventies we picked up after the considerable bash of the decade gone by. But for many, the unambiguous structures of an earlier time—military, state and church—would never be given the same authority. We had matured, left the warm web-nest and turned into something akin to the fiercely vigilant humpbacked loners, fly-fattened and sitting in wait in the junipers along the front of the house or strung along the ends of the clothesline.

Two decades later, as I cringe to hear the local folk group hiccup through "Be Not Afraid," or see what has become of the dream that was Nicaragua, or shudder for a fragile peace in the Middle East, I do not despair. Dreams will come and go. Where we have been and will be are perhaps less important than that we are, and will continue to be, alert to new springtimes in unanticipated places.

Mary Rose Donnelly, an associate editor of *Compass* from 1991 to 1997 and subsequently a director of the Compass Foundation, is coauthor with Heather Dau of *Katharine: A Biography of Dr. Katharine Boehner Hockin* (1992).

From Boom to Economic Crisis

by Mel Watkins

The 1970s were the in-between decade: between the good times that preceded it and the bad times that came after.

In his monumental history of the twentieth century, *Age of Extremes* (1994), the British historian Eric Hobsbawm dubbed the fifties and sixties the Golden Age of Capitalism, the greatest period of economic growth that the world has ever seen. Others have called those decades the era of the Keynesian Welfare State. There was full employment much of the time— and governments were explicitly committed to its achievement—with only minimal inflation. In theory, and to a lesser degree in practice, governments pursued active budget policies to fine-tune the economy. With memories of the Great Depression of the thirties still fresh, governments built safety nets to protect the unemployed and the sick and in the process put a floor on how far the economy could go down.

The years that followed the seventies are, in sharp contrast, marked by recurring crises: slow economic growth, high unemployment, deep recessions, drastic restructuring in the private and public sectors. There was some growth in the eighties, but later even the *Wall Street Journal* would call that "the false boom." When the nineties had no more than started, they were already being labelled the decade of "jobless recovery"; at least here in Canada, we saw more joblessness than recovery.

The seventies, then, were the decade when the world economy turned from generalized boom to generalized crisis, from mostly good times to mostly bad times. We seem to be still waiting for the turn back.

A new and unpleasant-sounding term was invented to describe the depressing mix of stagnation and inflation that took hold in the seventies: stagflation. The stagnation foretold what was to come. The inflation was reminiscent of what was supposed to happen only in an overheated, booming economy. The two together exposed a fresh contradiction of capitalism that was to prove deadly: to try to stop the inflation by deflating the economy meant further slowing the economy and worsening the stagnation.

Three specific shocks shook the world economy in the 1970s. On August 15, 1971, the Bretton Woods international financial system, established in the mid-forties, collapsed, along with the exchange stability associated with it. Underlying its demise were the weakness of the American dollar, which was the world's key currency, and the vast sums of money coursing about the world and subject to no particular control. It is not characteristic of great powers to arbitrarily devalue their currency and throw up a surcharge on imports. That the United States did these things was an indication of its reduced status: America, still bogged down in the Vietnam War, was apparently no longer the world's hegemonic economic power.

While orthodox economists tended to welcome the fluctuating exchange rate system that resulted (the market, by their assumption, being always good), they were probably wrong to do so even in their own terms. Without the discipline imposed by fixed rates, which required governments to deflate their economies when they were in balance of payments difficulties, the inflation those economists so deplored became more common and tended to spread more quickly from one country to another. And there was a yet deeper irony: the very orderliness of the world economy that had permitted rapid economic growth risked being eroded when there was no hegemon clearly in charge and able to impose its will.

As well there were the two oil price shocks, of 1973–74 and of 1978–79. The Organization of Petroleum Exporting Countries, dominated by Middle Eastern countries, got its act together as a marketing cartel. Not once but twice, it radically ratcheted up the price of oil, and hence of gasoline. Again it seemed that the U.S. was no longer able or willing to run the world economy. The cheap energy that had powered the great boom of the postwar years and was—at least in retrospect—essential to that boom was now put at risk. Importing countries found the price of energy rising; this simultaneously pushed up their prices and, by leaving consumers with less to spend on other goods, slowed their economies. The tendency to stagflation in the industrialized countries of the world received a powerful additional impetus.

To be sure, there were aspects to the situation that, at least at the time, did not seem so bleak. U.S. President Richard Nixon, who had gotten to the top of the swamp by red-baiting, went to the People's Republic of China. The worst of the Cold War appeared to be over; first with Nixon, and then with Presidents Ford and Carter, there was a thaw, a détente. Countries, Canada included, found that they had a bit more room to manoeuvre than they had before and were freer to pursue more nationalist policies. In Canada these were the Trudeau years, marked by the creation of the Foreign Investment Review Agency to monitor foreign investment and the state-owned oil company PetroCan at the beginning of the decade, and by the National Energy Program at the end.

Arguably the greatest achievement of the two decades of growth for the developed countries had been the building of the modern welfare state. The further growth of the welfare state slowed, but in the seventies what had been done still seemed firmly in place.

The real conundrum was inflation and what to do about it. The classic Keynesian analysis and prescription that had come to dominate political discourse about the economy were irrelevant, even wrongheaded, for they assumed that inflation resulted from too much growth rather than too little. The initial impulse, even in Nixon's America, was to move to neo-Keynesian policies: to have government impose some kind of wage and price controls. Here in Canada, Robert Stanfield of the Progressive Conservatives advocated controls in the early seventies. Trudeau ran against him on that issue, defeated him in 1974, and then brought in the controls.

The political consensus that saw controls proliferate was ephemeral. Business didn't like price controls because it just doesn't like government interference with its capacity to do business. It had learned, halfheartedly, to live with Keynesianism, but neo-Keynesianism was another matter. It wanted less government, not more. Labour doesn't like wage controls because they are seen as negating the hard-won right to collective bargaining; pushed to the wall, labour prefers to remain simply Keynesian.

Meanwhile, both unemployment and inflation were flourishing as the seventies progressed. Governments could not use Keynesian weapons to deal with the two simultaneously, and they were under powerful pressure from their better-off citizens who saw their real wealth eroding with inflation. As a result, they let central bankers obsessed with price stability take over the world.

There had long been growing within the economics profession a gang of monetarists who preached fiscal orthodoxy and tight money as the only way to bring inflation under control: there could be no long-term gain without that short-term pain that "got the fundamentals right." Under such malign influence, real interest rates, after allowance for inflation, reached unprecedented levels by the close of the decade—according to then–West German Chancellor Helmut Schmidt, the highest since the time of Christ. These high rates were, in any event, hardly conducive to stimulating the investment that would be helpful to creating economic growth and employment.

Of course, not all economies stagnated equally. Relative to the United States, both Japan and West Germany did better. Most impressive of all were the so-called Newly Industrializing Countries, a.k.a. the Asian Tigers —Taiwan, South Korea, Thailand and Singapore. They achieved sustained

The seventies were the last time there was a fork in the road. The world economy moved to the right and those in charge refuse to look back at the chaos that has resulted for so many ordinary people.

growth by exporting manufactured goods; they were able to take advantage of their vast pools of cheap labour and the increasing ability of transnational corporations with headquarters in the rich countries to allocate labour-intensive activities to these economies. Their entry into the world economy swung the balance between capital and labour at the world level more towards capital. The key to their growth was not free markets but strong, nasty, authoritarian states, but this point was played down in the western business press.

Within countries, capital, specifically big business, demonstrated an increasing ability to get its act together. In Canada in the mid-seventies, in the face of Trudeau's neo-Keynesianism, the Business Council on National Issues was formed, the better to lobby government. It consisted of the chief executive officers of the one hundred and fifty largest private-sector companies, Canadian- and foreign-owned. Predictably, the issue of foreign ownership began to disappear from the political agenda, to be replaced by free trade as part of a Canadian corporate bill of rights.

There was talk, even by otherwise serious academics and journalists, about the increasing maturity of the Canadian business class. As it happened, we now know that this maturity consisted of having the courage of the comprador: to go into a free trade arrangement with the United States that risked selling out Canada's sovereignty. Meanwhile, a Canadian labour movement long under the thumb of American unions became increasingly restive and moved towards autonomy, even independence. As capital became increasingly continental, labour became increasingly nationalist; that this strengthened the Canadian labour movement is a remarkable tribute to the weakness of the labour movement in the world's leading economy.

And while its hegemony lessened, the U.S. remained Number One and hastily created a new board of directors for the world economy with itself as chairman of the board. Under American leadership, the world's leading industrialized countries came together to set the rules for the world economy, particularly on financial matters—sometimes as the G-5, more often as the G-7 (with Canada included in the latter). Among the world's industrialized countries, the U.S. was (the arms industry excepted) by far the most market-oriented; the maintenance of global stability on American terms in the midst of the protracted economic crisis guaranteed a continuing drift to the right in both political discourse and political practice.

The decade closed, ominously, with the election of Margaret Thatcher in Britain. What would come to be called neoconservatism had carried the day—in fact, the decade. Government, seen in the time of the Keynesian consensus as part of the solution, had now become part of the problem. Central banks were an exception, of course, but having been created by governments, they were now to be left alone to do as central bankers saw fit, accountable to no one but themselves. The full package was monetarism plus privatization plus deregulation plus free trade plus union-busting plus deficit-cutting plus the gutting of the just-created-and-still-inadequate welfare state. The alternative to neo-Keynesianism sounded suspiciously like pre-Keynesianism; in these ahistorical times, the thirties had simply been forgotten.

The worst was yet to come. After Thatcher came Reagan. Détente was over. A weakened America turned bully and, standing tall in the saddle (choose your own John Wayne–Marlboro Man metaphor), redeclared the Cold War and insisted that its friends, like Canada, do as they were told. Nationalist initiatives that interfered with American trade and investment were not to be tolerated. Trudeau, never much of a nationalist, turned and fled without a fight. After Reagan came Mulroney; neoconservatism was snuck into Canada via the Free Trade Agreement. After Mulroney came Klein and Harris and Martin and the full flowering of neoconservatism.

The seventies can be seen as the last time there was a fork in the road. The world economy moved to the right and those in charge refuse to this day to look back at the chaos that has resulted for so many of the world's ordinary people.

Mel Watkins, a longtime professor of political economy at the University of Toronto and member of the editorial board of *This Magazine*, chaired the federal task force that produced the landmark 1968 report on foreign investment in Canada. During the 1970s he was a leading member of the Waffle movement within the New Democratic Party.

Christians Made Justice a Vital Concern

by Michael Czerny

Throughout the 1970s the church's increasing concern with social justice was an important part of my life. An authentic baby boomer, I had entered the Jesuits after high school, and when the seventies began I was in an interdisciplinary program in social philosophy at the University of Chicago. Ordained a priest in 1973, I later joined a small Jesuit community in the South Riverdale neighbourhood of Toronto, and in 1979 helped found the Jesuit Centre for Social Faith and Justice.

If the late 1960s were the spark, then the 1970s could only expect to be a glorious decade-long bonfire. The whole decade was an explosion of life, with everything opening up. One rallying cry came from Bobby Dylan: "Get out of the new road/if you can't lend a hand/for the times they are a-changin'." Another came from 1 John 4: "God is love" rather than law. All the revolutions (Vatican II, universities, TV, sexuality, you name it) seemed to come at once. For anyone too young or too old to enjoy "those years," they seem a maelstrom of banners and slogans, demos and marches, collectives and sit-ins, all in a fog of pot.

Today the upheaval looks a bit less glorious than ideological, but the enthusiastic desires that impelled people then cannot be denied. What were those desires? Specifically, how did social justice become a vital concern within the Roman Catholic Church (along with the other mainline Christian churches in Canada) in the 1970s?

Awake! Awake! The church at Vatican II acknowledged its real situation, intrinsically coresponsible not just for its own faithful and even all peoples but also for society and social structures. The conciliar decree par excellence seemed to recognize this in its very title: "The Pastoral Constitution on the Church in the Modern World."

Borrowing tools of analysis from Parsons, Weber and Marx, Christians began discovering the world in a critical way. The bishops at the 1971 synod on Justice in the World concluded that "action on behalf of justice and participation in the transformation of the world fully appear to us as a constitutive dimension of the preaching of the Gospel, or—in other words —of the church's mission for the redemption of the human race and its liberation from every oppressive situation."

Society used to exist as given by God or by Nature, like the horizon existing beyond human knowledge and control. But when society was found to be something human-made, then the consequence came quickly and unavoidably. In 1975, a document of the 32nd General Congregation of the Jesuits—the congregation that put social justice work at the centre of the Jesuits' mission—maintained that "it is now within human power to make the world more just." In other words, we are responsible for what we make and, if it is unjust, we can and must remake it. The document went on: "But we do not really want to. Our new mastery over nature and man himself is used, often enough, to exploit individuals, groups and peoples rather than to distribute the resources of the planet more equitably."

Throughout North America, the Vietnam War was a great teacher. It revealed the unjust economic, social, political and militarist structures underlying the war and taught the interconnectedness of everything. It showed everyone to be involved, not just those fighting the Viet Cong or resisting the U.S. draft. Everyone caught up in the (North) American way of life was complicit.

Meanwhile, the Latin American bishops were adapting key ideas of the Council to the Latin American reality. Instead of automatically blessing the status quo and standing by every dictator, the church began to assume a new optic, that of the poor in their millions who are poor not because God wills it but because of someone's choices and decisions. Sin may be an utterly private matter between God and the individual in confession, but it is also radically social: serious sins build up and petrify in rigid unjust structures. When with more or less radical change, society could assure the great majority of people a decent standard of living, what could possibly justify the continuation of misery and powerlessness?

Rereading the sacred Scriptures as opened up by biblical scholars and theology professors, the new theology applied great biblical texts like Exodus and the prophets to the reality of the poor millions of Latin America. The mission of Jesus Christ, to save us all from our sins, was experienced and expressed anew as liberation from everything that oppresses—not only spiritually but also politically, socially and economically. Liberation was within reach. After centuries of exploitation and repression, any further delay would only multiply the sufferings of the poor and our complicity. The question was: how to help?

Charity had its limits. "Give a hungry man a fish and you feed him for a day," but that did not provide for tomorrow and next year. The first insight beyond charity was development: "Teach a man to fish and you feed him for life." But how is development possible if social structures (oligarchy, dictatorship, repression, multinational corporations, imperialism) stand in the way, now and always? As the story goes, a good priest used to rush down to the river every day, sometimes two or three times a day, to rescue someone floating by at the very point of drowning. One day a young revolutionary challenged him: "Padre, why don't you go upstream and find out who is pushing the people into the river?"

The second insight, beyond charity and development, was the struggle of Third World masses for justice and liberation. Unjust social structures must change if the poor are to rise above famine, chronic disease, illiteracy, poverty and unfair practices of international trade. (What happened when the padre came upon the perpetrators is a Christian classic of the 1970s not yet written.)

Years earlier, many young Canadians had volunteered overseas as missionaries or church workers in Latin America, the Caribbean and Africa, where they learned to analyse society and to enculturate faith in practice. They perceived exploitation, repression and injustice not as inevitable and much less as God's will, but as sin to be denounced, resisted and overcome. Returning to Canada, they became the architects and pioneers of the Christian social justice movement in Canada.

Perhaps because Canadians tend not to separate church and state in a rigid manner, the church learned to speak out fairly effectively in the social realm. Every September (beginning in 1956!), the Canadian Catholic bishops used to publish a "Labour Day Message." The titles of the messages written in the 1970s give a pretty clear idea of how the Canadian church was implementing the Vatican Council in the social sphere:

- 1970: "Liberation in a Christian Perspective"
- 1971: "A Christian Stance in the Face of Violence"
- 1972: "Simplicity and Sharing"
- 1973: "Inequality Divides—Justice Reconciles"
- 1974: "Sharing Daily Bread"
- 1975: "Northern Development: At What Cost?"
- 1976: "From Words to Action: On Christian Political and Social Responsibility"
- 1977: "A Society to be Transformed" (actually published in December, and the last in the series)

The Christian critique of injustice learned in the Third World was more/less adapted and applied to the poor in Canada and Native People and Quebec, to Canadian multinationals operating in Third World countries, to our government's policies on human rights, refugees, development and trade.

Events like the coup in Chile against Salvador Allende in 1973 and the United Nations Conference on Population at Bucharest in 1974 demanded the most urgent and immediate response. Voilà, an ad hoc working group formed instantly and began to communicate by phone, telex and telegram (before fax!) with those in trouble overseas. Given the enormity of the challenge and the disproportionate power of the "enemy," the need to work together seemed obvious: therefore, the work was done ecumenically and in coalition. Those who picked up the challenge did so as highly motivated individuals *and* as church people (members, staff, clergy, officers). As a result the churches became institutionally involved, and the work was interchurch.

When the initial event or emergency dragged on, making manifest the persistent underlying unjust structures, a long-term response seemed called for, and an interchurch coalition was born. The list of such coalitions again speaks volumes about the Canadian churches in the world in the 1970s:

- 1972: China Working Group (which six years later became the Canada China Programme)
- 1972: "Ten Days for World Development": Inter-Church Committee on Development Education
- 1973: PLURA, a national agency devoted to the poor of Canada
- 1973: Interchurch Fund for International Development
- 1973: GATT-Fly, to monitor Canadian trade policies with the Third World (later the Ecumenical Coalition on Economic Justice)
- 1973: Inter-Church Committee on Chile (which in 1977 became the Inter-Church Committee on Human Rights in Latin America)
- 1974: Inter-Church Project on Population, to influence government policies at the Bucharest Conference (became, in late 1979, the Inter-Church Committee for Refugees)
- 1975: Inter-Church Project on Northern Development, "Project North" (later evolved into the Aboriginal Rights Coalition)
- 1975: Taskforce on the Churches and Corporate Responsibility, to monitor the behaviour of Canadian banks and multinational corporations, especially overseas
- Mid-1970s: Project Ploughshares, officially set up in 1977 to work on arms control and disarmament
- 1977: Canada-Asia Working Group, to concentrate on the Canadian connection with important issues in Asia

Combining personal dedication and institutional weight, these coalitions represent a wonderful Canadian achievement rarely seen elsewhere. They made common cause with many other groups working for justice at home and abroad—trade unions, political parties, development education groups, community organizations and many social movements—and their memberships overlapped a lot. Everyone had in common a future of shared justice, and a basic criterion of action.

The not-so-distant utopia for which all were struggling was sometimes expressed in New Testament terms: "Now the whole group of those who believed were of one heart and soul, and no one claimed private ownership of any possessions, but everything they owned was held in common" (Acts 4:32). Whether this primitive ideal foreshadowed contemporary communism, or socialism democratic or real, or "red" as in Red Tory was the occasion for much debate!

And a basic criterion of action was found in Matthew's great parable of the last judgement, where the Judge never asked which church you belonged to, if any, but how you responded to your neighbour in need. Given the electric importance of the many social causes at stake, whether one was RC or United or Anglican hardly seemed to matter—as long as one's denomination was "on board."

Christians could also turn to Luke's account of the mission of Jesus in the synagogue at Nazareth, which expressed a most important religious (but often also social and political) experience. After reading the prophecy of liberation from the prophet Isaiah, Jesus declares, "Today this scripture has been fulfilled in your hearing," and takes his seat. Just so it seemed that passages of Exodus, the prophets, the Gospels came to life before one's very eyes.

The remote age of martyrs like Marcellinus, Felicity or Perpetua became contemporary as well: in 1977 gentle Rutilio Grande, Jesuit seminary professor turned pastor, was cruelly martyred near his home village in El Salvador. The terrifying dangers run by courageous and long-suffering people, some of whom one knew personally, was nothing short of galvanizing.

The most telling image of the Vatican Council is Pope John XXIII opening the window and letting in the fresh light and air. But rather than something new coming into the church, what seemed to typify the 1970s was a general rush out of the familiar convent, sacristy and pew into the bright sunshine and primary colours of "the world."

The church of the 1970s seemed in full renewal, modernizing and declericalizing and sharing many human and material riches accumulated over centuries. Who thought the church itself needed attention? On the contrary, many seemed to be jettisoning ballast in a great hurry, not to keep the ship from sinking—impossible and unthinkable—but to help the spacecraft to lift off.

In our rush to implement the teachings of Vatican II, we tended to forget that major church councils in the past had set a very lengthy process of reform and renewal in motion that did not reach a lived consensus for centuries. Karol Wojtyla was elected Pope John Paul II in October 1978. The Sandinistas triumphed over Somoza in Nicaragua in July 1979. In March 1980 a death squad assassinated Archbishop Oscar Romero in El Salvador. Amid all these events the 1970s ended.

Michael Czerny SJ was a member of *Compass*'s publishing policy committee until 1990, and has been secretary for social justice at the Jesuit Curia in Rome since 1992.

New Horizons for Canada

by Doug Smith

If I might engage in reckless generalization (always a temptation in this sort of article), as I lived through the 1970s they seemed to languish in the shadow of the mighty sixties. Coming to maturity in the seventies, I always felt that I was living in a bit of an aftermath. Everything had been tried and everything had failed. Youth culture had brought about a consumer revolution, not a cultural revolution. Radical politics had dissolved into smaller and smaller sects with ever more grandiose titles. The expansive ambitions of the sixties simply existed to mock the illusory nature of any dreams of transcending a world mired in corruption and co-option. There was always Quebec—but to someone growing up in Winnipeg, Quebec was another country.

In retrospect, however, it seems that the seventies were a golden age. You truly don't know what you've got until it's gone. Or maybe it's just that (to engage in more reckless and unverifiable generalization) the sixties did not come to Canada until the seventies. The Conservative *deux nations* policy may have fallen flat on its face (remember Robert Stanfield and Marcel Faribault?), but the seventies were a period when it seemed that two nations might well be able to flourish north of the forty-ninth parallel. And it appeared that Canada might evolve into a North American social democracy. The 1970s were the golden age of nationalism and social democracy in Canada. And the fact that Canadian nationalism and Canadian social democracy have never really known what to make of each other is at least one reason why both of them have undergone such a beating in recent times.

The Golden Age of Social Democracy

At one point in the decade the New Democratic Party held power in three provincial capitals and controlled the balance of power in Ottawa. The Parti Québécois that came to power in 1976 was the most social democratic of all PQ governments (although it wasn't long before labour lawyer Robert Burns left the caucus). Even oil-rich Alberta ended up with a vastly expanded social sector. If it weren't for Peter Lougheed's expansiveness in the seventies, Ralph Klein would have had nothing to cut in the nineties. And it was Ontario's 1970s Tory premier Bill Davis, not Bob Rae, who created the social safety net that Mike Harris took the axe to. During the 1970s when an Ontario premier stole ideas from his opponents he was moving to the left.

There was a role for government in creating jobs, stimulating the economy and addressing social problems. Human rights, rent controls, occupational safety and health agencies, regional development programs, community development—these all became part of the common political coin of the 1970s. This was also a golden age for feminism. The injustices seemed so plain while an expanding economy appeared to offer the chance to eliminate them painlessly.

I remember speaking with Saskatchewan's deputy labour minister, Robert Sass, about his vision for occupational health and safety. In a reflective moment Sass said, "Maybe all these studies about carcinogenic chemicals are wrong. Maybe repetitive work isn't harmful. So what? I want to know what is wrong with trying to make work pleasant. What is wrong with trying to give workers more influence over the way they do their work?" Breathes there a deputy minister in Canada today who would utter such a heretical thought?

Even the Conservatives' doomed 1974 platform of wage and price controls rested on a twisted social democratic approach to the economy. By the nineties politicians had discovered that the ideal way to control inflation is to ensure that 10 per cent of the workforce is unemployed. The visible hand of the state had been exchanged for the invisible hand of the corporations.

Not too long before he was voted out of office, Manitoba NDP Premier Ed Schreyer made headlines by musing that the highest corporate salary should be something like two-and-a-half times the average industrial wage. Schreyer drew plenty of heat for the comment at the time, but it turns out that he made it just as the gap between the suits and the streets started to widen dramatically.

The Golden Age of Nationalism

In the 1970s Pierre Trudeau sought to undercut Quebec nationalism by strengthening Canadian nationalism. The changes were made in large and small ways. The word *Canada* was tacked onto every federal institution—usually at the end. Soon we were swimming in Air Canada, Health Canada, Labour Canada, StatsCan, InfoCan and so forth. In response to growing concerns over the influence that multinational corporations were exerting, a Foreign Investment Review Agency (FIRA) was established, while PetroCan was meant to give us a window on the oil industry. In 1979, during Joe Clark's brief term as prime minister, the NDP was able to mount a spirited petition campaign designed to save PetroCan from Clark's plans to privatize the company. A decade later the privatization sailed through with barely a whisper of protest.

At the time nationalists thought that FIRA was little more than a smoke-and-mirrors job, designed to steal a march on the NDP and the Committee for an Independent Canada. It still seems that way, except that in the 1980s Brian Mulroney found it objectionable enough to make FIRA one of the first federal agencies he dismantled. Mulroney transformed it into Investment Canada, made his way to Wall Street as fast as his knees would carry him, and announced that Canada was open for business.

There was a period in the 1970s when people did not talk of cultural industries but of culture. I read the snappy little *Books in Canada* once a month, and furthermore I read Canadian books. There were regional publishers and regional writers. Even poets seemed to enjoy a measure of fame and notoriety (I was young enough to think this was normal). This was when Atwood, Laurence and Davies became superstars. Little presses published books that I have been lugging around for more than two decades now. The New Canadian Library assembled a canon that people could read their way through. (Much of the older work was bleak, dreary or dreadfully overwritten. But even this had its upside—after all it underlined the fact that there was no better time to be a Canadian reader than the present.)

There were Canadian folksingers, Canadian rock stars, even an award named for a Canadian cultural czar (the Junos, after Pierre Juneau, who as head of the Canadian Radio and Television Commission had introduced the Canadian content rules for radio). Culture could happen here—although success was still validated south of the border. And it was never very easy to make a case that there was something truly distinctive about our culture. Rock and roll was rock and roll, and Canadian literature was too hydra-headed to admit of easy generalization.

Quebec nationalism went from the violent crisis of October 1970 to the PQ victory of 1976 to defeat in the 1980 referendum. Measuring the distance from René Lévesque and Gérald Godin to Jacques Parizeau and Lucien Bouchard, it is hard not to think that we are looking at the decline and fall of a good idea.

Canadian nationalism never achieved the goals Pierre Trudeau set for it. Quebec remained a separate country and Quebec nationalism has survived several funerals on CBC prime time. And the nationalism that dared not speak its name, the nationalism of English Canada, was a stunted and twisted child. It approached Quebec nationalism with liberal guilt and nativist intolerance—but rarely as an equal. Social democrats were always at sixes and sevens about what to think of nationalism. Like Trudeau they associated nationalism with the horrors of the Second World War. But it was also apparent that nationalism was more than backward-looking mumbo-jumbo—whatever one might think of Walter Gordon or René Lévesque, no one ever said they weren't modern. Social democrats were supposed to be internationalists—but they could not avoid noticing that all the successful social liberation movements of the postwar period were simultaneously socialist and nationalist.

And in the midst of all this, the real golden age, the postwar economic boom, collapsed. On Thanksgiving 1975 Trudeau imposed a system of wage and price controls. We were warned that the time for belt-tightening had arrived. The following year the National Union of Students was passing out buttons that said "No Cutbacks" at the University of Manitoba. I barely understood the concept. I certainly did not understand the magnitude of the coming change. According to the Trilateral Commission, democracy was in crisis: students, journalists, unions, minorities were putting too much pressure on the system. It was ungovernable. For much of the next two decades considerable political effort was expended to make it abundantly clear who does the riding and who is ridden in our society.

But golden ages are a long time in gestation. The short-lived good life of the seventies came from the suffering of the thirties and the fighting of the forties. It was not a gift but a legacy. And to quote Alexander Cockburn quoting Claude Lévi-Strauss, "The golden age is within us."

Doug Smith is a Winnipeg writer and labour historian whose books include *Let Us Rise!: An Illustrated History of the Manitoba Labour Movement* (1985).

Canadians Listened to "Ni-wha Judge"

by Louisa Blair

In 1968 the Atlantic Richfield company was just about to cease its oil explorations in Alaska when the company president received a request from the field to drill just one more test well. He reluctantly agreed, and Prudhoe Bay became the largest oilfield in American history.

As a result of the discovery, in the early seventies when Pierre Trudeau was settling in at 24 Sussex Drive with his new wife, twenty-nine years his junior, plans were being made for what Eric Kierans called the costliest project in Canadian history, the Mackenzie Valley Pipeline. Estimated at $6 billion and soon rising to $10 billion, as these things usually do, the 3,860-km pipeline was to carry 4.5 million cubic feet of natural gas per day (with potential to double that capacity) from Prudhoe Bay across the northern Yukon, and then south from the Mackenzie River delta to southern Canada and the United States.

Two companies vied for the contract. The more formidable was Canadian Arctic Gas Pipeline Ltd., an international consortium of twenty-seven companies including Exxon, Shell and Gulf. They planned the greatest construction enterprise ever undertaken, with the monumental engineering problems of freezing the gas and transporting it in pipes laid in ground chronically destabilized by permafrost. Foothills Pipe Lines Ltd., a smaller company backed by Calgary and Vancouver interests, had a more modest proposal that would link Alaskan pipelines only with existing pipes in Alberta and British Columbia. It called this proposal the "Maple Leaf Line" and complained that Arctic Gas was planning to supply primarily U.S. markets through a pipeline that would amount to a "Panama Canal" across Canada, interfering with Canadian sovereignty and, moreover, using Canadian money to do so.

The big companies may have understood appeals to Canadian nationalism, but they were far less equipped to deal with Aboriginal land claims. The chair of Arctic Gas, W.P. Wilder, said that the company could easily negotiate with northern Aboriginal people for the 100 square kilometres under which the pipe would be buried.

In January 1974 a forty-one-year-old B.C. judge, Thomas Berger, received a phone call from Indian Affairs and Northern Development Minister Jean Chrétien asking him to conduct an inquiry into the proposed pipeline. Berger—who liked to read Hunter Thompson, had served a brief spell as his province's NDP leader, and had a special interest in Aboriginal rights—enthusiastically agreed.

At the time, Aboriginal sovereignty claims were just beginning to elicit something other than contempt from the non-Aboriginal population. A 1965 headline in the Vancouver *Sun* saying "Lawyer says Indians own B.C," was seen at the time as a big joke, another B.C. lawyer noted. "No one is laughing now," he remarked in 1974. In 1975 the Dene declared themselves a nation and called for recognition. The minister of Indian Affairs dismissed their declaration as "gobbledygook," but the churches took it more seriously. In a support statement, the Canadian Catholic bishops called the development plans for the north "a serious abuse." They were joined by the Anglicans and the United Church, and together the three churches founded Project North to support northern Aboriginals and to mobilize the churches to consider northern development an ethical issue. The next year the Mennonites, Lutherans and Presbyterians joined them as well.

Thomas Berger

Berger, who came to be known to the Dene as "Ni-wha judge," or Our Judge, travelled for three years throughout the western Arctic. He listened to 317 expert witnesses, and 1,000 more witnesses at community hearings. In 1996, back working at a law office in Vancouver, he recalled that "we slept in schoolrooms and log cabins, and occasionally out in the open. There hasn't ever been a royal commission like it, and there won't be another." Hearings were held in tents, community halls and fishing camps, many reachable only by Twin Otter and freighter canoes. "The fact that the hearings took place not only in Yellowknife with the usual cast of expert witnesses but also in villages all along the Mackenzie Valley caught people's imagination," Berger said.

Meanwhile, the big companies were getting nervous at the interest the country was showing in the inquiry. Arctic Gas chair Wilder warned that without the pipeline, by 1990 Canada would have a "staggering" energy shortfall. He quoted an article in *Foreign Affairs* predicting a world oil shortage and a price increase of 25 to 50 per cent. (In the event, the price dropped and Canada, along with the rest of the world, now has an oil surplus.) But even the panic about the imminent energy crisis did not scare Canadians enough to resist Berger's impassioned recommendations.

By March 6, 1977, the day the report was released, the Queen's Printer had received orders for 16,000 copies. The report was light, readable, highly informative and illustrated. "It was the best-selling document ever printed by the Queen's Printer," said Berger, "and it was on the *Maclean's* bestseller list for a month or two, until another series of biographies of the Royal Family came out." It is still a textbook used in schools and universities across the country. At least 100,000 copies have been sold altogether.

Berger recommended that there be a ten-year moratorium on the proposed pipeline until Aboriginal land claims had been settled, an institutional infrastructure set up, and a truly diversified economy for the North established. In the end, the pipeline was never built. There are no more drillships in the Arctic Ocean. The oil companies all rushed off to places where drilling is cheaper.

If the inquiry changed Thomas Berger, it also changed Canada. The report challenged southern Canadians to see the future of the north as a profound testing of its identity and worth as a respectable country. "What happens here, here on the northwest frontier, here in the northern homeland," said Berger, "will tell us what kind of country Canada is, what kind of people we are."

No one who read the report could ever again think of the north as a vast, uninhabited, hostile wasteland. In April 1977, Martin O'Malley wrote in the Toronto *Globe and Mail*, "It is not surprising to find people in Regina or Halifax who now know Eskimos are Inuit, or that the singular of Inuit is Inuk, or that Indians in the Mackenzie Valley are Dene, which rhymes with Rene." Southerners learned about the immense linguistic and ethnic variety of the people in the north and their intricate economic and spiritual relationship with their land and with the settlers of the last century or so. The report destroyed the fallacy that the hunting economy of the northern Aboriginal peoples was moribund, and that little of the land used by Aboriginal hunters forty years before was still being used by their children and grandchildren.

The report also made it clear that much more was involved than a pipeline going down south, taking up 100 square kilometres of land. The pipeline couldn't be assessed in isolation, but would be the start of a series of related projects whose ripple effects would change the destiny of the northern Aboriginal people. As Louise Frost of the village of Old Crow put it, "I can see our country being destroyed and our people being pushed onto reservations, and the white man taking over as they please....The pipeline is only the beginning of all this."

In addition to Aboriginal rights, Canadians were asked for the first time to take environmental values seriously, and they did. Berger described northern ecosystems made particularly vulnerable by their exquisite simplicity. In one area, he noted, lemmings are the sole herbivore link between mosses and grasses (primary producers) and foxes, snowy owls and weasels, who are the only three predators. The extinction of just one of those species would have a far greater impact than in a tropical or temperate climate, where these essential links are made by hundreds or thousands of different species.

Perhaps the most dramatic environmental issue was the Porcupine caribou herd, at 100,000 strong the last of the world's great caribou herds (in the mid-nineties it stood at 160,000 beasts) and the means of survival for the Aboriginal communities scattered along its migration routes. Gwi'chin means "caribou people," and for generations they have depended on the caribou for food, clothing, shelter and tools. With the threat of the pipeline, the Gwi'chin felt deeply that the caribou were now dependent on them and they must speak up.

Berger was convinced that anyone seeing this herd would be converted to his recommendations. He later recalled:

> I had lunch with Trudeau, and I told him he should go up to the northern Yukon and see the caribou when they come down from the mountains on to the coast. It's one of the great sights on earth. In June, I noticed in the paper that Trudeau had gone with his boys to the northern Yukon as I had urged him, and I said to my wife, "Once he's seen this sight, one of the marvels of the planet, it will be difficult to say yes, let's build a pipeline through it. It's over," I said, "they're going to buy my report." And they did.

Would he have been so confident twenty years later? In the 1970s the time was ripe for the inquiry. At what other time in Canadian history would the word of one relatively unknown young man have held sway against a multinational oil consortium such as Arctic Gas? As Allan Fotheringham, then a columnist for the Vancouver *Sun*, pointed out, it was the equivalent of one person being given the power to "make his own pronouncements on the social, environmental and economic impact of the building of the CPR."

At the time of writing in 1996, the Dene Nation, which was in its heyday in the 1970s, had broken up; Prime Minister Chrétien had not even commented on the report of the Royal Commission on Aboriginal People; and the federal environmental review process, which was initiated as a result of the Mackenzie Valley Pipeline Inquiry, had been gutted.

Meanwhile, every last square metre of the Northwest Territories had been staked out for diamond mines, and the first major mine had been given the go-ahead after a rushed environmental review that had all of $250,000 at its disposal. It's the next gold rush, but this time without Thomas Berger.

Louisa Blair was an associate editor of *Compass* from 1989 to 1997 and subsequently a director of the Compass Foundation. She lives in Quebec City and is Quebec editor of the *Canadian Forum*.

Nobel Moved Away from the Mainstream

by Malcolm Reid

In my daydream, I'm in Stockholm on the last day of December 1969. I've been here as a reporter doing a story on the war crimes tribunal that Bertrand Russell and Jean-Paul Sartre have been holding at the invitation of the Swedes, who are very opposed to the Vietnam War. I've also looked in on the American draft resisters in Sweden. And I've inquired how Swedish social democracy is doing in the sixties.

What a decade it's been!

But in my daydream I'm seated with a friend named Sven. There is a bottle of schnapps. Before the bottle is finished, the famous decade will be over. Midnight! We'll be into the 1970s.

Our conversation gets around to the Nobel Prizes.

"I think you'll be seeing a change in the Nobel Prizes in the 1970s,"

Nobel Prizes for Literature

1970: **Aleksandr Solzhenitsyn** (b. 1918), Russian novelist, then in exile

1971: **Pablo Neruda** (1904–1973), Chilean poet

1972: **Heinrich Böll** (1917–1985), West German novelist

1973: **Patrick White** (1912–1990), Australian novelist

1974: (jointly) **Eyvind Johnson** (1900–1976), **Harry Martinson** (1904–1978), both Swedish novelists

1975: **Eugenio Montale** (1886–1981), Italian poet

1976: **Saul Bellow** (b. 1915), American novelist

1977: **Vicente Aleixandre** (1898–1984), Spanish poet

1978: **Isaac Bashevis Singer** (1904–1991), American novelist, writing in Yiddish

1979: **Odysseus Elytis** (b. 1911), Greek poet

nobels, 1970s

Elytis

Johnson

Montale

Böll

Solzhenitsyn

Neruda

Singer

White

Martinson

Bellow

Aleixandre

Sven says. "The mentality has changed here, you know. We're very connected with the Third World now.

"Old Alfred Nobel was a strange bird, eh? In his lifetime he was a fairly typical tycoon, and spent more time on the Riviera than back here in Sweden with his dynamite factories. He was into Russian oil wells too—and this was well before we had any idea that Russia would end up Bolshevik. Alfred didn't live to see the twentieth century. He died in 1896.

"Then, suddenly, his will is opened. Consternation! There's this strange idea of honouring the world's most humane and brilliant minds with a prize. Mostly scientists—he was a scientist himself—but he had his peace and literature prizes too.

"Well, it takes until 1903 to actually get the system going.

"The prize for literature is to honour writers who lift humanity up to higher things; the winners will be chosen by the Swedish Academy and receive their prizes from the hands of the king. No less! The winner then gets to make a short speech in his language on what it is he's trying to lift humanity *to*. What *he's* trying, or what *she's* trying—for early on, some women writers were chosen, like Sigrid Undset and Gabriela Mistral.

"In our youth, Malcolm, we've seen the great western bestsellers win the prize. Quality writers, yes, but world-famous, like Camus, Hemingway, Hermann Hesse.

"That's where I think you're going to see a change."

Sven's eyes crinkled with pleasure as the schnapps went down. Snowflakes swirled outside the window.

"Because you see, we Swedes speak a little-known language ourselves. We're very concerned about small cultures, and culture as a tool for economic development. I think you'll be seeing some literatures honoured that have never been honoured before. I think you'll see more politics, left, right, centre. And hence I think the big French, English and German guns will be silenced a little. The prize will move away from mainstream taste to a sort of Lutheran intellectual missionary work. That's my guess. The prize will throw in its influence with this cultural revolution we've been seeing, a little. It will try and help the century end a little less imperialistically than it began.

"You know, with his millions and his arms-maker's troubled conscience, old Alfred has had a damned strong influence on this century of ours. No? It's partly the quarter of a million dollars the winner receives. But it's not *just* that."

Sven poured me some more schnapps, in a nice Danish schnapps glass. He grinned, as well he might. For every prediction he made came true.

Quebec City writer **Malcolm Reid** is a former Quebec correspondent of the Toronto *Globe and Mail* and the author of *The Shouting Signpainters*, a study of Quebec left-wing movements in the 1960s. His articles have appeared in the *Last Post, This Magazine, Canadian Dimension* and other magazines, in addition to *Compass*.

Watergate: We Still Don't Know Why

by Rae Murphy

I was in Washington as the tangled skein of the Watergate scandals finally unravelled in the summer of 1974. The day the televised congressional hearings moved towards the actual vote to impeach Richard Nixon—which Nixon would soon finesse by becoming the first president to resign from office—I ducked into a bar to catch the action.

I remember noticing from the corner of my eye that the young woman sitting on the stool next to me seemed to be naked. Nonsense, I thought, and turned my full attention to the sonorous voice of Barbara Jordan. When the time came for Chairman Peter Rodino to cast his vote, the young woman sighed, rose from her stool, and walked to the tiny stage at the other end of the barroom. "Aah, big deal," she said, dismissing the whole event. She *was* naked, or nearly so. She was a "go-go dancer," and like everyone else in the bar, in Washington, in North America, she was enthralled with the pathos, the bathos, the glory and the grot of Watergate. Unlike most, she was somewhat underwhelmed by the occasion.

In the intervening years, the Watergate industry has pumped out scores of books, documentaries, docudramas and movies—I even read somewhere that an opera was being mounted. However, one of the famous "W's" is missing. We know the who, what, when and where, but we still have no why. And as Watergate has become trivialized by the use of the suffix *gate* for every real and imagined scandal, it seems unlikely that we ever will.

Watergate began as a break-in at the Democratic National Committee headquarters, a simple operation that was bungled. Why it was bungled became obvious when the weird cast was introduced. Central Casting could not have provided a more comedic gang of incompetents. No coherent reason for the break-in was ever advanced, although several incoherent reasons were speculated on. But it would seem obvious that Nixon, who has been called everything but a fool, couldn't have known of the break-in in advance. Or could he? Remember these were the days when the CIA

Richard Nixon

was trying to booby-trap Fidel Castro's cigars.

The scandal spread to other break-ins by the so-called Plumbers, enemies lists, tax evasions and a whole set of "dirty tricks," of which the actual Watergate break-in was neither the first, the worst nor the most bizarre. Perhaps the most notable was the break-in at Daniel Ellsberg's psychiatrist's office. Ellsberg, the author of the Pentagon Papers, was in Nixon's eyes the perfect poster boy for the duplicitous and treasonous Eastern Establishment intellectual. Let's hold that idea for the moment. In the end it all came down to the break-in at the Watergate office complex and the "cover-up"—in the words of Senator Howard Baker, "What did the president know, and when did he know it?"

To all lefties and liberals, Nixon was the personification of evil. As the attack dog of Senator McCarthy, he was a creature of the Cold War and did not deserve public office. However, Nixon also had critics who were far more right-wing or anti-Communist than he was. The whole American Establishment, although expunged of any traces of progressive liberalism, was then—as it still is now—the essential enemy of a wing of American conservative thought, which Nixon represented. McCarthy, after all, had targeted the Establishment—the government bureaucracy, the pointy-headed intellectuals who had "lost us China" and the State Department poohbahs who had committed thirty years of treason. And "tricky Dick" Nixon was the ultimate opportunist who rode on the coattails of the great crusaders, gaining prominence on the prosecution of that personification of the Eastern Establishment, Alger Hiss.

So nobody liked Nixon—right or left. Reelected in 1972, Nixon made no secret of some scores he intended to settle and some far-reaching plans to change the nature of governance and power in the United States.

In his second term he was going to deal with what Vice President Spiro Agnew called "the nattering nabobs of negativity." For openers he was going to make an example of the powerful publisher of the Washington *Post* by revoking her television licences. Then he was actually going to take over the government and change forever the relationship between the presidency and the other institutions of state. There would be a new balance and few checks. And, with a little help from his friends, he would do it himself.

Foreign affairs were no longer run out of the State Department. Domestic matters were handled by White House staff (quite effectively, actually—there were environmental legislation, a health care plan and antidiscrimination proposals). Nixon's aides H.R. Haldeman and John Ehrlichman were virtually prime minister and minister of the interior. But the action was on the world stage and Nixon, all on his own with his favourite lapdog Henry Kissinger, overturned the postwar international economic regime by breaking the Bretton Woods Agreement, played the "China Card," brought Anwar Sadat onside and courted Leonid Brezhnev.

Congress was generally ignored and, even more important, the permanent government and its institutions were firmly put out of the loop. The Plumbers were organized in the teeth of FBI opposition and the break-ins were the work of former or current CIA operators who had gone freelance. Even the political party structure was bypassed. Just consider the grief Nixon would have saved himself if he had let the Republican Party apparatus rather than the Committee to Reelect the President (CREEP) extort the campaign money, if he had trusted the FBI rather than the Plumbers to do the break-ins and illegal wiretaps—if, in general, he had tried to use the existing structures to do his deeds. But then he couldn't because they were his enemies.

For several decades, probably since the mobilization for the Second World War, the Cold War and the triumph of Keynesian economics, big central government has become the hallmark of all modern states. In the United States this growth and power, multiplied massively by the militarization of every aspect of society, has come to be associated with the Imperial Presidency. Nixon craved this power, splendor and isolation, and he saw the need for all the levers of power to be in his hands. And so he was finally brought down by those great grassroots organizations: the Washington *Post*, CBS and the New York *Times*.

So I believe there was both more and less to Richard Nixon and Watergate than what met the eye back then. But even with the insight that time and events provide, I think the go-go dancer was wrong. It *was* a big deal. Besides, I didn't like Richard Nixon either.

Rae Murphy taught journalism and Canadian studies at Conestoga College in Kitchener, Ontario, from 1972 to 1996 and is the author of numerous books on Canadian and world politics, most recently a biography of Finance Minister Paul Martin, written in collaboration with Robert Chodos and Eric Hamovitch (1998).

Woody's World: Beyond Sex and Death

by Marc Gervais

Nineteen seventy-seven and *Annie Hall*. Woody Allen, stand-up comic *extraordinaire*, gag writer, actor, playwright and screenwriter who also could make movies that were wild and brilliant extensions of loosely linked skits, now emerges as a veritable film *auteur*, destined to become one of the greatest comic film directors of all time. Let's go back and savor one of those *Annie Hall* moments.

Woody and Annie (Diane Keaton) are queuing up at a Manhattan art cinema, forced to listen to a Columbia prof in the lineup behind them doing his intellectual thing on Marshall McLuhan for the benefit of his young female companion and anyone else blessed enough to be within reach of his voice. Human endurance can take only so much, and Woody is going out of his mind. The inevitable happens: an irate Woody turns on the pedant, and in no uncertain terms explains to him that he is completely missing the point. Finally, Woody walks over to the neighbouring queue and drags in the real-life McLuhan. Marshall proceeds to vindicate Woody, echoing his very words. We, of course, are delighted, roaring with approval in a benign shared complicity, that recognition of ourselves as cultured, hip, educated and refined, genuine seventies types seeing through things.

Woody Allen, that Chaplin/Bergman/Marx Brothers/Absurdity cocktail mixed in a seventies shaker, and all of it sparkling with intellectual ice, shaped by education, immense reading and profound cultural insight. For Woody, there could be no ideologies to adhere to, no heroic gestures, no causes: in his public persona, he kept repeating, seriously or jokingly, that there were only two facts, two realities he could believe in: Sex and Death.

But seventies culture was surely not exclusively dominated by a kind of *eros/thanatos* Freudian nihilism. Woody was reaching us because he was also looking for something else—dare we say happiness? Or love? He thrilled all of us theological souls by persistently telling us that he could not believe in God while still, in film after film, constantly referring to the Judeo-Christian deity. But it goes beyond that: in Northrop Frye's terms, for Woody "romance" is never vanquished by "irony."

As understood in retrospect, the seventies were a kind of exhausted intermission, schizophrenically squeezed between the sixties, with their naïve idealism, their dreams, their recreating of culture, their revolution mystique, and the reactionary eighties, complete with the reinstitutionalization of the American Dream and all it stands for. Inevitably, gleefully, the stand-up comic in Woody was feasting on the sixties posturings of the ever-present Diane Keaton. But there was no question of going back to what the sixties had demolished. Ronald Reagan, after all, was still just a bad joke from Woody's least favourite place, California.

In *Manhattan* (1979, and the film many still feel is his greatest achievement), Woody shares with us a list of what he loves, things that make life worth living: Groucho Marx, Willie Mays, the second movement of the Jupiter Symphony, Louis Armstrong's recording of "Potato House Blues," Swedish movies, Flaubert's *Sentimental Education*, Marlon Brando, Frank Sinatra, those "incredible apples and pears by Cézanne," the crabs at Sam Wo's—still not a bad list twenty years later, and so representative of a certain East Coast American lifestyle. The movie itself is nothing less than a love affair with Manhattan, and the glorious music of the Gershwins. It's all so lovely and impermanent, small, limited and limiting. That, at least, the culture of the seventies could connect with: a pleasant, sophisticated lifestyle, a basic kind of human decency, and don't ask for too much more.

But Woody, being Woody, needs to add one more item to the love list: "Tracy's face" as the strings of Gershwin's "He Loves, She Loves" sneak onto the sound track, gradually filling the theatre and our hearts. Tracy, symbol of a seventies kind of innocence, whom, just maybe, Woody loves. Desperately he tries to phone her hotel before she leaves for London, but the line is hopelessly busy. He races out onto the street, but no cab is free. So our tiny, semineurotic hero runs and runs through those familiar Manhattan blocks, finally reaching Tracy just in melodramatic time. He tries to convince her to stay: yes he really loves her. But Tracy must leave, promising to come back in six months; Woody must learn to trust. And that heart-rending final closeup of Woody's face, beseeching, wistful, daring/not daring—his tribute to Chaplin's *City Lights*.

Wasn't it Woody himself, earlier on in the film, who confided to us that his story "is about people creating real unnecessary problems for themselves because it keeps them from dealing with more unsolvable, terrifying problems about the Universe"? Come to think of it, maybe that is not such a bad epitaph for the entire decade, not totally bereft of hope, but very bewildered, vulnerable and exhausted.

Woody Allen

Marc Gervais teaches film in the communications department at Concordia University in Montreal. He was a member of *Compass*'s publishing policy committee in the 1980s and a contributing editor of *Compass* from 1993 to 1997.

Finding Feminism, Rediscovering Faith

by Denise Nadeau

I step over the rotted grey wooden door sill into the dimly lit living room of a squat in East Oxford. A bald light bulb swings over the circle of about twenty women seated on benches and old chairs. It is January 1972, and this group is Oxford Women's Liberation. Some of the women are students like me; some are welfare claimants; a few are working-class activists with autonomous groups like Big Flame and Wages for Housework; some identify as socialist feminists.

I sit on the outside, drawn into the discussion and the energy flying around the room. We are debating the Family Allowance Campaign and the role Wages for Housework should play in it. These women are talking revolution—how to change the economic structures of society to reorganize domestic labour, childcare, the family, waged work and the welfare state. The debate is fierce. Wouldn't fighting for the family allowance further institutionalize women's unpaid labour in the home? Or would it challenge and expose how women's unpaid labour holds up the base of the capitalist economy?

This is not just a theoretical debate. We are deciding whether to participate in the Family Allowance Campaign in Oxford. With no clear resolution a sheet is passed around to see who wants to work on the campaign. I sign up.

Oxford Women's Liberation was a long way from my comfortable upper-middle-class upbringing in Montreal. I had attended Sacred Heart Convent, a private English school for girls from well-connected Catholic families, and then studied history at McGill and later the University of British Columbia. I read Kate Millett's *Sexual Politics* in 1969 and joined my first consciousness-raising group in 1970, but until Oxford I had been an armchair feminist. I read books, talked about feminist ideas and tried to get the men in my life to do the dishes and take up less space at meetings. The Family Allowance Campaign changed all this.

I was part of the door-to-door campaign in two working-class suburbs. We talked to women about the government's plan to replace the family allowance with a family tax credit (after much protest a similar scheme was introduced in Canada in 1993). We were demanding that the family allowance be increased and paid directly to women. For the first time I met women whose husbands drank away their pay-packets; who were afraid to talk to us because their husbands might find out; who, tired from night-shift jobs, answered the door with three kids around their knees. I became painfully aware of the contrast between their grinding poverty and the elegant and mannered wealth of the Oxford university community that I was part of.

In the next year and a half I became passionately involved in the British women's movement. We won the family allowance campaign, and I attended two national women's liberation conferences where, with hundreds of women, I debated theory and strategies, attended workshops, passed resolutions and danced through the night. On International Women's Day, 50,000 women strong, we marched through the streets of London chanting the Four Demands—free contraception and abortion on demand, equal pay, twenty-four-hour nurseries, and equal education opportunity. It was an exciting time—women were starting to create their own women's centres, bookstores and health collectives, and vision, not reaction, fuelled our energy and actions. The women's movement caught my imagination and my passion for justice. It was a place where at last I felt I belonged.

It's midnight and I'm exhausted as I crawl into my sleeping bag on the floor. This is the organizers' shed. We hadn't had time to set up our tents before it began to rain. All night we have been driving over the mountain on the rough logging road, picking up truckloads of women. This shed is now crowded with women and children, latecomers to the first Vancouver Island Women's Festival.

For three days we camp, gather in circles and attend an amazing variety of workshops in the fields or on the rocky beach: how to run a chainsaw, natural birth control, herbal medicine, self-defence, spirituality, midwifery and fighting rape in your community. Organization is voluntary and cooperative—as you register you sign up for a shift on daycare, kitchen, first aid or cleanup.

I returned from Britain in late 1973, and after a year in Vancouver I moved to Courtenay on Vancouver Island. I was hungrily searching to replicate the political fervor and clarity of analysis of the British women's movement. Some of this analysis I found with my first women's group in Courtenay. Most members were recent mothers, with some involved in the women's health movement and the politics of birthing. When I became pregnant I too became involved in the natural childbirth and midwifery movements, opting for a home birth when I had my son in 1977. For the next few years I cared for two young boys in an isolated homestead, feeling not only the delights of mothering but also depression as I watched my life evaporate into endless dirty diapers, sleepless nights and hungry little mouths.

There were six Vancouver Island Women's Festivals between 1976 and 1982. They were started by a group of us who were living with men, had young children, and were struggling to understand what feminism meant for us as women living in a rural area. Many who attended were urban feminists without children; some were childless lesbians; some called themselves separatists. Some of these women moved to the country to set up women's land or find a part-time refuge from the city. With such a large seasonal influx of lesbians it became easier for some of the rural women to come out as lesbians. By the fourth year of the festival, workshop topics included talking to one another: lesbians, bisexuals and straight; building a women's land trust; and raising sons. But many of the heterosexual rural women felt alienated by the separatist tone of a few and the festivals eventually ended as some of the old organizers dropped out.

In 1979 I entered a four-year working period that changed my perspective on rural feminism. From a pilot project educating women about wife assault, we formed the Women's Self-Help Network which trained women to run self-help groups in four single-industry resource communities. Most of the women we met were wives of miners, loggers and fishers who worked in the home as mothers; a few had also managed to find paid jobs as store clerks or waitresses. Most were unfamiliar with feminism and distrusted it. They came to the self-help groups for a wide variety of reasons: they were fed up with the isolation of living in a small trailer with three children and a husband always away on shift work; their husbands drank and were beating them and they were thinking of leaving; they had already left and were isolated single parents. We provided popular education, assertiveness training, peer counselling training and community organizing skills.

Working with these women I began to realize just how middle-class my own feminism was. They had far fewer options than I. Leaving their husbands usually meant a life of poverty for themselves and their kids. I realized it was no accident that most of the women who came to our country women's festivals were middle-class. Many of these small-town women already knew how to run a chainsaw and saw cutting wood as one extra job they wanted to avoid. The spectre of a bare-breasted group of women chanting in the woods had little relevance to their lives.

I see now that much of my energy in those years was involved in the personal feminist politics of taking control of your life. I flirted with non-traditional work such as commercial fishing and built my own little cabin (with a lot of help from my friends). Having a home birth was a refusal to have the medical establishment control my body. Organizing the women's festivals and self-help groups was an extension of this principle that women could support and grow together as women, on our own. It was a climate in which claiming my own lesbian identity seemed a logical progression in my development as an autonomous woman. But as a mother, and as a woman who had been exposed to the class politics of British feminism and the class divisions in resource-based towns in rural B.C., I distanced myself from separatism and anti-men values. Feminism for me was not about opting out of the world but about the struggle to change it.

The seventies were my secular years; I had stopped going to church in 1968—not out of anger but because it seemed irrelevant to my life. The feminist journey that I began in the seventies would eventually lead me back to my Christian roots. British feminism was my first introduction to acting for justice; my experience of Canadian feminism, largely in British Columbia, helped me in the process of claiming my own voice. It would only be in the early eighties, when I experienced a deep personal crisis, that I began to feel that something was missing for me in secular feminism. As well I realized that it was important to include spirituality and religion in the work I was doing with women. I would transition back into my faith almost as easily as I had transitioned out. Liberation theology and feminist spirituality were for me logical progressions in my feminist journey.

Denise Nadeau is a writer and activist living in Vancouver.

I Came Too Late for Sixties Magic

by Charlie Angus

When I was born in 1962, my parents were sharing a house with my grandparents. It was a typical Timmins, Ontario, dwelling—a cramped, poorly insulated house built for the families of miners. My parents were born into such housing and probably thought they would die in such housing.

Luck and fate intervened. In 1964 the Kidd Creek mine, the biggest base metal deposit in the world, was discovered just outside of town. My father happened to be friends with the crew that mapped out the orebody. He took what little savings two generations had been able to amass and invested them in Kidd Creek. It was a good move.

To celebrate, we moved into a new split-level modern home. I took this for granted. Families on television had the latest of everything—why shouldn't we? I was a complete stranger to the fix-it and make-do world my parents had grown up in.

My father, however, was a child of the Depression, and he was exceptionally sensible with the money he had made. A split-level was as flashy as it got. He invested his remaining earnings in something that had been beyond the reach of a working-class kid of the 1940s—a university education. He spent five years trekking back and forth between out-of-town colleges and his northern home. With his degree our family got a legitimate toehold into the middle class.

I assumed it would all be gravy after that—university, if I wanted it, a job of my choice. I wanted to get through childhood and into my teen years as fast as possible. I was in a hurry to share in the magic of a generation that believed that anything was possible, and probably not too difficult. For even if I was too young to be a part of the sixties, the sixties were a part of me. As a child watching this turbulent and exciting decade unfold, I developed certain expectations and attitudes.

But I was too late. The magic dried up, as a result more of the Arab oil boycott than of the dissipation of a cultural zeitgeist. Like many in my generation I have grown up carrying an unresolved grudge towards the sixties.

The sixties were about rising expectations, and the decades since have been about coming to terms with the failure of these expectations.

In 1973 I turned eleven. Nixon was in trouble, the Vietnam War was ending, the oil crisis had the world economy in a panic and the Club of Rome had issued its grim report about the prospect of an ever-increasing scarcity of resources. It was also the year my father got a job in Toronto.

I vividly remember the twelve-hour bus ride from our dream house down to a small row house in Scarborough, Ontario. There were seven of us living almost on top of one another in a bleak subdivision. For my parents our new home was just a more modern version of the housing they had grown up in. For my siblings and me, however, it was a major shock.

I sometimes think that the resentment I felt at moving into that faceless row house was akin to the resentment my age group felt at the manner in which the sixties ended. When the contorted face of Johnny Rotten finally spewed across the television in our suburban basement in the late seventies, his anger expressed what many of us teens felt: "Where there's no future, how can there be sin? We're the flowers in the dustbin." Unlike the rock bands of the sixties, Johnny Rotten was less interested in shocking parents than in shocking the baby boomers. We were feeling pretty ripped off and we blamed our older brothers and sisters.

The seventies have often been written off as a time of "burnout" after the excitement of the sixties. It was more complicated than that. We weren't tired. We were worried. I recall class discussions in 1973 about the future. Many of us believed that by the time we were in our late teens there wouldn't be any oil, or even enough food. Those dire predictions didn't come true but the sense of foreboding and uncertainty has remained. We became the first generation since the Second World War to think that our future might not be as rosy as the one our parents had.

My generation has come into adulthood feeling that it has never hit its stride. We grew up in the shadow of the boomers, always comparing our accomplishments as an age to theirs. This shadow has only lengthened with time—as movies like *Forrest Gump* and *JFK* continue to dwell on the myths of the age of peace and love. This nostalgia reflects our cultural unwillingness to come to terms with a world that has grown more complex and much more fractured.

My generation is unlikely to shed the sixties' shadow. The problem is ours. We have remained in the shadow because we haven't thought to look beyond it. If we are to look at another generation for inspiration, we would do better to look back to the 1930s. Instead of struggling with the boomers and the twentysomethings for whining rights, we need to learn to be self-reliant and finally, with a modicum of grace, grow up once and for all.

Charlie Angus is editor of *HighGrader* magazine in Cobalt, Ontario, and a member of the folk-rock band The Grievous Angels. He is coauthor of *We Lived a Life and Then Some: The Life, Death and Life of a Mining Town* (1996) and *Industrial Cathedrals of the North* (1999).

Oscar Romero: El Salvador's Archbishop to the Poor

by Frances Arbour

I first saw Archbishop Oscar Romero in 1978. It was at Sunday Mass in the San Salvador Basilica, a cold, unfinished cement structure that filled up every Sunday with the colour and noise of the poor.

He was their "Monseñor Romero." He would say Mass, and preach, and his every word was broadcast by radio throughout El Salvador and to much of Latin America. Inside the basilica, the people interrupted his words with applause, recognizing themselves in his descriptions of the pain of their lives. Here they heard God's call to liberation. And they loved Romero.

Born in 1917 in the Salvadoran countryside, Oscar Romero was named archbishop of El Salvador on February 3, 1977. At the time he was known only as a quiet-spoken, deeply spiritual priest, a conservative. The country's elite expected he would not even address the tense and polarized political and economic conditions in the country.

They were wrong. Romero changed. The killing of Rutilio Grande, a Jesuit priest from a rural parish, along with a small boy and an old man, had an especially profound impact. Romero began to raise his voice to denounce the violence and the widespread injustice that caused so much death. He drew strength from the sufferings of these people and learned from them to speak prophetic words of truth about the war against the poor of El Salvador. He and his diocese lived a renewal, faithful to the teachings of Vatican II and the 1968 Medellín Conference and to the preferential option for the poor. For this, Oscar Romero was assassinated, the church attacked, and priests and sisters and catechists killed.

When I first met Romero, I was working with the Canadian ecumenical coalition, the Inter-Church Committee on Human Rights in Latin America (ICCHRLA). It was shortly after the government promulgated the Law of Defense and the Guarantee of Public Order, a law that legitimized arbitrary imprisonment, systematic torture and the suppression of freedom of speech and of assembly. Archbishop Romero condemned the law, opening his diocesan office to the multiplying number of persecuted people. He unlocked the seminary grounds to internal refugees, and gave his support to a legal aid and human rights office, Tutela Legal, to protect and defend the victims of human rights violations.

I went to his offices at the seminary, an austere building whose waiting room and patio were filled with poor people—mostly women, mostly frightened, waiting to speak to their archbishop. Romero wore a simple black suit. He greeted foreign visitors with the same graciousness and humility as he did everyone who came to his door. In our discussions, he often turned to his lay assistants to get an explanation of a human rights situation. He spoke of the suffering of the people, and the commitment of the church to them. While El Salvador's elite and military portrayed Romero as an agent of the left, he was always a man of the church.

Oscar Romero

Eventually Romero asked to be excused: "There are many women waiting to speak to me—they come every morning knowing that I am here." He said goodbye and went out to the patio. For all of the national and international politics that engulfed him, this was the most important thing for Romero: taking time to listen to the poor and the oppressed.

This daily contact with the persecuted continued Romero's own conversion. As the blood and pain escalated, the archbishop wrote a public letter to President Jimmy Carter demanding that the U.S. discontinue military aid to the Salvadoran military. In the basilica, his Sunday homilies denounced the Salvadoran government and military for their savage repression against the poor and against the church. In his final Sunday homily, he pleaded with soldiers to stop killing their own sisters and brothers: "In the name of God, stop the repression."

Oscar Romero was assassinated while celebrating Mass on March 24, 1980, his death an offering to the people of El Salvador and to people everywhere who struggle for justice. Every year since, my family and friends have marked this date with remembrance services, to recognize a saint of our times and to strengthen our own resolve to fight for social justice.

Then in April 1996, a high school in Ottawa mounted a play based on the life of Oscar Romero. My son Michael auditioned and won the part of Romero. Sixteen years after his death, these Canadian students immersed themselves in studying the history of the Salvadoran people and their archbishop. And they found themselves moved—by Romero's courage, by his commitment to the poor, by his clarity amid great political confusion. When the play was presented, I sat in the audience crying, less as a proud mother than as a witness to Romero's spirit still alive today.

Frances Arbour is a consultant on international development, gender, Guatemala and health issues. She lives in Ottawa.

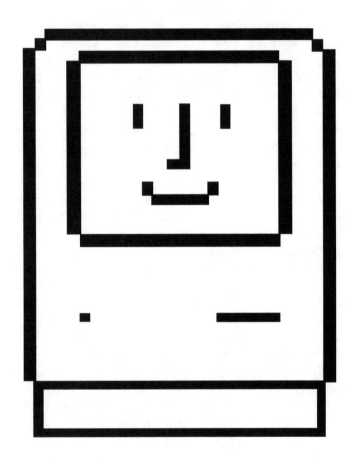

The Eighties

331 The Decade in Our Blind Spot — by Louisa Blair

333 The Rise of Neoconservatism — by Rae Murphy

339 The Church in Canada: A Golden Autumn and a Dark Night — by Doug McCarthy

343 Quebecers Were Asked a Question, and Gave their Answer — by Daniel Latouche

348 Revolution on the Desktop — by Gail van Varseveld

354 The Eighties' Environmental Legacy: Death (of Nature) by Natural Causes? — by Moira Farr

359 Jean Vanier: Community Builder — by Carolyn Whitney-Brown

The Decade in Our Blind Spot

by Louisa Blair

The eighties are both too far away and not far enough away to say any-thing intelligent about them. They are in that blind spot: you just know you can't trust your vision entirely. But the eighties were a decade in which a lot of people did trust their visions, and a decade in which others' visions were shattered.

The Russians trusted their vision enough to send 800,000 troops into Afghanistan, but by the end of the decade the entire vision of the Soviet Union had crumbled to dry dust, and they pulled them all out again. The Berlin Wall came tumbling down, but Chinese authorities shot thousands of protesters in Tiananmen Square.

A popular poster of the era summed up the unholy U.S.-U.K. alliance: Ronald Reagan waltzed with Margaret Thatcher in his arms, against a backdrop of the nuclear mushroom. It read, "She said she'd follow him to the end of the world, and he said he'd organize it." It was the decade in which one had persistent nightmares of Reagan waking up in the night and pushing that little red button that flashed permanently on his bedtable just in case he felt like ending the world, out of sheer boyish exuberance.

Thatcher made war on Argentina and Reagan matched her with Gre-nada.

Meanwhile in Canada there was burgeoning consumerism. People perhaps saw the signs that all this bounty would end one day but while they had it, by golly they were going to spend it. Big cars, real estate and fax ma-chines dominated the economy. The word Yuppie came into common parlance and never left.

As Moira Farr demonstrates, the environment began to show us, writ large, that such consumerism had a price: this was the decade of Chernobyl, Bhopal and the Exxon Valdez. My beautiful *Reader's Digest Book of World Animals*, which I saved up for as a child and was hoping to pass on to my daughter, will be hopelessly out of date because so many of the species will have been eradicated.

Louisa Blair was an associate editor of *Compass* from 1989 to 1997 and subsequently a direc-tor of the Compass Foundation. She lives in Quebec City and is Quebec editor of the *Canadian Forum*.

But at the same time the social justice movement was also in its prime. Parts of the church were putting the social teachings into practice with fierce energy and commitment; justice centres and ecumenical programs were coming into maturity—but perhaps losing sight of liturgy, spirituality and individuality. At the same time, revelations of sexual abuse by priests threw cold water on any new credibility the church might have gained in the public eye. Doug McCarthy SJ suggests that these revelations, painful as they were for the church, eventually led to a new awareness of issues sur-rounding power, authority and the celibate male priesthood.

The eighties managed to encompass these and other contradictions. To look back on them is to see the entire century in a single decade.

The Rise of Neoconservatism

by Rae Murphy

The 1980s were vintage years for Canada's Constitutional Crisis, the "Neverendum Referendum"—call it what you will. And in retrospect, that was a good thing for the country.

It created a whole new industry for many of Canada's stressed-out academics and constitutional experts. The industry even found a modest export market as these experts were sought out in some eastern European countries, notably the former Czechoslovakia. But most important, our more or less permanent constitutional crisis allowed Canadians to escape the full impact of the rebirth of Social Darwinism that marked the 1980s. At the very least, we postponed our encounter with the hurricane until it was downgraded to a tropical storm (if one can apply that metaphor to such cold places as Alberta and Ontario) called Ralph or Mike.

In retrospect, we can be grateful that Canada ushered in the decade with Pierre Trudeau's "Well, welcome to the eighties," rather than with Margaret Thatcher's hectoring about the "Nanny State" or Ronald Reagan's idiotic non sequitur, "Government is not the answer, it's the problem." In Canada, how could government be a problem when the need for strong government was one of the things Canadian federalists and Quebec sovereignists agreed on? For federalists, a strong federal government was all that could keep Canada together, while for sovereignists, a strong national government in Quebec City would be the guarantor of sovereignty.

In both cases, strong government meant power to get their constituencies where they wanted to go. Interestingly enough, the two governments were able to assist each other to achieve opposite goals. What we came to call Quebec Inc. was a product as much of federal largesse as of Quebec's "Quiet Revolution." In Quebec, big government replaced the church. In English Canada, big government tried to replace American economic domination, especially in the oil fields. In the end we had to capitulate to a much more powerful force, the "global economy" (read the global American economy), but for Canada the eighties at least began with promise. To

Margaret Thatcher

give one small example of the mood of the times, in 1981 the United States attempted to block construction of a natural gas pipeline from the Soviet Union to western Europe. Pierre Trudeau seized on this issue:

> I think that suddenly the Europeans have realized how serious a situation is when a country as powerful as the United States can impose the application of its own laws, especially in the economic field, on other countries. Now perhaps they will understand a bit better that a country which is economically dominated, as Canada is, has a right to attenuate the effects of that economic domination.

The right to attenuate the effects of economic domination is one thing. The ability—even more to the point, the political will—is something else. The decade that began with some promise reached an embarrassing nadir when Prime Minister Brian Mulroney, who had grown up singing "When Irish Eyes are Smiling" for his father's American boss, Colonel Robert McCormick, took the stage to croon the same song with President Reagan in 1986.

This rather parochial Canadian perspective is important, because on a global scale the decade in question was nasty, brutish and unfortunately not very short. Thus we should acknowledge our good fortune in being able to postpone much of it by remaining almost totally consumed by our domestic affairs. This circumstance may help explain why Canada is now, according to Jean Chrétien's favourite statistic, the choice of the United Nations for best country in the world.

There are, however, some important qualifications. The operative words here are "postpone" and "much of." As the decade wore on, we were forced to accommodate ourselves to the monstrous series of frauds we remember as Thatcherism, Reaganism, perhaps Kohlism. And so we need to look more closely at what these frauds were.

In 1930, the Spanish philosopher José Ortega y Gasset published *The Revolt of the Masses*. In it he ruminated on the collapse of the old world order in the wake of the Great War, which ushered in what Eric Hobsbawm so aptly described as the Age of Catastrophe. Not only were the masses misbehaving—history is littered with doomed insurrections—but this time they were out of control and "the political domination of the masses" threatened to bring about the collapse of western civilization.

Regardless of what one may think of Ortega's observations or conclusions, western civilization almost did collapse in the Second World War and its immediate aftermath. As the Duke of Wellington said of Waterloo, "It was a close run thing." Indeed, the irony for Ortega would be that the country he regarded as the most frightening example of the revolt of the masses, the Soviet Union, played the key part in saving civilization. It did this both through its role during the war and through the role assigned to it after the war as international menace. The Soviet fact alone would concentrate the mind of everyone. There could be no return to the multifold prewar crises.

A new social contract had to be drawn up. In exchange for rebuilding the world economies, workers would receive a greater share of the wealth they produced. Furthermore, because of a whole range of social policies promised and administered by the government, they would remain consumers of goods and services even when they were unemployed. In the aftermath of the war—for North Americans it had actually started during the war—the Welfare State was born. It was the answer to Communism.

Ronald Reagan

The new world order was created and ratified in 1944 at Bretton Woods, New Hampshire, and it lasted for thirty years. Institutions created at Bretton Woods, such as the International Monetary Fund and the World Bank, and others that flowed from it such as the Marshall Plan established the postwar world. Even the Cold War, which by accelerating the arms race intensified the need for effective government oversight of the economy, was Keynesianism writ large. With the exception of the Marshall Plan, the wheels on the other postwar institutions didn't start to wobble until the seventies. What was created with such hope as the Welfare State was denounced by Margaret Thatcher as the Nanny State. The contract drawn up in 1945 was dead by 1979. The eighties represented the search for a new equilibrium, based on very different premises.

In contrast to Ortega, the American philosopher Christopher Lasch looked back on the 1980s and wrote *The Revolt of the Elites*. Like Ortega's, Lasch's work was largely a rant about the decline of morality and indifference to old-fashioned bourgeois values, real or mythical. But he made many points about structural changes in American society, the polarization of society, the growing gap between rich and poor, and the relatively new values of the newly rich:

> The privileged classes...have made themselves independent not only of crumbling industrial cities but of public services in general. The send their children to private schools, insure themselves against medical emergencies...hire private security guards to protect themselves against the mounting violence. It is not just that

they see no point in paying for public services they no longer use; many of them have ceased to think of themselves as Americans in any important sense....

The market in which the new elites operate is now international in scope....They are more concerned with the smooth functioning of the system as a whole than with many of its parts. Their loyalties—if the term is not anachronistic in the context—are international rather than regional, national or local.

One could argue that it was forever thus. Internationalism was always a quality of the rich. They took the curing waters in central Europe, skied the Alps and scattered châteaux along the Riviera. John Kenneth Galbraith once tried to estimate the impact on the U.S. balance of payments problem of the flow of rich American heiresses marrying impecunious members of the British aristocracy. Old John D. Rockefeller, J.P. Morgan and their colleagues went to their graves protesting the principle that their wealth should be taxed by any country in any shape or form.

But that is hardly the point. Freed from the threat of advancing Communism, however real that ever was, and with a docile body politic at home (Lasch established that the masses are now more conservative than the elites), the elites have opted out of the nation and the society it reflects. And this includes support for any of the provisions of the Welfare State:

> Any sense that the masses are riding the wave of history have long since departed. The radical movements that disturbed the peace of the twentieth century have failed one by one, and no successors have appeared on the horizon. The industrial working class, once the mainstay of the socialist movement, has become a pitiful remnant of itself. The hope that "new social movements" would take its place in the struggle against capitalism, which briefly sustained the left in the late Seventies and early Eighties, has come to nothing. Not only do the new social movements—feminism, gay rights, welfare rights, agitation against racial discrimination—have nothing in common; their only coherent demand aims at inclusion in the dominant structures rather than a revolutionary transformation of social relations.

Lasch overstated the contrast between the industrial working class and the new social movements: elements aiming at "inclusion in the dominant structures," and other elements aiming at "a revolutionary transformation of social relations," could be found within both. But his larger point about the lack of any challenge to the capitalist system is difficult to argue with. And if there is no such challenge, then clearly one could repeal the implicit social contract that had been drawn up to save the system from the real or imagined challenge of Communism. And so Keynes, who always insisted that this theories saved the system, found himself out of favour in the eighties. But as we began to discover in the nineties, the partial rejection of Keynes rested on a number of fallacies.

In the first instance there was the notion—which became the mantra of the business and financial elites throughout the West— that we could no longer afford social policies enacted when the country was much poorer and in greater per capita debt. In Canada, this notion was well expressed at the very outset of the eighties by the Toronto *Globe and Mail's Report on Business*, which chose John Crosbie, finance minister in Joe Clark's Conservative government, as its man of the year for 1979. Crosbie won the praise of the *Globe and Mail* for repudiating the Tories' election promise of introducing a stimulative fiscal policy:

Brian Mulroney

> [He] preached restraint, hard work and self-denial to a people inclined to forget that sooner or later the bill for credit card living must be paid....Mr. Crosbie gained the respect of the business and financial community...who believe that the country's massive and increasing economic problems need to be confronted squarely and decisively....[He] has come to be seen by many as Canada's best hope for making a successful adjustment to the harsher environment that has followed the long post-war boom.

Unfortunately for the *Globe*, the government of which Crosbie was a member had just been defeated in the House of Commons, and it would soon be defeated by the electorate. But the *Globe* and just about every other media outlet sang that same note throughout the decade, and they found new heroes in politicians such as Michael Wilson, finance minister under Mulroney, and later Paul Martin, finance minister under Jean Chrétien.

Of course it was true that there was a growing gap between government income and expenditures. It was also true that our growing dependence on the United States created the conditions where the U.S. could export its increasing economic problems into Canada, forcing up Canadian interest rates and thereby accelerating the debt spiral.

Furthermore, government finances were being starved by corporate Canada. In his 1998 book *Dismantling the State: Downsizing to Disaster*, Walter Stewart wrote that when everyone began to get excited about the debt in 1980, federal corporate taxes totalled $12.6 billion. By 1994 corporations paid only $7.4 billion. Corroborating these figures, tax expert Neil Brooks has shown that if the government had simply maintained 1974 levels of taxation, the deficit in the early 1980s would have only been half the size it actually was. Studies have shown that declining tax revenues were a much more important contributor to increasing deficits than growth in government spending.

Nevertheless, the rising deficit was used as the excuse to cut back social services and in effect renege on the promises of the postwar contract. This was the essential fraud of the eighties. But if the eighties were the time of laissez-faire triumphalism, it is also important to remember how the decade turned out. Margaret Thatcher's revolution was a failure, and she was dumped by her own party in 1990. Ronald Reagan dug the largest deficit hole in modern times. Brian Mulroney's unpopularity had reached the terminal stage by 1990, and his legacy destroyed his party in 1993. In contrast to the thirty-year lifespan of the postwar social contract, the counterrevolution of the eighties barely reached the age of ten. As the folk singer said about another era, "The times they are a changin' "—and fast.

Times may change, but they never change back. The rampaging free market and the new globalism made possible by the technological revolution are not about to be uninvented or rescinded. If a new equilibrium is established, it will balance the freedom of the global market with the overriding interests of a global society. Only then will the damage done in the eighties finally be repaired.

Rae Murphy taught journalism and Canadian studies at Conestoga College in Kitchener, Ontario, from 1972 to 1996 and is the author of numerous books on Canadian and world politics, most recently a biography of Finance Minister Paul Martin, written in collaboration with Robert Chodos and Eric Hamovitch (1998).

The Church in Canada: A Golden Autumn and a Dark Night

by Doug McCarthy

For ten days in September 1984, Canadians stuck to their TVs viewing the spectacular pageant of a papal tour of their country. People of all faiths were moved as they watched Pope John Paul II literally touch his people as they reached out to him in vast crowds wherever he visited. His words were at times challenging and at times consoling, and overall his message was vigorous. Even though this papal tour had little effect on how Canadian Catholics lived their faith in the months to come, it did leave a memory of a golden autumn for the church.

Looking back, it might now be seen as a last hurrah for the Catholic Church in Canada. For shortly after that splendid event, widespread scandals of priestly sexual abuse confronted the church. These scandals unleashed a plague of shame, hurt and disillusionment throughout the late 1980s. Yet this crisis was a kind of purging dark night for the church in Canada, which was led through a searing humiliation to a fresh humility and a new awareness of issues concerning the celibate priesthood.

The clerical power of the priest, his loneliness and his unpreparedness for the rigors of celibacy all came under scrutiny. No longer would revelations of sexual misconduct be covered up by protective clerical secrecy. Independent committees were established to investigate all complaints of sexual impropriety among the clergy. The priesthood became somewhat demystified as the human fragility in its ranks became all too apparent. People in charge of priestly formation began to look, with varying degrees of success, for ways to teach young men to live celibacy. In some places, such as Newfoundland, the institutional church was so weakened by the scandals that people began to discover a new power and authority in themselves.

While the sexual abuse scandals offered a cleansing for the church, another form of purge was underway with divisions that had their origins in the Second Vatican Council. These divisions, which had begun to emerge with Pope Paul VI's encyclical *Humanae Vitae* in 1968, now gelled around the moral and theological teachings of Pope John Paul II.

There was much upheaval in the church after Vatican II. Many pushed for further change while others resisted all change. Within this tension, the church experienced a new liberalization in its structures. Still, ten years after the council ended, I remember theologian Rosemary Haughton saying that the changes made so far were only scratching the surface of what the council called for.

In the eighties we were not to go much beyond surface-scratching. In fact, some people thought that there was a reversal of the directions the council had set for the church. As in many areas of society, the enthusiasm of the sixties could not be translated into the eighties. But in the church a retrenchment seemed to be taking place, and there was much conflict and discontent as a result.

The hierarchy, under the direction of the pope, seemed to think it was a time now for regathering, and this meant a stricter adherence to the dogmatic teaching of the church. The Holy See appointed more and more bishops who were known for their orthodox dogmatism. The pastoral bishops of Paul VI's time were fast becoming a dying breed. All of this would culminate a decade later in the promulgation of *Ad Tuendam Fidem* which forbade any kind of dissent from church teaching.

The role of women in the church remained a contentious issue throughout the eighties. In particular, the cause of the ordination of women did not go away, and if anything the debate intensified. This issue too would come to a head in the nineties with a papal ban on even discussing the matter. Many thought that the whole question was the burning concern only of a minority of radical feminists. For many others, however, the church's growing rigidity, as they saw it, was a source of pain, and some questioned the theological foundation of the church's seeming intransigence.

The power structure in the church remained male-dominated, but more and more women were demanding their rights in the church, and radical feminists and their loud protests may well have been the catalyst for a widespread consciousness among women. I remember a time when women friends of mine failed to see the problem with exclusive language in the liturgy. There were few places in the late eighties where a priest would get away with addressing the congregation (most likely with a female majority) as "brothers."

In 1974, I joined the ministerial association in a small city in Ontario. Apart from a Presbyterian deaconess, the membership was male. In 1986, when I left that ministerial association, almost half the membership was female. Some of the members were Protestant ordained women, but many were Catholic religious sisters and lay women who held pastoral positions that would have traditionally been the domain of priests. Accommodations were being made to women—probably because there was a shortage of priests and women were the best and most available pastoral ministers to fill the empty sacerdotal shoes.

Even though we still have a long way to go, the deepening consciousness in both women and men of the injustice to women in the church grew much in the eighties. But maybe it is as Rosemary Haughton said about Vatican II: we had just scratched the surface.

The number of vocations to the priesthood and religious life continued to drop during this time. In some religious congregations, the trickle of one or two novices a year dried up completely and active novitiates were closed. Departures from the ordained and vowed life persisted, although at a slower pace than in previous decades. On the surface, statistics indicated that the church was heading for disaster.

Pope John Paul II

On closer inspection, however, one could see that there were still vocations. Men and women were still responding to the "call" with dedication and commitment, but the response was less likely to be directed along traditional lines. Instead, it followed a path being traced by many new forms of lay service in the church. More and more lay people were becoming involved in formal ministry—some as volunteers, but many others as paid pastoral workers. A new age for the laity was emerging.

Statistics compiled in the eighties suggested contradictory tendencies. Nine out of ten Canadians believed in God and had some form of religious experience—a majority of these would have been Catholics. Yet only three Canadians in ten attended church regularly, and more and more middle-aged and elderly Catholics complained that their children did not go to church any more. Still, the number of nominal Catholics was growing, and daily mass attendance rose. The relatively healthy state of church attendance primarily reflected the large number of immigrants flooding into urban areas.

People who fell away from the church at this time spoke about its being too rigid (especially in its moral teaching) and about its being irrelevant ("I don't get anything out of it"). There may be some truth in these assertions. On the other hand, Canadians were also becoming more and more affluent and self-centred at this time, and these developments surely contributed to religious indifference.

And so on one level, the church in Canada in this decade could be seen as beset with troubles and tensions. Yet at the core it remained quite vibrant. Catholics still had a hunger for Eucharist and were experiencing a

Doug McCarthy SJ is associate pastor of Holy Cross Church in Wikwemikong, Manitoulin Island, Ontario. He was an associate editor of *Compass* from 1994 to 1997 and subsequently vice-president of the Compass Foundation.

deep spiritual thirst. Many people sought to deepen their spiritual lives at retreat centres and through spiritual direction. Prompted by the social teachings of the bishops in the first half of the decade, there were enough Catholics involved in issues of justice to give the church a concrete presence in that area.

Despite its troubles, the church has always been able to fulfil its basic mission. At the heart of the church, there are enough believers who know that no matter how much the Bark of Peter is tossed about on the stormy seas of our times, it is always securely anchored.

Quebecers Were Asked a Question, and Gave their Answer

by Daniel Latouche

The Quebec referendum of 1980 has now gone the way of all "traumatic" political events: down the road to oblivion with stopovers for nostalgia, misinterpretation and reinterpretation. This is especially so in Canada since we are not too good at moving forward, but feel safer with staging well-rehearsed debates, fighting old battles and reenacting past events.

One of the most puzzling reconstructions of the events of 1980 has to do with the so-called solemn "exchange of marital vows" that presumably took place between Quebec and Canada. In May 1980, it is often remembered, Quebec said "I do" to federalism, but with the understanding that the terms of the agreement would eventually be redrawn and made acceptable to its special needs. This was Prime Minister Trudeau's "promise" to reshape the constitutional environment in such a way that Quebecers would feel comfortable living within Canadian borders.

It is time to set the record straight before it is too late. In 1980, Quebec voters did not massively support the No option on the basis of Pierre Trudeau's promise to revamp federalism. The prime minister's speech, along with the Quebec Liberal Party blueprint for a renewed federation, did play an important role in the rhetoric of the campaign. So did the weather and the speeches of Joe Clark.

Quebecers voted No on May 20 because they believed that a Canadian political and economic framework was a better proposition than a strictly Quebec one. Period. This was not an endorsement of Canada, English Canadians or the Rocky Mountains. Nor was it the expression of a strongly held conviction that federalism constituted a more appropriate and morally better constitutional formula than sovereignty. They were asked a question and they gave their answer. Nothing more, nothing less. True, a majority of the electorate believed that the particularly Canadian brand of federalism could and should be renewed, but their support for Canada was not made conditional on the implementation of such reforms.

If their approach had been rational and well thought out, they could have voted themselves out of Canada a long time ago. Quebecers have a strong emotional and irrational attachment to Canada, including the queen, Moose Jaw and the Toronto Blue Jays. This is a well-kept secret. But they balk when they are told to express their attachment in a specific format.

In 1982, the promised reforms came and were deemed unacceptable to all Quebec political parties. Pundits talked of treason and constitutional hijacking. Maybe. But the Quebec electorate's reaction suggests, rather, that its referendum vote of only a few months earlier had not been a calculated gesture. If the 1982 constitution was a collection of broken promises, why did Quebecers pay so little attention to it?

The 1980 referendum was never intended to be a contract, marital or otherwise. It was never considered by its Parti Québécois initiators as anything other than a major component of their electoral strategy and a way to set the table for the inevitable constitutional negotiations with the rest of the country. No thought was ever given to the possibility—I know, I was there—that the Quebec government might lose this *appel au peuple*. Nor was it ever envisaged that a victory would settle the matter once and for all.

As a matter of fact, very little thought was ever given to the drawbacks of forcing such an overdose of electoral democracy on the Quebec and Canadian electorates. Nor was much thought given to what should be done the day after the referendum. "We'll see," was René Lévesque's favourite answer. Again, I should know since it was my job, and my sole source of bureaucratic gratification, to plan ahead for the "day after."

First and foremost, the decision to hold a referendum was made in 1974 as a way for the Parti Québécois to get out of what was fast becoming an NDP-like situation: a host of moral victories punctuated by demoralizing electoral defeats. One has to return to the reality of the early 1970s, and not to the mythical image of a period of intense mobilization and high political consciousness. In 1970 and 1973, the PQ experienced massive defeats at the polls. Even Lévesque could not succeed in getting elected in his own riding. So much for the figure of the charismatic hero in tune with the aspirations of his people. The 1973 defeat was especially painful, with the loss of one seat in relation to 1970. The party was broke, torn with dissension, and unsure of the best strategy to adopt the next time around. One thing was certain: a simple repetition of the 1973 scenario would mean a third catastrophe.

Computer simulations revealed that only a significant breakthrough among supporters of federalism could increase the PQ's share of the vote. All other scenarios spelled defeat. Surveys also revealed that the only strength of the PQ, outside of its nationalist platform, lay in the positive and honest image of its leadership, especially René Lévesque. The problem was thus a simple one: how to best use this high level of trust in the honest and straightforward leader to get around the suspicion and outright rejection of the separatist option by the same electorate.

The situation had certain Catch-22 aspects to it: any repudiation of the independentist platform would not be believed by the electorate and thus would destroy the PQ's only asset. Any attempt to redefine the content of sovereignty-association in a more acceptable way would cause turmoil within the party and would play into the hands of the Liberal government.

In short, the PQ could not resort to a gimmick to get out of its no-win situation. Honesty was its strength and could not be bypassed. A strange situation for any political party, but one in which the Parti Québécois revelled as it confirmed its sense of moral superiority.

René Lévesque

The promise to hold a referendum on the future status of Quebec was both a clever and a democratic solution—a rare combination. Never could the Liberal Party and the federal government convince the Quebec electorate that it was an empty promise and that the PQ could not be trusted with its "solution." As subsequent events would confirm, Pierre Trudeau himself had always been a strong believer in the value of referendums, and would eventually suggest such a procedure to break the 1981 constitutional impasse. The more the PQ was attacked for this promise, the more the party's democratic nature was highlighted, in contrast with Premier Bourassa's vague promise about the need for Quebec to obtain its "full cultural sovereignty." In the end, the PQ was swept into power in November 1976 because the promise of a referendum built on its strength: its image as an honest political party. In the post-Watergate era, such an image was money in the bank (as Jimmy Carter also found out).

Born out of electoral necessity, the referendum rapidly developed a life of its own. It fit marvellously with the PQ's self-image as a party of the people, by the people and for the people. No one in the party's reigning circle ever doubted the existence of a special bond with the Quebec people, who would answer the call of destiny when the time came. *Le peuple allait parler.* Well, they did.

The promise to hold a referendum became such an integral part of the PQ's ideology and image that the party was eventually reelected in 1981 after having lost the referendum—in part, because it came through on its promise to hold one in the first place. Rarely has a party's democratic image both helped and hindered its fortunes to such an extent.

As the months went by after November 1976—and once in power they tend to go by faster—the referendum was transformed from being a political process, even a democratic one, to the mythical status of a "rendezvous with destiny." Two issues rapidly moved to the top of the agenda: when the referendum should be held, and what the question should be. The first issue dominated all internal debates during the 1977–78 period and lasted well into 1979. As is often the case, it was never really decided on its face value. With the passage of time, the number of potential windows of opportunity dwindled until it was almost too late. Only in August 1979 was the decision finally reached (by default) not to have the referendum in 1979.

Then there was the question of the question. Until the spring of 1979, a small group of advisors to Claude Morin, then minister of intergovernmental affairs, worked on the scenario of a simple "yes and no" question along the lines of "Do you agree with Bill 147?" Bill 147, or whatever number would have been selected, was to have been an "ordinary" bill introduced in the Quebec National Assembly which, in the tradition of the BNA Act, would have listed the "legislative" powers that the Quebec government had every intention of patriating from Ottawa. In the words of Claude Morin, the idea was to keep it "short, sweet and very parliamentary." Unfortunately, the idea was shot down in midair when it was realized that the referendum-enabling legislation made it almost impossible to use such a question. A referendum could not bind Parliament! The British parliamentary tradition, of which René Lévesque was an almost maniacal admirer, had struck back with a vengeance.

Back to the drawing board.

It is true that polls taken at the time indicated that a straight and simplistic question along the lines of "Are you in favour of political independence for Quebec?" would have brought defeat. But I do not believe that this was the major motivation for the question that finally emerged, asking Quebecers for a mandate to negotiate sovereignty-association. Why make it simple when one can make it complicated? For the government, the referendum was part of an ongoing dialogue among the Quebec people, Ottawa and the rest of the country. Everyone knew that in the end, some day and in some way, Québécois would opt to stand on their own two feet. This conviction was never in doubt and it would have been useless to organize the referendum for the simple pleasure of being confirmed in this belief.

There was to be more to the referendum than a simple show of constitutional force. The referendum was to be the *acte de naissance* of a new Quebec, which only needed this confirmation to step out side its Canadian maternal pouch. Strategically, the objective was to arrive at the negotiating table with the best set of cards, and in Péquiste ideology a clear popular mandate offered the best hand.

The awakening was a brutal one, made even more brutal by this paternalistic and grandiose vision. Fortunately for the PQ, the Quebec people never shared this vision. They voted because they were asked to pass judgement. Quebecers were not told this was to be a marriage. There was no wedding reception. Canadian federalism was never first on their priority list. They pronounced on an important issue, yes, but an "issue" nevertheless, not a rendezvous with their destiny.

As the 1980 results revealed, Quebecers were not willing to take a position that would have led to sovereign status down the road. No single set of reasons explains that decision. For many, the fear of economic reprisal was sufficient. For others, sovereignty was still a fuzzy idea. Many objected to the idea because of its socialist overtones. Age was also a factor—as a matter of fact, the significant variable (outside of language of course) explaining the propensity of a voter to support or not to support the Yes side.

As this is written in 1990, it has become fashionable to argue that Quebecers were not "ready" to support independence in 1980. Notwithstanding its paternalistic overtones, this line of argument implies the existence of a collective maturity threshold beyond which Quebecers had moved a decade later. But could ten years make such a difference?

The attachment to Canada and Canadians is still there. What has changed, though, is the context against which this attachment plays itself out. Events in eastern and western Europe have shown political situations to be infinitely adaptable to changing conditions. Ideological and political alliances are being transformed before our eyes. Borders are there to be crossed—and changed. Society is taking over politics. In short, there is nothing dramatic about Quebec's wanting to redefine its relationship with Canada. Compared to 1980, this sets the tone for a completely different type of debate.

Political scientist **Daniel Latouche** was an adviser to Premier René Lévesque at the time of the 1980 Quebec referendum, and at the time of writing in 1990 worked at the Institut National de la Recherche Scientifique—Urbanisation in Montreal.

Revolution on the Desktop

by Gail van Varseveld

Summer 1969. Research into violence and land reform during the Mexican revolution of the early twentieth century kept me in a small, windowless room, at a keyboard that resembled a large typewriter, except that it punched holes in cards instead of transferring ink to paper. If you hit the wrong key, the machine punched a hole in the wrong place and you had to redo the entire card. Another machine, taking up a whole wall, shuffled the cards into stacks, "reading" their holes and transmitting the data over a cable to yet another machine, which lived in specialized isolation in another building and did the actual processing. I never saw that machine, a mainframe computer, and only inferred its existence by the large sheets of correlations it produced. The correlations, which once would have taken weeks or even years to calculate, now appeared within hours or days.

To write the report, the information was reentered onto long sheets of wax, where a small mistake could be corrected by applying what looked like fluorescent pink nail polish, letting it dry, and typing over. If a paragraph was omitted, the whole stencil had to be redone. When the stencils were all cut, someone stood at the Gestetner and cranked the handle to produce a rough impression on paper, sheet by sheet, until there were the required number of copies.

Summer 1979. In another tiny, airless room at another university, editing a thesis (not mine) on international treaties and war, I worked on a keyboard attached to a monitor, entering characters a line at a time—too many or too few on a line and the paragraph would not format properly. For tables, there were special codes; graphs had to be pasted in later. When the editing was done, I entered some codes—the card sorter was gone —and impulses went over a cable to the mainframe. If I had done everything correctly (I found out when I picked up my printout, hours—or days—later), the computer formatted the text and produced a report. That computer too lived elsewhere in its special environment and I never saw it.

Summer 1980. In the large, airy office of a computer components manufacturer, I used another "dumb" terminal—a monitor and keyboard that did nothing if not connected to a computer. By now the computer, called a "mini" although it was the size of two large refrigerators, lived down the hall, next to the coffee room. It had special power hookups and lots of wiring, but no particular environmental controls. I could visit it any time the system "sludged up" (a technical term) and bookkeeping data entry became slower than writing with quill and ink. When the system was "up" (another technical term), data entered at the terminals was sent in batches to the computer, and hours (or days, depending on the system load) later, we got back the results and found out our books didn't balance.

Summer 1984. Planning classroom requirements for universities, in an office with windows that opened, I typed on a keyboard, watching my input on a monitor, correcting mistakes as I went. To run the analysis, I keyed in the "calculate" command and class sizes and required classroom capacities appeared right before my eyes. I typed up the results at the same keyboard, added some strange-looking characters (control commands), and the report appeared on the screen, formatted with justified paragraphs and neatly aligned tables. To reproduce it, I saved it to a five-inch plastic disk, carried it across the office to the machine attached to the daisy-wheel printer and, after a good deal of clickety-clacking, had a printout that looked for all the world as if it had been typed on an IBM Selectric. The computers that did all this were fully in evidence, one on my desk, one beside the printer. They didn't get any special consideration: they lived as we did—heat, humidity, dust, smoke—and they ran off standard office power.

Summer 1989. Similar office, similar work, except that my monitor had full colour, my data were saved on a slightly larger piece of plastic permanently stored in the computer, my reports appeared on screen without the ugly control commands and with graphs and charts in place, just (or almost) as they would appear on the printout. When it was finished, I entered the print command and electronic impulses went over a cable to the printer where I could collect it as soon as I walked across the office. There was no noise, save a slight whir as the printer spat out the pages, and the report could print in any typeface the company had fonts for. All the pieces —computer, keyboard, monitor and printer—would fit inside one household refrigerator with room to spare.

The change in "information technology" between the 1960s and the 1990s was staggering, but the most profound aspect was the advent of the desktop computer in the 1980s. From rare and exotic machines requiring enormous resources to operate and thus only available to large institutions such as the military in the 1940s and 1950s, general-purpose computers have evolved into compact, relatively easily usable tools now found everywhere in offices, homes and carry-on baggage.

Looking back at the development of what we came to think of as "the computer," it seems like a logical progression from the gigantic ENIAC, the electronic programmable calculator which first ran in November 1945, weighing 30 tons and using 174 kilowatts of power, to the late-nineties desktop computer which weighs about 30 pounds (not counting the monitor) and runs off standard household current. But the path was anything but clear to those on it. The quotes that follow have been kicking around the Internet for some time and may be apocryphal, but the attitudes they express were real:

"I think there may be a world market for maybe five computers."

—Thomas Watson, chair of IBM, 1943

"Computers in the future may weigh no more than 1.5 tons."

—*Popular Mechanics*, 1949

"But what...is it [the microchip] good for?"

—IBM engineer, 1968

"There is no reason why anyone would want a computer in their home." —Ken Olson, president, chair and founder of Digital Equipment Corporation, 1977

"640K ought to be enough [memory] for anybody."

—Bill Gates, cofounder of Microsoft, 1981

Miniaturization of both price and components (my father stores his address book in his wristwatch, and this miniature computer costs so little that he simply replaces it when it "wears out") has contributed a great deal to the prevalence of personal computers at the end of the twentieth century. But two other factors also played major roles: hobbyists with their computer games, and GUI, the "Graphical User Interface" pioneered by Apple Computer and subsequently the basis of Microsoft Windows.

The microprocessor, the gizmo that made the desktop computer possible, was developed between 1969 and 1971. In 1977, the Apple II, Commodore PET and Tandy TRS-80 came on the market. In between, hobbyists using kits advertised in magazines like *Popular Mechanics* built computers which they used to write programs in BASIC. But small BASIC programs are, well, basic, and these machines didn't do much else. The first personal computer kit, the Altair 8800 based on the (then) new Intel 8080 microprocessor, was announced in *Popular Mechanics* in 1975. It had no keyboard, no monitor and no language or programs to run it.

Once prebuilt, affordable machines became available, people needed a use for them, and the first was to play games, many of them adapted from video games. For those who remember Pong and text-based adventure quests, this use may seem a far cry from our current computers, but as Martin Kelly-Campbell and William Asprey wrote in their useful 1996 book *Computer: a History of the Information Machine,*

> Programming computer games created a corps of young programmers who were very sensitive to what we now call human/computer interaction. The most successful games were ones that needed no manuals and gave instant feedback.

However, games were not enough. Serious (i.e., business) people needed serious applications. The first of these, a spreadsheet program called VisiCalc (for Visible Calculator), was released in December 1979 and changed computing. According to Kelly-Campbell and Asprey,

> Because the personal computer was a stand-alone, self-contained system, changes to a financial model were displayed almost instantaneously….The fast response enabled a manager to explore a financial model with great flexibility, asking…"what if?" questions. It was almost like a computer game for executives.

At US$3,000, a desktop computer was a realistic possibility for small businesses and individuals. With the appearance the following year of computers able to display both upper- and lower-case characters *and* eighty of them across the screen, applications like WordStar could provide WYSIWYG ("what you see is what you get") document editing previously only possible on dedicated—and expensive—word-processors.

An outpouring of business-related software followed: spreadsheet, word-processing and database applications, many of which did not survive the decade. Who remembers Multiplan, PFS:Write, Symphony? The availability of software that could be bought off the shelf (mainframe and minicomputer programs had to be written for the specific machine they were to run on) and used by people without computer science degrees meant that the desktop computer became a serious—indeed, indispensable—business tool. *Time* magazine's Man of the Year for 1982 was a desktop computer.

The desktop computers taking the business world by storm were known as PCs, for the Personal Computer produced by IBM, or "clones" for those made by its imitators. Apple Computer, whose hobby-market Apple II was becoming elderly, tried to get into this market with the Lisa in May 1983. But with a price tag of US$17,000, it was too rich for personal users and even, it seems, for the corporate world. A commercial failure, the Lisa's technological achievements contributed significantly to Apple's next effort: the much more affordable "information appliance," the Macintosh.

The release of the Macintosh with its Graphical User Interface–based operating system in January 1984 was the next major shift in desktop computing. Previously, the computing metaphor had been a programming one where, simply to move a file from one location to another, one entered (carefully) instructional strings such as:

```
COPY A:\COMPASS\JUNE\LEADER.DOC B:\COMPASS\ARCHIVES\JUNE\
LEADER.DOC DEL A:\ COMPASS\JUNE\LEADER.DOC
```

GUI changed the metaphor to the virtual office: a desk cluttered with file folders and papers, notebooks, a calculator and even a wastebasket. Using a "mouse," you clicked a folder to open it, clicked a document to load it into its application or dragged it to the wastebasket to delete it. Not all of us found the graphical interface as intuitive as it was meant to be. Using a Mac, I spent at least half an hour trying to delete some files. Then the Mac's owner came by and pointed out the tiny trash can symbol in the corner of the screen. I'd tried everything *but* hauling the files to the garbage!

Time was when I argued that those of us who weren't "graphically oriented" would never take to the virtual office metaphor, even though, in a command-line interface, each application had different screen layouts and required learning different commands. For a time, Macs dominated graphics-related industries such as publishing, while PCs were the choice of the rest of the business world. Then, in 1985, came Microsoft Windows.

Version 1 of Windows didn't make much of an impact. The cutting-edge PC, the "286" (for the Intel microprocessor 80286), couldn't run a GUI-based system with any speed, and besides you couldn't do much in Windows except play Reversi. Windows 2, released in 1987 to take advantage of the faster 386 processor, heralded the beginning of the shift from command-line to graphical interface in the PC world. Beginning with Microsoft's Excel spreadsheet (originally released for the Mac), application software was rewritten so that a user who could work in one application could very quickly be functional in another. By 1992 and revision 3.1, Windows on a 486 PC actually almost did what it promised, allowing multiple simultaneous computer operations: the "multitasking" we now expect from our computers as a matter of course.

What did all this mean for people like me? When I began in facilities planning in 1974, secretaries booked our meetings and typed up our reports. Draftspeople drew up our plans (and redrew them when things changed over the course of a project), and graphic artists sketched elevations and site layouts.

At the small firm where I worked in the 1980s, the first desktop computer, a DEC Rainbow with 64K of memory and dual diskette drives, was determined by the availability of time-billing accounting software. Word-processing software came next, and since revision was so much easier than on a typewriter, we did more drafts. Those of us who typed found ourselves doing our own, and soon the clerical staff disappeared.

Spreadsheets were next, a real boon for those of us doing twenty-year student enrolment projections with graph paper and adding machines. Need to change the starting assumptions for the projections? Simply change those numbers and the computer corrected the rest. Then came desktop publishing, and every document had to look professionally de-signed and printed. The replicate-the-typewriter daisywheel printer was replaced by a faster, quieter laser printer, which printed graphics. Now our spreadsheets generated pie charts and scatter graphs to insert into the report, and we got vector-drawing software for organizational charts and fancy cover designs. No report could go out without illustrations.

Drafting software (CAD for Computer-Assisted Drawing) had required high-end workstations (basically minicomputers on a desk) found only in large architectural firms or firms specializing in CAD. But in 1986, we too got CAD —one computer and one software licence, so we worked around the clock in shifts. Now, no planning session was complete without full-size layouts to show the clients. And one by one our draftspeople disappeared (although un-like the clerical staff, eventually they came back, as CAD specialists).

By the end of the eighties, planners booked their own site visits (straight into Personal Information Managers, computerized appointment/ address books), designed and laid out data collection forms, inputted the collected data, analysed it, wrote up the reports, developed the supporting graphs and charts, completed vector-drawn layouts, and fancied it all up in desktop publishing. One thing hadn't changed: we still had a manual Cerlox machine to bind the finished product.

By the end of the 1980s my computer, except for the printer, fit on a 27-by-42-inch table in the corner of my living room. By then, or soon af-ter, I used it to do all my work, both planning and desktop publishing (and subsequently, Web design), to send faxes and e-mail, keep my accounts and submit my taxes, even play the odd game. If I wanted, I could have had all that and more in something about the size of a large three-ring binder.

The impact of the "desktop revolution" continues to play out. Lots of old skills became obsolete, lots of capable people had to find new careers. Lots of us "brain workers" learned to do our own scut work. And not a few of us moved out of the office, because of the advent of those machines we now think of when we hear the word "computer."

Gail van Varseveld, in keep-ing with the times, pursues ca-reers in desktop publishing, Website design and develop-ment, facilities planning and, oc-casionally, writing. She was *Compass*'s desktop publisher from 1990 to 1997 and is treasurer of the Compass Foundation.

The Eighties' Environmental Legacy: Death (of Nature) by Natural Causes?

by Moira Farr

Kermit the Frog was right: it's not easy being green. In fact, if the eighties taught us anything about our relationship to what we now routinely refer to as "the environment," it may have been that not only is it not easy, but in the long run of our species' life, it's impossible.

If nothing else, the eighties were a decade of heightened environmental anxiety, and for good reason. Previous decades of this century had their share of environmental Cassandras warning of troubles to come. But in the eighties there was a difference: we could no longer so easily ignore the doomsayers and their increasingly alarming messages of imminent disaster, from global warming to deforestation, from radioactive landfill to mass species extinction. By the eighties we had no excuse for not seeing the glowing writing on the contaminated wall; we knew all too well that the things we were doing as human beings weren't good for our health, for the health of other species, or for the health of the planet. We knew—and for the most part kept right on doing them.

A few honest souls had taken the trouble to enlighten us before it came to this. In the 1940s American writer Aldo Leopold, in his famous *Sand County Almanac*, offered enlightening thoughts on how to preserve the remaining environment from the ravages of mass industrialization. In the 1950s Marjory Stoneman Douglas almost singlehandedly saved the Florida Everglades from complete degradation with her immensely readable and heartfelt *River of Grass* —and by example gave environmentalists everywhere a durable template for responsible conservation based on both a scientific and a spiritual sense of place. It was Rachel Carson's turn to warn the human race to stop racing technologically and chemically in the 1960s with the bestselling *Silent Spring*, which detailed the disastrous effects of DDT on bird populations and spawned a whole new environmental consciousness among North Americans.

By the 1970s, an entire movement of mainly first-wave baby boomers was going "back to the land," armed with rebellion against the prevailing consumerist notions they were spoonfed through their fifties childhoods and naïve ideas of what it would take to eke out a satisfactory rural existence on the margins of mainstream society, in all its wasteful and avaricious glory. Some stayed on in their wilderness paradises; others left for less extreme ways of living. Many retained their sense that "green" is good and became community activists, doing their bit by recycling, campaigning to preserve local habitats, joining Greenpeace, buying phosphate-free detergent, shopping at health-food stores, cooking with vegetarian recipes from such popular books as *Diet for a Small Planet*, and protesting against corporate polluters with product boycotts and demonstrations.

Unfortunately, we began to understand in the eighties that it might be too little too late. There were, after all, so many of us, more all the time, pushing other species out of existence as we exponentially asserted our own. In 1979, biologist Norman Myers ushered out the old decade and dubiously heralded the new one with his gloomy book on species extinction, *The Sinking Ark*. During the politically hawkish early and mid-eighties, environmental anxieties skyrocketed in our fears over the potential for nuclear Armageddon, causing parents to worry over the state of their children's doom-nourished psyches. Who would not respond emotionally to the stirring eloquence of the distinguished scientist Dr. Helen Caldicott, painting from her lecture podium a dark and tragic portrait of a post-fallout world in which all the greatest achievements of humanity would be catastrophically nullified overnight? *If You Love This Planet*, the National Film Board of Canada's documentary consisting primarily of Caldicott's devastating speech, won an Oscar for best documentary in 1985.

Later in the decade our fears surrounding nuclear war may have eased somewhat in the midst of global geopolitical shifts, but we couldn't exactly relax once the Brundtland Report was in the public realm, with its unequivocal assertion that global warming and all its attendant negative environmental effects were upon us. (It would take another decade for the majority of mainstream scientists to admit that this was so, once weather patterns began to become so markedly distorted that they could no longer be characterized as part of some normal cycle. At the time, it was still possible for some to dismiss the report's findings as exaggerated or false.) Bhopal, Love Canal, the St. Clair River Blob, ozone holes over Antarctica—the decade was littered with real evidence of the destruction in our midst. How could we rest easy when children born near nuclear generating plants were exhibiting higher rates of leukemia, when mothers in their millions were said to have traces of dioxins in their breast milk, when beluga whales were turning up dead in the St. Lawrence, so infused with deadly chemicals they were declared toxic waste in themselves?

By 1989, it seemed more fitting for writers to dispense with metaphor and cut to the chase: Bill McKibben offered us his eloquent lament for what we were losing with the bluntly titled book *The End of Nature*. Around the same time, Exxon offered us a massive oil-tanker spill in the hitherto pristine waters of Alaska. Operators at the company's switchboards began having nervous breakdowns as the vicious calls of public protest flooded in. It was hard for many not to get emotional looking at photographs and video footage chronicling the devastation to marine wildlife, in endless horrifying images of animals and birds sickening and dying in oceans of crude oil that covered their coats and wings in the evil black substance—the evil black substance that fuels the lives of everyone living in modern society. Exxon might provide it, but how could we deny that we were the ones consuming it? Perhaps some of us were ready to accept guilt by association. Still, the task of turning the tides, environmentally speaking, would be a mammoth one. It could no longer be borne on the backs of a few enlightened idealists, but would rather have to involve a sea change in global human habits of consuming the earth's increasingly damaged and diminishing resources.

During the eighties, we began to understand as well that the politics of it all had become a lot more complicated. With everyone from the militant Paul Watson to Prince Philip and Sting calling themselves environmentalists, just what did it mean to take a stand that had merit and a chance of success? Shopping for unbleached coffee filters and "green" brand bleach at Loblaw's might be the start of a general evolution in public environmental awareness, but many questioned the environmental commitment of any profit-driven corporation. Were they not simply responding to a trendy new consumer demand that would keep customers filing through the cash lineups?

Was it better to choose cotton clothing over synthetic, when producing it meant massive earth-stripping crop monocultures managed at the expense of impoverished Third World peasants? What clothing was it okay to buy anyway, be it cotton or polyester, once we learned that much of it was produced by miserably exploited children in squalid sweatshops? Maybe Greenpeace was right to save the seals and the whales, but what about the human populations, many of them indigenous, that suffered as a result of lost hunting livelihoods? Organic produce might be preferable to commercially grown, but poor people could not afford to buy it and mostly lived in crowded urban spaces where it would be difficult if not impossible to grow it. Consumers might not have been as resistant to recycling as some politicians and corporations had thought (or hoped), but without the infrastructure to handle old newspapers and other recyclable goods, much of the stuff people thought they were recycling ended up in landfills anyway. Just how ethical were those ethical mutual funds when companies like the environmentally questionable MacMillan Bloedel were showing up in their investment mix? Was it okay to own a car so long as it was small, driven only occasionally in car-pool situations, and fuelled on the cleanest gasoline on the market—or were bikes the only way to go? And was it okay to take a fuel-guzzling airplane to a distant conference to discuss these matters with other concerned environmentalists?

Despite these conundrums, there were on occasion some glimmers of hope: it was scientific research into the acidification of Canadian lakes that convinced large companies like Proctor and Gamble to remove phosphates from their detergents; it was a Canadian school children's protest that prompted McDonald's to switch from Styrofoam containers to (allegedly) less wasteful paper wrapping for its burgers (but was that beef provided at the expense of the Amazon rainforest?). Cree Grand Chief Matthew Coon-Come and several elders from northern Quebec made history—and an arresting image—when they paddled a canoe down the Hudson River into New York City, where they convinced state politicians not to sign up with Hydro-Quebec for its hydroelectric power. With this success they won a reprieve for the Cree and their ancestral lands, already largely destroyed by the first phase of Hydro-Quebec's massive dam project.

Such victories, however small or large in their significance, might have given us some heart. But during the late 1980s I began to feel that with the alarming increase in the rate of environmental degradation, we were experiencing a profound loss on a far more subtle level than we were acknowledging—one that had to do with our spirits and souls, not just lungs and blood cells, and could not be easily mitigated with the odd saved bit of land or resource here and there. Maybe it struck me forcefully because in response to all the bad news about the environment I had begun to be drawn to the writings of essayists of nature. As a result I ended up reading such things as Annie Dillard's remarkable *Pilgrim and Tinker Creek* (published in the early seventies) at the same time as I was reading McKibben's *The End of Nature*.

The juxtaposition of the two sensibilities was a saddening shock to me, and I eventually wrote about it in an essay called "The Death of Nature Writing" (*Brick*, Winter 1993). What struck me most was that when Dillard had gone into nature on her pilgrimage, she had done so in a time-honoured tradition that took nature to be, even at its most violent and wild, an intact place of refuge for the seeker of enlightenment. It was a place where you could contemplate and discover truths about yourself and the universe, not questioning its essential integrity. By the end of the eighties, such a pilgrimage might still be physically possible, but encroachments on the environment had made it impossible to have that same unsullied, optimistic faith in the abiding sacredness of nature. You might find some peace, but if you were at all honest you would have to mention the garbage you tripped over, the lack of fish, the absence of certain birdsong, the deformed frogs, the noisy planes flying overhead. In a few short years, an age-old way of seeing, a cast of consciousness, had been forever ruined along with the forests and oceans. I'm not sure we've come to fully acknowledge this loss even yet.

For a final sense of the environmental legacy of the eighties we need only look at what is going on in the late nineties. Yes, MacMillan Bloedel did decide to stop clearcutting its forest holdings in British Columbia, but most of the recent environmental news has been bad. According to statistics published in 1998 in *Shift* magazine, although only 8 per cent of the world's population lives in North America, we produce 50 per cent of the world's garbage. Since 1988, paper packaging in Canada has increased by 11 per cent, while the amount of Canadian garbage washing up on the shores of Scotland has increased by 1,000 per cent. A hundred thousand marine mammals die yearly from ingesting plastic debris dumped in U.S. waters. The food Americans discard could feed a hundred million people. The amount of paper going to landfill sites has decreased by 60 per cent as a result of recycling, but the bottom line is, we still create a ridiculous, unconscionable amount of garbage. It takes only four months for Metro Toronto to make enough to fill the SkyDome.

And so environmental optimism post-eighties is awfully difficult to maintain. Just read David Quammen's article "Planet of Weeds" in the October 1998 issue of *Harper's*, in which the author of many fascinating and informative books on the state of nature tells us he went to a paleontologist looking for answers to the question of what the future holds for the earth because he "wanted answers unvarnished with obligatory hope." He got them:

> Biologists believe that we are entering another mass extinction, a vale of biological impoverishment....In the next fifty years, deforestation will doom one half of the world's forest-bird species....Even by conservative estimates, huge percentages of Earth's animals and plants will simply disappear....We confront the vision of a human population pressing snugly around whatever natural landscape remains.

Not being a paleontologist, I suppose I am in Quammen's estimation among those who are obliged to hope, and I do try, though since the eighties it is harder. I live beside a large, thriving river, and it clears my head to walk along its banks. I recycle. I support a few environmental causes as best I can. But I'm realistic and I try to be honest. Nothing we did or learned or knew in the eighties has significantly altered the overall destructive course the human population is taking on the planet. That's the truth, and truth hurts. It remains to be seen whether it will set us free. Post-eighties it's as good as environmental hope gets.

Moira Farr, a writer specializing in environmental and scientific topics, lives in Ottawa. She is a former managing editor of *This Magazine* and the author of *After Daniel: A Suicide Survivor's Tale* (1999).

Jean Vanier: Community Builder

by Carolyn Whitney-Brown

Jean Vanier, internationally respected spiritual leader and founder of several influential movements worldwide, was offering an afternoon talk to members of the L'Arche Daybreak community in Toronto. David Harmon, long-term member of Daybreak, dragged a mattress to the front and sprawled out at Jean's feet. "You always put me to sleep, Jean," he commented.

Jean smiled delightedly and addressed the group. "This is that dangerously sleepy time after lunch. It's all right if you go to sleep. I'll keep talking as long as one person is still awake." Then he leaned forward and spoke quite earnestly. "But when you wake up, listen. That is the prophetic word for you, the word for which you've been awakened."

I see three essential aspects of Jean in this moment: first, his extremely nondefensive and playful humour; second, his realistic and affectionate acceptance of the peculiarities and vulnerability of being human; and third, his absolute conviction that for each of us there are prophetic moments that God will initiate, the wake-up calls of our lives. Every person, no matter how socially marginalized, has a unique call and purpose from God in the world.

Jean Vanier, fourth child of Pauline and Georges Vanier, was born in 1928 into a privileged, respected and generously public-spirited French Canadian Catholic family. His father's military and ambassadorial postings took the family around Europe, before the Vaniers settled in Canada during the Second World War. Jean, aged thirteen, arranged entirely on his own to enter the Royal Military College at Dartmouth, England, and while his parents were justifiably apprehensive (it was the height of the war), they let him go. His father said simply, "I trust you." A younger friend in England recalls fourteen-year-old Jean Vanier coming for holidays with her family:

> He was very dashing in his naval uniform, delightful, unusual, full of energy. He was not shy, quite at ease with himself. He taught me an American pop song, *My mama done told me, when I was in knee pants.*

Jean Vanier

After eight years, Jean left the navy. He was an officer on the HMS *Bonaventure*, with a promising military career ahead of him, having learned an interior discipline and a quality of trustworthiness that remain with him still, but feeling that "my place in the world was somewhere else." He spent the next fourteen years preparing to discover that place. He studied philosophy and theology, travelled, taught, and lived in contemplative solitude for long periods. Gradually growing was his theological, intellectual, personal and absolutely heartfelt conviction that the most rejected and poor are at the centre of the Church and of society.

In 1964, at the urging of his Dominican friend Père Thomas Philippe, Jean invited three men from an institution for the mentally handicapped to Trosly, France, to create a home with him. The first night, one man was so needy and disturbed that the next day Jean regretfully returned him to the familiar routines of institutional life. The other two men endured the primitive comforts, military-style schedule and playful celebration that Jean offered, gradually teaching Jean deep truths about building authentic community. Jean knew, too, that with these two men, Raphael and Philippe, he had made an irrevocable choice for his life. This was the beginning of L'Arche: a vision, a desire, an audacious risk, an immediate wrenching failure and new wisdom gained even that first night.

By the 1980s L'Arche and its cousins—Faith and Light, and Faith and Sharing—had become worldwide movements of life-sharing with mentally handicapped people. Each is founded in Jean's fundamental insight—which can sound sentimental, but most radically is a mystical orientation—that the cornerstone of all community is the weakest person. It is the rejected "chief cornerstone" of the Gospels, the spirit of the Beatitudes, announcing the infinite value and beauty of each life in a way that doesn't minimize the pain, anguish and rejection in those lives.

A sabbatical year in the late 1970s living with the most profoundly disabled members of his community pushed Jean to explore more deeply his own pain, anger, fear, even violence. Through the 1980s the fruitfulness of that time grew as Jean continued to articulate the radical message of L'Arche: there is a real alternative to competitive greed and isolating individualism. In 1987, Jean was invited by the pope to participate in a synod focused on vocation and mission: there too he urged the church to recognize the crucial if often intangible gift of the poor, and to pursue the challenge of ecumenism. But even as his international stature grew, Jean did not become protective of his own image. It's not only the ubiquitous blue jacket with its overstuffed pockets even for most formal occasions. While Jean takes his responsibilities seriously, he doesn't take himself seriously. There is an impish humour in this six-foot-four-inch man flicking orange peels across a dining room.

An assistant at L'Arche in Trosly in the early 1980s returned for a visit some fifteen years later and found herself deeply moved over and over by the maturity of the people with handicaps she had lived with twenty years before. "I realized that Jean can see all along who people are, and can walk the long walk with them while they grow into it," she observed. It wasn't that Jean could see who they would become: it was that he could see the essential gift of someone's life already present. The gift of our lives is for Jean always deeper than the disability or struggle.

People commonly experience even a brief time with Jean as one that leaves them feeling bigger, their horizons, imagination and commitment wider. It is Jean's fearless confidence in God's work in every person, the unconditional "I trust you" of his father that stood Jean on his feet so many years ago. A young Jesuit asked him more than twenty-five years ago what to do with his life. "It doesn't matter what you do," responded Jean, "as long as you build community."

Carolyn Whitney-Brown is a writer and artist, and was for seven years part of the L'Arche Daybreak community in Toronto.

The Nineties

363 **The Age of America** by Judy MacDonald

365 **After the (Cold) War Is Over...** by Rick Salutin

372 **A Gambler's Society: The End of Job Security** by Jamie Swift

377 **Hannibal's Mirrors: Cyberintelligence and
the Zapatista Revolution** by Louisa Blair

382 **Canada in the Information Age** by Ronald Deibert

385 **Spirituality in the Nineties: Rediscovering Sacred Spaces** by Peter McIsaac

391 **Is Aboriginal Self-Government a Mirage?** by Miles Morrisseau

397 **Rwanda: Alone with Its Deep Wounds** by Augustin Karekezi

402 **South Africa's Election: Inspiring yet Sobering** by Josephine C. Naidoo

407 **Mother Teresa: Champion of the Poor** by Lucinda Vardey

The Age of America

by Judy MacDonald

"Just as the reckless laissez-faire capitalism of the nineteenth century spawned Marxism, so the indiscriminate globalism of the 1990s may generate a worldwide assault on the concept of the free financial markets." It was former U.S. Secretary of State Henry Kissinger who said this, and in 1998, a year that happened also to mark the 150th anniversary of the Communist Manifesto.

Kissinger's alarm presents a jarring contrast with the great bellicose hurrah that opened the last decade of the twentieth century. The United States declared victory in the Cold War, and the end of history had arrived. Economic doctors went forth from winners' universities and think tanks to apply their bromides to the world. But as Rick Salutin notes, the euphoria hasn't lasted. Mexico, Indonesia, Russia, Brazil: one after another, the newly minted free-market economies fell like the dominoes we heard so much about in the olden days of two superpowers. As we enter the last half of the last year ending the last decade of a millennium, assuring sounds are being made that these were simply sobering corrections in an otherwise vibrant structure.

"When you are asked, you just say he was going, he said, to America." With these words, a wastrel landlord shot himself dead in Dostoyevsky's *Crime and Punishment*. More than a century after this was written, we see whole nations self-immolate while chanting a similar sentiment. These days it seems we might all be going to America. Or else America is coming to us, thanks to Mickey Mouse and smart bombs.

Of all decades, perhaps this one begs for reflection before it's done: maybe it is appropriate to write a historical perspective for an era suffering from chronic amnesia. Weeks after another volley of bombs hits Iraq, the media skitter on to the next event. What led to the first Gulf War all those years ago takes on the patina of old war stories set way-back-when. And in the age of globalization, there are so many bits and pieces of information to try to keep up with. Rwanda, Korea, Colombia, Sierre Leone, Kosovo; Lewinsky, Furbies, national unity: there's no telling what is important. Do events not consumed really exist? What would be the sound of a revolution not packaged and simulcast?

Well, let's take Sierra Leone and compare it to the much more highly publicized crisis in Kosovo, then match these two horrors to the smaller, more marketable tragedy of two kids killing themselves and thirteen others one spring afternoon in America. There is no contest: it is the last place mentioned where we all seemed to go.

Still, there is something strange in reflecting on a decade while it is still in progress, especially when there is one big question hanging in the air right up to the minute. What *will* Y2K do to the stock excanges and rusting Soviet arsenal? Tune in at 12:01 a.m., January 1, 2000. Or, depending on your power source, maybe not.

The nineties have shown that technology isn't all bad, however: the very tools that define the electronic elite can now be exploited to great effect by marginalized communities. Louisa Blair reports on the flourishing Zapatista presence on the Web. Opponents of the Multilateral Agreement on Investment e-mailed one another with details of the secret negotiations, playing a part in shelving the MAI.

And yet most of the world is not wired. And the breathless cheerleading for the information age cloaks the fact that all this busy-busy leaves little time for the simple act of reflection. It is a culture suffering from a kind of intellectual bulimia. Those privileged few hurtle forward to whatever, leaving the rest of the planet ravaged and destitute. Yet there is a hunger for meaning greater than material gain, for knowledge deeper than the latest software program application.

At the beginning of the great new age after the Cold War, democracy and capitalism were seen as one and the same. At the close of the nineties, the falsity of this equation has been layed bare. Just as one era faced the daunting task of separating church from state, perhaps we are almost ready to separate democracy from the machinations of the market. Perhaps the present hysteria about globalization and competitive edge can then calm down. And in the pause, around the world, we can revel in the simple notion, the miracle, of being.

Judy MacDonald was a contributing editor of *Compass* from 1995 to 1997, an associate editor in 1997, and subsequently a director of the Compass Foundation. She is a former managing editor of *This Magazine* and currently chair of the editorial board of the *Canadian Forum*. Her first novel, *Jane*, was published in 1999.

After the (Cold) War Is Over…

by Rick Salutin

In September 1990, right at the beginning of the end of history, I happened to be unpacking my bags in the Hotel Europejski in Warsaw, one of the few hotels not totally taken over by travelling American businessmen. The irksome thing about those carpetbaggers wasn't the way they gobbled up large and small enterprises in the name of the new free-market millennium, but that they talked so loud you couldn't avoid their lectures on all the new eternal verities. A Polish economist I knew came to the door and said Milton Friedman was meeting a group of academics and journalists just across the street and I could probably slip in.

Friedman was near the end of a regal tour through the former Soviet satellites, during which he dispensed advice. He told the assembled Polish intellectuals to think of themselves on the model not of the United States in 1990, but in 1890. Rather than go into the silliness of this analogy, let me just recount the collective reaction of his audience. They began to noisily jiggle the samovars of coffee and tea on the tables in front of them and rattle the cups and saucers as they passed them back and forth. They were like kids in class with a supply teacher. Each time Friedman, who had received the Nobel Prize for economics in 1976, made another point similar to his parallel between Poland and the era of America's robber barons, the Poles renewed the clatter. Yet almost all these people had rejected any version of Marxist or socialist economics at that point, and embraced the need for capitalism and free markets in their country. They were all Reaganites, even Friedmanites.

At the time I thought their reaction meant simply that they were sophisticated Reaganites and Friedmanites, unlike Friedman himself. They weren't prepared to sit still for patent economic and historical idiocy. But looking back now, from the fall of 1998, I wonder if there wasn't something else in their peevish response to this embodiment of neoconservative economics who had come to call. I wonder if they weren't trying to drown out a terrifyingly familiar sound, the sound of socioeconomic dogma and certainty, the sort of thing they had had quite enough of during the previous half century. The kind of voice that promises, like a parent to a child, "If you do A in your life, you will always get B; I guarantee it, I have the proofs and arguments right here in my little answer kit." That sound was now coming from the right and the West, rather than the left and the East, but little had actually changed in the tone, the timbre and the odor.

One remarkable aspect of the transition from the Cold War to the post–Cold War era was the way in which mindsets, thought patterns and intellectual habits and markers which had seemed to dog and colour left-wing thinking for more than a century transferred seamlessly to the thoughtways of the right. Francis Fukuyama's well-known essay "The End of History," which first appeared in *The National Interest* in 1989 and was widely reprinted, is one example—but a striking one, if you think of it as filling the vacuum left by Marxist styles of thought. Fukuyama parodied or simply repeated many traditional claims and nostrums of Marxists, especially on the subject of "history": that history would absolve "us"; that history led to a "final conflict" beyond which a period of tranquillity, more or less, would commence; that all previous history (in the future to be known, according to Marx, as prehistory) would be superseded. In other words, the end of history. But in Fukuyama's case, the claims were made in the name of liberal capitalism and its political sidekick, electoral democracy, rather than the name of socialism and the withering of the state in a classless society.

This sort of intellectual cross-dressing by the ascendant right characterized what you could call the short tenth decade, 1990–1998, on the analogy of Eric Hobsbawm's notion, the short twentieth century, 1914–1991. The beginnings of the style can already be found in the anti-Keynesian shift of *The Economist* during the 1970s. Editor Doug Henwood of the *Left Business Observer* found in it "a heavy dose of British attitude that insecure Americans find intoxicating." But I think you can also see in it many of the typical mannerisms of left-wing writing. Those traits include a Rolodex of economic formulas and definitions: for example, deficits always mean this and always lead to that; labour "markets" are too "rigid" and provide "disincentives"; they must become "flexible." Governments are inherently inept at best; human beings are fundamentally individuals—which, when you come down to it, means shoppers. Those formulas were cited the way fundamentalists revert to Scripture, and the way leftists of an earlier age cited Marx, Lenin or Mao: not to illustrate a point but to end an argument.

The implication was that any challenge to this set of premises was ignorant or obsolete, and not worthy of a response. "If some ideas don't receive discussion in the mainstream media," wrote Andrew Coyne in the Toronto *Globe and Mail* about alternate views of economic reality, "it may be because they are not worth discussing." It reminds me of American new left student leader Mark Rudd in the 1960s refuting every argument of his university's administration by shouting, "Bullshit!" It's an energetic, confident style that has its appeal, though for myself I found it more attractive coming from someone attacking entrenched corporate power than from someone justifying it. In some ways it's the intellectual style of youth who see themselves as revolutionary: cocky, theoretical and callow. In an article in the *New York Times Magazine*, Andrew Sullivan, a right-winger himself and former editor of the *New Republic*, said the American new right and especially its younger intellectuals and journals showed a style of thinking which he called "characterologically leftist."

As I say, I remember this style well, and personally I found its transfer from left to right a relief. Smugness and arrogance aren't appealing traits, especially when you hear them coming out of your own mouth—even as you express your belief in the common people at the same time. But on thinking about it, I'm not sure this style isn't more a matter of being characterologically human than left. Speaking again for myself, before I was a leftist and noticed those offputting markers in my own thinking, I was for a serious amount of time a religious and theologically inclined person. It seems to me that earlier phase contained a similar style: calm certainty (too calm); a ready answer for everything (too ready); the absence of uncertainty. Just because a behaviour appears in a particular historical guise doesn't mean its source lies in that era.

To take a similar case, I had anticipated that with the end of the Cold War the tendency by both sides to dualize reality into forces of good and evil and to dehumanize, demonize and if at all possible demolish the "other" would be replaced by something better, or at least subtler. That hasn't happened. If it's no longer Communists that are the menace, it's terrorists or fundamentalists or gays or just the plain old adulterers and senusalists. There's a deep Manicheanism in human nature, or at least in that part of it stoked by theologians, economists, journalists and other intellectual pacesetters. Perhaps even back when the Christians won out against the original Manicheans in the late days of the Roman Empire, people were surprised to find the dualism just went on grinding anyway.

At any rate the current guise, what you might call the leftism of the right, already seems to have passed its peak. The crisis that began in 1997 in Thailand spread to Indonesia, South Korea, Japan, Russia and then Latin America, and as it did so the wall of neoconservative dogma began to disintegrate like the one in Berlin less than ten years before. By the fall of 1998, the dogmas about a free market, unrestrained compeitition, globalization, the evil of government and regulation had been in one degree or another abandoned by many mainstream voices. The World Bank suddenly announced that "markets alone are not adequate" to deal with, well, markets. The International Monetary Fund demanded "forceful action." *Business Week* ran a series of covers with headlines like "Global Crisis: Time to Act" and "Global Risk: How to Reshape the World Financial System." The latter article said, "The first and biggest task is to tame the anarchy of markets that globalization has unleashed."

The zealots of unhindered capitalism carried on, to be sure, but they began looking more like a well-financed cult and less like the latest world-conquering religion. Milton Friedman seemed more like a lonely kook once more, the way he used to. They were all Keynesians again. This doesn't mean the born-again Keynesians will try to do anything but continue to line their own pockets at the economic and social expense of the rest of the human race. But at least we may not have to listen to quite as much neoconservative economic triumphalism.

I wonder if any of them experienced relief at losing the burden of a perfect and unchallengeable worldview. For leftists like myself—to try to empathize again—probably our last source of hope lay in the revolutions of the Third World. As Hobsbawm wrote, for the western left from the 1960s on, those became "the central pillar of the hope and faith of those who still put their faith in social revolution." It wasn't easy to sustain a belief based on societies which weren't our own and which we understood very imperfectly from a distance, and it was unfair to lay such a responsibility on those societies themselves. So when the Sandinistas lost the Nicaraguan election of 1990 it was a sort of last call for an unsupportable faith. Of course there were reasons for that election defeat. The United States of Reagan and Bush had held a gun to the heads of Nicaraguans for more than a decade and had refused to recognize the perfectly legitimate election of 1984 in which the Sandinistas did win. Anyway, the loss of one flawed election does not negate an entire way of seeing the world. Still, speaking personally again, I experienced that result as a sort of licence to let go of unrealistic expectations.

The trouble with all-embracing explanations of how the world works is that those who hold them will inevitably be embarrassed, whether by an economic collapse or by an unexpected election result somewhere. In one of the wise asides in a wise book, Hobsbawm writes that one appeal of the laissez-faire dogma of the Reagan-Thatcher years, which "helps to explain the brief vogue for the neo-liberal utopia, was precisely that it purported to bypass collective human decisions." Human efforts to control our fate will inevitably be frustrated because we always get it wrong, more or less, in the end. Laissez-faire tried to have it both ways: claiming to know how it all worked, but refusing to try to do anything about it, other than staying out of the way. In that light the neocon faith was an impressive, almost noble, effort to avoid inevitable embarassment in the face of social reality's unpredictability and uncontrollability.

But the results of "doing nothing" turned out to be other than expected and pretty disastrous too. The faith fizzled and will fizzle whenever it's tried again. When I was in theological seminary in the early 1960s, I had a teacher, Abraham Joshua Heschel, who wrote about our inevitable "ontological embarrassment": that what we think we are doing and what we end up doing are almost never the same and are often in sharp contradiction. Heschel, who had a viciously effective way with English though it wasn't his native tongue, was once asked in a seminar, "Dr. Heschel, would you say my idea is far-fetched?" "I would say," said Heschel, "that it is near-fetched," which you could say about most of the all-embracing faiths of our century, the ones put forward in the name of objective truth.

The conflicts of the Cold War were often portrayed as debates: capitalism versus socialism, planning versus laissez-faire, democracy versus tyranny (or people's democracy versus bourgeois democracy), Marxist class analysis versus whatever the western sociological riposte was. The issue would in one way or another be argued by invoking evidence from history, past or present. Yet none of these debates were ever really about truth or about science in any verifiable way. They were always rooted in values. All sides proceeded from what Hobsbawm calls "an a priori view of human society."

It's not that you can't attempt to make relatively dispassionate judgements on the merits of different economic systems or philosophies. You surely can. And though the judgements won't be utterly conclusive or persuasive to everyone, few important issues in personal or social life are ever resolved with utter certainty. But it's not on the basis of an intellectual estimate that people ultimately take their stands on these matters—especially given the degree of uncertainty and the incalculability of future discoveries or unpredicable outcomes. In the end what you stake your life on is the things you value. History, in the end or at any immediate point, won't ever absolve anyone.

If this point—that the roots of idoleological conflicts lie in conflicting values—seems obvious, let me add that people on all sides nevertheless appear determined to fight on as if things could eventually be decided by one last shattering proof or argument. Among the things that most perplex me about life on the left as I knew it—that is, until the nineties—was a certain obsession with being on the right side of history. History would absolve us, Castro said. The prehistory of humanity was bound to end, Marx said, because the proletariat had nothing to lose but its chains. Why did it matter so much to us that history was on our side, that we knew our side would win? If we hadn't been sure of victory, or even if we'd been certain of defeat, would we have given up the fight or switched sides? These questions still perplex me.

As the nineties draw to a close, there has been a kind of shift in the balance of intellectual forces: those on the right who said a few years back that we were at the the end of history have been "proven," in various ways, wrong. You could even claim we're now at the end of the end of history. But doesn't that just put us back on the old treadmill, still caught up in a dependence on the historical outcome? As if history were a horse race, or a pennant race, in which everyone roots for their own team (or cause) to win, and gets depressed, just like a true blue fan, when their team lets them down—but hey, even when that happens, there's still next year, or next decade, or next century.

Back in the 1960s, for instance, it looked to those of us on the left as if our side was winning the race to the end of history, and we would get to declare what it looked like once we were there. A couple of decades later the other side declared that they had won, the finish line had been crossed. Now it appears they were wrong, and though that doesn't mean we've won after all, just by virtue of reinstating the status of the race we've scored a few points and edged back into contention. In other words, we've climbed back onto the treadmill. But is there a way to step off it altogether, or at least move into a different game?

Alan Watts, in one of his books explaining the philosophies of the East to westerners, gave such short shrift to history that his account is a little breathtaking for an average dweller in the western tradition.

> The Western equivalent of reincarnation is our obsession with history...the fruitless attempt to move forward to a satisfactory future by the logic of an impoverished past....History is the refusal to "let the dead bury their dead." History, or better, historicism is a chronic hoarding of trash in the hope that it will someday "come in useful."

I find those words both frightening and seductive, but above all they have the ring of truth. Watts's cavalier dismissal of history makes me realize how deeply committed I am to it. If we give up on history or devalue it along the lines Watts proposes, it feels like an abandonment of two of our major sources of orientation and inspiration: the socialist-Marxist tradition, rooted in Hegel and Marx, and the Judeo-Christian tradition, reaching back through the universalism of the New Testament to the demands made by the biblical prophets for social justice and collective moral accountability.

But hold on. When the author of Deuteronomy said, "Justice, justice shalt thou pursue," he didn't add, "Because history will absolve you." It's true the prophets sometimes promised retribution to those who failed to heed their call, often at the hand of historical forces like Babylonian or Assyrian kings. But that retribution was not a matter of human concern or control. God would see to the appropriate use of various nations, armies or wars or—later in the apocalyptic tradition—cosmic powers. It was not up to the people the prophets were addressing.

If you eliminate the messianic and apocalyptic elements and promises in the Judeo-Christian tradition, you're left with the simple demand to pursue justice because it is just and because it is what is demanded. If you look around and note that the promises of reward and punishments have yet to be fulfilled, well, that's not really your area of concern. And if you start complaining or whining about it, the God of the later biblical texts might just answer you out of the whirlwind and tell you to shut the hell up. The Hegelian and Marxist traditions, by including both the promised results and the ethical demands on the same human and historical level rather than keeping them separate as the Bible does, stirred up a mess of trouble for themselves.

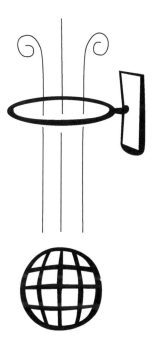

These thoughts occur to me because the sense of parody of Marxism created by the right during the 1990s, in Fukuyama's declaration of the end of history and the general doctrinaire stance of neoconservatives, has given me pause. It has driven me back towards that other source of western leftism: the biblical and especially the prophetic tradition. I'm quite aware there are far different ways to draw on the biblical tradition, towards different political ends. I'm also aware it's not part of everyone's heritage, and that there are other routes by which one can arrive at a left viewpoint. Thus, the prescriptive elements in Kant, unlike those in Hegel, are derived from an essentially moral as opposed to historical base—not to mention the endless philosophical and ethical resources available outside the western heritage altogether.

Anyway, you don't draw on a tradition for political or ethical purposes the way you choose a supermarket to shop at. A tradition can provide a sort of context and vocabulary, even a way of looking at things; but the convictions had better stand on their own or they're unlikely to stand at all. Some time between the sixties and the nineties, I ran into a friend I'd been active with in the new left. "Are you still a Maoist?" she asked tentatively. "I don't think so," I said. "Are you, um—" she went on, "an anybodyist?" To the extent that many of us on the left have drawn intensively from the well of Marxism, and other anybodyisms, it might be worthwhile to think of the 1990s as a good time to take a breather.

Rick Salutin is a former rabbinical student, playwright, novelist and longtime member of the editorial board of *This Magazine*. His column on media and politics appears in the Toronto *Globe and Mail*.

A Gambler's Society: the End of Job Security

by Jamie Swift

Visiting Montreal at the end of 1994, I learned that Loto Quebec's new casino had attracted nearly a million visitors from outside the region in its first year of operation. The aging autoroutes (always a minefield of potholes) were now upgraded, everywhere emblazoned with fresh new ace-jack logos—the perfect blackjack hand—directing gamblers to the flashy casino near the former Expo 67 site on Île Sainte-Hélène.

Tourism, the world's biggest employer, is a way of life in Montreal. The Film Festival, Jazz Festival and Comedy Festival heat up the summers. The recession had finally lifted and restaurants were fending off the winter chill with an endless round of Souvlaki Festivals. The hard-hit island and surrounding suburbs seemed in full recovery. An economist for the huge Desjardins credit union said he found the job rebound so strong that it was "a little shocking." Bombardier had just hired 350 people, mostly engineers, at its South Shore plant.

But on Christmas Eve a newspaper article on charity hampers and free church hall turkey dinners stopped me in my tracks. One in four households brought in under $10,000 annually. Nearly half of Montreal's people lived below the poverty line, and the city was "the poverty capital of Canada." Grizzled men standing, palms outstretched, at the bottom of escalators on the Metro had become permanent fixtures of the Montreal scene. Many were older, some still young, but all looked like veterans of life on the street in a city where joblessness had become entrenched. Montreal's unemployment rate was 12.1 per cent in 1994. In March 1995, defending his harsh budget, federal Finance Minister Paul Martin noted that in his working-class Montreal riding, unemployment was at 22 per cent—a situation the budget would not ease.

Meanwhile, workers at the General Motors plant in Sainte-Thérèse went on a wildcat strike, not over wages and benefits, but because of overwork. A potent brew of speedup on the Camaro assembly line mixed with too much overtime was making work humanly impossible. Here, in a nut-

shell, was Canada's fin-de-siècle job predicament. On the one hand, opportunities opened up for well-paid engineers and factory workers were
forced into the frenzy of overtime. On the other, people with bad jobs,
part-time jobs or no jobs at all competed for work at the bottom of the service sector. Prosperity and poverty jostled one another in a society increasingly characterized by polarization and uncertainty—a Gambler's Society.

The End of Security

It seems that the only certainty is uncertainty in the brave new world of
work. It is a world ruled by the market and the unaccountable corporations
that dominate it, a place where jobs scatter about like so many shards of
glass from a bottle that has crashed to a cement floor.

By the mid-1990s the economy had gone through one of its familiar cy-
cles. In the 1980s, the record unemployment of 1983 (11.3 per cent) slowly
gave way to a partial job recovery; growth soared and business boomed. But
unemployment remained stubbornly high—by 1989 it had declined only to
7.5 per cent, a level that in the 1960s would have been seen as a scandal.

As early as 1983 the Canadian Manufacturers Association was predicting a return to full capacity with 10 per cent fewer workers. By 1992 the
CMA's chief economist was warning that "there is no job in Canada that is
secure." In 1994, Canada had emerged from the deep recession of the early
nineties and enjoyed robust economic growth of 4.5 per cent, the highest
percentage among the leading industrialized countries. And yet the jobless
level remained close to 10 per cent.

Workers not spooked by firms heading south worried about a generalized "downsizing." Managers became aware of "delayering" as organizations eliminated administrators by contracting out as many functions as
they could. Employment in the welfare state industries—health, education,
welfare—shrank in the face of Bob Rae's social contract in Ontario and
Ralph Klein's frontal attack on the public sector in Alberta.

Poverty and productivity, inequality and competitiveness, dollar stores
and chic boutiques coexisted very nicely. In Montreal, industry and the
middle class relocated to the suburbs, leaving an inner city deprived of jobs
and a solid tax base. In many ways, the situation was not so different from
the plight of inner-city U.S.A. In *The Culture of Contentment*, his book
about the glaring duality of American society, John Kenneth Galbraith observed that "the normal upward movement that was for long the solvent for
discontent has been arrested. The underclass has become a semipermanent
rather than a generational phenomenon."

During the early postwar years rising incomes and the birth of the welfare state tended to make Canada a more egalitarian society. But since the

seventies there has been a trend towards polarization. "The volatility of in-comes," the Economic Council concluded in its 1992 report *The New Face of Poverty*, "implies that roughly one-third of working-age Canadians face the risk of being poor at some time in their working lives."

The postwar boom—a period that is seeming more like a historical hiccup—brought increased real wages until 1976. From that year until the start of the depression of 1990 real wages shrank by an average of 0.3 per cent annually. By the 1980s a new change was well underway. In that de-cade, fully 44 per cent of all jobs added to the economy were in low-wage consumer and retail services. Many of these new jobs were in precarious or "nonstandard" employment: part-time, temporary or contract work. Tem-porary help agency work, mostly done by women, tripled in the 1980s.

"Wage levels are generally well below those for full-time workers and fringe benefits are usually minimal," reported the Economic Council. "The labour market is offering economic security to fewer Canadians."

The Training Gospel

Conventional wisdom has it that these changes, painful as they are, are part of a Second Industrial Revolution that will lead to a New Economy. This economy is based on skill, knowledge and access to information.

Just before the dramatic recession of 1990 the Economic Council of Canada published a landmark report with a portentous title. "Good Jobs/Bad Jobs: Employment in the Service Economy" underlined one of today's ap-parent truisms: "No longer can prosperity come straight from the ground: increasingly, it must come from the minds of the Canadian people."

Of course, Canada has always based its prosperity both on its resources and on the skills of the workers who caught the fish, cut the trees, dug the mines and transformed natural resources into goods—often semifinished ones to be sent elsewhere for further processing. The workers of the nineties have been renamed. They are routinely called "human resources" by those who employ them. There is a sort of brutal honesty here. In this scheme of things, workers must be recycled when their skills are rendered obsolete.

This is what the training gospel so popular with politicians and busi-nesses is all about. Workers become so many empty bottles that must be topped up with new skills, trained and retrained almost continuously as their skills are rejected as inadequate. The tools of the nineties—the hard-ware and software that drive the Second Industrial Revolution—become obsolete faster and faster. So do the skills of people who use them.

"I have an absolutely dominating belief," said then–New Brunswick Premier Frank McKenna, a leading training booster. "In this chicken-and-egg conundrum of whether you should have jobs or training first, the answer is that you need the training first. If you have the training, the jobs will take care of themselves."

Just before Christmas 1994 I attended a town hall meeting on Ottawa's green paper on social policy reform. Maurizio Bevilacqua, parliamentary assistant to Human Resources Minister Lloyd Axworthy, explained that though his Italian immigrant father had worked in construction all his life, he expected to see his children change "careers" a dozen times. "Lifelong learning" and "learning a living" had become the clichés of the day.

In the face of these changes, governments began to link public provision—welfare or unemployment insurance—to training. This was not quite "workfare" of the old "give 'em a shovel" variety. "Learnfare" was more liberal-sounding and meshed smoothly with the notion of workers as empty bottles in constant need of a skill refill.

However, training is no guarantee of good jobs. It is entirely possible to train people for bad jobs and marginal participation in a contingent labour force of just-in-time workers who can be let go when no longer needed. Faced with this supply-side approach to the labour market equation, it's not surprising that people on the training treadmill ask, "Training for what?"

Such social policy is in fact industrial strategy by omission. The problem it addresses is not how to create good jobs, but how to get people to be "job-ready" for bad ones, keeping them close to the labour market in a grey area between bad jobs and welfare. It's about handcuffing people to the expanding bottom of the labour market. The goal—implicit or explicit, stated or understated—is to develop what Galbraith calls a "functional underclass."

Taking a Chance

Governments funding learnfare programs also put their money on gambling as a source of both revenue and jobs. Montreal, Winnipeg and Windsor all had casinos by the mid-1990s. Every community seemed to want one. Debate over casino gambling raged in Vancouver, dividing the labour movement.

At the gala opening of Windsor's Las Vegas–style casino, trade-unionist-turned-Ontario-NDP-cabinet-minister Frances Lankin described it as a "terrific jobs effort." The head of Circus Circus Corporation, a casino partner, added with no apparent irony that the jobs being created would give rise to "a tremendous economic upheaval." More than three million American tourists visited the casino in its first seven months of operation.

The United States is very much a Gambler's Society. The idea that anyone has a chance of hitting the jackpot, making it to the pinnacle of wealth and power, has always been a central element in the American myth. Even as the economic power of the United States declined and it became stymied by its violence and poverty and the anguished malaise of its modernity, people from around the world still wanted to come and take a

chance in the Gambler's Society. Canadian newspapers ran ads offering to help people with the American "Green Card Lottery." They were attracted by the chance to spin the wheel of fortune and come out a winner.

For Canadians—and particularly English Canadians insecure about our identity—this attraction to the United States remains tempered by our search for things that separate us from Americans. For the Gambler's Society has its dark side. Mutual affiliation and solidarity are foreign to the Gambler's Society. It's far easier to find yourself "out on the street"—both figuratively and literally—in the United States, where employment regulations are much looser than in other industrial countries. Poor Americans have little in the way of public support.

Canada too has become more of a Gambler's Society. On the most obvious level, we have witnessed governments scrambling to maximize their tax take, not by making the tax system fairer but by bringing in new lotteries. Malls offer specialized lottery kiosks. "Imagine the freedom," said the ads for the 6/49. By extension, our political vocabulary is saturated with "win-win" solutions. Everyday discourse disparages someone who is either poor and disreputable or just plain unsuccessful: "a loser." More of us are poorer—and more still are insecure—as the market is left to sort the good-job winners from the bad-job (or no-job) losers.

In the polarized labour market, education and training are held out as the sine qua non for winners. But formal learning is increasingly becoming the prerogative of the few. University tuition increased 58 per cent in the first half of the nineties, with individual students (or their parents) paying a larger share of university costs. Yet so pervasive was the faith in education as the key to the future that the nagging question of who gets it—the well-born? the poor?—was shunted aside in favour of a myth of meritocracy. If you don't make it as a winner, it's because you lack the requisite skills.

Education becomes another marketplace. When they don't secede from the public system by joining the accelerating rush to private education, parents shop around for the best schools in the best neighbourhoods. High-school graduates compete for admission to the universities at the top of *Maclean's* magazine's fervid ratings. Even a university degree, however, is no longer a ticket to a secure job with decent pay.

And so, early in 1995, 20,000 people lined up in bitterly cold weather to get their hands on applications for work on the General Motors assembly line in Oshawa, Ontario. Rumors flew. Frazzled GM workers were working six-day weeks and the company was thinking of adding a third shift. The union jobs paid $22 an hour, plus benefits.

"Life's a chance," observed one man in the lineup. "So why not take a chance on getting a job?"

Jamie Swift is a writer living in Kingston, Ontario. His books include *Wheel of Fortune: Work and Life in the Age of Falling Expectations* (1995) and *Civil Society in Question* (1999).

Hannibal's Mirrors: Cyberintelligence and the Zapatista Revolution

by Louisa Blair

Hannibal is much less famous for mirrors than for elephants trudging grimly across the snow-covered Atlas Mountains. But it was the mirrors, clutched by chilly observers standing on hilltops, that kept the Carthaginian generals informed of Roman movements, and won Hannibal the Second Punic War.

Information has always been crucial in war. Consider the Mongols of the thirteenth century who, although always outnumbered by their enemies, created the largest continental empire the world has ever seen. Their success lay in their "arrow riders," messengers who rode nonstop at a full gallop across the steppe, changing horses whenever one wore out. The result was that field commanders, often separated by large distances, were in daily communication. Even the Great Khan, sometimes thousands of kilometres away, was told of an event only days after it had happened.

The Mongols were finally stopped short by the Mamelukes in Egypt. Their secret was carrier pigeons.

And in the 1990s, we have the arresting image of the Zapatista revolutionary Subcomandante Insurgente Marcos, sitting in a beat-up pickup truck in the mountains of southern Mexico with a laptop plugged into the lighter socket, writing his letters and communiqués in a kind of poetic frenzy, giving birth to the world's first postmodern revolution.

For the Zapatistas, the first stage of communication was prehistoric. In an letter to three newspapers just days after the Zapatistas launched their uprising on January 1, 1994 (the day the North American Free Trade Agreement went into effect), Marcos wrote that his letters have to "travel for days along ancient trails and steep dirt roads, through mountains and valleys, past war tanks, military vehicles, and thousands of olive-green uniforms."

But once a diskette had made it to a telephone line, the next stage of the process was an entirely new form of warfare: what two Rand Corporation analysts named "netwar," which they defined as "societal-level idea-tional conflicts waged in part through internetted modes of communica-tion." The raw material consisted primarily of Marcos's voluminous com-muniqués, which were converted in full to e-text by Mexico's daily *El Jornada* and broadcast on the Net.

Soon after the military confrontation in 1994, the netwide broadcasts be-gan to include eyewitness reports by religious groups and other humanitarian delegations, local and international human rights reports, and newspaper arti-cles that appeared in small sympathetic local papers. These were swiftly trans-lated, typed and scanned, often by cooperative groups of volunteers, and posted on one of the many websites and Internet lists (at the time of writing there were thirty-two and nine respectively) devoted to the Zapatistas.

Flashing instantly around the world, this information often provoked an international response within hours of actions by President Ernesto Zedillo's government. The Net made Mexico's attempts to limit media coverage (such as shutting down the Televisa TV station and Radio Huaya in Veracruz) look pathetic. Demonstrations, mass marches, candlelight vig-ils, embassy occupations, and fax and letter-writing campaigns were all or-ganized over the Net. Pierre Leblanc of the Ottawa Committee for Soli-darity with Chiapas recalled the feeling of immediacy during the early days:

> We were able to interact very quickly, generating a live, flowing, continuous picture of events, sometimes in great detail. If some-thing happened, we knew it from the horse's mouth within hours, and could contradict the official version that the Mexican govern-ment was putting out. Our organization had an e-mail address bank which grew to 800 people and included people as far away as South Africa. We could put communications from the federal government on our list, and within a day the minister would be getting letters telling him to smarten up.

Using the Internet, Leblanc's organization linked up with the Assembly of First Nations, churches (mostly United) and trade unions (especially the Canadian Union of Public Employees), and organized several joint demon-strations and two joint meetings with the Canadian secretary of state for Central America. "If the money-changers can use the Net to make millions of dollars every day, other groups have to learn that those tools are there for us, too," said Leblanc.

What captured the world's imagination, other than the compelling glow of the computer screen, was that the spokesperson for the indigenous rebels of Chiapas was proposing something that did not follow the familiar rubric of Latin American revolutions. As novelist Carlos Fuentes said in an interview with *New Perspectives Quarterly* in the spring of 1994,

> Many people with cloudy minds in Mexico responded to what happened in Chiapas by saying, "Here we go again, these rebels are part of the old Sandinista-Castroite-Marxist-Leninist legacy. Is this what we want for Mexico?" The rebels proved exactly the contrary: Rather than the last rebellion of that type, this was the first post-communist rebellion in Latin America.

The rebels did not want to seize power themselves, but wanted rather to open up a free and democratic space in Mexican "civil society" where, as Marcos said, "Political parties will see themselves as obliged to confront that majority [of the people] instead of each other." Their ambitions went beyond democracy in Chiapas and Mexico, though, to challenging the whole project of "neoliberalism," and in this they found echo in countless grassroots movements across the networld.

"In other places, if it is not Indians that will dramatize this conflict," said Fuentes, "it will be immigrants who are the bearers of different cultures entering Germany, France and Britain; it will be the large Third World underclass in the U.S. that is shut out of the global village every bit as much as the Indians of Chiapas."

In 1996 the Zapatistas organized a worldwide meeting in Chiapas, attended by people from forty-two countries and five continents, to discuss the struggle against neoliberalism. At that meeting, Marcos suggested the creation of "an intercontinental network of alternative communication against neoliberalism...to tie together all the channels of our words and all the roads of resistance."

A certain element of the Zapatista movement appeals mightily to hackers, who see themselves as the pioneers in the cyberfrontiers, undermining commerce by creating shareware, cutting through the electronic barbed wire of security codes, intellectual property rights and private ownership of the net, to freedom and—the key word—autonomy. As University of Texas economist Harry Cleaver wrote, "Just as the campesinos of Morelia under the leadership of Zapata cut barbed wire to liberate the land in 1910, electronic hackers have chopped down electronic barriers and liberated information, creating a pirate underground of free activity constantly slipping beyond corporate and state control."

Marcos himself has done little to discourage this tendency to internationalize the issue of autonomy. To his proposal for an intercontinental network he added, "It will have no moderator, central control, or any hierarchies....[It] will be all of us who speak and listen."

While the Internet has made it easier for activists in different countries to link up and coordinate strategies more successfully, it has also made it easier for businesses to operate transnationally and to move their operations out of areas of high wages and strict environmental controls to areas like Mexico where controls are laxer.

Moreover, it is still just a fragment of the 2 per cent of people worldwide with computer access who are cyberactivists. Employees of human rights organizations and NGOs, academics with free e-mail accounts at universities, the independently wealthy with time to browse, and those who live in the thirty or so North American cities with freenets must represent all the rest of the shut-outs. "Teledensity," the number of telephones per hundred people, still averages 1.5 in developing countries, and in some, such as Cambodia, there is one telephone per thousand people.

Even this exclusive aspect of the Net has its apologists, who say that "netwar" no longer needs the participation of the masses. In an electronic book published by the Critical Art Ensemble of the University of Texas in Austin, the authors write,

> This is post-modern civil disobedience: it requires a democratic interpretation of a problem, but without large-scale action. In early capital, the only power base for marginal groups was defined by their numbers. This is no longer true. Now there is a technological power base, and it is up to cultural and political activists to think it through....Perhaps it is time to reassess the idea of quantity as power.

Such a statement begs an important question: what is "democratic" about this kind of activism when it is left "up to cultural and political activists to think it through"? By what authority do they act, if the people for whom they act are not involved? It is an ironically far cry from the democratic space that the Zapatistas want to open up so that ordinary people, such as the indigenous majority of Chiapas, can finally participate.

And one wonders what the indigenous villagers of Chiapas would make of the Electronic Disturbance Theater, a group of cyberactivists and artists led by someone who calls himself Sub-cyber-commandante Z of the Intercontinental Cyberspace Liberation Army. Using the Net for direct action as well as communication, they have focused their experiments with electronic civil disobedience on the Zapatista struggle, and created a software device called Flood Net that is used to flood and block an opponent's website.

On April 10, 1998, more than 8,000 participants intermittently blocked access to President Zedillo's website. The Electronic Disturbance Theater, thrilled with this success, hopes that they can promote a "swarm" of other Flood Net-like devices, "arising, acting and dispersing simultaneously against an array of cyberspacial political targets." Two months later, however, a similar action against Mexico's Secretaria de Gobernación, which oversees immigration and security services, was ineffective. Mexico had taken the threat seriously, and struck back with a counterprogram.

In Canada these phenomena have provoked a flurry of interest from the Canadian Security Intelligence Service, the RCMP, and the Department of National Defence. At an NGO conference in September 1998, Canadian Foreign Affairs Minister Lloyd Axworthy remarked that "the mouse is mightier than the missile."

So has the Internet really made a difference to the Zapatistas' struggle? Some claim that it forced the Mexican government to maintain negotiations with the rebels for two years and stopped it from simply ordering the army to finish them off. Others argue that it was NAFTA that put a new spotlight on Mexico's behaviour. Both are surely part of the same movement, breaking borders and speeding up transactions, giving new power both to those in control and to those who resist it.

Meanwhile the struggle for autonomy in Chiapas is soberingly parochial. There are thirty-two autonomous townships (in Chiapas these are enormous territories embracing hundreds of villages) under Zapatista control. Some townships go so far as to issue birth and death certificates, run clinics and schools, and judge and punish local criminals. In July 1998 the Mexican government sent in a thousand additional troops and police to recapture some of these autonomous townships.

"The government knows perfectly well that as long as these autonomous communities exist, they will never defeat the [Zapatistas], because there the indigenous people have real power," said Father Pablo Romo, a leader of the Fray Bartolomé de las Casas Human Rights Center in San Cristóbal, in an interview with the Los Angeles *Times* in September 1998. "These are Zapatista power bases [where] the leaders are faceless; the individual leaders change often. The communities are self-regulated, with a great elasticity in power."

For the villagers who still live under the intimidation of huge army encampments throughout the state, the struggle is far from virtual. Murders and disappearances continue, and no cyberwar seems to be a match for the violence of local vigilante groups, who in December 1998 massacred forty-five peasants in the community of Acteal.

It was a somewhat subdued group of Chiapans who gathered in the damp village of La Realidad on January 1, 1999, to celebrate the fifth anniversary of the Zapatista uprising. Instead of appearing through the mist on horseback at the last minute to deliver one of his eloquent and eminently quotable speeches, Subcomandante Marcos sent a taped message that was crackled out to the assembled crowd: "We have turned inward to organize the resistance among our people."

Louisa Blair was an associate editor of *Compass* from 1989 to 1997 and subsequently a director of the Compass Foundation. She lives in Quebec City and is Quebec editor of the *Canadian Forum*.

Canada in the Information Age

by Ronald Deibert

In April 1998, a conference was held in Toronto to honour Mel Watkins, the University of Toronto economist whose account of the economic developments of the 1970s can be found on page 295 of this book. In his presentation to the conference, Ronald Deibert, professor of political science at the U of T, related Watkins's work to that of his great predecessor, Harold Innis, and applied Innis's insights to the situation of the 1990s. What follows is an edited version of Prof. Deibert's presentation.

—Editor

In my mind, what makes the work of Harold Innis unique in political economy is his skilful combination and appreciation of the interplay between material factors and ideas:

- between environmental and geographical conditions on the one hand, and dominant belief systems on the other;
- between material technologies of communication and transportation on the one hand, and prevailing symbols and signs on the other;
- between core-periphery relations of uneven economic development on the one hand, and the prevailing temporal and spatial biases of a time on the other.

I would like to focus on Innis's concern with time-space biases. One of the more novel aspects of Innis's work was his concentration on the way different civilizations or societies apprehended the categories of space and time. Innis argued that different societies exhibited a bias towards either space or time, a bias that was often closely related to the dominant mode of communication of the time.

The biases were the warp and woof of history, according to Innis, with a happy medium between them rarely being achieved. They reflected the character or underlying preoccupation of the civilization in question, and so were like a lens into prevailing power relationships and dominant concerns.

In *Empire and Communications, The Bias of Communications* and *Changing*

Concepts of Time, Innis canvassed civilizational history to reveal this interplay, from ancient Sumeria right up to the mid–twentieth century. How would Innis have interpreted the space/time biases of our times?

Near the end of his life, Innis believed that there was an imbalance in western civilization towards the bias of space with a corresponding neglect of time. In his essay "A Plea for Time," Innis urged a correction to this imbalance, believing that the time dimension had been reduced to a superficial "present-mindedness," reflected in an obsession with statistics in the social sciences and the fetish of newspapers with current events and catastrophes.

Harold Innis

Needless to say, much has changed since Innis made these reflections. I think if were he around today, Innis would zero in on a new kind of temporal bias that has emerged: what I call the Empire of Speed.

What is the Empire of Speed? It is a complex of forces working in the general direction of unleashing the velocity and flow of information across borders and around the world. At its heart are the swift currents of capital that circuit the globe twenty-four hours a day, shifting astronomical sums in a swarm of electrical impulses.

It is manifested in the dream of unleashing friction-free capitalism over the Net, and the rise of e-commerce and digital cash. It is formed in and around the space of flows that define the just-in-time production networks and the virtual corporations of so-called Kanban capitalism. It is driven by the mass obsession for ever faster computing and communication technics, which has ripped through governments and consumer culture: greater bandwidth, more baud-rate, faster Ethernet connections, speedier processors.

As Lewis Mumford remarked not so long ago, "The power complex today is preoccupied only with acceleration." Forget the "megamachine," this is the megabyte society.

Relating this complex to the Canadian experience, I believe Innis would have pointed to this preoccupation with speed as an explanation for the urgency felt among elites to get people wired, to extend networks to rural communities, winding ever tighter the electronic ties that bind and speeding up the currents inside. And he would have likely asked, "To what end?"

If every society is established with a view to some good, as Aristotle said, then what is the good to which the information superhighway leads, and why do we need to get there so fast? Searching around today, he would likely find as a response from those in positions of power: "We are building an information society and a knowledge economy."

Now knowledge has been defined in many different ways, but I think Innis would have to be restrained not to remark on how narrowly it is being used today in this connection. What is this so-called "knowledge economy" that we are working to create?

Reading Industry Minster John Manley's comments in a speech to the University of Toronto in early 1998, I can't help but believe that it is simply a desire to reorder the Canadian system in ways congruent with global market forces. "Knowledge" here is not the knowledge of Plato and Aristotle, of the arts and humanities, of music and literature and spiritual fulfilment. It is simply the extension of technique to more domains of life: building knowbots for the information economy.

Concerned about Canadian culture? Let's digitize, put it on a CD and export it. That'll save it. Can you imagine what Innis would have made of that idea?

Speaking of Canadian culture, there is something pathetic about those Molson beer commercials. Flashing images of toothless hockey players, shouts of "I am Canadian!" pounded into the retinas of the viewers. I think people looking back on this generations from now will see it as a reflection of a society in panic and desperation. I think Innis would have too.

Most of all, I think, Innis would have been troubled about—but would have had no problem explaining given contemporary monopolies of knowledge—how the entire process is being played out and wrapped up in what Lou Pauly calls "the language of inevitability." We have no choice but to go along with the whirlwind of change, so the harbingers of globalization tell us. We have no choice but to deregulate, to open up borders. It is inevitable for reasons of competitiveness. New technologies make old regulations obsolete. We must adapt, change, or get left behind in the dust.

Is it any coincidence, though, that the combination of velocity and abundance of information creates an environment in which pausing and reflecting and indeed questioning where we are headed is placed at a disadvantage?

Indeed, there is an end to the information society we are building after all—it is what Lewis Mumford once called the "goods life." Not the "good life" but the "goods life." In the goods life, information and knowledge are commodities. Efficiency, speed and technological proficiency are virtues of the highest sort. And the end to which all is directed is nothing more than a society where every home and workplace has been converted into a computerized box office, shopping mall, video arcade and slot machine, open for business all day long, every day of the week. That is the Empire of Speed and those are the biases of our time.

Indeed, were he alive today I think Harold Innis would have no trouble explaining the biases and monopolies of the contemporary period. I think he would have looked for ways to decelerate, to slow things down, put on the brake, place checks and balances around unrestrained power in the form of speed limits.

Spirituality in the Nineties: Rediscovering Sacred Spaces

by Peter McIsaac

Into the sea all rivers flow,
and yet the sea is never filled,
and still to their goal the rivers flow....
What was will be again;
what has been done will be done again;
and there is nothing new under the sun.

—Ecclesiastes 1:7–9

Standing at the threshold of a new millennium, who can resist the delusion of every generation, believing that it is poised at the end of history, ushering in a new age of enlightenment, prosperity and justice? We are now, some say, a postmodern people, globally aware and spiritually ennobled. According to others, we are spiritually apathetic, thoroughly secularized, and sophisticated beyond the primitive religious notions of our predecessors. In either case, the hubris or the pessimism of those announcing the end of modernity continue to incarnate the implicit biases of positivism.

The tendency to immanentize the end of history or the dawn of a new era has manifested itself in various social movements: political and cultural imperialism, ethnocentrism, religious sectarianism and apocalypticism. The ideologies that emerge from these diverse social phenomena can be radically dissimilar and even contradictory, but they share an underlying historical presupposition: a specific social group has appropriated a privileged place in history, by virtue of intrinsic superiority, divine election, or even historical accident.

Thus the ancient Christian gnostic, the enlightened nihilist, the early-twentieth-century communist and the postmodern New Age globalist may all share a strange kinship. For all, history has progressed to a point of culmination, centred on various personal, collective or social embodiments of self. This self-centredness inevitably involves distinguishing "self" from "others": certainly all past generations, but also those contemporary persons or groups that are not privileged. The "others" are not at the centre and so are "on the margins." In routine political and economic processes, the marginalized are manipulated or exploited to the advantage of the "centre" of power, and thus their ideological significance (or insignificance) can be largely ignored.

In the context of the immanent anticipation of a new era, however, the fulfilment or completion of history cannot tolerate the tensions and divisions intrinsic to process. There can be neither centre nor margins, and thus the marginalized must be either eliminated—as has happened far too often in the twentieth century—or else incorporated by coercion, education, socialization or other means. An ideology that is self-centred and immanentizes the final age makes a number of assumptions concerning the perspective of the "centre": it is absolute (no longer subject to the vicissitudes of history), exhaustive (subsequent correction or substantial addition is precluded) and universal (not conditioned by, or concerned with, cultural or historical context).

On the eve of a new millennium, then, we see the growth and propagation of a self-centred and dominating ideology. We are said to be moving to an unprecedented globalism, in which the ideals of neoliberal capitalist society wear the guise of universality and transnational political and economic structures cultivate values that leave out the particularity of culture and ethnic history. Flung headlong towards an apparently inevitable completion of history, the traditions of religion and communities of faith find themselves on the margins: either sidelined by a sophisticated and self-preoccupied apathy or diluted by a notion of universal, "New Age" spirituality.

For the task of describing spirituality in the nineties, then, I choose the margins of spirituality as my perspective: the viewpoint of those who by choice or by circumstance belong to communities of faith distinguished by long spiritual traditions, self-defining histories and differentiated cultures. My experience has largely been among two substantially different marginal groups: first, various impoverished urban and rural dwellers of the South; and second, economically secure urban North Americans whose religious affiliation with a denominational community makes them extraneous both to contemporary modern secularism and to a nondescript "global" spirituality.

From the viewpoint of the marginal, the form of globalism that attaches cultural and ideological uniformity to emerging international political and economic structures carries with it the demands of ideological hegemony. One must either conform to the "universal and absolute truths" of the dominant historical agents, or else deny any and all particular truth claims, so that religion is prohibited or sidelined as irrelevant to the mundane tasks of secular society.

In either case, spirituality is lifted out of the ordinary movements of daily life. It becomes entirely transcendent—rather than radically incarnational as a contemporary spirituality of the margins seeks to be. An incarnational spirituality is fundamentally opposed to a dichotomy between the spiritual and the secular, or between the sacred and the profane. Its primary task is the discovery or rediscovery of sacred spaces, rather than their contrived reconstruction.

In traditional cultures, an incarnational spirituality is expressed in the integration of very ordinary patterns of nature and social relationships with religious cosmology and ritual processes. For peoples outside the direct influence of "western" society, the needs of a contemporary spirituality are largely concerned with the cultural disintegration that comes with greater participation in world social structures and conversion to "world" religions. It is an immense task to attempt to preserve the cultural traditions and maintain the vital symbolic matrix that provides for the possibility of an incarnational spirituality, while avoiding a self-imposed isolation that is neither socially beneficial nor realistic.

This need has profoundly influenced the Christian project of contextual theology in Africa, Asia and Latin America. On the grassroots level, the proliferation of small, seminal worship and prayer communities has generated incarnational spiritualities that attend to the specific issues of economic and political marginalization as well as to the cultural importance of preserving and integrating indigenous symbolic and ritual traditions.

In the West, those who have voluntarily chosen a religious tradition and community live in a situation of much greater heterogeneity and pluralism. In this situation, it is difficult to isolate common cultural features and symbolic traditions that facilitate an easy integration of one's daily world with the symbols of sacred time and space. North American societies, for example, are founded more on ideological agreement than on common culture, history or ethnicity. This may account for the development of "transcendent" spiritualities that under the dubious banner of universalism dismiss any form of social diversity and social concern.

In the face of the vacuousness of secularism or the exotic fascination of New Age religion, many Christians seek a simple and communal way to develop and express their spirituality. There are three interrelated components to this "marginal" spirituality: (1) participation in a community of faith that shares a common field of religious experience as well as a communally recognized language of faith expression (creeds, symbols, rituals and forms of worship); (2) concrete methods of prayer that facilitate the integration of people's awareness of God with their "ordinary" lives of work and relationships; and (3) some form of spiritual companionship.

Apart from the psychological need to belong to a group for a sense of self-identity, placing a priority on the communal expression of faith allows for a spirituality that encompasses the ordinary and complex web of all social relationships. A community creates (or discovers) symbols to sanctify and re-express in ritual the life-processes that constitute one's "world." Personal sanctity, in this way, is primarily communally based, for the life of holiness is sanctified in the process of social relationships.

The emphasis on community is not unique to the nineties, but what is perhaps novel—particularly among marginal faith communities in the affluent West—is the nonapologetic and unselfconscious attitude towards the communal beliefs and rituals that express membership and a common religious experience. I would call this movement a new form of traditionalism, but contrast it with the coincidental emergence of neoconservatism, which at times appears similar but is in fact quite different.

Neoconservatism tends to preserve the tradition in reaction to a prevailing modern secularist ideology, but does so from within the modern worldview. In a sense, neoconservatism presents a counterideology, making itself the marginalizing centre, and its method of proselytizing tends towards various forms of "incorporation." Being ideological, neoconservatism is concept- rather than symbol-based. As a result, incorporation usually favours a broad uniformity, with little attention to cultural and historical divergence.

By contrast, the new traditionalism is much less ideologically concerned or invested. It accepts its position on the margins. Rather than propagating a counterideology that seeks external affirmation or acquiescence, it emphasizes confirmation and growth from within the community. Self-acceptance that is no longer concerned with general social approval indicates a moment of growth in spiritual maturity. It expresses itself in a satisfaction and confidence with the quality and depth of community rather than its size and influence. The emergence of small, dynamic and charismatic spiritual communities in the West in the nineties has perhaps been hidden by virtue of their comfort with obscurity or "marginality."

Attentiveness to the central importance of metaphor likewise distinguishes the spirituality of the margins as "traditional." This spirituality's nonideological character means that its principal interest at the outset is with the discovery rather than the construction of "sacred spaces." In the face of modernity's preoccupation with progress as "novelty," the spiritually marginalized nevertheless seek progress through the development of spiritual and church metaphors, the symbols and rituals of the community's tradition. The new traditionalism, therefore, is an ongoing reinterpretation of the community's scriptural, dogmatic, theological and liturgical inheritance in the cultural and historical context.

By incarnating the prayer of the community through the cultural symbols and rituals of a particular historical tradition, the marginal spiritualities of the nineties effectively integrate social relationships and the experience of the sacred, leaving no room for the radical separation of sacred and profane. The sense of the immanence of the divine also gives rise to a corollary desire for simple forms of individual prayer that integrate one's spiritual experience and concern with the ordinary unfolding of daily life. Many people seem satisfied neither with "spiritualities" that focus on esoteric experiences and prescribe exotic disciplines of meditation nor with an occasional worship whose rituals become unconnected with life and thus empty of meaning. Instead, the "communities of the margins" seek God in the ordinary events and relationships of work and recreation.

The fundamental desire is the awareness of God in all things: an attentiveness that calls them to a habit of solitude and silence, not as a form of monastic separation from the world but as a means of discerning the Spirit of God who is present to the solitude and silence of all moments of social life. It is an orientation in prayer that calls them to greater social concern and action, communal and liturgical participation, and an ongoing awareness of themselves as a spiritual people.

The strong sense of the need for community and the quest for an orientation of divine immanence in prayer intersect in the desire for spiritual companionship—the natural tendency to seek more individual and more intimate friendships with those who share a similar spiritual path. Spiritual companionship provides the possibility for a kind of interpersonal sharing that cannot be sustained by larger community but may yet mediate the discernment of new forms of community. And in the contemporary context of exaggerated, hierarchical institutions, it develops an image of God—reflected in the "other"—that is both intimate and informal.

The recent and growing popularity of individually directed retreats and ongoing spiritual direction provides a good example of the movement towards greater interpersonal spiritual intimacy. Being formal and structured, however, these forms of companionship can also be prone to the manipulation of various ideological agendas. Direction can confuse itself with therapy or analysis, or even become a platform for "incorporating" others into a particular worldview. Perhaps as a result, more informal spiritual friendships—in which there is an exchange between equals, sharing with friends the simple experiences of God in daily life—are becoming more central to contemporary "marginal" spiritualities.

While compensating psychologically for the inevitable isolation of being on the margins and providing necessary interpersonal support, spiritual companionship is also the retrieval of the wisdom of many ancient traditions. The rise of Christian religious orders and congregations was sometimes the fruit of this kind of interpersonal intimacy shared among individuals, both within and outside structured communities. An excellent example of this is the ongoing spiritual companionship of monks and laypeople at the end of the first millennium in Ireland. The Irish cultural tradition of having a spiritual intimate, a "soulmate," led to its sacramentalization in the form of a rite of "penance" and in some sense provided the practical, incarnational spirituality that western Europe needed at the time to renew its Christianity.

Of course, I am not so optimistic as to compare the spirituality of this decade to the birth of the Irish church. But I do find hope in the many emerging spiritualities of the margins, steeped in tradition and seeking the elements of integration, community and intimacy. The spirituality of the nineties—at least at the margins—rediscovers the wisdom of Ecclesiastes that contemplates the wonder of God: centred not on our own novelty and narcissism, but rather on the ongoing relationships and cyclical patterns of all of creation.

Peter McIsaac SJ is assistant pastor of St. Anne's Church and community in Kingston, Jamaica.

Is Aboriginal Self-Government a Mirage?

by Miles Morrisseau

Canada's ongoing constitutional controversies reached a peak of sorts in the early 1990s. The demise of the Meech Lake Accord in June 1990 led to a wave of pro-sovereignty sentiment in Quebec, followed by a new round of constitutional talks. An unprecedented feature of these talks was the presence of Aboriginal leaders; the urgency of Aboriginal issues had been highlighted by Manitoba MLA Elijah Harper's key role in the scuttling of Meech Lake and by the armed standoff at Oka later in 1990.

The new constitutional agreement formalized at Charlottetown in August 1992 included proposals for Aboriginal self-government. The Charlottetown Accord was put to a referendum in October 1992 and went down to a decisive defeat in Quebec, in English Canada and among Aboriginal people.

During the referendum campaign, *Compass* published an issue (November/December 1992) focusing on Aboriginal self-government. The following article, which appeared in that issue, placed the Charlottetown proposals in broader historical perspective.

—Editor

The symbolism surrounds us, like signs on a deserted highway. It has been such a long time since we could read these signs and so the message remains unclear. The ability to hear, to comprehend and to act has been washed away by the tide. The teeming waters of assimilation and oppression have left us spinning on the bottom, like a pebble being rounded and rounded into nothingness.

And now it appears that there is an oasis shimmering on the horizon. It whets our appetite, because we can still remember what it was like. We heard the legends and the stories of the time before the coming of the white man—of the kind of freedom we could only dream about, of a way of life unmatched; of a connection to Mother Earth and all living things, of a respect for human life and dignity, of spiritual freedom. The desire to return to this way aches within us as it has for the many generations that we have longed for these things.

But as we get closer to the vision, it appears no clearer to us. At times it even fades from view and something stiffens within our oppressed spirit: the fear of a thou-

sand broken promises.

With the coming of the Europeans, aboriginal nations entered into treaties based on friendship and peace with European nations. It has been said that the treaties were broken before the ink dried, but it has been a commonly held belief among aboriginal people that the treaties would be valid for "as long as the grass grows and the rivers flow...."

In 1763, a royal proclamation that has been dubbed the Magna Carta of Aboriginal Rights recognized that aboriginal people are sovereign nations. The proclamation formed the basis for the historical relationship between the aboriginal nations and the British crown. It was not until the creation of the country of Canada in 1867 that Native people were stripped of their sovereignty. By virtue of the British North America Act, the newly formed federal government assumed jurisdiction and authority over "Indians, and Lands reserved for the Indians."

Nine years after Confederation, the federal government went one step further in the oppression of aboriginal people, crafting the most racist, destructive legislation ever written in this country. The Indian Act, which went into effect in 1876, is a distinct set of laws that assumed absolute control over Indian people, their lands and their resources in Canada. For Indian people, everything from birth through school and work to death was now in the hands of the government. Traditional ceremonies were outlawed. Children were removed from their homes, brainwashed with the knowledge of the Europeans and taught about the failings and inferiority of their own people. Traditional ways of hunting and gathering were limited or banned outright.

The Indian Act created forms of "government" commonly referred to as band councils, which are little more than bureaucratic arms of the Department of Indian Affairs and bear no resemblance to the kind of self-governing institutions that existed before contact. In a further Orwellian twist, the Indian Act made the band councils responsible to the minister of Indian affairs and his department and not to the people of the reserves.

As part of the process of assimilation, the void left by the removal of cultural and spiritual practices was filled with a crippling bureaucratic mindset. The Indian Act institutionalized the age-old practice of divide and conquer, dividing aboriginal people into a number of categories. Some of these categories receive special privileges; others don't. The divisions are often more statistical than anything else.

A list of status Indians, to whom the government gives a limited number of special privileges, was developed by the Department of Indian Affairs. Each status Indian was issued a card and number. Native people could

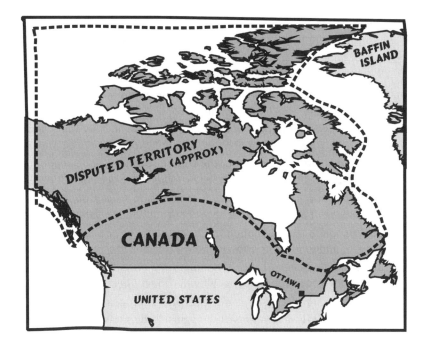

be removed from the list of status Indians in a number of ways. They could "enfranchise" (sell their rights back to the government) for money if they wished to join the army or the priesthood or to move freely off the reserve in search of employment. If a status woman married a nonstatus man, she lost her status; on the other hand, a man who married a nonstatus woman did not. This continued until 1985, when Bill C-31 was enacted to change this sexist clause. After generations, Indian people accepted the divisions created by the act.

As a result of the divisive nature of the Indian Act, a new group of Native people called nonstatus Indians emerged. In recent years they have banded together with off-reserve Indians to gain a political voice through the Native Council of Canada. Off-reserve Indians lose a number of privileges they would have on the reserve, but that would be weighed against the lack of employment and educational and social services on the reserve.

The Métis were another Native group excluded from the Indian Act's list of people with status. The Métis were regarded as the people with mixed blood, based largely in the Red River area of southern Manitoba. Following the Red River Insurrection of 1869–70, the Métis had negotiated their own relationship with the Canadian government in the context of the Manitoba Act. But as with all agreements or treaties made with Native people, the government has yet to live up to its end of the bargain.

Perhaps having learned that it's better not to write down agreements you have no intention of keeping, the Canadian government did not sign treaties with the Inuit. The Inuit were also excluded from the list of status Indians.

Over the years, although aboriginal people continued to fight to have control over their lives returned to them, for the most part the battles were isolated and had little impact. Aboriginal people were reduced from independent sovereign nations to "the Indian Problem," which became a buzzword for those who regarded aboriginal people with contempt and for bleeding hearts who felt guilty over the Native reality.

In 1969, the federal government led by Prime Minister Pierre Trudeau introduced a white paper announcing its intention to abolish aboriginal rights in Canada. The white paper gave rise to political awareness among aboriginal people across the country. They became united to fight its implementation and won. The white paper was shelved and Native lobbying groups such as the National Indian Brotherhood (which evolved into the Assembly of First Nations) began to become a real force in the country.

In 1978, the Trudeau government began the process of patriating the constitution. In 1981, delegations of aboriginal leaders travelled to England to protest patriation. Since all treaties were signed with the British crown, aboriginal people feared their treaties and aboriginal rights would not be fully recognized and protected in the newly patriated constitution. When the Constitution Act was proclaimed in 1982, it did include several provisions on aboriginal rights, although they were developed without the consent of aboriginal peoples. Section 35 of the constitution stated, "The existing aboriginal and treaty rights of the aboriginal peoples of Canada are hereby recognized and affirmed."

The patriation of the constitution was followed by a process established to allow aboriginal leaders and the first ministers to define and elaborate on the provisions of section 35. The process ended in March 1987 with no agreement. Within weeks of this final failure to reach an agreement on aboriginal self-government, the first ministers reached an accord to bring Quebec into the constitution by recognizing it as a "distinct society."

Native leaders were appalled that after they had spent years in futile negotiation, Quebec secured a deal in a weekend, but the Meech Lake Accord was doomed to fail. In June 1990, Manitoba Member of the Legislative Assembly Elijah Harper effectively killed the accord by refusing to give his consent in the provincial legislature. Harper's actions sent the country spiralling into its current constitutional crisis.

Following the death of Meech, Quebec refused to participate in any first ministers' conference and the fires of nationalism began to rage as never before. But within days, the Sûreté du Québec (Quebec provincial police) botched a raid on the Mohawk community of Kanesatake near Montreal; the whole country watched in astonishment and cries of outrage and anger were heard from the First Nations of Canada. Incredibly, the Oka Crisis was sparked by the desire of the Oka municipal government to extend a golf course: a police officer died and hundreds of people were held under siege by the police and then the army because someone wanted to hit a little white ball around.

Obviously, a lot more than a golf course was at stake. Underlying the Oka Crisis was the same issue that has been at the centre of Native-white relations from contact to present: sovereignty and who controls the lands and resources. The colonists and their successive governments have always struggled to ensure that aboriginal people would lose the right to their traditional territory and its resources.

The Oka Crisis put Native issues on the front burner of the national agenda. Less than a year after the crisis ended, the government of Canada had a new constitutional package on the table. The package included the recognition of a "justiciable right" to self-government. The cracks within a Native leadership that held together throughout the first ministers' conferences in the 1980s began to show. The leader of the most powerful Native organization, Ovide Mercredi of the Assembly of First Nations, flatly rejected the self-government proposal, calling it a "betrayal." The Métis National Council supported the proposal even though it did not recognize an "inherent" right. The other Native groups, the Inuit Tapirisat and the Native Council of Canada, both responded cautiously to the deal.

It became obvious that a "justiciable" right to self-government would not fly in Native communities. In February 1992, Mercredi raised the stakes by announcing in Quebec that Native people wanted "distinct society" recognition. The ensuing political controversy had Quebec politicians crying foul, but it also had Constitutional Affairs Minister Joe Clark saying "inherent" for the first time.

As Canada celebrated its 125th birthday on July 1, Native elders and others from a group calling itself the Protectors of Mother Earth were arrested. The group had formed a roadblock to stop the clearcutting of a massive area of forest. The blockade was a peaceful one and received little attention in the national media. In August, a constitutional proposal containing recognition of aboriginal peoples' inherent right to self-government was accepted by the government of Canada and all provinces, including Quebec. At almost the same time as the deal was agreed to, Mohawks and the Sûreté du Québec were engaged in a standoff eerily similar to the Oka Crisis two years before. The standoff ended without incident.

The next day, the traditional government of the Mohawks rejected the deal. A spokesperson for the Kahnawake Mohawks, Billy Two Rivers, challenged Mercredi on national television, telling the AFN leader that he doesn't speak for the Mohawk people. Mercredi insisted that he does. Overall, Native people remained relatively quiet about the new self-government package, even though if the deal is ratified it will probably rank with the Indian Act of 1876 in the potential impact it will have on their lives. What would our ancestors have done if they had known then what we know now? Today aboriginal people know, but they are not the same people they were 125 years ago. In that time they have been divided, assimilated, oppressed and abused.

And now they are expected to believe that the same process that has oppressed them all these years, government legislation, will be the thing that will set them free—that somehow, with the stroke of a pen, they will be returned to the freedom and independence they had before the coming of the Europeans. With the October 26 referendum coming up, Prime Minister Mulroney began his yes campaign by putting the Native package at the forefront. During trips to British Columbia and Saskatchewan in September, Mulroney touted the aboriginal package as one of the accomplishments of the Charlottetown Accord. He said it was time to say yes to Native people's rights and that Canadians who voted yes in the referendum would be doing just that. The implication was that Canadians who vote no for whatever reason will be denying aboriginal people once again.

In many ways, the referendum is a perfect example of the kind of government Native people fear will be forced on them with the self-government package—a kind of government in which people are deluded into believing that they actually have a say even though when they are given a chance to vote it is unclear to everyone what they are actually voting about. Self-government must come from the self, through consensus and the full involvement of people in the governing process. And for that to happen, before any vote takes place there must be discussions, information and clear understanding—not fake, illusory consultations of the kind currently taking place in Canada but consultations carried out with complete honesty and integrity. Otherwise, no matter what is written in the constitution, self-government will remain a utopian dream.

At the time of writing in 1992, **Miles Morrisseau** was editor of *Nativebeat*, a monthly newspaper published on Kettle and Stony Point First Nation, Forest, Ontario.

Rwanda: Alone with Its Deep Wounds

by Augustin Karekezi

Who knew about Rwanda before April 1994? This little country, until then of little importance and seemingly without a history, was dragged brutally from anonymity as if from a deep sleep.

At first glance, the Rwandan drama represented all of the evils that afflict Africa: tribal conflict, a colonial pattern of opting for one group against another, struggle for influence by world powers, despotic corruption, poverty, population pressure, lack of leadership by people of cultural or religious standing. But what makes Rwanda so talked about is a special evil unlike the others, which even before the mass killings was referred to as "Nazi-type ethnic totalitarianism." Rwanda now holds the unenviable record for the maximum number of people killed in the minimum time and with unequalled savagery, for the sole reason of ethnic difference.

The repeated questions are: How are such crimes possible? How can they be committed so openly and with such impunity? By all evidence, the holocaust was prepared and even announced. The world press was there. United Nations military were in Kigali and, for the first days of the genocide, France was on the spot. Nonetheless, the horror was carried through to the end as if the international community was powerless or an accomplice.

Background to the Massacres

Three social groups, the Bahutu, Batutsi and Batwa, inhabit the country. They speak one language, share one culture, and live intermingled in the same territory. From this perspective, there is only one ethnic body in Rwanda: the Banyarwanda.

Two major economic activities, grazing and agriculture, are undertaken by diverse sectors of the population. The Bahutu were more familiar with agriculture and the Batutsi with grazing, but neither of these activities was ever the exclusivity of one group. As for the Batwa, they were specialists in pottery, hunting and making weapons.

The first Europeans to arrive were the Germans, who presented themselves to the court of King Rwabugili in 1884. In 1885 the Berlin Conference initiated a division of Africa, and Rwanda became a German territory. In 1900, the Missionaries of Africa, the White Fathers, established the first mission at Save. After the First World War Rwanda was entrusted to Belgium.

A striking element in the colonial and missionary literature is the insistence on the differences among demographic groups in Rwanda. This was undoubtedly the approach of the time: the comparative studies of the nineteenth century. All was seen and judged by comparison. Thus, the social categories such as Bahutu, Batutsi and Batwa were classified as "races" or "ethnic groups." Colonial writers even used terms such as "caste", "feudalism" and "serfs," concepts borrowed from other types of society and applied to Rwanda without any effort at analysis. Inaccurate references to the "minority of Tutsi nobles" and the "mass of Hutu serfs" are still heard today. This, then, is the origin of the Rwandan ethnic problem that has claimed so many victims.

Between 1926 and 1930, the Belgian government introduced administrative reforms that deepened the divide at the heart of Rwandan society. Here is how a Belgian writer explained the rationale behind these decisions in 1933: "The Batutsi were destined to rule. Their dignity assures this already, compared with the inferior races around them, and confers on them a significant prestige: their qualities—and even their faults—elevate them even further." Before the reform, the Bahutu and the Batutsi shared power and all the advantages that this brought. After the administrative reforms, power was almost exclusively in Batutsi hands.

A census was organized in 1933–34. The Belgian administration established that the criteria for belonging to the Tutsi ethnic group would be the fact of owning at least ten cows. The population with such wealth numbered 15 per cent. The remaining Rwandans were identified as Hutus or Twa, according to whether they were agriculturalists or potters. This fatal manoeuvre took the socioprofessional categories of agriculturalist, grazer and potter, set them in place and retyped them as races or ethnic groups. It is worth noting the paradox that the few Bahutu who were big cattle owners could be counted among the Batutsi; in the same way a large number of Batutsi became Bahutu. Since this pseudocensus of 1934 there has been no attempt at a more sensible demographic study.

Missionary practice relied on the approach taken by the colonial administration. Once established that the Batutsi were superior, the logical conclusion was that their conversion should lead the rest of the population to the church. Therefore it was important to play the Tutsi card. Baptized in 1943, the king Mutara III Rudahigwa (a Tutsi like all Rwandan kings) encouraged his chiefs and subchiefs to accept the Catholic faith. This was the "golden age" of the Catholic mission in Rwanda, which culminated in the consecration of the country to Christ the King in 1947 and the blessing in 1952 of the first Rwandan elevated to the episcopate.

After the king died on July 25, 1959, the colonial administration and the Catholic Church turned against the Batutsi and from then on played the Hutu card. The division in the country grew deeper from then on. What should have been claims for sociopolitical reform turned instead into ethnic claims. The Hutu-Tutsi polarization culminated in the war of November 1959, in the course of which thousands of Tutsi were liquidated or forced to flee abroad.

A political party whose name is itself a program, the Permehutu (party for Hutu emancipation), led the country to independence in 1962. A year after independence, the country adopted a one-party system—all opposition parties were suppressed. Those Tutsis who had agreed to be aligned with the republican institutions became official members of the state party which, by definition and by ideology, excluded them. Henceforth, the ethnic policies of Rwanda would determine the institutions and become the Rwandan problem par excellence.

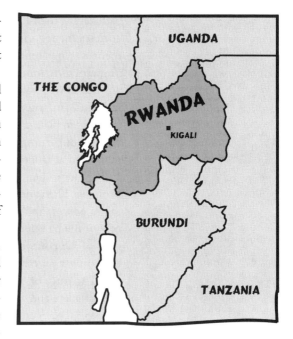

When General Juvenal Habyarimana took power in 1973, many thought for a while that he might cure the country of its ethnic demon. He had at any rate put to death a myth. In effect, when one Hutu topples another Hutu in order to take power by force, it is clear that ethnicity is not the sole determining factor in Rwandan politics. There was hope that the military authorities might restore the rule of law. The state of grace was short-lived, and by 1980, ethnicity had become a national obsession maintained by law: thanks to "ethnic balance" there was balance in the schools, balance in employment, balance everywhere except the army, diplomatic service and parliament, which were always Hutu reserves with rare exceptions.

From 1959 on, there were periodic massacres of Tutsis in Rwanda (1959, 1963, 1967, 1973). However cruel all these killings were, they were not planned except for 1973. It is important to recall that no one has ever been punished for any of these killings. The international community considered that this was a small, purely internal affair. As for the Rwandan government, it could not punish that which it had ordered.

In 1990, the war initiated by the Rwandan Patriotic Front (FPR) offered a pretext for imprisoning thousands of people suspected of being sympathizers of the FPR. Almost all were Tutsi, plus a few Hutu who dared to criticize the regime. They were released after six months. Their imprisonment was apparently an intimidation measure, which nonetheless entailed numerous victims.

Faced with the continuous pressure of the FPR and the action of political parties opposed to the president and his party, the authorities systematically put in place a reign of terror against all who did not favour them. This was no longer imprisonment, but death. In 1992, hundreds of Tutsi were massacred at Bugesera, in a sort of rehearsal for what would take place in 1994. These then were essentially political crimes with an ethnic colour. President Habyarimana's regime could not envisage for an instant the sharing of power, and took all opposition as the work of a mortal enemy. The official media referred constantly to those who opposed his party as "enemies of the country." As always, this confusion could be made to polarize the conflict on ethnic lines: the Tutsi became the enemy to fight.

The party of the president created a militia called "Interahamwe," free to intimidate and to kill. The militia was administered by the army and had access to whatever weapons it needed. It is worth mentioning also the setting up of the CDR (Coalition for the Defence of the Republic), a radical and overtly racist political party which, in its meetings, preached only hatred and suppression of the Tutsi. Finally, for long periods each day, the extremist radio, the "Radio-Télévision Libre des Milles Collines," broadcast the concepts of hatred and extermination of the "enemies"—understood as Batutsi.

On August 4, 1993, the Accords of Arusha put an end to the war between the government and the FPR and promised a bright future for all Rwandans. The country knew moments of enthusiasm and many believed that harmonious coexistence between Hutu and Tutsi was possible. People were sure that only through reconciliation could the Rwanda problem be solved.

Unfortunately, while some were doing everything to defuse the time-bomb of hatred, another merciless plan was in preparation: the Apocalypse. When it was first said that the president was distributing weapons to the people, no one paid much attention. These are the very weapons which, within two months, laid waste the country. Seeing that the "Interahamwe" militia and the CDR were preparing themselves without let-up, one can ask what the reason was for the accords, signed by President Habyarimana himself. These are the militia who covered the country with blood with the speed and effectiveness of lightning.

The Role of the Church

In late 1994, during a meeting, a missionary stated strongly, "In Rwanda reconciliation between Hutu and Tutsi is impossible." Such a statement is a public confession that is equivalent to saying we should simply close up the Christian church. There is no doubt that reconciliation may be difficult, even very difficult. But it is unhealthy for a "bearer of the Good News" to conclude that it is impossible.

Many books have been written on Rwanda. I know very few that are devoted to the questions of peace, reconciliation and unity between Rwandans. Even conventional language used to speak about the country and its culture is affected by ethnic polarization. Some propositions regarding Rwanda reveal an intellectual laziness that is neither acceptable nor understandable, at least in the church.

The long history of hatred and contempt for life puts our very identity as Christians in question. The definitive raison d'être of our action should be to refocus on the foundational experience of the church. We must work in humility so that the church can still speak to Rwandans a word that sets free, warms hearts, and disposes them to welcome the tenderness of God.

Originally from Rwanda, **Augustin Karekezi SJ** was at the time of writing rector of Hekima College, the Jesuit theologate in Nairobi, Kenya.

South Africa's Election: Inspiring yet Sobering

by Josephine C. Naidoo

The agony of apartheid became apparent to me as a girl. I remember the hillsides of lush seaside Durban swollen by hundreds of wretched squatter shacks within a stone's throw of First World affluence; the countless maids at the beck and call of their "madams"; the gardeners toiling in the blazing sun for a pittance; the bent, chapped-footed hawkers plying their homegrown peanuts, chilies and sticky "madumbie" potatoes from door to door; and the long lines of workers waiting in the chilly evenings for crowded black buses to transport them to their dusty neglected black township "homes."

My anguish deepened on my arrival in Johannesburg, city of gold for privileged whites and potential danger and death for blacks exposed to the physical and chemical hazards of mining. I was just seventeen and entering university and, as was typical of Asian Indian girls at the time, I had basically no experience of life and the outside world. I was accompanied by my father, a benevolent authoritarian school principal, torn between his certainty about the merits of higher education for his daughter and his fears of leaving her alone in the difficult segregated living conditions designated for Asian Indians. "Nonwhites" were not allowed to live on the campus of the esteemed white liberal University of Witwatersrand, and they were barred from all sports facilities. On course-related field trips there was nowhere to eat, no restroom to use, no one to talk to. Nonwhite medical students were not allowed to witness a post-mortem on a white body. Apartheid clearly defined the boundaries between white and nonwhite.

Since blacks and Asians shared common space, I saw for the first time the violation of human rights and dignity on which was built the precarious life of ease and privilege for a white elite. Hundreds of black workers "ran the gauntlet" each morning in the subway we used, as they ran to catch their trains to the mines. White plainclothes police would stop them at random, demanding the hated passbook. Those who did not carry it on their person were arrested. These unfortunates were shipped to white-owned farms, providing ready, cheap labour. People simply disappeared—no good-byes, no messages, no phone calls.

Every train, bus, telephone booth, elevator, store entrance, restaurant, city bench and restroom was segregated. "Blankies" and "Nie-Blankies" read the signs in Afrikaans. The claim of apartheid was that facilities would be separate but equal; in reality they were always unequal. A philosophy of blatant racism, divide and rule, and Eurocentric superiority penetrated all the institutions of South African society. Schools, hospitals, job opportunities, residential areas, housing—all were created with a view to cultivating the races for the role they were destined to play in the God-given scheme espoused by a Chosen People, in covenant with God.

The churches, including the Catholic Church, were not exempt. Residential segregation ensured that Christian parishes would be ethnically clean. All Catholic schools were segregated. The best schools were sealed tight from nonwhites. The front pews of the Catholic cathedral in Durban were roped off to nonwhites on important occasions. Public processions celebrating church festivals were assembled by race. God, the Virgin Mary and the Holy Family were portrayed as white, surrounded by white angels. Nonwhites fell victim to a norm of exploitation, subjugation, powerlessness and self-destruction.

A ruthless Security Police Force terrorized anti-apartheid groups and individuals. The united front against apartheid by Indian and coloured political activists in collaboration with the African National Congress (ANC), demonstrated in the Defiance Campaign of 1952, petered out under the ever-widening battery of laws. People avoided political topics. There was fear of "spies" among friends. The word "Communist" evoked terror. Even minor political activists disappeared. In a 1970 visit to South Africa, it seemed clear that I could not engage in the research and teaching activities for which I had been trained, under an American scholarship, at the University of Illinois. I felt certain that the "winds of change" would not come in my good years. On my return to Canada, I promptly became a Canadian citizen.

It was to be twenty-one years before I returned to South Africa. In the summer of 1991, I visited the country with my Scottish-Irish, Canadian-born husband and three university-aged children. It was their first visit to South Africa, which they had heard so much about from me.

The Mixed Marriages and Immorality acts, which had prohibited white-nonwhite marriage and sexual relations, had been repealed. This change facilitated our trip, as did the removal of "petty apartheid." However, unrest continued, fuelled by strident calls by the South African Council of Churches for more vigorous international sanctions, by African trade unions for mammoth industrial boycotts, and by the military wing of the African National Congress to "render South Africa ungovernable." A state of emergency had been declared in townships around Johannesburg.

There was great concern about our safety. Did we have a gun?, family and friends asked. Fear of criminally motivated violence had prompted people to surround their property with security gates, barred windows, vicious dogs, high walls and security alarms. Children were not allowed out of sight; they were escorted and transported by car everywhere.

Surprisingly, people recognized us as "strangers" wherever we went; mostly they thought we were "Americans." My husband was impressed with how nice black Africans were to him, a white man whom they might have identified with their oppressors. We also wondered whether there would be "place at the inn" for us when we went to isolated parts of Afrikaner country. There always was, and with courtesy and concern. This was a profound reversal of how people of colour were treated at the height of the apartheid era.

In fact, a visitor was immediately struck by the generous and conciliatory interpersonal relations between people of different ethnicities in public settings. One was equally struck by the lack of interaction across ethnic lines in private, social life. Apartheid successfully created an "ethnic cleansing" along racial lines; emotional bonding was essentially "in-group." When questioned, people said it would "take time" for them to reach out beyond their ethnic boundaries.

Durban, largely peopled by South Africa's 1.2 million Asian Indians, descendants of indentured labourers, professionals and entrepreneurs who had dared to seek a better life in the nineteenth century, had special appeal for my Canadian-born children. They were excited to learn that their maternal great-grandfather, an English teacher and Tamil scholar, was Mahatma Gandhi's confidential secretary for six years when Gandhi was in South Africa as a young lawyer. Equally, they were distressed to learn that their paternal great-grandparents, who established a wholesale fruit business for half a century in Grahamstown, a city of colleges and universities in the Cape Province, were forced to send their sons to Ceylon (now Sri Lanka) for their higher education. At the time, no Catholic teaching order would have the children of the single Catholic Asian Indian family in their all-white schools!

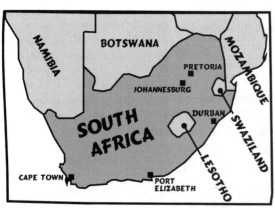

In September 1993, I joined the psychology department at the University of Durban-Westville in

Durban as a visiting professor on sabbatical leave from Wilfrid Laurier University in Waterloo, Ontario. Built as a showpiece university for Asian Indians under apartheid, it was in the process of moving to serve a larger black clientele. The transition was not easy; discontent, turmoil, destruction and violence were a constant feature of campus life.

In my own discipline, reconstruction of a divided psychological association was underway. By strange coincidence, my application to the parent organization in 1956 had triggered the schism and subsequent acrimony between racially liberal and conservative psychologists. I was the first "black" psychologist to make such an application, which—I now discovered thirty years later—created an unprecedented stir. In his letter to me the association's president, the late Dr. Simon Biesheuvel, today considered a "giant" of South African psychology, wrote, "Owing to social circumstance in South Africa, the Association cannot accept your application." I subsequently went to see Dr. Biesheuvel in Johannesburg about this response. He patted me on the back and said, "My dear, try to understand if we have you in the organization, the whole thing will break up." At the September 1993 meeting of the South African Psychological Association in Durban, I was asked to stand up, and the audience applauded.

As election day, April 27, 1994, approached, tension, fear and uncertainty peaked. The Inkatha Freedom Party and its leader, Chief Mangosuthu Buthelezi, resisted all attempts to bring them into the election process until a few days before April 27. The major bodies responsible for transition and election organization were in disarray. Politically motivated black-on-black violence, in particular, escalated. Innocent women, children and young people met horrific deaths.

The daily diet of criminally motivated violence fed us by the news media frightened people out of their wits. Indian doctors became vulnerable targets. The typical attack strategy was for an armed bunch of black men to enter a doctor's surgery, tie up the (often black) receptionist-nurse, and rob the doctor of money and car. The lives of the more fortunate doctors would be spared. The robbers would disappear. In the prevailing political climate it was impossible to bring such people to justice.

Rumors and myths abounded. People hoarded tinned goods, candles and lamps in the belief that food supplies and electricity would be cut. An extra contingent of armed guards was deployed around the reservoir serving Durban. Others feared their homes would be taken over by black people desperate for better housing. People repeated horror stories of robbery, murder and rape that came to their attention. Looking up to heaven, one humble black woman said to me that she was going to vote for God!

Mercifully, throughout this period peace messages and voter education intensified, and hundreds of election monitors and observers and local and international peacekeeping forces provided a reassuring presence. The churches, in a massive ecumenical movement, organized voter education, peace processions and support for the interim constitution, the bill of rights and the new South African flag. Blue and white doves clutching an olive branch formed the peace logo that appeared everywhere—in the media, advertisements, songs, buttons and t-shirts. Huge rallies were organized, at which ANC leaders tried to allay the fears of each ethnic community.

When I went for my training as an election observer at Durban's Ecumenical Centre, all present were young black South Africans; the conscientious facilitator was a young black woman. Among the tasks of an observer were to ensure that voting was fair, secret and without pressure of any kind, to observe sealing of ballot boxes and to report any irregularities to the presiding officer. The experience fed my excitement, wonder and hope for a better South Africa, which continued as I lined up for hours and got my voter's card (although I am a Canadian citizen, I was eligible to vote because I was born in South Africa). I marvelled at the hundreds of black people who had travelled long distances to do likewise. Voting was an inspiring yet sobering exercise. I never thought it would happen in my lifetime. Nor did the hundreds of people who stood in line in the sun, three to four hours on average, at the two polling stations at which I was deployed. One Afrikaner news reporter cited the words on the gravestone of Dr. John Dube, founder of the ANC: "Out of the darkness into the glorious light."

Dr. Josephine C. Naidoo, a professor of psychology and multicultural researcher at Wilfrid Laurier University in Waterloo, Ontario, spent several months during the academic year 1993–94 in the department of psychology at the University of Durban-Westville in Durban, South Africa, engaged in cross-cultural research and community experience.

Mother Teresa: Champion of the Poor

by Lucinda Vardey

When I first saw Mother Teresa she was signing autographs. A group of Korean nuns were crowding around her, shoving and pushing to get a photograph, and there was another crowd of people right behind them also pushing for the opportunity to be touched by her.

She always blessed everyone she met by touching their heads while saying, "God bless you." And there in the Missionaries of Charity Mother House in Calcutta she, the champion of the poor, the sick and the dying ("there is so much work to do," she always said), was finding time to encounter the hungry autograph hunters. One of Mother Teresa's many simple but profound qualities was to smile, to be a "cheerful giver" and to reach out and touch. Such qualities, she emphasized, were vital for "wholehearted service to the poorest of the poor."

Everyone wanted a part of her, to talk to her, be photographed with her, be at Mass with her, recite the rosary alongside her. Everyone was thirsting to be near holiness itself: to be touched by a saint. She always managed to deflect this attention by insisting that we too can *experience* God's work with the poor. "Go and see what you can do, see what's needed, and then you'll know the joy of giving yourself," she would say. "We all have what it takes to be holy. Holiness is not a luxury for the few; it is not just for some people. It is meant for you and for me, for all of us."

It is by knowing and experiencing the work of the Missionaries of Charity, by working alongside them in the leper villages, hospices and homes for the dying, clinics, soup kitchens, orphanages, shelters for the homeless, the downtrodden, the forgotten, that one gains an understanding of Mother Teresa and her legacy. It's tough work—in fact it's straight labour—but her brothers and sisters radiate a joyful peace while they work. Mother Teresa said that to labour without love is slavery.

Her call to serve the poorest of the poor came in 1946: when she had been sick with tuberculosis in a time of hardship and food rationing in India. On a train to Darjeeling, where she was sent on retreat, she heard Christ's call

Mother Teresa

Lucinda Vardey compiled the bestselling *A Simple Path with Mother Teresa* (1995) and is the editor of *God in All Worlds: An Anthology of Contemporary Spiritual Writing* (1995) and *The Flowering of the Soul: A Book of Prayers by Women* (1999).

and all she could do, she said, was answer it. She had been a geography teacher and later principal of a convent school in Calcutta, a member of the Loreto order. Her act of leaving Loreto and living in poverty following the Gospel teaching to the letter, relying solely on divine providence, was a leap of faith of heroic proportions. Following the teaching of her patron saint, St. Thérèse of Lisieux, she began to do ordinary everyday things with extraordinary love, dedicated to serving Christ in others, to relieving the suffering of isolation in sickness and death in the slums of Calcutta.

Within forty years, nearly 3,000 members of the Missionaries of Charity were serving worldwide, and Mother Teresa had received the Nobel Peace Prize and the highest honours bestowed on an Indian. She had the skill and ability to be utterly in the world, doing God's work, and yet able to practise the fine balance of contemplation within action. Prayer and the Eucharist were central in her daily life. She exclaimed that "without prayer we can do nothing." She was a highly attuned woman of enormous faith and trust in God's will, and at the same time a courageous, down-to-earth, easy-to-talk-to, no-nonsense, clear-thinking and straight-talking nun.

She had the charisma and the ability to seize international opportunities to carry out her mission and could clean a toilet like no other. She had the skill of a CEO; she kept one eye on the big picture and the future while the other saw clearly and concisely the present moment. She had the great ability to listen—whoever you were she made you feel the most important person in the world. She became a beacon of hope in the darkness of the world; from her fragile four-foot-ten-inch frame her soul towered above us.

She spoke eloquently and clearly, borrowing many phrases from the Gospel and other people she admired, especially St. Thérèse of Lisieux and her contemporary Dorothy Day. Never shy, always reminding us of the poor, always insisting that poverty is right in our families and our communities, she reminded us that God offers us opportunities to share, to give and to serve and puts them right in front of us. Calcutta is in our own backyards, she said, certainly camouflaged but there. Spiritual poverty and lack of love were her greatest concern, especially in the West. She always emphasized that to love and be loved was the prominent message she was here to give. "Love has no meaning if it isn't shared," she instructed. "Love has to be put into action."

She lived and worked and came among us in the latter part of the twentieth century, when material wealth surpassed all previous generations and the gap between rich and poor widened considerably. She instilled hope by showing us that acts of loving kindness, however small, can transform the world. She worked into her eighties and now that she is dead the message she conveyed in her life hopefully will live on in ours.